Jus Post Bellum

Leiden Studies on the Frontiers of International Law

Editors

Carsten Stahn
Larissa van den Herik
Nico Schrijver
(*Grotius Centre for International Legal Studies, The Hague*)

VOLUME 8

The titles published in this series are listed at *brill.com/lsfi*

Jus Post Bellum

The Rediscovery, Foundations, and Future of the Law of Transforming War into Peace

By

Jens Iverson

BRILL
NIJHOFF

LEIDEN | BOSTON

Library of Congress Cataloging-in-Publication Data

Names: Iverson, Jens, author.
Title: Jus post bellum : the rediscovery, foundations, and future of the
  law of transforming war into peace / by Jens Iverson.
Description: Leiden, The Netherlands : Koninklijke Brill NV, [2021] |
  Series: Leiden studies on the frontiers of international law, 2212-4195; volume 8 |
  Includes bibliographical references and index.
Identifiers: LCCN 2020045549 (print) | LCCN 2020045550 (ebook) | ISBN
  9789004331020 (hardback) | ISBN 9789004331044 (ebook)
Subjects: LCSH: Peace-building--Law and legislation. | Peace. | Postwar
  reconstruction--Law and legislation. | Just war doctrine. | War
  (International law)
Classification: LCC KZ6745 .I94 2021 (print) | LCC KZ6745 (ebook) | DDC
  341.6/6--dc23
LC record available at https://lccn.loc.gov/2020045549
LC ebook record available at https://lccn.loc.gov/2020045550

Typeface for the Latin, Greek, and Cyrillic scripts: "Brill". See and download: brill.com/brill-typeface.

ISSN 2212-4195
ISBN 978-90-04-33102-0 (hardback)
ISBN 978-90-04-33104-4 (e-book)

Copyright 2021 by Koninklijke Brill NV, Leiden, The Netherlands.
Koninklijke Brill NV incorporates the imprints Brill, Brill Hes & De Graaf, Brill Nijhoff, Brill Rodopi, Brill Sense, Hotei Publishing, mentis Verlag, Verlag Ferdinand Schöningh and Wilhelm Fink Verlag.
All rights reserved. No part of this publication may be reproduced, translated, stored in a retrieval system, or transmitted in any form or by any means, electronic, mechanical, photocopying, recording or otherwise, without prior written permission from the publisher. Requests for re-use and/or translations must be addressed to Koninklijke Brill NV via brill.com or copyright.com.

This book is printed on acid-free paper and produced in a sustainable manner.

Dedicated to my parents, my sisters, my brothers, my daughters, and always to Kate

∴

Contents

Introduction 1
- A Introducing the Theme of *Jus Post Bellum* 1
- B Summary 2
- C Problematization 3
- D Research Aims 7
- E Research Questions 7
- F Propositions 8
- G Conceptual Framework 12
- H Addressees of *Jus Post Bellum* 14
- I Explanation of Structure 19

PART 1
Foundations and Functions: Rediscovering the Peace-Oriented Law in the Just War Tradition

1 **Past – The Deep Roots of *Jus Post Bellum*** 23
- A Introduction 23
- B Historical Development 28
    1. *Augustine of Hippo (354-430)* 28
    2. *Institutes of Justinian (533)* 38
    3. *Raymond of Penafort (1175-1275) (Decretals of Gregory IX)* 41
    4. *Thomas Aquinas (1225-1274)* 42
    5. *Baldus de Ubaldis (1327-1400)* 48
    6. *Francisco de Vitoria (1492-1546)* 50
    7. *Francisco Suarez (1548-1617)* 58
    8. *Alberico Gentili (1552-1608)* 60
    9. *Petrus Gudelinus (1550-1619)* 71
    10. *Hugo Grotius (1583-1645)* 76
    11. *Christian Wolff (1679-1754)* 79
    12. *Emer de Vattel (1714-1767)* 84
    13. *Immanuel Kant (1724-1804)* 88
- C Conclusion 90

2 **Exploration of Sister Terms** 94
- A *Jus In Bello* 94
- B *Jus Ad Bellum* 108
- C Import for *Jus Post Bellum* and the Trichotomy 112

3   **Three Approaches to *Jus Post Bellum*** 115
    A   Introduction   115
    B   Temporal Approach   115
    C   Functional Approach   116
    D   Hybrid Approach   116
    E   Lex Specialis and Lex Generalis   118
    F   Interplay   120
    G   Hybrid Approach to *Jus Post Bellum*   121

4   **Present – An Exploration of Contemporary Usage**   128
    A   The Existing Matrix of Definitions: A Review of Contemporary Scholarship   128
        1   *Introduction*   128
        2   *Identifying the Definitional Dichotomy — Functional vs. Temporal*   130
        3   *Problems of the Dichotomy*   133
        4   *Importance*   135
        5   *Empirical Analysis*   136
    B   Contrasting *Jus Post Bellum* and Transitional Justice   138
        1   *Introduction*   138
        2   *The Grotian Tradition*   139
        3   *Basic Definitions*   144
        4   *Contrasting the Content of Transitional Justice and* Jus Post Bellum   146
        5   *Temporal Contrast – The Dynamics*   156
        6   *Specific to Global Contrast*   169
        7   *Legal Contrast*   171
        8   *Historical Foundations*   172
        9   *Going Forward – Continuing the Grotian Tradition*   177

5   **Empirical Analysis of the Literature**   180
    A   Introduction   180
    B   Method   180
    C   Findings   182
        1   *Summary Findings*   182
        2   *Unclassifiable*   183
        3   *Functional Definitions*   186
        4   *Temporal Definitions*   188
    D   Conclusion   196

PART 2
Substance and Promise: The Utility and Potential of Focusing on the Goal of Just and Sustainable Peace

6   *Jus Post Bellum* in the Context of International and Non-International Armed Conflict   203
  - A   Introduction   203
  - B   *Jus In Bello* in IAC and NIAC   204
  - C   *Jus Ad Bellum* in IAC and NIAC   208
  - D   *Jus Post Bellum* in IAC and NIAC   211
    1   *Complications*   212
    2   *Prohibitions and Facilitations*   213
    3   *More Procedural Aspects*   213
    4   *Mixed Procedural and Substantive Aspects*   215
    5   *More Substantive Aspects*   229
  - E   Conclusion   230

7   **Contemporary Legal Content of** *Jus Post Bellum*   232
  - A   Introduction   232
    1   *Chapter Focus*   232
    2   *Responses to Critical Approaches to* Jus Post Bellum   233
  - B   Procedural Fairness and Peace Agreements   238
    1   *Article 52 of the Vienna Convention on the Law of Treaties*   238
    2   *Other Considerations of procedural fairness*   240
  - C   The Responsibility to Protect   244
  - D   Territorial Dispute Resolution   248
    1   *Prohibition of Annexation*   248
    2   *Self-determination*   250
  - E   Consequences of an Act of Aggression   252
  - F   International Territorial Administration and Trusteeship   253
  - G   The Law Applicable in a Territory in Transition   258
    1   *The Law of State Succession*   258
    2   *Human Rights Law and the Rights and Interests of Minorities*   261
    3   *The Laws of Occupation*   267
  - H   The Scope of Individual Criminal Responsibility   272
  - I   Odious Debt   273
  - J   Alternative structuring of *Jus Post Bellum*   278
  - K   Conclusion   283

8   **Future? Rethinking Transformative Occupation and Democratization**   284
  A   Introduction   284
  B   The Interests of Groups in the Transition to Peace   284
  C   *Jus Post Bellum* and Democratization   288
  D   The Problem of Undemocratic Transitions to Peace   289
      1   *The Natural Tendencies of Unguided Transitions to Peace to Favor the Powerful*   289
      2   *The Limitations of Public International Law and Traditional International Humanitarian Law*   290
      3   *The Limitations of Human Rights Law, Transitional Justice, and International Criminal Law*   292
  E   Transformative Occupation and Democratic peace   293
      1   *The Problem of Transformative Occupation*   293
      2   *Kant's Concept of a Warlike Constitution*   295
      3   *Democratic Peace*   296
      4   *The Role of Protecting the Rights and Interests of Women in a Democracy*   297
  F   Argument for Democratization in the Transition to Peace   297
  G   Transformative Occupation that Considers Group Interests and Participation Aiding the Transition to Peace   298

9   **Conclusions**   302
  A   Key Strengths   304
      1   *Broad and Increasing Interest*   304
      2   *Foundation*   305
  B   Key Weaknesses   306
      1   *Lack of Consensus*   306
      2   *Difficulties of Integrating a Range of Sources*   309
  C   Key Opportunities   311
      1   *The Opportunity to Clarify a Range of Areas of Law and Practice*   311
      2   *The Opportunity to Contribute to the Establishment of Just and Enduring Peace*   312
  D   Key Threats   313
      1   *The Threat of Politicization*   313
      2   *The Threat of Discouraging Peace*   314
  E   Final Conclusion   314

Bibliography 321
    A   Literature 321
           a.   *Table of Cases* 339
           b.   *Table of Treaties* 340
           c.   *UN Documents* 345
           d.   *Miscellaneous Sources* 351
           e.   *Online Sources* 352

Index 354

Introduction

A   Introducing the Theme of *Jus Post Bellum*

Sir Hirsch Lauterpacht once asserted that "if international law is, in some ways, at the vanishing point of law, the law of war is, perhaps, even more conspicuously, at the vanishing point of international law."[1] Lauterpacht was not arguing that there was no law to apply—something antithetical to his approach.[2] Rather, he was suggesting that there was work to do. He makes this observation after a stunning list of problems that require clarification,[3] suggesting that the

---

1 Lauterpacht, H, The Problem of the Revision of the Law of War, *British Year Book of International Law* 29 (1952) 360, 381–382.
2 See generally, Lauterpacht, Hersch. Function of Law in the International Community. Oxford: Clarendon Press, (1933); "Non Liquet and the Function of Law in the International Community'(1959)." BYIL 35: 124; Lauterpacht, Hersch. "The Doctrine of Non-Justiciable Disputes in International Law." *Economica* 24 (1928): 277–317. The emphasis of the present work on the *function* of *Jus Post Bellum* is in part a homage Lauterpacht's historic work, The Function of Law in the International Community. It was based on an earlier 1928 work in *Economica* in which Lauterpacht argues against the doctrine of non-justiciable disputes in international law and expanded into a general exploration into the principal issues of the philosophy of international law. Lauterpacht suggested "a hypothesis which, by courageously breaking with the traditions of a past period, incorporates the rational and ethical postulate, which is gradually becoming a fact, of an international community of interests and functions." Lauterpacht, Hersch. Function of Law in the International Community. Oxford: Clarendon Press, (1933), p. 422. This hypothesis, that an international community of interests and functions exists, informs this work.
   The cover art for this volume is from the Franklin Delano Roosevelt memorial. The full quote is "I have seen war. I have seen war on land and sea. I have seen blood running from the wounded…I have seen the dead in the mud. I have seen cities destroyed…I have seen children starving. I have seen the agony of mothers and wives. I hate war." President Roosevelt spoke these words on 14 August, 1936. This visceral, tangible disgust with war that predated the Second World War helped motivate his vision of a post bellum world. The accomplishments of restructuring the international legal order after that war is very much in the spirit of *jus post bellum* this work describes. Other relevant quotes from President Roosevelt, also inscribed upon this memorial, include:
   "Unless the peace that follows recognizes that the whole world is one neighborhood and does justice to the whole human race, the germs of another world war will remain as a constant threat to mankind." February 12, 1943.
   "The structure of world peace cannot be the work of one man, or one party, or one nation… it must be a peace which rests on the cooperative effort of the whole world." March 1, 1945.
        https://www.nps.gov/frde/learn/photosmultimedia/quotations.htm, last visited 18 October 2019.
3 The list is 36 lines long. Lauterpacht, H, The Problem of the Revision of the Law of War, *British Year Book of International Law* 29 (1952) 360, 381.

lawyer must "do his duty regardless of dialectical doubts—though with a feeling of humility[.]"[4] What is that duty? To "expound the various aspects of the law of war."[5]

One might continue the observation—if the laws regulating war are at the vanishing point of international law, the laws regulating the transition from war to peace are at the vanishing point of laws regulating war. The transition to peace is at the frontier of efforts to govern human conduct, both at the global and local level. As an armed conflict concludes, the victor's comparative strength is often at its apogee, and the opposing side may be at its most desperate. How can either side be constrained by law under these challenging circumstances?

Characterizing the transition to peace as a phenomenon at the frontier of law only hints at the rich, complex nature of this difficult area. The transition to peace is often a period of intense instability and complex legal interplay and flux. New states, constitutions, inter-state agreements and peacekeeping agreements may come into existence, crimes may or may not be amnestied, old institutions may lose their legal existence and lawgivers of the *ancien régime* may lose their role as a source of law. The causes of the conflict, the conflict itself, and actions taken within the conflict may be the subject of legal action as the transition to peace moves forward.

B   Summary

This study focuses on legal and normative principles of the transition from armed conflict to peace, often called *jus post bellum*. *Jus post bellum* is self-consciously named in relation to its sister terms, *jus ad bellum* and *jus in bello*, terms that have been exhaustively developed and theorized. *Jus post bellum*, in contrast, is comparatively under-developed. It is a phrase frequently used without definition, or with little understanding that others may use the term to mean something else. It is almost never used with anything approaching a full exposition of the intellectual history upon which it is built. Before the scholarship in recent years, the laws and principles that constitute the *jus post bellum* were rarely expounded. This study helps to consolidate a firmer theoretical grounding for the term, as well as a clearer intellectual history and analysis of

---

4   Lauterpacht, H, The Problem of the Revision of the Law of War, *British Year Book of International Law* 29 (1952) 360, 381. Referring to lawyers generically as male was common in 1952.
5   Ibid 382.

its content. *Jus post bellum*, like *jus gentium* or *jus civile*, is best understood as *by definition* primarily a system or body of law and related principles.

In addition to the positive objectives identified above, it may be helpful to identify what this work argues against. Throughout the volume, explicitly or implicitly, the suggestion that *jus post bellum* does not exist is rebuffed, as is the idea that it has no content. In the introduction and conclusion to Chapter 1 (Past – The Deep Roots of *Jus Post Bellum*) the claim that the just war tradition is devoid of discussion of the subject matter of *jus post bellum* or that discussing the just war tradition is meritless is specifically rejected. Chapter 2 situates *jus post bellum* with its sister terms, *jus in bello* and *jus ad bellum*. The particular content and contours of *jus post bellum* are explored in Chapter 3 (Three theories of *Jus Post Bellum*) and Chapter 4 (Present – An Exploration of Contemporary Usage). Chapter 4 also specifically rejects the idea that transitional justice, post-conflict international criminal law and *jus post bellum* are interchangeable ideas. Chapter 5 provides an empirical analysis of the trends in the literature on *jus post bellum*. Chapter 6 provides a closer examination of *jus post bellum* in international and non-international armed conflict. Chapter 7 examines the contemporary legal content of *jus post bellum*. Chapter 8 provides an analysis of *jus post bellum* and counterinsurgency. Chapter 9 concludes with an overall analysis of the current state and future of *jus post bellum*.

C   Problematization

This study focuses on legal and normative principles of the transition from armed conflict to peace, often called *jus post bellum*. *Jus post bellum* is named in relation to its sister terms, *jus ad bellum* and *jus in bello*, terms that have been exhaustively developed and theorized since they were coined in the early-1900s, a subject that will be discussed in detail below. *Jus post bellum*, in contrast, is comparatively under-developed. For *jus post bellum*, there is no foundational treaty text equivalent to the Hague Regulations of 1899[6] or 1907[7] or

---

6   Short title: Hague Declaration (1899); International Peace Conference 1899, Declaration (IV, 3) concerning Expanding Bullets. The Hague, adopted 29 July 1899, (entry into force 4 September 1900).
7   Short title: Hague Regulations (1907); International Conferences (The Hague), Hague Convention (IV) Respecting the Laws and Customs of War on Land and Its Annex: Regulations Concerning the Laws and Customs of War on Land, 18 October 1907.

the Geneva Conventions of 1949[8] for *jus in bello* or Articles 2 and 51 of the United Nations Charter[9] for *jus ad bellum*.

While this is primarily a work of legal analysis, given the deep roots of *jus post bellum* analysed in Chapter 1, normative aspects will also be considered. Larry May's work on the normative principles of *jus post bellum* is noteworthy. May advocates that six normative principles of *jus post bellum* be recognized: rebuilding, retribution, reconciliation, restitution, reparation, and proportionality.[10] Given the normative content of his work, he rightly suggests that the addressee of these principles are not only political leaders but average citizens.[11] The goal of May's conception of *jus post bellum* is the same as the hybrid functional approach outlined in this work,[12] namely, one that emphasizes the *functional* aspects of *jus post bellum* (establishing a just and lasting peace) while nonetheless rooting it in a general timeline of transition from armed conflict to peace.[13] As May and Elizabeth Edenberg put it:

> It is not merely peace that is at issue, but a just peace, where mutual respect and the rule of law are key considerations. [...] The *jus post bellum* literature focuses, as one might expect, on the achieving of peace. [...] While *jus post bellum* theorists want a just peace, not merely any peaceful settlement of hostilities, they focus on the stopping of hostilities.[14] *Jus post bellum* principles all are aimed at securing a just and lasting peace at the end of war or armed conflict. Discussion of these principles has been standard fare in the Just War Tradition for several thousand years, even if

---

8   International Committee of the Red Cross (ICRC), Geneva Convention for the Amelioration of the Condition of the Wounded and Sick in Armed Forces in the Field (First Geneva Convention), 12 August 1949, 75 UNTS 31 ("GCI"); International Committee of the Red Cross (ICRC), Geneva Convention for the Amelioration of the Condition of Wounded, Sick and Shipwrecked Members of Armed Forces at Sea (Second Geneva Convention), 12 August 1949, 75 UNTS 85 ("GCII"); International Committee of the Red Cross (ICRC), Geneva Convention Relative to the Treatment of Prisoners of War (Third Geneva Convention), 12 August 1949, 75 UNTS 135 ("GCIII"); International Committee of the Red Cross (ICRC), Geneva Convention Relative to the Protection of Civilian Persons in Time of War (Fourth Geneva Convention), 12 August 1949, 75 UNTS 287 ("GCIV").

9   United Nations, Charter of the United Nations, 24 October 1945, 1 UNTS XVI.

10 See e.g. May, Larry. "Jus Post Bellum Proportionality and the Fog of War." European Journal of International Law 24.1 (2013): 315–333, p. 316.

11 Ibid 318–319.

12 See particularly Ch. 3.

13 May, Larry. "Jus Post Bellum Proportionality and the Fog of War." European Journal of International Law 24.1 (2013): 315–333, p. 320.

14 May, L. and Edenberg, E. (2013) 'Introduction,' in May, L. and Edenberg, E. (eds.) *Jus Post Bellum and Transitional Justice:*. Cambridge: Cambridge University Press, p. 1.

jus post bellum principles are not usually given the status afford to *jus ad bellum* and *jus in bello* principles.¹⁵

This work principally reflects on the historic meaning of normative principles that inform contemporary law and practice in Chapter 1, *Past —The Deep Roots of* Jus Post Bellum. Recognition that the application of law in this area has, as May and Edenberg state, the *aim* of a just and lasting peace (and is not neutral with the application to these normative goals) is necessary for understanding and development of *jus post bellum*.

Another way to frame the normative emphasis on a "just and sustainable peace" so often referenced in the literature of *jus post bellum* is to tie it to concepts form peace studies such as Johan Galtung's "positive peace" being differentiated from a mere "negative" peace,¹⁶ without a just resolution of the causes of the war and conduct within the war. The specific nature of what constitutes a "just" peace depends in large part on what the causes of the war and conduct of the war were. The fundamental aspect of what is "just" with respect to a "just and sustainable" peace is that *jus post bellum* is not simply focused on peace at any price with respect to justice; it rejects, for example, the goal of a sustainable peace founded on annexation, the denial of self-determination, rewarding aggression, denying the responsibility of trusteeship, violation of laws of occupation or human rights, or complete impunity for international criminal law violations. Attention should be paid not only to the justice demanded under international law but the particular priorities of those who will live in the constructed peace.¹⁷ Legal scholars interested in *jus post bellum*

---

15 Ibid. 2–3.
16 The concepts of "negative" and "positive" peace were developed by Johan Galtung in his seminal 1964 article: Galtung, J. (1965). An Editorial. *Journal of Peace Research*, 1(1), 1–4. For more on Galtung's work on structural analysis of peace, *see also* Galtung, J. (1969). Violence, Peace and Peace Research. *Journal of Peace Research*, 6 (3), 167–191. Galtung, J. (1981). Social Cosmology and the Concept of Peace. *Journal of Peace Research*, 17 (2), 183–199. Galtung, J. (1985). Twenty-Five Years of Peace Research: Ten Challenges and Some Responses. *Journal of Peace Research*, 22 (2), 141–158. Galtung, J. (1990). Cultural Violence. *Journal of Peace Research*, 27 (3), 291–305.
17 For more on subjective and objective public reasoning in the area of distributive justice, the foremost scholar on the subject may be Amartya Sen. *See* e.g. Sen, Amartya Kumar. *Collective choice and social welfare*. Vol. 11. Elsevier, 2014; Sen, Amartya. *The Idea of Justice*. Harvard University Press, 2011 (particularly Part IV); Sen, Amartya. *Development as freedom*. Oxford Paperbacks, 2001. For those particularly interested in a philosophical approach to the evaluation of post-conflict justice, the works of Larry May on the subject are recommended, particularly May, Larry. "Grotius and Contingent Pacifism." *Studies in the History of Ethics* (2006): 1–24; May, Larry. "Jus Post Bellum Proportionality and the Fog of War." *European Journal of International Law* 24.1 (2013): 315–333; May, Larry. "Jus Post

cannot shy away from principles, including normative principles, that inevitably arise in discussions of *jus post bellum*.[18]

For international lawyers, the transition to peace may be at the frontier, or the vanishing point. For those surviving armed conflict and that must live in the society created by the peace, the possibilities and risks inherent in creating a potentially novel social structure with new rules and power relations are not at the edge but at the centre of their reality. There is a chance of creating a new moment that is in a sense "pre-constitutional"—indeed peace agreements and similar documents often serve a constitutional function. One might argue that this period when the new core of a future society or relationship between states can be formed is, perhaps, controlled purely by non-legal forces, that it is the outcome solely of the use of force. But upon reflection, most jurists will reject that notion, adopting instead the notion espoused by Lauterpacht, that where there are questions, there is work to do in determining the international law that applies to the transition to peace.

Without answering the type of questions described above, there is an increasing gap between the references to *jus post bellum* and providing a coherent, well thought out theoretical and historical basis for the concept. By exploring definitional aspects of *jus post bellum*, including its relationship to *jus ad bellum*, *jus in bello*, and related concepts such as transitional justice and international criminal law, this work will seek to provide a coherent view of how scholars consider the term, closing the gap between the varied definitions scholars use for the term (when a definition is supplied at all). There is an unfortunate tendency by some scholars to treat *jus post bellum*, transitional justice, and post-conflict justice as interchangeable—this idea or assumption of interchangeability is a tendency this work argues against. By exploring the historical roots of *jus post bellum* within the just war tradition, it will address the gap between scholars such as Grégory Lewkowicz[19] who insist that there are no such roots and the many authors who think such roots exist. With these

---

Bellum, Grotius and Meionexia." Eds. Carsten Stahn, Jennifer S Easterday and Jens Iverson. *Jus Post Bellum: Mapping the Normative Foundations* (OUP 2014) 15–25; May, Larry. *After war ends: a philosophical perspective*. Cambridge University Press, 2012.

18   For an example of an approach to define the principles of just peace from an international studies perspective, see Williams, Robert E., and Dan Caldwell. "Jus Post Bellum: Just war theory and the principles of just peace." *International Studies Perspectives* 7.4 (2006): 309–320.

19   Lewkowicz, Grégory. "Jus Post Bellum: vieille antienne ou nouvelle branche du droit? Sur le mythe de l'origine vénérable du Jus Post Bellum." *Revue belge de droit international* 1 (2011).

foundations laid, this volume will address the gap implicit in the uncertain question of the potential of *jus post bellum*.

D Research Aims

This volume has three overarching objectives. First, it will evaluate the history of *jus post bellum avant la lettre*, tracing important writings on the transition to peace from Augustine, Aquinas, and Kant to more modern jurists and scholars. Second, it explores definitional aspects of *jus post bellum*, including current its relationship to sister terms and related fields. Third, it will explore the current state and possibilities for the future development of the law and normative principles that apply to the transition to peace. *Jus post bellum* has received an increasing amount of attention in recent years, but remains comparatively[20] under-theorized, and frequently referenced without realizing that many authors be talking past each other, meaning different things while using the same term. The author's hope for the volume is not only to help clarify the debate over the term, but also to move the consensus towards a hybrid functional (rather than temporal) approach to *jus post bellum*, that is, to define an approach to this area of law that focuses on the goal of achieving a just and sustainable peace (with an awareness of temporal context) rather than a mere discussion of law that applies during early peace.

E Research Questions

It is not enough to simply invoke the existence of *jus post bellum*, as many scholars and practitioners do. Rather, it is helpful to, first, test the existence and meaning of *jus post bellum* and second, examine the added value of *jus post bellum*. The overarching research question is to identify the function and content of *jus post bellum*. More specifically, the primary research questions discussed in this work are:

1) What are the historical roots of *jus post bellum* and how does this impact present-day conceptualizations of *jus post bellum*?
2) To what extent do sister terms shape the contours of *jus post bellum*?
3) What is the present-day function of *jus post bellum*?
4) To what extent do competitive notions such as transitional justice shape the contours of *jus post bellum*?

---

20 As compared to the last century's theorization of *jus in bello* and *jus ad bellum*.

5) How does *jus post bellum* operate in international and non-international armed conflict?
6) What is the contemporary legal content of *jus post bellum*?
7) How should *jus post bellum* evolve as a concept?

For maximum clarity, each research question is paired with a chapter. Research question 1 (historical roots) is addressed in Chapter 1 (*Past — The Deep Roots of Jus Post Bellum*). Research question 2 (Sister terms) is addressed in Chapter 2 (*Exploration of Sister Terms*). Research question 3 (function) is addressed in Chapter 3 (*Three theories of jus post bellum*). Research question 4 (competitive notions) is addressed in Chapter 4 (*Present — An Exploration of Contemporary Usage*) and Chapter 5. Research question 5 is addressed in Chapter 6 (*Jus Post Bellum in the context of International and Non-International Armed Conflict*). Research questions 6 and 7 are addressed in Chapters 7 (*Contemporary Legal Content of Jus Post Bellum*), 8, and 9.

F   Propositions

The following propositions are presented as a numbered list, not strictly orthogonal with the structure of this work, but bringing forth certain major points that are referenced throughout.

1. "*Jus post bellum*" is a useful and meaningful term, best used to examine and structure the laws and principles applicable to the effort to transition from an armed conflict to a just and sustainable peace. While meaningful, the phrase "*jus post bellum*" is not always used consistently by various authors. This plurality in intended meaning comes from the newness of the term, the complexity of the problem, and the relative under-theorization of the concept. Despite the newness of the term, the concept has deep roots.[21]

2. The function of *jus post bellum* is the successful transition from armed conflict to a just and sustainable peace. A hybrid functional approach to *jus post bellum* is superior to a primarily temporal approach to *jus post bellum* in terms of coherence, efficacy and scholarly depth.[22]

    a. The simplest but least useful theorization of the *jus ad bellum/jus in bello/jus post bellum* tripartite division is that these areas cover the beginning, middle, and end of armed conflict. This might be called a "temporal" tripartite division. It might be thought of as a "horizontal"

---

21 See generally Part I.
22 See generally Ch. 2, 3.

approach, where *jus ad bellum* covers the moment of entry into armed conflict, the *jus in bello* covers the period during armed conflict, and *jus post bellum* covers the period after armed conflict.

    b. With a hybrid functional conception, *jus ad bellum, jus in bello*, and *jus post bellum* can overlap temporally, but differ in terms of function. While the emphasis of application may change over time, with *jus ad bellum* taking the lead during peace, *jus in bello* taking the leading during periods of armed conflict, and *jus post bellum* playing a role during the transition to peace, their definition is rooted more in their function than in their sequence.

3. The concerns and laws of *jus post bellum*, like those of *jus ad bellum* and *jus in bello*, predate the terms themselves. A review of the works of Augustine and his peers, the Institutes of Justinian, the Decretals of Gregory IX, Thomas Aquinas, Baldus de Ubaldis, Francisco de Vitoria, Francisco Suarez, Alberico Gentili, Petrus Gudelinus, Hugo Grotius, Christian Wolff, Emer de Vattel, and Immanuel Kant demonstrate that the issue of the transition from armed conflict to peace is of enduring importance.[23]

    a. The writings of international jurists regarding the successful transition from armed conflict to a just and sustainable peace are deeply rooted in the same just war tradition that informs contemporary *jus ad bellum* and *jus in bello*.

    b. The legal and normative tradition regarding the transition to peace has been under-examined in part due to the retrospective application of the terms of the twentieth century (*jus ad bellum* and *jus in bello*) to encompass the entirety of thinking about armed conflict. This reductive pattern of thinking poorly serves contemporary understanding of these important works.

    c. It is a fair criticism to note that there are limits to the import of a tradition primarily based in Europe. A truly comprehensive, encyclopaedic approach to the history of legal and normative thinking regarding the transition from armed conflict to peace would be of great value, but is beyond the scope of this work. While not universal, there remains a good deal of value in analyzing a discrete tradition that has been largely historically rooted in Europe, given its impact on contemporary law and practice.

    d. It is far from useless to discuss the ancient traditions of normative and legal thinking on the justice of war and peace, and indeed failure to reevaluate and consider the traditions that gave rise to

---

23   See generally Ch. 1.

contemporary international law is to doom oneself to a curious form of self-imposed blindness—not only to the beneficial analysis of past authors, but also to their errors (such as using *jus post bellum* as a general license to violate other norms).

4. While *jus post bellum*'s function in aiming to establish a just and sustainable peace is in many ways more complex than the function of *jus ad bellum* or *jus in bello*, it is no less coherent in its basic aims.[24]

   a. The transition to peace is often a period of intense instability and complex legal interplay and flux. New states, constitutions, interstate agreements and peacekeeping agreements may come into existence, crimes may or may not be amnestied, old institutions may lose their legal existence and lawgivers of the *ancien régime* may lose their role as a source of law. The causes of the conflict, the conflict itself, and actions taken within the conflict may be the subject of legal action as the transition to peace moves forward.

   b. One benefit of including *jus post bellum* as part of a trichotomy rather than limiting analysis of armed conflict and peace to the *jus ad bellum*/*jus in bello* trichotomy is it encourages a reevaluation of the coherence and purpose of *jus ad bellum* and *jus in bello* as well.

5. *Jus post bellum*'s sister terms *jus ad bellum* and *jus in bello* extensively shape the contours of *jus post bellum*, helping jurists take a comprehensive view of the challenges of armed conflict and the transition to peace.[25]

6. Transitional justice is clearly distinguishable from *jus post bellum*. Transitional justice, properly understood, is a conception of justice associated with periods of political change, characterized by legal responses to confront the wrongdoings of repressive predecessor regimes.[26] *Jus post bellum* is rooted in transition from armed conflict to a just and sustainable peace.[27]

   a. While *jus post bellum* is substantively broader than Transitional Justice in many respects, *jus post bellum* is also clearly inapplicable in certain scenarios where Transitional Justice is applicable. Similarly, one can imagine a change in regime in which no significant human rights violations were perpetrated by the previous regime, deposed by armed conflict. Armed conflicts can happen without massive human rights violations. Additionally, armed conflicts occur without

---

24 See generally Chs. 2–5.
25 See generally Ch. 2.
26 Teitel, "Transitional Justice Genealogy," 69.
27 See generally, Ch. 4.

regime change. In these instances, Transitional Justice would tend not to apply, but *jus post bellum* would.

b. Similarly, Transitional Justice and *jus post bellum* are both distinguishable from post-conflict justice. Transitional Justice does not require armed conflict, while post-conflict justice obviously does. *Jus post bellum* is broader than post-conflict justice, although clearly can include it.

7. A review of the contemporary legal content of *jus post bellum* provides a clear indication of the need for *jus post bellum*. Procedural fairness is generally necessary for peace to succeed. Territorial disputes must be resolved, and aggression condemned. No longer is it acceptable and commonplace to exterminate or enslave the defeated population. The prohibition on the annexation of territory is central not only in determining the legality of particular post-conflict settlement, but also in underpinning the entire order of stable and pacific interstate relations. The possibility of holding individuals to account must be available, and the possibility of freeing a post-conflict state from odious debt must be considered.[28]

8. *Jus post bellum* should push back against the prohibition on transformative occupation in certain situations.[29]

9. *Jus post bellum* addresses an issue of vital concern for the international community and for post-conflict societies. Relapse into armed conflict is too frequent in modern history,[30] with devastating results. *Jus post bellum* should be developed to help all participants manage the complex process of ending armed conflict and developing early peace as successful as possible.[31]

The promise of peace lies not only in the cessation of the suffering of war but also in the wide variety of forms that peace can take. Navigating the path to a just and sustainable peace is notoriously difficult. There is work to be done on this frontier. Before looking at the laws and norms that apply and could apply to the transition to peace, it may help to take a step back and think generally about how to approach law and norms with respect to armed conflict in general.

---

28   See generally Ch. 7.
29   See Ch. 7.
30   From 1945–2009, 57 percent of all countries that suffered from one civil war experienced at least one subsequent conflict. UCDP/PRIO Armed Conflict Dataset, vol. 4, 2009. Barbara F. Walter, Conflict Relapse and the Sustainability of Post-Conflict Peace, World Development Report Background Paper, 2010, World Bank, p. 1.
31   *Passim.*

G   Conceptual Framework

How should the law and principles regarding armed conflict be approached? At least since the terms *jus ad bellum* and *jus in bello* were invented in the early 20th century,[32] there has been a strenuous emphasis on the distinction between two sets of legal and normative questions regarding armed conflict. The law applicable to armed conflict is typically divided into two parts, the first governing resort to force (*jus ad bellum*), and the second the conduct within the conflict (*jus in bello*). While imperfect, the laws restricting aggressive war (*jus ad bellum*) and codifying war crimes and other international humanitarian law violations (*jus in bello*) have matured considerably since the Second World War. In contrast, transitions out of armed conflict are less regulated and frequently fail. The post-conflict pause in violence often collapses into renewed armed conflict, or persists as a mere "negative" peace,[33] without a just resolution of the causes of the war and conduct within the war. From 1945–2009, 57 percent of all countries that suffered from one civil war experienced at least one subsequent conflict.[34]

There has been a push in recent years to approach the law that governs the use of force not as a dichotomy, but as a trichotomy. But adding *jus post bellum* to *jus in bello* and *jus ad bellum* has proven difficult, much as rebuilding a viable post-conflict society is more complicated than a general prohibition on armed conflict. To find the legal core of *jus post bellum*, one cannot simply reference a single document such as the prohibition on aggressive war in the Charter of the United Nations[35] or a set of treaties governing conduct in war such as the

---

32   See Robert Kolb, "Origin of the Twin Terms Jus Ad Bellum/Jus In Bello" (1997) 37 *International Review of the Red Cross* 553; see also Carsten Stahn, "Jus Post Bellum: Mapping the Discipline(s)" (2008) 23 *American University International Law Review* 311, 312.

33   The concepts of "negative" and "positive" peace were developed by Johan Galtung in his seminal 1964 article: Galtung, J. (1965). An Editorial. *Journal of Peace Research*, 1(1), 1–4. For more on Galtung's work on structural analysis of peace, see also Galtung, J. (1969). Violence, Peace and Peace Research. *Journal of Peace Research*, 6 (3), 167–191. Galtung, J. (1981). Social Cosmology and the Concept of Peace. *Journal of Peace Research*, 17 (2), 183–199. Galtung, J. (1985). Twenty-Five Years of Peace Research: Ten Challenges and Some Responses. *Journal of Peace Research*, 22 (2), 141–158. Galtung, J. (1990). Cultural Violence. *Journal of Peace Research*, 27 (3), 291–305.

34   UCDP/PRIO Armed Conflict Dataset, vol. 4, 2009. Barbara F. Walter, Conflict Relapse and the Sustainability of Post-Conflict Peace, World Development Report Background Paper, 2010, World Bank, p. 1.

35   United Nations, Charter of the United Nations, 24 October 1945, 1 UNTS XVI; see in particular Articles 2 and 51.

Geneva Conventions of 1949[36] and their additional protocols.[37] Rather, the law that governs the transition to peace is contingent and cross-cutting. Different laws may apply to each transition, and the applicable laws in any particular transition will be drawn from legal areas often considered separately. For example, transitions to peace occur in the context of conflict exclusively between states and also in conflicts involving non-state actors, with the involvement of the United Nations Security Council or without its involvement, with the dissolution of states or the creation of them, with a military victory for those with criminal culpability or without that difficulty.

Why make the distinction between two or three different areas of regulation and norms relating to armed conflict? Why not one unified theory of the justice of war? Why not a highly atomized field with each sub-element of the current two or three areas treated as one of scores of separate areas (e.g. why think of *jus in bello* protections for those *hors de combat*, civilians, prisoners of war, and weapons law under one umbrella term)? The terms *jus ad bellum* and *jus in bello* were coined in large part to protect one set of concerns (governed by *jus in bello*) from another (governed by *jus ad bellum*). Again, *jus ad bellum* regulates recourse to the use of force. *Jus in bello* regulates the conduct of the armed conflict, seeking to limit the damage caused by war without resort to adjudicating the justice of the conflict as a whole.[38]

---

36   International Committee of the Red Cross (ICRC), Geneva Convention for the Amelioration of the Condition of the Wounded and Sick in Armed Forces in the Field (First Geneva Convention), 12 August 1949, 75 UNTS 31 ("GCI"); International Committee of the Red Cross (ICRC), Geneva Convention for the Amelioration of the Condition of Wounded, Sick and Shipwrecked Members of Armed Forces at Sea (Second Geneva Convention), 12 August 1949, 75 UNTS 85 ("GCII"); International Committee of the Red Cross (ICRC), Geneva Convention Relative to the Treatment of Prisoners of War (Third Geneva Convention), 12 August 1949, 75 UNTS 135 ("GCIII"); International Committee of the Red Cross (ICRC), Geneva Convention Relative to the Protection of Civilian Persons in Time of War (Fourth Geneva Convention), 12 August 1949, 75 UNTS 287 ("GCIV").

37   International Committee of the Red Cross (ICRC), Protocol Additional to the Geneva Conventions of 12 August 1949, and relating to the Protection of Victims of International Armed Conflicts (Protocol I), 8 June 1977, 1125 UNTS 3 ("API"); International Committee of the Red Cross (ICRC), Protocol Additional to the Geneva Conventions of 12 August 1949, and relating to the Protection of Victims of Non-International Armed Conflicts (Protocol II), 8 June 1977, 1125 UNTS 609 ("APII"); and to a minimal degree International Committee of the Red Cross (ICRC), Protocol Additional to the Geneva Conventions of 12 August 1949, and relating to the Adoption of an Additional Distinctive Emblem (Protocol III), 8 December 2005 ("APIII").

38   *See, e.g.*, François Bugnion, Jus ad bellum, jus in bello and non-international armed conflicts, Yearbook of International Humanitarian Law, T.M.C. Asser Press, vol. VI, 2003, pp. 167–198.

There are extremely good reasons to make this distinction between *jus ad bellum* and *jus in bello*, beyond any qualitative difference that allows for the creation of a convenient typology. Chief amongst these reasons is to protect *jus in bello* from *jus ad bellum*—that is, to prevent the asserted justice of one's cause[39] in war from being an excuse for one's conduct. Without a strict distinction between questions of *jus in bello* and *jus ad bellum*, the regulations of *jus in bello* tend to crumble under the emotional force of *jus ad bellum* claims, leaving the humanitarian concerns at the heart of *jus in bello* wholly unprotected.

Since the terms *jus in bello* and *jus ad bellum* became commonplace, this distinction has been the starting point for answering the question of how the law and principles regarding armed conflict should be approached. First, one determined if a particular question related to the laws and norms of entering into armed conflict. If that was not the concern but it still related to armed conflict, the question was generally determined to be one within the body of laws and norms known as *jus in bello*. Thus, *jus in bello* grew to cover many diverse wartime and peacetime concerns, as long as they were not reducible to *jus ad bellum*.

H   Addressees of *Jus Post Bellum*

Additional information regarding the addressees of *jus post bellum* will become clearer throughout this work, particularly in Chapter 2 (Exploration of Sister Terms) and Chapter 6 (on the contemporary legal content of *jus post bellum*). Introducing the range of addressees at the outset, however, may help to clarify the concept somewhat.

Discussing addressees can be unexpectedly complicated.[40] Even in the simple case of domestic law, there can be debate as to whether the addressee is the nationals of that state or the government officials and agencies.[41] Classical

---

39   Or the injustice of one's opponent's cause.
40   For a foundational work on the modern complexity of this issue (without emphasising the terminology "addressee") Kelsen, Hans. *Pure theory of law*. Univ of California Press, 1967.
41   For more on this general issue, see e.g. Stevenson, Drury. "To Whom Is the Law Addressed?." Yale Law & Policy Review 21.1 (2003): 105–167; Stevenson, Drury D. "Kelsen's View of the Addressee of the Law: Primary and Secondary Norms." *Hans Kelsen in America-Selective Affinities and the Mysteries of Academic Influence*. Springer International Publishing, 2016. 297–317; Stevenson, Drury D., Kelsen's View of the Addressee of the Law: Primary and Secondary Norms (June 21, 2014). Kelsen in America Interdisciplinary

commandments such as "do not murder" directly address all persons, but typical modern domestic legislation often more directly regulates the state apparatus that may arrest, try, and punish (alleged) murderers.⁴²

To take an example closer to the subject of this work, consider the question of the addressees of *jus ad bellum*. The standard response as to the addressees of *jus ad bellum*, is simple: states are the addressees, because *jus ad bellum* involves international armed conflicts, which are between states. On further reflection, scholars and practitioners might consider that the United Nations is also regulated and in a sense a source of specific regulation of *jus ad bellum*, in the form of one its organs, the United Nations Security Council.⁴³ The issue of which organ or subsidiary organ of the United Nations is addressed by *jus ad bellum* is further complicated by the trend towards more "robust" peacekeeping mandates,⁴⁴ historic examples such as the Uniting for Peace Resolution,⁴⁵ or the role of the Secretary General; and if the term "addressee" is not limited to restrictive regulation but also the possibility of license or facilitation. Addressees of *jus ad bellum* arguably also go beyond states when one looks at the role of collective self-defence organizations such as the North Atlantic Treaty Organization or for example organized armed groups that play a role in internationalized armed conflicts. While some may argue that *jus ad bellum* only regulates the act of aggression and not the crime of aggression, given that the act is a constituent part of the crime, those "in a position effectively to exercise

---

Conference hosted by Valparaiso University School of Law at the Lutheran School of Theology at Chicago, June 27 – 28, 2014.

42   Stevenson, Drury D., Kelsen's View of the Addressee of the Law: Primary and Secondary Norms (June 21, 2014). Kelsen in America Interdisciplinary Conference hosted by Valparaiso University School of Law at the Lutheran School of Theology at Chicago, June 27–28, 2014.

43   *See e.g.,* United Nations, Charter of the United Nations, 24 October 1945, 1 UNTS XVI, Article 51.

44   I.e., with greater authorization to use force, in particular to protect civilians. *See* e.g. Tardy, Thierry. "A critique of robust peacekeeping in contemporary peace operations." *International Peacekeeping* 18.2 (2011): 152–167; Terrie, Jim. "The use of force in UN peacekeeping: The experience of MONUC." *African Security Studies* 18.1 (2009): 21–34; Ocran, T. Modibo. "The Doctrine of Humanitarian Intervention in Light of Robust Peacekeeping." *BC Int'l Comp. L. Rev.* 25 (2002): 1.

45   UN General Assembly, *Uniting for peace*, 3 November 1950, A/RES/377; for more on the Resolution *see* e.g. White, Nigel D. "The relationship between the UN Security Council and General Assembly in matters of international peace and security." *The Oxford Handbook of the Use of Force in International Law.* 2015; Johnson, Larry D. "'Uniting for Peace': Does it Still Serve Any Useful Purpose?" *American Journal of International Law* 108 (2014): 106–115; Carswell, Andrew J. "Unblocking the UN Security Council: The Uniting for Peace Resolution." *Journal of Conflict and Security Law* (2013).

control over or to direct the political or military action of a State"[46] who may be liable to be convicted of the crime of aggression may consider themselves at least indirectly addressed by *jus ad bellum*. To ask "who are the addressees of *jus ad bellum*" is thus an imprecise question, allowing a general answer such as "generally states" but requiring a specific legal question applied to a precise fact pattern to provide an answer as to who is addressed by which specific legal provision. Noting the need for precision when amplifying a question such as "who are the addressees of *jus ad bellum*" in no way suggests that *jus ad bellum* has no meaning in terms of legal responsibility, it merely suggests the need for clarity.

Jus in bello is a more complex body of law than *jus ad bellum* in many respects, regulating a great diversity of conduct within armed conflict and occupation as opposed to largely prohibiting conduct (albeit with notable exceptions). The potential addressees of *jus in bello* grow as one includes non-international armed conflict in the phenomena addressed. Nonetheless, a general answer to the question "who are the addressees of *jus in bello*" can be ventured: generally belligerent states, and also in non-international armed conflict organized armed groups, although properly conceived a wider array of actors from the International Committee of the Red Cross to local humanitarian groups to intergovernmental organizations are also regulated. A more precise question is needed for a more specific answer, but that in no way lessens the importance, coherence, or validity of *jus in bello*.

Jus post bellum is more complicated still, involving what is in many respects a more complex set of challenges (ending conflict and building a positive peace, not restricting force and protecting the vulnerable). Most importantly with respect to the question of "who are the addressees of *jus post bellum*," many questions of *jus post bellum* properly conceived involve a greater diversity of potential actors. That said, it is worth describing at the outset some general answers to the question of the addressees of *jus post bellum*. The general summation might be "usually states, sometimes other parties to peace agreements and international organizations," but of course specifying the particular law applied and factual scenario clarifies the answer.

With respect to *jus post bellum* and the regulation of the procedural fairness of peace treaties between states emerging from international armed conflict, the addressees are primarily states, although for example depositories may also be involved. More generally peace processes (including the crafting of

---

46 Rome Statute of the International Criminal Court, July 1, 2002, 2187 U.N.T.S. 3 (last amended 2010) Article 8 *bis*.

peace agreements) may have a distinctive self-determination role bound to questions of state legitimacy and human rights protections that may involve both governments and organized armed groups.[47] Peace agreements often have a hybrid international/domestic legal status and may create obligations that may need to be interpreted from both a treaty or contract law framework and a constitutional law framework; and distinctive types of third-party delegation,[48] but primarily can be said to address those entities who are party to the agreements.

Jus post bellum is informed by The Responsibility to Protect doctrine,[49] particularly the Responsibility to Prevent and the Responsibility to Rebuild as part of this doctrine. These responsibilities lie primarily on the territorial state, but secondarily to the international community as a whole.

Certain specific legal restrictions that are part of *jus post bellum* apply to governments due to their state-based nature. The prohibition of annexation as a forbidden conclusion to an armed conflict is addressed to states. The prohibition of the threat of the use of force as guaranteed by the Article 52 of the Vienna Convention on the Law of Treaties[50] with respect to fairness in peace treaties applies to states, as do other areas of treaty law. Similarly, the duty to extradite or refer for prosecution (*aut dedere aut judicare*) certain criminal violations bind states or state actors, limiting their ability to grant amnesties or to simply refrain from acting. This is in tension with the duty of states in non-international armed conflicts a duty to "endeavour to grant the broadest possible amnesty to persons who have participated in the armed conflict, or those deprived of their liberty for reasons related to the armed conflict, whether they

---

47   See generally Christine Bell, *On the Law of Peace: Peace Agreements and the Lex Pacificatoria* (Oxford University Press 2008).
48   Christine Bell, *Peace Agreements and Human Rights* (Oxford University Press 2000) 407; see also Christine Bell, *On the Law of Peace: Peace Agreements and the Lex Pacificatoria* (Oxford University Press 2008).
49   See International Commission on Intervention and State Sovereignty, *The Responsibility to Protect: Report of the International Commission on Intervention and State Sovereignty* (International Development Research Centre 2001) 39–45; see also United Nations Secretary General's High-Level Panel on Threats, Challenges and Change, *A More Secure World: Our Shared Responsibility, Report of the High-level Panel on Threats, Challenges and Change* (2004) 65–7; UN General Assembly, *2005 World Summit Outcome : resolution / adopted by the General Assembly*, 24 October 2005, A/RES/60/1, paras 138–9; United Nations General Assembly, *Implementing the Responsibility to Protect: Report of the Secretary-General*, UN Doc. A/63/677 (12 January 2009) para. 48.
50   Vienna Convention on the Law of Treaties (adopted 23 May 1969, entered into force 27 January 1980) 1155 UNTS 331, Art. 52.

are interned or detained,"[51] arguably limiting this type of amnesty to conduct other than, for example, genocide,[52] torture,[53] destruction of cultural property,[54] and terrorism.[55] When a question of law in the transition from armed conflict to peace relies on the law of state succession or occupation, these laws are also primarily addressed to states.

The addressee of a question of *jus post bellum* with respect to the right to self-determination is more complex. Self-determination has historically been the goal of many armed groups, and may be a necessary part of a just and sustainable peace. The right to self-determination is a peremptory norm.[56] Under Additional Protocol II it is made clear that an "International Armed Conflict" "include[s] armed conflicts in which peoples are fighting against colonial domination and alien occupation and against racist régimes in the exercise of their right of self-determination[.]"[57] The primary addressee of these norms are states, but other groups such as international organizations may also be regulated.[58] Similarly, human rights law, when applied in the context of the transition from armed conflict to peace with an aim towards establishing a just and

---

51 Art. 6(5) of Protocol Additional to the Geneva Conventions of 12 Aug. 1949, and relating to the Protection of Victims of Non-International Armed Conflicts (Protocol II) (signed 12 Dec. 1977, entered into force 7 Dec. 1978) 1125 UNTS 609.

52 UN General Assembly, Convention on the Prevention and Punishment of the Crime of Genocide, 9 December 1948, (Entry into force: 12 January 1951) United Nations Treaty Series, vol. 78, p. 277.

53 UN General Assembly, *Convention Against Torture and Other Cruel, Inhuman or Degrading Treatment or Punishment*, 10 December 1984, (Entry into force 26 June 1987) United Nations Treaty Series, vol. 1465, p. 85.

54 UN Educational, Scientific and Cultural Organisation (UNESCO), *Convention for the Protection of Cultural Property in the Event of Armed Conflict*, 14 May 1954 (Entry into force: 7 August 1956).

55 United Nations, *Convention for the Suppression of Unlawful Seizure of Aircraft*, 16 December 1970, (Entry into force: 14 October 1971) UN Treaty Series 1973; UN General Assembly, *International Convention against the Taking of Hostages*, 17 November 1979, (Entry into force: 3 June 1983) No. 21931; UN General Assembly, *International Convention for the Suppression of Terrorist Bombings*, 15 December 1997, (Entry into force: 23 May 2001) No. 37517; UN General Assembly, *International Convention for the Suppression of the Financing of Terrorism*, 9 December 1999, (Entry into force: 10 April 2002) No. 38349.

56 International Law Commission. "Draft articles on Responsibility of States for Internationally Wrongful Acts, with commentaries." Report of the International Law Commission on the Work of its 53rd session (2001), Commentary on Article 26, paragraph 5, p. 85.

57 International Committee of the Red Cross (ICRC), Protocol Additional to the Geneva Conventions of 12 August 1949, and relating to the Protection of Victims of Non-International Armed Conflicts (Protocol II), 8 June 1977, 1125 UNTS 609, Article 1.

58 *See e.g.* Emerson, Rupert. "Self-determination." *Am. J. Int'l L.* 65 (1971): 459 (on obligation to support self-determination efforts).

sustainable peace, is primarily addressed to states but is increasingly applied to international organizations and non-state actors as well. The law of International Territorial Administration, as indicated by the term, historically is addressed to international organizations, albeit with impacts on other entities.

While the obligation to extradite or refer for prosecution may apply only to states, the scope of international criminal responsibility and its impact on the transition from armed conflict to peace regulates more than states. A central theory behind international criminal responsibility (thus saving most prosecutions from challenges regarding legality) is that conduct can be criminalized regardless of domestic law. This addresses states by limiting the effectiveness of state decriminalization, amnesty, or inaction. The application of international criminal law, regardless of whether this occurs in international, hybrid, or domestic fora, can play an important role in building a just and sustainable peace. It is addressed primarily to individuals, but also to others subject to the authority of court or tribunal, as well as the court or tribunal itself.

If state debt can be discharged during the transition from armed conflict to peace due to its "odious" nature, the law regulating the discharge or validity of such debt is addressable both to the state debtor and the creditor, whether that creditor is a governmental, intergovernmental, or non-governmental entity.

I   Explanation of Structure

This work is structured in nine chapters. The first five chapters form Part 1, the theoretical foundation for the work. Chapter 1 establishes the existence and use of *jus post bellum* within the just war tradition, ranging from Augustine of Hippo to Immanuel Kant. Chapter 2, *Exploration of Sister Terms* roots the discussion of *jus in bello* in the "sister terms" *jus ad bellum* and *jus in bello*. One of the main concepts this work seeks to introduce and reinforce is outlined in Chapter 3, *Three Theories of Jus Post Bellum*. Chapter 4, *Present – An Exploration of Contemporary Usage*, has two major sections. The first section reviews contemporary scholarship, evaluating the functional/temporal definitional dichotomy. The second section contrasts *jus post bellum* and transitional justice.[59] Chapter 5 provides an empirical analysis of the trends in the literature on *jus pos bellum*.

---

59   This sub-chapter builds upon Iverson, Jens. "Contrasting the Normative and Historical Foundations of Transitional Justice and Jus Post Bellum: Outlining the Matrix of Definitions in Comparative Perspective": 80–101." *Jus Post Bellum: Mapping the Normative*

Part II builds upon the foundation of Part I, covering in four chapters the substance and future of *jus post bellum*. The question of why *jus post bellum* is useful for both International Armed Conflict and Non-International Armed Conflict and how it applies in each is explored in Chapter 6, *Jus Post Bellum in the context of International and Non-International Armed Conflict*. Chapter 7 surveys the contemporary legal content of *jus post bellum* with an eye towards some areas (such as the Responsibility to Protect) that are more *lex ferenda*[60] than *lex lata*.[61] Chapter 8 provides an analysis of *jus post bellum* and counterinsurgency. The work concludes in Chapter 9 with an overall analysis of the current state and future of *jus post bellum*.

Foundations. New York: OUP (2014); and Iverson, Jens. "Transitional Justice, Jus Post Bellum and International Criminal Law: Differentiating the Usages, History and Dynamics." *International Journal of Transitional Justice* 7.3 (2013): 413–433.

60   Law as it should be.
61   Law as it exists.

PART 1

Foundations and Functions: Rediscovering the Peace-Oriented Law in the Just War Tradition

∴

CHAPTER 1

Past – The Deep Roots of *Jus Post Bellum*

A   Introduction

To discuss *jus post bellum* is inevitably in part to consider the Just War Tradition. This tradition holds that questions regarding the morality and legality of war are worth answering and require close examination to properly answer. Consider, in contrast, Realism, which holds either prescriptively that these question are not worth answering or are not answerable, or descriptively that whatever one's answer to these question, they have no bearing on what states actually do. Or from another perspective, consider Pacifism, which holds that the questions of the morality of war are worth answering but do not require close examination to properly answer in any particular instance, because regardless of the conditions, the answer is always going to be against violence— against fighting of armed conflict in general, against any permitted methods of waging war, and always in favor of armed conflict's termination.[1]

Brian Orend considers James Turner Johnson to be the authoritative historian of the Just War Tradition.[2] Johnson's early volume *Ideology, Reason, and the Limitation of War: Religious and Secular Concepts 1200–1740*[3] is a good starting point to introduce the basic historical framework for the tradition. Johnson posits that there before about 1500 C.E., the classic just war doctrine did not really exist.[4] This means that to speak of the "just war tradition" without further qualification or explanation with respect to Aristotle, Cicero, Augustine, or the theologians or canonists of the High Middle Ages (pre-1500) is misleading. Not that there was no writing on the moral and legal questions of war before that point, but rather, it had not resolved itself into a single tradition.[5] Before around 1500 C.E., Johnson identifies two traditions, a religious (theological and canonical) tradition focused on the right to make war (*i.e., jus ad bellum*) and a secular, chivalrous code focused exclusively on allowable

---

1   For more on this division between Just War Theory, Realism, and Pacifism see Orend, Brian. The morality of war. Broadview Press, 2013.
2   See Orend, Brian. The morality of war. Broadview Press, 2013.
3   Johnson, James Turner, *Ideology, Reason, and the Limitation of War: Religious and Secular Concepts 1200–1740*, (Princeton University Press 1975).
4   Ibid 8.
5   Ibid 8.

methods of fighting (*i.e.* the Law of Arms, or *jus in bello*).[6] *Jus in bello* in medieval Europe was defined primarily by the knights' chivalric code.[7] The principal divide in the late Middle Ages regarding war doctrine was between two approaches to *jus ad bellum* particularly with respect to war for religion (*bellum sacrum*): the approach that took war for religion to be the most just kind of war imaginable, and another that ruled out religious justifications for war and emphasized only natural law (mainly political) just causes for war.[8]

It is a fair criticism to note that there are limits to the import of a tradition primarily based in Europe. A truly comprehensive, encyclopaedic approach to the history of legal and normative thinking regarding the transition from armed conflict to peace would be of great value, but is beyond the scope of this work. While not universal, there remains a good deal of value in analyzing a discrete tradition that has been largely rooted in Europe. A critique that a particular analysis is Eurocentric holds particular weight if the analysis is blithely unaware of its bias or selectivity. The following analysis is fully aware of the selectivity employed, and acknowledges its limitations, while insisting on its continued value.

Over time, there were three positions that went by the name "just war doctrine."[9] The first, the medieval just war doctrine, was itself the product of at least two distinct traditions, religious and secular.[10] Within those two broader traditions, the religious tradition included the canon law after Gratian and the theological tradition (to which Thomas Aquinas made a vital contribution), and the secular tradition included the renewed work of civil lawyers to understand and make current the concepts of Roman law, and the influence of the chivalric codes.[11] One can see the separate roots combining in the idea of noncombatant immunity for example: for the church this derives from the right of the (often religious) noncombatant, for the knight this derives from the magnanimity of the knight and his obligations under the chivalric code.[12]

---

6   Ibid 8.
7   Johnson, James Turner, *Just War Tradition and the Restraint of War: A Moral and Historical Inquiry*, (Princeton University Press 1981), p. 47.
8   Johnson, James Turner, *Ideology, Reason, and the Limitation of War: Religious and Secular Concepts 1200–1740*, (Princeton University Press 1975), pp. 8–9.
9   Ibid 29.
10 I 8–9, 29.
11 Johnson, James Turner, *Just War Tradition and the Restraint of War: A Moral and Historical Inquiry*, (Princeton University Press 1981), pp. 79, 122.
12 Ibid 138–9.

The second, post-Reformation holy war doctrine, applied the term "just war" to the doctrine generally described by Roland Bainton[13] and others as a "crusade."[14] Medieval Christian "just war" also did not apply to infidels or heretics the restrictions on warfare they applied to themselves,[15] but the context changed to actively justify war post-Reformation. The third "just war" is the modern "just war doctrine" which emerged in the 1500s and 1600s, developing into secular international law.[16] Modern attempts to limit war have, in part, their origin in the demise of "Christendom" and the rise of the sovereign state—in the attempts by scholars such as Francisco de Victoria and Hugo Grotius to ground the already existing limits on war in universal, natural law.[17] The first (medieval) doctrine spawned both the second holy war doctrine and the third secular tradition.[18]

For those focused exclusively on the secular international law doctrine, it is worth noting the role of the medieval as the parent to the secular doctrine, and the arguable incomprehensibility of such modern developments as the "Responsibility to Protect" doctrine without reference to the grander, richer, Just War Tradition. The rhetoric, mind-set, and accusations of "crusade" are also not without contemporary relevance. In all, a broader intellectual history is necessary for a fully formed theory of *jus post bellum* and its place in the Just War Tradition.

The pre-Christian influence analyzed in this work is limited, because its influence is limited. Take the Roman practice limiting warfare of demanding redress formally through a *repetio rerum*.[19] This diplomatic document would list the wrongs allegedly done and the conduct needed to satisfy Rome. After thirty-three days, if satisfaction had not been obtained, the next step was legal authorization in the name of the Senate and the people of Rome. Only then

---

13   Bainton, Roland H., *Christian attitudes toward war and peace: a historical survey and critical re-evaluation*. Wipf and Stock Publishers, 2008. In short, Bainton asserted that Christian thought began primarily in a pacifist mode, then developed the medieval just war doctrine, then developed the idea of holy war and crusade. This work was originally published in 1960.
14   Johnson, James Turner, *Ideology, Reason, and the Limitation of War: Religious and Secular Concepts 1200–1740*, (Princeton University Press 1975), p. 29.
15   Ibid 149.
16   Ibid 29.
17   Johnson, James Turner, *Just War Tradition and the Restraint of War: A Moral and Historical Inquiry*, (Princeton University Press 1981), p. 149.
18   Johnson, James Turner, *Ideology, Reason, and the Limitation of War: Religious and Secular Concepts 1200–1740*, (Princeton University Press 1975), p. 29.
19   Johnson, James Turner, *Just War Tradition and the Restraint of War: A Moral and Historical Inquiry*, (Princeton University Press 1981), pp. 153–154.

would the fetial priests issue a formal declaration of war, and military measures could commence. While of potential interest when discussing later methods of addressing abrogations of a peace treaty, the particulars role of fetial priests did not outlast Rome.

In contrast, Cicero's Republic was a source for Augustine and others,[20] who was the foundation for Aquinas, who laid the foundation for the theological strain of law that was fundamental to the medieval just war tradition. The continuity of the modern tradition on the restraint of war and its growth out of medieval just war thought became evident in the decades between World War I and World War II. Studies such as Alfred Vanderpol's *La Doctrine scholastique du droit de guerre*,[21] James Brown Scott's *The Spanish Origin of International Law*,[22] John Eppstein's *The Catholic Tradition of the Law of Nations*,[23] the Carnegie Institute series *Classics of International Law*, and Reinhold Niebuhr's *Moral Man and Immoral Society*[24] were all important in rediscovering and making the connections between medieval just war thought and contemporary law clear.[25]

It is worth noting that there have been specific challenges against the existence of any historical pedigree to the concepts now referenced as *jus post bellum*. Most notably, Grégory Lewkowicz contributed an article to an issue of the *Revue belge de droit international* focused on *jus post bellum* critiquing existing references to the historical development of the subject.[26] In part, Lewkowicz could be taken to argue that further development of this area of scholarship is needed. Lewkowicz goes further, however, arguing that by disagreeing with a few selected examples of basing *jus post bellum* on historical sources, "*il n'existe pas dans cette tradition de droit de la transition du conflit à la paix.*"[27] This is an

---

20   Ibid 154.
21   Vanderpol, Alfred, and Emile Chénon. La doctrine scolastique du droit de guerre. A. Pedone, 1919.
22   Scott, James Brown. The Spanish Origin of International law: Francisco de Vitoria and his Law of Nations. Oxford University Press, 1934.
23   Eppstein, John. The Catholic Tradition of the Law of Nations. The Lawbook Exchange, Ltd., 2012. Originally published: Washington, D.C.: Published for the Carnegie Endowment for International Peace by the Catholic Association for International Peace, 1935.
24   Reinhold Niebuhr, *Moral Man and Immoral Society* (New York: Charles Scribner's Sons, 1932).
25   See more generally *The Contribution of the Medieval Canon Lawyers to the Formation of International Law*, James Muldoon, Traditio, Vol. 28, (1972), pp. 483–497.
26   Lewkowicz, Grégory. "Jus Post Bellum: vieille antienne ou nouvelle branche du droit? Sur le mythe de l'origine vénérable du Jus Post Bellum." *Revue belge de droit international* 1 (2011).
27   Ibid.

extremely broad claim, one which would require a more exhaustive study that Lewkowicz provides, and it is one which the following section should certainly complicate.

In *Law and the Jus Post Bellum* Robert Cryer sounds a somewhat different note of caution than Lewkowicz.[28] He seems to be arguing that it is not defensible for *jus post bellum* scholars (he primarily cites Brian Orend and Carsten Stahn) to reference the just war tradition to discuss *jus post bellum*, if *jus post bellum* is taken to be the area of law that applies to the post-conflict phase (what will be discussed in Chapter 3 *infra* as a temporal approach). But, as Cryer seems aware, other conceptions of *jus post bellum* (such as they hybrid functional approach discussed in Chapter 3 *infra*) emphasize laws and principles that have an explicit normative goal (achieving a just and sustainable peace) in mind. If this is what is meant by *jus post bellum*, then it becomes clear not only that the just war tradition cannot be understood without reference to its treatment of the transition to peace, but that contemporary thinking on the transition to peace benefits from an awareness of how the problem has been conceptualized historically.

The legal and normative tradition regarding the transition to peace has been under-examined in part due to the retrospective application of the terms of the twentieth century (*jus ad bellum* and *jus in bello*) to encompass the entirety of thinking about armed conflict. This reductive pattern of thinking poorly serves contemporary understanding of these important works. While the following authors did not use the term *jus post bellum* just as generally they did not use the terms *jus ad bellum* or *jus in bello*, the understanding of these concepts is enriched by looking at the substance of the works with an eye towards understanding how the difficult problems of our present moment were dealt with in the past.

A note on the methodology and structure of this chapter—each of these authors have earned hundreds of years of secondary writing. Each could merit a lifetime of study. The purpose of this chapter is not to summarize their work or impact, but to trace to the source some of the most important writings on what might be called *jus post bellum avant la lettre* to provide an inevitably partial genealogy of a venerable line of thought.

---

28 Cryer, Robert. "Law and the Jus Post Bellum," *Morality, Jus Post Bellum, and International Law*. Ed. Larry May and Andrew Forcehimes. 1st ed. Cambridge: Cambridge University Press, 2012. pp. 223–249, p. 226 ff (see generally the section *Jus Post Bellum: Historically Defensible?*).

B Historical Development

1 *Augustine of Hippo (354–430)*

a) Introduction

The influence of Aurelius Augustinus, more commonly known as St. Augustine of Hippo (hereafter "Augustine") on western religion and philosophy is profound, pervasive, and enduring. He played a pivotal role in in merging Greek philosophy and Judeo-Christian religion. His writings were cited as deeply authoritative not only in early philosophy but in the medieval (e.g. Aquinas and Gratian) and modern (e.g. Descartes and Malebranche) periods. He was a North African Bishop and Doctor of the Roman Catholic Church, living and teaching mainly in Thagaste (now in Algeria) and Carthage (now in Tunisia) with a brief but important period in Milan, where he was baptised, became a professor of rhetoric, and developed what would later be called a Neoplatonic framework that would organize his later writings. He was enamoured of Latin classical works, particularly Cicero and Virgil.

Several important elements come out when Augustine's writings are examined with an eye towards discovering thoughts on the transition to peace. First, war is seen as evil, even when just. Second, war has purposes that may or may not be fulfilled by the transition to peace. Third, Augustine is primarily concerned with the effect on the individual, not the state—and his concern is not death or suffering per se, but vice, and is brutal and fatalist by modern standards. Fourth, the transition to peace is not always better than war—he is concerned about achieving a just peace. He describes a positive peace like a body with harmonious appetites. Fifth, mercy must guide war and allow a successful transition to peace.

b) Writings and Relation to *Jus Post Bellum*

Augustine is credited with deriving the original principles in much of Christian thought, including Christian thought about war. He did not provide the formulas or lists of criteria commonly referred to when discussing the just war tradition, but he provided the authority to which others such as Aquinas and Gratian would later refer.[29]

The following passage from *Ad Bonifacium* is repeated by both Aquinas and Gratian:

---

[29] Johnson, James Turner, *Ideology, Reason, and the Limitation of War: Religious and Secular Concepts 1200–1740*, (Princeton University Press 1975), p. 27.

For Peace is not sought in order to the kindling of war, but war is waged in order that peace may be obtained. Therefore, even in waging war, cherish the spirit of the peacemaker, that, by conquering those whom you attack, you may lead them back to the advantages of peace.[30]

For Aquinas, in *Summa Theologica*, this statement by Augustine is authority for the criterion of right intention in what we would now call the *jus ad bellum*. Aquinas defines the concept of right intention in part in the negative, using Augustine's words: "the desire for harming, the cruelty of avenging, an unruly and implacable animosity, the rage of rebellion, the lust of domination and the like—these are the things which are to be blamed in war."[31] So for Aquinas, as he creates the rules for what makes a just war, the key thing to derive from the earlier passage ("For Peace...") has to do with the right to wage war in general—without the right intention, a potential party to an armed conflict (the sovereign) lacks the right to wage war. That is, it has to do with what is normally described as *jus ad bellum*.

For Gratian, the focus is different. Instead, he uses this same passage to discuss not the sovereign but the general question of whether Christians may without sin participate in war.[32] This does not fit neatly within *jus ad bellum* or *jus in bello*. Unlike *jus ad bellum* considerations, it is not addressed to the sovereign. Unlike *jus in bello* the concern is not directly the conduct within and armed conflict but the intent behind overall participation. This helps to demonstrate that the just war tradition does not always neatly divide into the modern *jus ad bellum/jus in bello* dichotomy.

Returning to the original passage from Augustine, one can find the type of principle that lies at the root of *jus post bellum*—the obligation during armed

---

30 Aquinas, *Summa Theologica*, II/II, Quest. SL, Art. 1; CJC, *Decretum*, Quaest. I, Can. III; Augustine, *Ad Bonifacium*, CLXXXIX. Referenced in Johnson, James Turner, *Ideology, Reason, and the Limitation of War: Religious and Secular Concepts 1200–1740*, (Princeton University Press 1975), p. 40.

31 Aquinas, Summa Theologica, II/II, Quest. XI, Art. 1.) Referenced in Johnson, James Turner, *Ideology, Reason, and the Limitation of War: Religious and Secular Concepts 1200–1740*, (Princeton University Press 1975), p. 40. Also translated as: "What is the evil in war? ... The real evils in war are love of violence (*nocendi cupiditas*), revengeful cruelty (*ulciscendi crudelitas*), fierce and implacable enmity, wild resistance, and the lust of power (*libido dominandi*) and such like. (Against Faustus, Augustine, 887:301) AUGUSTINE *City of God, De libero arbitrio, Against Faustus,* and *Commentary on the First Letter of John*, Book XV, p. 595.

32 CJC, *Decretum*, Quaest. I, Can. IV. Referenced in Johnson, James Turner, *Ideology, Reason, and the Limitation of War: Religious and Secular Concepts 1200–1740*, (Princeton University Press 1975), p. 40.

conflict and afterwards to preserve the possibility of a transition to a just and sustainable peace. "Therefore, even in waging war, cherish the spirit of the peacemaker, that, by conquering those whom you attack, you may lead them back to the advantages of peace."[33] When does this obligation apply? Both during armed conflict ("in waging war") and plausibly afterwards during early peace ("conquering those whom you attack"/ "lead them back to the advantages of peace"). This is precisely the time span discussed in the theoretical discussion *supra*. More importantly, it plays the functional role emphasized by the theoretical discussion *infra*. One waging war is obliged to make choices that may lead the opposing party to see the advantages of peace, and not return to war. This means avoiding "the desire for harming, the cruelty of avenging, an unruly and implacable animosity, the rage of rebellion, the lust of domination and the like."[34]

The nature of the peace following war, whether it is just or unjust, is of interest to Augustine. This appears to be true more due to the inner morality of the individuals involved than the external effects—for Augustine, peace is a natural goal, but a corrupted nature seeks an unjust peace.[35] Augustine's concern to minimize the evils of war can be characterized as an ethics of personal virtues (concerned with how to be good) rather than an ethics of principles (concerned with how people can live together to each other's benefit).[36] This approach seems to be widespread amongst contemporaries. See for example, Aphrahat's Demonstration v "Of Wars," which refers to the internal effect as the most important aspect of wars.[37]

Augustine says "The natural order conducive to peace among mortals demands that the power to declare and counsel war should be in the hands of

---

33 Aquinas, *Summa Theologica*, II/II, Quest. SL, Art. 1; CJC, *Decretum*, Quaest. I, Can. III; Augustine, *Ad Bonifacium*, CLXXXIX. Referenced in Johnson, James Turner, *Ideology, Reason, and the Limitation of War: Religious and Secular Concepts 1200–1740*, (Princeton University Press 1975), p. 40.

34 Aquinas, Summa Theologica, II/II, Quest. XI, Art. 1.) Referenced in Johnson, James Turner, *Ideology, Reason, and the Limitation of War: Religious and Secular Concepts 1200–1740*, (Princeton University Press 1975), p. 40.

35 Augustine, 1950:687–690, The City of God, tr. Marcus Dods. New York: Modern Library.

36 The Elements of St. Augustine's Just War Theory, John Langan, The Journal of Religious Ethics, Vol. 12, No. 1 (Spring, 1984), p. 32.

37 Nicene and Post Nicene Fathers: Series II, Volume XIII, Ephraim the Syrian and Aphrahat, Select Demonstrations of Aphrahat, Demonstration v "Of Wars," Phillip Schaff et al. For more on Aphrahat, writing in 337, see Nicene and Post Nicene Fathers: Series II, Volume XIII, Ephraim the Syrian and Aphrahat, Introductory Dissertation, Ephrahat the Persian Sage, Philip Schaff et al.

those who hold the supreme authority."[38] Augustine's vision is ultimately not one of pure self-defence, or a state of anarchy and war of all against all, but rather one in which there is a system of international peace and authority, and those who violate that peace and authority can be rightly punished. In a sense, Chapter 7 authorization under the UN Charter for acts not clearly characterized as self-defense echo this ancient conception. It is modern, but in a sense deeply conservative, again strongly biased in favor of the *status quo*.

In *City of God*, (Book XIX, Ch. 7 "Of the Diversity of Languages, by Which the Intercourse of Men is Prevented; And of the Misery of Wars, Even of Those Called Just.") discusses the evil and suffering of war, even just war.[39]

> But, say they, the wise man will wage just wars. As if he would not all the rather lament the necessity of just wars, if he remembers that he is a man; for if they were not just he would not wage them, and would therefore be delivered from all wars. For it is the wrongdoing of the opposing party which compels the wise man to wage just wars; and this wrong-doing, even though it gave rise to no war, would still be matter of grief to man because it is man's wrong-doing. Let every one, then, who thinks with pain on all these great evils, so horrible, so ruthless, acknowledge that this is misery. And if any one either endures or thinks of them without mental pain, this is a more miserable plight still, for he thinks himself happy because he has lost human feeling.[40]

Augustine is not in love with war. Even a just war is terrible,[41] and the misery that they cause must be acknowledged, at the risk of dehumanization.

In *Against Faustus*, Augustine describes an explanation for war that will be widely discussed by subsequent authors, such as Aquinas.

> Now, if this explanation suffices to satisfy human obstinacy and perverse misinterpretation of right actions of the vast difference between the indulgence of passion and presumption on the part of men, and obedience to the command of God, who knows what to permit or to order, and also

---

38   Contra Faust. xxii, 75.
39   Augustine 1950 *The City of God*, tr. Marcus Dods. New York: Modern Library, Book XIX, Ch. 7.
40   Ibid.
41   For more on the horrors of civil war, what today might be called non-international armed conflict, *see e.g.*, Augustine 1950 *The City of God*, tr. Marcus Dods. New York: Modern Library, Book III, Ch. 23 "Of the Internal Disasters Which Vexed the Roman Republic, and Followed a Portentous Madness Which Seized All the Domestic Animals."

the time and the persons, and the due action or suffering in each case, the account of the wars of Moses will not excite surprise or abhorrence, for in wars carried on by divine command, he showed not ferocity but obedience; and God in giving the command, acted not in cruelty, but in righteous retribution, giving to all what they deserved, and warning those who needed warning. What is the evil in war? Is it the death of some who will soon die in any case, that others may live in peaceful subjection? This is mere cowardly dislike, not any religious feeling. The real evils in war are love of violence, revengeful cruelty, fierce and implacable enmity, wild resistance, and the lust of power, and such like; and it is generally to punish these things, when force is required to inflict the punishment, that, in obedience to God or some lawful authority, good men undertake wars, when they find themselves in such a position as regards the conduct of human affairs, that right conduct requires them to act, or to make others act in this way.[42]

This is an exceedingly interesting passage. It is putting forward the inverse of what Kenneth Waltz put forward in *Man, the State, and War*:[43] instead of arguing that war happens because of the faults of individuals (what Waltz puts forward as a "first frame" analysis) Augustine is asserting that war is evil because it makes individuals faulty, that is, sinful.

To Augustine, God commands wars for 1) "retribution" and 2) "warning those who needed warning." In other words, just deserts and deterrence, two of the cornerstones justifying criminal law. These are arguably well tied to *jus post bellum* – if the purpose of the war is retribution, as the transition from war to peace proceeds one would ask whether and to what degree that purpose has been fulfilled. If it is deterrence (general or specific) one would ask whether and to what degree the unwanted conduct is deterred. In a modern context, if the purpose of engaging in armed conflict is in response to aggression, one might question whether a peace agreement that effectively rewards aggression was just. Later in the passage, participation in war is justified because of "public safety," another classic justification of criminal law and governmental use of force outside of criminal law.

The passage also discusses the evil of war, not from a consequentialist view (suffering, violence) and more from a perspective of human virtues ("The real

---

42 Nicene and Post-Nice Fathers: First Series: Volume IV: Against Faustus, Edited by Philip Schaff, pp. 300–301, para. 74.
43 Waltz, Kenneth Neal. *Man, the State, and War: a theoretical analysis*. Columbia University Press, 2001.

evils in war are love of violence, revengeful cruelty, fierce and implacable enmity, wild resistance, and the lust of power") – these are the evils in war and also the evil conduct war is meant to punish and deter. It also discusses the ethics of serving in the military, basically blessing it because striking, wounding, or disabling people in war, when authorized by law, and when not carried out from a soldier's vengeance but to defend the public safety.

In the *City of God*, (Book III, Ch. 28 "Of the Victory of Sylla, the Avenger of the Cruelties of Marius.") Augustine uses Roman history to emphasize the importance of a *just* peace.[44] After the surrender, he discusses mass murder, gruesome torture, and injustice after a victory.[45] The peacetime atrocities seem to derive from the fact that "when hostilities were finished, hostility survived."[46]

> These things were done in peace when the war was over, not that victory might be more speedily obtained, but that, after being obtained, it might not be thought lightly of. Peace vied with war in cruelty, and surpassed it: for while war overthrew armed hosts, peace slew the defenceless. War gave liberty to him who was attacked, to strike if he could; peace granted to the survivors not life, but an unresisting death.[47]

Augustine favors peace, as the natural order, over war—but he is not pushing for peace at any cost.[48] While he is well-aware of the evils of war, he is also wary, based on the lessons of history, of peace that leaves innocent people defenseless and subject to collective punishment for wrongs, perceived or actual, during the previous conflict. Similarly, in Book XXI, Ch. 15, Augustine emphasizes the need for a just peace, preferring a hard conflict to a peace "under the dominion of vice":

> Better, I say, is war with the hope of peace everlasting than captivity without any thought of deliverance. We long, indeed, for the cessation of this war, and, kindled by the flame of divine love, we burn for entrance on that well-ordered peace in which whatever is inferior is forever subordinated to what is above it. But if (which God forbid) there had been no hope of so blessed a consummation, we should still have preferred to

---

44 Augustine 1950 *The City of God*, tr. Marcus Dods. New York: Modern Library, Book III, Ch. 28 "Of the Victory of Sylla, the Avenger of the Cruelties of Marius."
45 Ibid, Book III, Ch. 28 "Of the Victory of Sylla, the Avenger of the Cruelties of Marius."
46 Ibid, Book III, Ch. 28.
47 Ibid, Book XXI, Ch. 15.
48 See, e.g., Nicene and Post-Nice Fathers: First Series: Volume IV: *Against Faustus*, Edited by Philip Schaff , p. 301: "for the natural order which seeks the peace of mankind."

endure the hardness of this conflict, rather than, by our non-resistance, to yield ourselves to the dominion of vice.[49]

In contrast, in Book III, Ch. 19, Augustine describes the possibility of a war being so protracted that the victors, in the end, were more liked the conquered than conquerors.

> As to the second Punic war, it were tedious to recount the disasters it brought on both the nations engaged in so protracted and shifting a war, that (by the acknowledgment even of those writers who have made it their object not so much to narrate the wars as to eulogize the dominion of Rome) the people who remained victorious were less like conquerors than conquered.[50]

So how does one build peace, according to Augustine? Not through monuments, apparently. In *The City of God*, Book III, Ch. 25, "Of the Temple of Concord, Which Was Erected by a Decree of the Senate on the Scene of These Seditions and Massacres," Augustine derides the idea that a temple of concord, built on the site of massacres, will create peace. What will create peace? In part, he suggests something akin to a protean version of the democratic peace hypothesis:

> The wicked war with the wicked; the good also war with the wicked. But with the good, good men, or at least perfectly good men, cannot war; though, while only going on towards perfection, they war to this extent, that every good man resists others in those points in which he resists himself.[51]

Augustine suggests that "good men" do not go to war with other "good men." He further seems to indicate that there are degrees of goodness, and as they approach perfection, the likelihood of war goes down. This is surprisingly reminiscent of the idea that as the democratic level of a dyad of states increases, the likelihood of armed conflict in a given year decreases, that is, the democratic

---

49 Augustine 1950 *The City of God*, tr. Marcus Dods. New York: Modern Library, Book III, Ch. 28.
50 Ibid, Book III, Ch. 19.
51 Ibid, Book XV, Ch. 5.

peace hypothesis.[52] It is also similar to Kenneth Waltz's "first frame" (peacemaking through a change in individuals) in *Man, the State, and War*.[53]

Of course, Augustine's vision of an omnipotent God controlling all that occurs is at odds with a human-centered vision of war. In *City of God*,[54] (Book v, Ch. 22 "The Durations and Issues of War Depend on the Will of God.") Augustine discusses evils of long-continued wars, but in the same register, one might talk about "natural evils," like an earthquake.

> Let them, therefore, who have read history recollect what long-continued wars, having various issues and entailing woeful slaughter, were waged by the ancient Romans, in accordance with the general truth that the earth, like the tempestuous deep, is subject to agitations from tempests— tempests of such evils, in various degrees[.][55]

For Augustine, the duration of wars is determined by God.

> Thus also the durations of wars are determined by Him as He may see meet, according to His righteous will, and pleasure, and mercy, to afflict or to console the human race, so that they are sometimes of longer, sometimes of shorter duration.[56]

This also undercuts the humanitarianism within the idea of Christian reluctance towards violence, as well as the underdeveloped state of the laws of war during biblical times. In *The Church History of Eusebius*, Book IV, Ch. 6, Augustine describes the law of war allowing an occupied country to be reduced to complete subjection.[57] He describes the indiscriminate killing of thousands of men, women, and children without describing it as a violation of those laws.[58]

---

52 Maoz, Zeev, and Bruce Russett. "Normative and Structural Causes of Democratic Peace, 1946–1986." American Political Science Review 87.03 (1993): 624–638; Russett, Bruce. Grasping the Democratic Peace: Principles for a Post-Cold War World. Princeton University Press, 1994; Russett, Bruce, et al. "The Democratic Peace." *International Security* (1995): 164–184.
53 Waltz, Kenneth Neal. *Man, the State, and War: a theoretical analysis*. Columbia University Press, 2001.
54 Augustine 1950 *The City of God*, tr. Marcus Dods. New York: Modern Library.
55 Ibid, Book v, Ch. 22.
56 Ibid, Book v, Ch. 22.
57 Nicene and Post-Nicene Fathers: Series II, Volume I, Church History of Eusebius, Book IV, Ch. 6, Philip Schaff et al.
58 Ibid.

> AS the rebellion of the Jews at this time grew much more serious, Rufus, governor of Judea, after an auxiliary force had been sent him by the emperor, using their madness as a pretext, proceeded against them without mercy, and destroyed indiscriminately thousands of men and women and children, and in accordance with the laws of war reduced their country to a state of complete subjection.[59]

But in the end, Augustine's vision of peace is as an underlying order—one that allows the possible existence of war. For Augustine, there is a universal peace which the law of nature preserves through all disturbances. Peace is not synonymous with equality or universal joy—some may be justly miserable in a well-ordered peace. In a chapter comparing international peace to the peace of a well-proportioned body, with harmonious appetites, Augustine describes peace as follows:

> The peace of all things is the tranquillity of order. Order is the distribution which allots things equal and unequal, each to its own place. And hence, though the miserable, in so far as they are such, do certainly not enjoy peace, but are severed from that tranquillity of order in which there is no disturbance, nevertheless, inasmuch as they are deservedly and justly miserable, they are by their very misery connected with order. [...] As, then, there may be life without pain, while there cannot be pain without some kind of life, so there may be peace without war, but there cannot be war without some kind of peace, because war supposes the existence of some natures to wage it, and these natures cannot exist without peace of one kind or other.[60]

In his letter to Darius, Augustine calls conflict prevention more glorious than war-making. The goal of good people is peace, even if good men fight.

> But it is a higher glory still to stay war itself with a word, than to slay men with the sword, and to procure or maintain peace by peace, not by war. For those who fight, if they are good men, doubtless seek for peace; nevertheless it is through blood. Your mission, however, is to prevent the shedding of blood.[61]

---

59 Ibid.
60 Augustine 1950 *The City of God*, tr. Marcus Dods. New York: Modern Library, Book XIX, Ch. 13.
61 Nicene and Post-Nicene Fathers: Series I, Vol I, Letters of St Augustin, Ch. 160.

Augustine's love for peace and distaste for war was not universally shared. For example, Theodoretus, Bishop of Cyrus, makes the striking claim that war brings more blessings than peace because of the effects on inner nature.[62]

> These wars and the victory of the church had been predicted by the Lord, and the event teaches us that war brings us more blessing than peace. Peace makes us delicate, easy and cowardly. War whets our courage and makes us despise this present world as passing away. But these are observations which we have often made in other writings.[63]

Contrast this with St Jerome:

> We must seek peace if we are to avoid war. And it is not enough merely to seek it; when we have found it and when it flees before us we must pursue it with all our energies. For "it passeth all understanding"; it is the habitation of God. As the psalmist says, "in peace also is his habitation." The pursuing of peace is a fine metaphor and may be compared with the apostle's words, "pursuing hospitality." It is not enough, he means, for us to invite guests with our lips; we should be as eager to detain them as though they were robbers carrying off our savings.[64]

A final note on Augustine is worth review, regarding his ideas on peace as the ultimate goal, even during war—demanding mercy due to the vanquished or captive:

> Peace should be the object of your desire; war should be waged only as a necessity, and waged only that God may by it deliver men from the necessity and preserve them in peace. For peace is not sought in order to the kindling of war, but war is waged in order that peace may be obtained. Therefore, even in waging war, cherish the spirit of a peacemaker, that, by conquering those whom you attack, you may lead them back to the advantages of peace; for our Lord says: "Blessed are the peacemakers; for they shall be called the children of God." If, however, peace among men be so sweet as procuring temporal safety, how much sweeter is that peace

---

62 Nicene and Post-Nicene Fathers: Series II, Vol. III, Theodoret, Ecclesiastical History, Book V, Ch 38, Philip Schaff et al.
63 Ibid.
64 Nicene and Post-Nicene Fathers: Series II, Vol. VI, The Letters of St. Jerome, Letter 125, Philip Schaff et al.

with God which procures for men the eternal felicity of the angels! Let necessity, therefore, and not your will, slay the enemy who fights against you. As violence is used towards him who rebels and resists, so mercy is due to the vanquished or the captive, especially in the case in which future troubling of the peace is not to be feared.[65]

c) Conclusion

As described above, several critical elements of Augustine's thought must be remembered as the work later scholars are considered. Even a just war is an evil. For a war to be just, it must have a purpose, and the purposes of war may not be fulfilled by the transition to peace. It is possible to evaluate the justice of war and the subsequent peace based mainly on the effect on the individual rather than the state. The transition to peace is not always better than continued warfare. Ultimately, mercy must guide the conduct of war and allow a successful transition to peace.

2 *Institutes of Justinian* (533)

a) Introduction

While Caesar Flavius Justinian (Justinian I) is credited as the author, in fact he was the sponsor of the text. The work was authored collectively, supervised by Tribonian.[66] The Institutes of Justinian is the core of a larger work known as the *Corpus Juris Civilis*, a codification of Roman law. The Institutes (or *Pandects*, roughly akin to encyclopedia, and signifying comprehensiveness) of Justinian is largely based upon the Institutes of Gaius,[67] a celebrated Roman jurist who wrote from 130–180 A.D, but also upon Marcian, Forentinus, Ulpian, and Paul.[68] It was intended as a textbook for new law students, but were essentially binding as law. Properly translated, the name of the Institutes (*Institutiones*) would be closer to "basic principles."[69] Justinian also called this work "*Elementa*," providing the sense of basic principles on which to grow.[70] It is essentially

---

65 Nicene and Post-Nicene Fathers: Series 1, Vol 1, Letters of St Augustin, Ch 142, Philip Schaff et al.
66 *Justinian's Institutes*, Introduction and translation Peter Birks and grant McLeod, Cornell University Press 1987, with the Latin text of Paul Krueger, Introduction, p. 8.
67 Gordon, William M., and Olivia F. Robinson. *The Institutes of Gaius*. Duckworth, 1988.
68 *Justinian's Institutes*, Introduction and translation Peter Birks and grant McLeod, Cornell University Press 1987, with the Latin text of Paul Krueger, Introduction, p. 12.
69 Ibid.
70 Ibid.

an anthology of excerpts of classical jurists. These excerpts were generally at least three hundred years old when Justinian's commission compiled the Institutes.[71]

b) Writings and Relation to *Jus Post Bellum*

The main text of the Institutes of Justinian is not principally concerned with the law of war and peace generally or the transition to peace specifically, the work itself is framed in the context of war, peace, conquest, and justice. From the preamble:

> The imperial majesty should be armed with laws as well as glorified with arms, that there may be good government in times both of war and of peace, and the ruler of Rome may not only be victorious over his enemies, but may show himself as scrupulously regardful of justice as triumphant over his conquered foes.
>
> With deepest application and forethought, and by the blessing of God, we have attained both of these objects. The barbarian nations which we have subjugated know our valour, Africa and other provinces without number being once more, after so long an interval, reduced beneath the sway of Rome by victories granted by Heaven, and themselves bearing witness to our dominion. All peoples too are ruled by laws which we have either enacted or arranged.[72]

Law and justice applied not only to Romans during peacetime. Rather, at least implicitly, government could be good or bad during war, Caesar could be judged as just or unjust with respect to defeated people, and dominion and promulgation of law after war is a chief result of war. The result of war, however, is not necessarily just.

From Book I, Title II:

> But the law of nations is common to the whole human race; for nations have settled certain things for themselves as occasion and the necessities of human life required. For instance, wars arose, and then followed captivity and slavery, which are contrary to the law of nature; for by the law of nature all men from the beginning were born free.[73]

---

71 Ibid 10.
72 Moyle, John Baron, ed. *The Institutes of Justinian*. Clarendon Press, 1906, p. 1.
73 Ibid 4.

This famous passage, describing the law of nations as common to the whole human race, based in natural law but directed towards human ends, dwells directly on one of the profound issues that arose in early history in the wake of armed conflict, the problem of captivity and slavery. These are contrary to the law of nature, but not barred by the law of nations. The issue of captivity arises repeatedly in the Institutes of Justinian.

Book I, Title III "Of the Law of Persons" states:

> Slavery is an institution of the law of nations, against nature subjecting one man to the dominion of another.
>
> 3 The name 'slave' is derived from the practice of generals to order the preservation and sale of captives, instead of killing them; hence they are also called mancipia, because they are taken from the enemy by the strong hand.
>
> 4 Slaves are either born so, their mothers being slaves themselves; or they become so, and this either by the law of nations, that is to say by capture in war, or by the civil law, as when a free man, over twenty years of age, collusively allows himself to be sold in order that he may share the purchase money.[74]

This possibility of capture and enslavement during war and recovery during the transition to peace touched on many areas of the law, including family law. As stated in Title XII "Of the Modes in which Paternal Power is Extinguished": "A captive who is recovered after a victory over the enemy is deemed to have returned by postliminium"[75]—that is, he will recover all of his former rights including paternal power over his children through the fiction that the captive has never been absent. *Postliminium* could serve as a restoration of the *status quo ante* in the aftermath of war, or simply the successful escape from captivity.[76] Capture of people was an extension of the capture of things from the enemy by the law nations: "Things again which we capture from the enemy at

---

74   Ibid.
75   Ibid.
76   *See also* Book I, Title XX "Of Atilian Guardians, and Those Appointed Under the Lex Iulia" Section 2 "On the capture of a guardian by the enemy, the same statutes regulated the appointment of a substitute, who continued in office until the return of the captive; for if he returned, he recovered the guardianship by the law of postliminium."; Book I, Title XXII. Of the Modes in which Guardianship is Terminated" Section 1 "Again, tutelage is terminated by adrogation or deportation of the pupil before he attains the age of puberty, or by his being reduced to slavery or taken captive by the enemy." Moyle, John Baron, ed. *The Institutes of Justinian.* Clarendon Press, 1906.

once become ours by the law of nations, so that by this rule even free men become our slaves, though, if they escape from our power and return to their own people, they recover their previous condition."[77] Captivity and return also influenced the disposition of property in wills.[78]

c) Conclusion

While the focus of the Institutes of Justinian is neither war nor peace, the legal effects of the transition to peace are integrated into the rationale of many issues. Because this work is largely compilations of earlier statements from Roman jurists, the treatment of the transition to peace reflects hundreds of years of past practice and law. The Institutes of Justinian became the core of Roman civil law for hundreds of years after its publication. While it had a limited influence on the development of medieval law and thought, it has proven influential in certain legal traditions over time.

3 *Raymond of Penafort (1175–1275) (Decretals of Gregory IX)*
a) Introduction

Raymond of Penafort was an older contemporary of Thomas Aquinas. Raymond compiled the Decretals of Gregory IX providing the basis for canon law for hundreds of years thereafter.[79] Raymond was ordered by Pope Gregory IX to take the expansive body of papal rulings (*Compilationes antiquae*) and tighten it into a definitive Book of Decretals.[80] More to the point for *jus post bellum*, Raymond also composed the *Summa de poenitentia* [*Summa de casibus poenitentialis*], which has sections specifically relating to the conduct of war.

b) Writings and Relation to *Jus Post Bellum*

Raymond lists five conditions, all of which are necessary, for a war to be just:
1. The person making war must be a layman and not an ecclesiastic, since the latter may not draw blood.
2. The object must be to recover goods or defend one's country.
3. The cause must be to obtain peace after all other means have failed.

---

77 Book II, Title I, "Of the Different Kinds of Things" Section 17, Moyle, John Baron, ed. *The Institutes of Justinian*. Clarendon Press, 1906.

78 Book II, Title XII, "Of Persons Incapable of Making Wills" Section 5, Moyle, John Baron, ed. *The Institutes of Justinian*. Clarendon Press, 1906. See also Book III, Title I "Of the Devolution of Inheritances on Intestacy" Section 4.

79 Kuttner, Stephan. "Raymond of Peñafort as Editor: The Decretales and Constitutiones of Gregory IX." *Bull. Medieval Canon L.* 12 (1982).

80 Kuttner, Stephan. "Raymond of Peñafort as Editor: The Decretales and Constitutiones of Gregory IX." *Bull. Medieval Canon L.* 12 (1982).

4. The intention must include no hatred, vengefulness, nor cupidity and must be to obtain justice.
5. The authority may come from the church, when the war is of the faith, but otherwise it proceeds from the order of the prince.[81]

Of particular note for *jus post bellum* are points three and four. While this list would ordinarily and simply be categorized as a precursor to Aquinas requirements for waging a just war in terms of *jus ad bellum*, points three and four oblige a party to an armed conflict to use the armed conflict to "obtain peace after all other means have failed." The only way this can make sense (waging war to obtain peace) is if the peace obtained is of a different quality than the alternative, specifically, a more just peace. This is clarified in the next point, stating that the intent must be to obtain justice. Further, a party to the armed conflict must avoid the intents that make the transition to a just and sustainable peace difficult: hatred, vengefulness, or cupidity.

c) Conclusion

Raymond sets the stage for Aquinas's important contributions to *jus post bellum* thinking. The goal of war is to obtain a just peace after all other means have failed, and to avoid war-making with intentions that make it difficult to sustain that peace.

4 *Thomas Aquinas (1225–1274)*

a) Introduction

Thomas Aquinas (St. Thomas, hereafter "Aquinas") wrote at a moment when the Latin West came into contact with the ideas of Greek, Jewish, and Arabian philosophers, including Aristotle, Avicenna, Algazel, Averroes, Avicebron, Maimonides, Alexander of Aphrodisias, Themistius, Philoponus, Simplicius and Proclus.[82] Aquinas continued the contemplative orientation of Augustine but with a practical approach received from Aristotle.[83] His *Summa Theologica* thus develops moral theology as applied to human action in a manner and breadth that was unequalled at the time.

---

81 *Summ. Ram.*, Lib. II, tit. V. 12; Vanderpol, Alfred, and Emile Chénon. *La doctrine scolastique du droit de guerre*. A. Pedone, 1919., p. 55; Johnson, James Turner, *Ideology, Reason, and the Limitation of War: Religious and Secular Concepts 1200–1740*, (Princeton University Press 1975), p. 49.

82 Anton C. Pegis, Introduction, in Basic Writings of St. Thomas Aquinas:, Volume 1, Anton C. Pegis ed., Hackett Publishing 1997, p. xxxv.

83 Jean-Pierre Torrel, *Thomas Aquinas (1224/1225–1274), Thomism*. In Encyclopedia of the Middle Ages, (Vauchez André ed., James Clarke & Co. 2002).

b) Writings and Relation to *Jus Post Bellum*

Aquinas's summary analysis of the law and normative principles of warfare is found in Question 40 of the *Secunda Secundae* in the *Summa Theologica*.[84] Aquinas begins, as is his custom throughout much of the *Summa Theologica*, with Objections to the questions posed. He poses four questions:

(1) Whether some kind of war is lawful?
(2) Whether it is lawful for clerics to fight?
(3) Whether it is lawful for belligerents to lay ambushes?
(4) Whether it is lawful to fight on holy days?

Of these, the first is of the most interest to *jus post bellum*. He makes four objections to the idea that it is sinful to wage war. Of those, two are of particular interest:

> Objection 2: Further, whatever is contrary to a Divine precept is a sin. But war is contrary to a Divine precept, for it is written (Mat. 5:39): "But I say to you not to resist evil"; and (Rom. 12:19): "Not revenging yourselves, my dearly beloved, but give place unto wrath." Therefore war is always sinful.

> Objection 3: Further, nothing, except sin, is contrary to an act of virtue. But war is contrary to peace. Therefore war is always a sin.

Peace is seen as a natural, good, virtuous thing. So why should the violation of that peace ever be just? Aquinas answers that three things are necessary for a war to be just: authority, just cause, and rightful intention. With respect to authority, he argues:

> First, the authority of the sovereign by whose command the war is to be waged. For it is not the business of a private individual to declare war, because he can seek for redress of his rights from the tribunal of his superior. Moreover it is not the business of a private individual to summon together the people, which has to be done in wartime. [...] Hence it is said to those who are in authority (Ps. 81:4): "Rescue the poor: and deliver the

---

84   Question 40, Of War (Four Articles), *Secunda Secundae* in the *Summa Theologica*. Available as Aquinas, Thomas. "Summa theologica. 3 vols." *Trans. By the Fathers of the English Dominican Province. New York: Benziger Brothers* 48 (1947). *See* The Elements of St. Augustine's Just War Theory, John Langan, The Journal of Religious Ethics, Vol. 12, No. 1 (Spring, 1984).

needy out of the hand of the sinner"; and for this reason Augustine says (Contra Faust. xxii, 75): "The natural order conducive to peace among mortals demands that the power to declare and counsel war should be in the hands of those who hold the supreme authority."[85]

Aquinas, quoting Augustine, espouses the idea of a natural order conducive to peace. War, *bellum*, is not a conflict between private individuals, *duellum*, but something commanded by the sovereign. Authority is important, at least in part, not simply because it is a requisite to a just war, but because it is conducive to peace. What are those with authority to do with that authority? To rescue the poor and deliver the needy from the hand of the sinner, presumably creating a link between the existence of poverty and need and a sin, an injustice. A major point of authority as a requisite for just war then is not only because it is conducive to the natural order of peace, but a just peace, where the poor are rescued and the needy delivered, and where the commonweal is defended.[86] This may seem to be a particularly modern focus not just on justice, but on distributive or transformational justice.[87] In fact, it is an ancient concern.

Aquinas also requires a just cause for any war to be considered just:

> Secondly, a just cause is required, namely that those who are attacked, should be attacked because they deserve it on account of some fault. Wherefore Augustine says (QQ. in Hept., qu. x, super Jos.): "A just war is wont to be described as one that avenges wrongs, when a nation or state has to be punished, for refusing to make amends for the wrongs inflicted by its subjects, or to restore what it has seized unjustly."[88]

Again, Aquinas leans on Augustine for authority, but derives a more general principle. The last point in the list, to "restore what [the nation or state attacked] has seized unjustly is perhaps most interesting to a modern audience, as it describes most clearly the desired state of peace after war, something like the *status quo ante*. Particularly in the case of territory acquired through aggression, the territory must be returned to the aggrieved sovereign for a just peace to return. This ties in with the original requirement given by Aquinas, that of authority—as without authority (usually given by just war

---

85   Question 40, Of War (Four Articles), *Secunda Secundae* in the *Summa Theologica*.
86   Ibid.
87   See e.g. Mani, Rama. *Beyond Retribution: Seeking Justice in the Shadows of War*. Polity, 2002.
88   Question 40, Of War (Four Articles), *Secunda Secundae* in the *Summa Theologica*.

scholars, but not by Aquinas here as "right authority) there can be no just return of that what has been seized unjustly from that authority. Then, as now, *jus ad bellum* places a positive value on the international *status quo* and a negative value on actions and powers that challenges and destabilizes that *status quo*. The obverse of this is a tendency of *jus post bellum* to emphasize, as a default position, a return to the *status quo ante*. This is not without its difficulties. The *status quo ante*, after all, was the situation that generated the conflict. Larry May, for example, asserts that total justice should not be demanded, but that it should be tempered by the principle of *Meionexia* (something akin to moderation in one's demands for justice).[89] It is uncertain May would go so far as to advocate that territory taken by aggressors not be disgorged and returned to the original sovereign.

Thirdly, and perhaps most importantly for the analysis of *jus post bellum*, Aquinas asserts that "it is necessary that the belligerents should have a rightful intention."[90] Again, Aquinas relies on Augustine as a source to make a generalizable principle: "Hence Augustine says (Contra Faust. xxii, 74): "The passion for inflicting harm, the cruel thirst for vengeance, an unpacific and relentless spirit, the fever of revolt, the lust of power, and such like things, all these are rightly condemned in war."[91] And again, citing Augustine (erroneously),[92] Aquinas states "True religion looks upon as peaceful those wars that are waged not for motives of aggrandizement, or cruelty, but with the object of securing peace, of punishing evil-doers, and of uplifting the good." While peace is not the only right intent listed, it is the first listed. As analyzed regarding Augustine *supra*, Aquinas can be read as saying that wars waged with the right intent to be in a sense "peaceful," perhaps in that they are not waged with the type of intent that makes a return to a just and sustainable peace difficult or impossible.

Aquinas makes a specific Reply to Objection 2, which is essentially the Christian pacifist objection based on Matthew 5:39: "But I say to you not to resist evil." He suggests, using Augustine as authority,[93] that this approach:

---

89   See e.g., *Jus Post Bellum*, Grotius, and *Meionexia*, in Jus Post Bellum: Mapping the Normative Foundations, edited by Carsten Stahn, Jennifer S. Easterday, Jens Iverson (Oxford University Press 2014); Larry May, *After War Ends: A Philosophical Approach* (Cambridge University Press 2012).
90   Question 40, Of War (Four Articles), *Secunda Secundae* in the *Summa Theologica*.
91   Ibid.
92   These words cannot be found in Augustine's works, but can be found in Can. Apud. Caus. xxiii, qu. 1.
93   Augustine, De Serm. Dom. in Monte i, 19.

should always be borne in readiness of mind, so that we be ready to obey them, and, if necessary, to refrain from resistance or self-defense. Nevertheless it is necessary sometimes for a man to act otherwise for the common good, or for the good of those with whom he is fighting. Hence Augustine says (Ep. ad Marcellin. cxxxviii): "Those whom we have to punish with a kindly severity, it is necessary to handle in many ways against their will. For when we are stripping a man of the lawlessness of sin, it is good for him to be vanquished, since nothing is more hopeless than the happiness of sinners, whence arises a guilty impunity, and an evil will, like an internal enemy.[94]

This is interesting to those interested in *jus post bellum*, both as a call to what Larry May has suggested using the Aristotelian concept of *Meionexia*,[95] and as a direct response to Christian concern for (even) those who cause harm. Aquinas is not saying that the idea of "turning the other cheek"[96] is irrelevant, but that indeed sometimes resistance and even self-defence should be refrained from. This is remarkable for those taking the mistaken approach that the Just War doctrine is essentially a simple apologia for war making. This, in a sense, mirrors Larry May's idea of *Meionexia*,[97] that total justice should not be demanded, in the service of something other than deontological (just deserts) justice.

In addition, the passages above suggest that the reason why pacifism is not obligatory is due to *concern for those with whom one fights*. For Augustine and Aquinas, one punishes with "kindly severity"[98] and vanquishes for the good of one's enemy. In a sense, Aquinas is performing a slight-of-hand, dividing the enemy into two entities, with the real war being fought against the "evil will"[99]

---

[94] Question 40, Of War (Four Articles), *Secunda Secundae* in the *Summa Theologica*.

[95] See e.g., *Jus Post Bellum*, Grotius, and *Meionexia*, in Jus Post Bellum: Mapping the Normative Foundations, edited by Carsten Stahn, Jennifer S. Easterday, Jens Iverson (Oxford University Press 2014); Larry May, *After War Ends: A Philosophical Approach* (Cambridge University Press 2012).

[96] The full Matthew 5:39 is as follows: "But I tell you, do not resist an evil person. If anyone slaps you on the right cheek, turn to them the other cheek also." (New International Version).

[97] See e.g., *Jus Post Bellum*, Grotius, and *Meionexia*, in Jus Post Bellum: Mapping the Normative Foundations, edited by Carsten Stahn, Jennifer S. Easterday, Jens Iverson (Oxford University Press 2014); Larry May, *After War Ends: A Philosophical Approach* (Cambridge University Press 2012).

[98] Question 40, Of War (Four Articles), *Secunda Secundae* in the *Summa Theologica*.

[99] Ibid.

and "guilty impunity"[100] of the opponent, not the opponent *per se*. This may seem self-deluding, but it has potentially interest regarding *jus post bellum*. Again, this would militate against the kind of war and warfare that would make improbable a successful transition to a just and sustainable peace. While it is too much to expect that the opposing side would truly accept that the intent of war was "kindly," this type of framing may none the less restrain those adopting it and make the framework both for prosecuting the war and transitioning to peace more restrained.

With respect to Objection 3, Aquinas is even more to the point. He states, again relying on Augustine:

> Reply to Objection 3: Those who wage war justly aim at peace, and so they are not opposed to peace, except to the evil peace, which Our Lord "came not to send upon earth" (Mat. 10:34).[101] Hence Augustine says (Ep. ad Bonif. clxxxix): "We do not seek peace in order to be at war, but we go to war that we may have peace. Be peaceful, therefore, in warring, so that you may vanquish those whom you war against, and bring them to the prosperity of peace."[102]

Again, we have an interesting entanglement of what might later be called *jus ad bellum*, *jus in bello*, and *jus post bellum*. Right intent is required for a war to be just, and is typically categorized as a *jus ad bellum* criterion. But that intent is shown in a specific way, according to Augustine (and highlighted by Aquinas), to conduct war in a fashion that does not foreclose the prosperity of peace-not an evil peace, but a prosperous, just peace.

c)   Conclusion

Aquinas' contribution to just war thinking was profound and well-acknowledged. Less well-acknowledged is his contribution specifically to the law and normative principles of the transition from armed conflict to peace. Following Augustine's lead, he espouses the idea of a natural order conducive to peace.[103] Right authority is important, not merely for its own sake, but because it is conducive to peace.[104] That peace should be a just peace, where the

---

100   Ibid.
101   Matthew 10:34 states in full "Think not that I am come to send peace on earth: I came not to send peace, but a sword." (King James Version).
102   Question 40, Of War (Four Articles), *Secunda Secundae* in the *Summa Theologica*.
103   Ibid.
104   Ibid.

poor are rescued and the needy delivered.[105] The right intent should be securing peace, punishing evil-doers, and uplifting the good.[106] Aquinas answers the argument for pacifism, not by an absolute demand for rights-based self-defence, but due to concern for the enemy, who has fallen into sinful conduct.[107] The ultimate goal of a prosperous peace controls not only post-conflict behaviour but the warring itself.[108]

5 *Baldus de Ubaldis (1327–1400)*

a) Introduction

Baldus de Ubaldis[109] was a student of Bartolus of Sassoferrato (d. 1352)[110] and Federicus Petrucci.[111] Bartolus and Baldus were both pre-eminent jurists of the late Middle Ages.[112] Bartolus also taught Johannes (Giovanni) de Ligano, who wrote an early, perhaps the first tract to focus exclusively on the law of war in 1360, *Tractatus de bello, de represaliis et de duello*.[113] This work was mostly influential through vulgarizations (translations from Latin), particularly in *L'Arbre des Batailles* by Honoré Bonnet. *Tractatus de bello, de represaliis et de duello* adds little to reflections *on jus post bellum*, mostly echoing Augustine with statements like "The end of war, then, is the peace and tranquillity of the world."[114] Amongst other accomplishments, Baldus and Bartolus provided a legal foundation for the modern conception of the state.[115] The conception of a state that transcended the position and prerogatives of the ruler and recognized

---

105 Ibid.
106 Ibid.
107 Ibid.
108 Ibid.
109 For more on Baldus de Ubaldis, see Canning, Joseph. *The Political Thought of Baldus de Ubaldis*. Cambridge, U.K.: Cambridge University Press, 1987; Kenneth Pennington, Baldus de Ubaldis, 8 RIVISTA INTERNAZIONALE DI DIRITTO COMUNE 35 (1997); Wahl, J.A. "Baldus de Ubaldis and the Foundations of the Nation-State." Manuscripta 21.2 (1977):80.
110 Magnus Ryan, Bartolus of Sassoferrato and Free Cities. The Alexander Prize Lecture, *Transactions of the Royal Historical Society*, Vol. 10 (2000), pp. 65–89. Published by: Cambridge University Press on behalf of the Royal Historical Society.
111 Baldus de Ubaldis, Petrus, The Oxford International Encyclopedia of Legal History, (Stanley N. Katz ed.), Oxford University Press, 2009.
112 Kenneth Pennington, Baldus de Ubaldis, 8 RIVISTA INTERNAZIONALE DI DIRITTO COMUNE 35 (1997).
113 Da Legnano, Giovanni, Thomas Erskine Holland, and James Leslie Brierly. *Tractatus de bello, de represaliis et de duello*. Printed for the Carnegie Institution of Washington at the Oxford University Press, 1917.
114 Ibid 244.
115 Wahl, J.A. "Baldus de Ubaldis and the Foundations of the Nation-State." Manuscripta 21.2 (1977):80.

the people's sovereignty was necessary for a more permanent conception of peace. Baldus wrote on the *Digest*, the *Codex Iustinianus*, including the last three books (*Tres libri*), the Institutes, the *Decretales* of Pope Gregory IX, the *Liber feudorum*, and *Liber de pace constantiae*, a commentary of the Peace of Constance of 1183.[116] This last work will be the focus here, as it has the greatest relevance to *jus post bellum*.[117]

b) Writings and Relation to *Jus Post Bellum*
In *Liber de pace constantiae*[118] when Ubaldis writes: "*Imperator vult istam pacem esse perpetua.... quia Imperator facit hanc pacem nomine sedis non nomine proprio ... et Imperium non moritur*"[119] Baldus is distinguishing between peace agreements (such as the Treaty of Constanz) and a private contract that a ruler might enter into. Under this understanding of the state and the methods the state has for transitioning from armed conflict to peace (peace agreements), the peace agreement can be the basis for a lasting peace, binding on successive rulers. He pioneered the idea of *dignitas* or Royal Dignity, which "referred chiefly to the singularity of the royal office, to the sovereignty vested in the king by the people, and resting in the king alone."[120] Royal Dignity was not something that touched the king alone, but rather his entire government.[121] Immortality was a characteristic of *Dignitas*—like a species or like the phoenix, the natural body of the king might die but the king's "public body" could not.[122] This idea of what would now be called a legal person or an international legal personality is a critical foundation for later developments in *jus post bellum*—most obviously for peace treaties that resolve international armed conflict, but also for non-international armed conflicts resolved by peace agreements to which a state is a party. Contracts made by the king must be

---

116 Baldus de Ubaldis, Petrus, The Oxford International Encyclopedia of Legal History, (Stanley N. Katz ed.), Oxford University Press, 2009.
117 For contextualization of Baldus de Ubaldis as a predecessor to later scholars, see Lesaffer, Randall. "A Schoolmaster Abolishing Homework? Vattel on Peacemaking and Peace Treaties." *Vattel's International Law from a XXI st Century Perspective/Le Droit International de Vattel vu du XXI e Siècle*. Brill, 2011. 353–384, 356.
118 Baldus, on *Liber de pace constantiae*, 'Nos Romanorum' in *Corpus iuris civilis* (Lyons, 1553), fol. 76, as cited in Wahl, J.A. "Baldus de Ubaldis and the Foundations of the Nation-State." Manuscripta 21.2 (1977):80, 81.
119 Very roughly translated: "Because the emperor, who wants this peace to be permanent, makes this peace not in their own name but in the name of the empire, it does not die[.]"
120 Ernst Kantorowicz, *The King's Two Bodies* (Princeton, 1957), p. 384.
121 Ibid.
122 Wahl, James A. "Baldus de Ubaldis and the Foundations of the Nation-State." *Manuscripta* 21.2 (1977): 80–96, p. 83.

honoured by his successors because such contracts were governed by natural law—and no prince was above natural law or divine law, nor free to disregard the public welfare.[123] The law of was only somewhat distinguishable from general contract law at this point.[124]

Personal crimes of the king could not be imputed to a successor, however, as that would affect the *dignitas* of the king.[125] This is interesting from the perspective of individual criminal responsibility of heads of government and heads of state, important *jus post bellum* issues. It is in tension with the idea of the king not only animating *ius* or justice (*iustum animatum*)[126] but the king *as the law* (*nota quod lex est princeps*).[127]

c) Conclusion

Baldus plays an important part in establishing that peace treaties and peace agreements could and should endure. Without the idea that such agreements could be permanent, outlasting the king, a key foundation of *jus post bellum* would be lacking. Baldus manages to lay this foundation without sacrificing the idea that kings should be individual responsible for their personal crimes.

6 *Francisco de Vitoria (1492–1546)*

a) Introduction

Since the pioneering work of James Brown Scott in the 1920s[128] and 1930s,[129] the Spanish neo-scholastics of Francisco de Vitoria (or Victoria) and Francisco Suarez have been recognized as the principal point of origin for the modern doctrine of the law of nations.[130] Vitoria had a wide influence, both in his time and thereafter. The New Laws of the Indies of 1542 relied heavily on his works

---

123 Ibid 84.
124 Randall Lessafer, "The Medieval Canon Law of Contract and early Modern Treaty Law," 2 *Journal of the History of International Law* (2000), pp. 178, 185; Randall Lesaffer (2002) An Early Treatise on Peace Treaties: Petrus Gudelinus between Roman Law and Modern Practice, The Journal of Legal History, 23:3, 223–252, DOI: 10.1080/01440362308539651, p. 224.
125 Wahl, James A. "Baldus de Ubaldis and the Foundations of the Nation-State."*Manuscripta* 21.2 (1977): 80–96, p. 84.
126 Ibid 88.
127 Ibid.
128 James Brown Scott, *The Spanish Origin of International Law: Lectures on Francisco de Vitoria (1480–1546) and Francisco Suarez (1548–16717)*, Washington, 1928.
129 James Brown Scott, *The Catholic Conception of International Law: Francisco de Vitoria, founder of the modern law of nations; Francisco Suarez, founder of the modern philosophy of law in general and in particular the law of nations; A critical examination and a justified appreciation*, Washington, 1934.
130 Randall Lesaffer (2002) An Early Treatise on Peace Treaties: Petrus Gudelinus between Roman Law and Modern Practice, The Journal of Legal History, 23:3, 223–252, DOI: 10.1080/01440362308539651, p. 224.

De Indis and *De Jure Belli*.[131] These theologians are the best known members of the "School of Salamanca" or the "second scholastic," building on Aquinas to address new issues.[132] Vitoria was a theologian, not a lawyer—a Professor of Theology in the University of Salamanca.[133] Vitoria moved away from Aquinas styling of *ius gentium* as purely a natural law phenomenon as opposed to one also based on agreements between humans, what would now be called positive law.[134] That said, Vitoria relied heavily on natural law, and held to Thomas Aquinas's belief that natural law could be known through reason, not revelation.[135] Using this approach, he legitimized the Spanish conquest of the Indies not based on arguments that indigenous inhabitants of the Americas were heathen or allegedly irrational, but because of the alleged violation of the *ius communicandi*, the right of communication.[136] Strikingly, he held that "Difference of religion is not a cause of just war"[137] and that a just war may only be waged for causes provided in natural law.[138]

b) Writings and Relation to *Jus Post Bellum*
(1) Peace as the Aim of Armed Conflict—and the Problems that can Cause

Like Thomas Aquinas, Vitoria relies on Augustine as weighty authority. With regards to the aim of armed conflict, Vitoria states:

> If after recourse to all other measures, the Spaniards are unable to obtain safety as regards the native Indians, save by seizing their cities and

---

131 Johnson, James Turner, *Ideology, Reason, and the Limitation of War: Religious and Secular Concepts 1200–1740*, (Princeton University Press 1975), p. 158.
132 Annabel Brett, *Francisco De Vitoria (1483–1546) and Francisco Suárez (1548–1617)*, The Oxford Handbook of the History of International Law, Edited by Bardo Fassbender and Anne Peters (Oxford University Press, 2012).
133 Johnson, James Turner, *Just War Tradition and the Restraint of War: A Moral and Historical Inquiry*, (Princeton University Press 1981), pp. 94–95.
134 Annabel Brett, *Francisco De Vitoria (1483–1546) and Francisco Suárez (1548–1617)*, The Oxford Handbook of the History of International Law, Edited by Bardo Fassbender and Anne Peters (Oxford University Press, 2012).
135 Johnson, James Turner, *Just War Tradition and the Restraint of War: A Moral and Historical Inquiry*, (Princeton University Press 1981), p. 76.
136 Annabel Brett, *Francisco De Vitoria (1483–1546) and Francisco Suárez (1548–1617)*, The Oxford Handbook of the History of International Law, Edited by Bardo Fassbender and Anne Peters (Oxford University Press, 2012).
137 Franciscus de Victoria, *De Indis et De Jure Belli Relectiones*, ed. Ernest Nys, in *The Classics of International Law*, ed. James Brown Scott (Washington: Carnegie Institute, 1917: *De Jure Belli*, Sect. 10).
138 Johnson, James Turner, *Ideology, Reason, and the Limitation of War: Religious and Secular Concepts 1200–1740*, (Princeton University Press 1975), p. 157.

reducing them to subjection, they may lawfully proceed to these extremities. The proof lies in the fact that "peace and safety are the end and aim of war," as St. Augustine says, writing to Boniface.[139]

Vitoria continues:

> And since it is now lawful for the Spaniards, as has been said, to wage defensive war or even if necessary offensive war, therefore, everything necessary to secure the end and aim of war, namely, the obtaining of safety and peace, is lawful[140]

This absolutist language demonstrates an old difficulty with *jus post bellum*—the aim of transitioning to a sustainable peace, instead of restricting practice *in bello*, can be used to serve as an unlimited license.

Post bellum concerns can also undermine *ad bello* restrictions. Again relying ultimately on Augustine, Vitoria states on the issue of whether Christians may make war at all:

> A sixth proof is that, as St. Augustine says (De verbo Domini and Ad Bonifacium), the end and aim of war is the peace and security of the State. But there can be no security in the State unless enemies are made to desist from wrong by the fear of war, for the situation with regard to war would be glaringly unfair, if all that a State could do when enemies attack it unjustly was to ward off the attack and if they could not follow this up by further steps.[141]

Similarly, he states shortly thereafter:

> Not only are the things just named allowable, but a prince may go even further in a just war and do whatever is necessary in order to obtain peace and security from the enemy; for example, destroy an enemy's fortress and even build one on enemy soil, if this be necessary in order to avert a dangerous attack of the enemy. This is proved by the fact that, as said above, the end and aim of war is peace and security. Therefore a belligerent

---

139   De Vitoria, Francisco. *Francisci de Victoria De Indis et De ivre belli relectiones*. No. 7. The Carnegie Institution of Washington, 1917, p. 155 (On the Indians, Section III).
140   Ibid.
141   Ibid 167.

may do everything requisite to obtain peace and security. Further, tranquillity and peace are reckoned among the desirable things of mankind and so the utmost material prosperity does not produce a state of happiness if there be no security there. Therefore it is lawful to employ all appropriate measures against enemies who are plundering and disturbing the tranquillity of the State. [...] This shows that even when victory has been won and redress obtained, the enemy may be made to give hostages, ships, arms, and other things, when this is genuinely necessary for keeping the enemy in his duty and preventing him from becoming dangerous again.[142]

(2) *Post-conflict Justice*

Vitoria also directly addresses issues of post-conflict justice.

> It is lawful for a prince, after gaining the victory in a just war and after retaking property, and even after the establishment of peace and security, to avenge the wrongs done to him by the enemy and to take measures against the enemy and punish them for these wrongs.[143]

Again, linking the aims of peace to potential over-reach, even *post bellum*:

> Not only is all this permissible, but even after victory has been won and redress obtained and peace and safety been secured, it is lawful to avenge the wrong received from the enemy and to take measures against him and exact punishment from him for the wrongs he has done. [...] It is, therefore, certain that princes can punish enemies who have done a wrong to their State and that after a war has been duly and justly undertaken the enemy are just as much within the jurisdiction of the prince who undertakes it as if he were their proper judge. Confirmation hereof is furnished by the fact that in reality peace and tranquillity, which are the end and aim of war, can not be had unless evils and damages be visited on the enemy in order to deter them from the like conduct in the future. [...] Moreover, shame and disgrace are not wiped away from a State merely by its rout of Its enemies, but also by its visiting severe punishment and castigation on them. Now, among the things which a

---

142 Ibid 171.
143 Ibid 163.

prince is bound to defend and preserve for his State are its honor and authority."[144]

Vitoria does, however, restrict some post-conflict measures:

> Merely by way of avenging a wrong it is not always lawful to kill all the guilty. [...] We ought, then, to take into account the nature of the wrong done by the enemy and of the damage they have caused and of their other offenses, and from that standpoint to move to our revenge and punishment, without any cruelty and inhumanity. In this connection Cicero says (Offices, bk. 2) that the punishment which we inflict on the guilty must be such as equity and humanity allow. And Sallust says: "Our ancestors, the most religious of men, took naught from those they conquered save what was authorized by the nature of their offenses."[145]

Similarly:

> [I]t would involve the ruin of mankind and of Christianity if the victor always slew all his enemies, and the world would soon be reduced to solitude, and wars would not be waged for the public good, but to the utter ruin of the public. The measure of the punishment, then, must be proportionate to the offense, and vengeance ought to go no further, and herein account must be taken of the consideration that, as said above, subjects are not bound, and ought not, to scrutinize the causes of a war, but can follow their prince to it in reliance on his authority and on public counsels. Hence in the majority of cases, although the war be unjust on the other side, yet the troops engaged in it and who defend or attack cities are innocent on both sides. And therefore after their defeat, when no further danger is present, I think that they may not be killed, not only not all of them, but not even one of them, if the presumption is that they entered on the strife in good faith.[146]

This idea, that individuals can enter into strife in good faith, even if there side is not just, is one of Vitoria's most influential ideas in the just war tradition. For

---

144 Ibid 172–173.
145 Ibid 182.
146 Ibid 182.

example, the English jurist Fulbecke takes the same approach on this subject, sometimes called "invincible ignorance" as Vitoria.¹⁴⁷

(3)   *An Integrated View of* Jus ad Bellum, *Jus In Bello, and Jus Ad Bellum*
Vitoria does not view the legal authority to make war and secure peace as separate domains, but rather, relying on Augustine, views them as an integrated whole.

> A prince has the same authority in this respect as the State has. This is the opinion of St. Augustine (Contra Faustum): "The natural order, best adapted to secure the peace of mankind, requires that the authority to make war and the advisability of it should be in the hands of the sovereign prince." Reason supports this, for the prince only holds his position by the election of the State. Therefore he is its representative and wields its authority; aye, and where there are already lawful princes in a State, all authority is in their hands and without them nothing of a public nature can be done either in war or in peace."¹⁴⁸

Vitoria also connects the just cause of war to the nature of the domestic regime, well before there was any thought of a "democratic peace." He extend this not just to the overall just cause of war (a *jus ad bellum* concern with important effects on *jus post bellum*) but to the rules of war (a *jus in bello* concern).

> Neither the personal glory of the prince nor any other advantage to him is a just cause of war. [...] [W]ere a prince to misuse his subjects by compelling them to go soldiering and to contribute money for his campaigns, not for the public good, but for his own private gain, this would be to make slaves of them.¹⁴⁹

The connection between *jus ad bellum*, *jus in bello*, and *jus post bellum* also extends to the question of acquiring territory as a fine, or mulct, during war and after war.

---

147   Johnson, James Turner, *Ideology, Reason, and the Limitation of War: Religious and Secular Concepts 1200–1740*, (Princeton University Press 1975), p. 189.
148   De Vitoria, Francisco. *Francisci de Victoria De Indis et De ivre belli relectiones*. No. 7. The Carnegie Institution of Washington, 1917, p. 169.
149   Ibid 170.

It is also lawful, in return for a wrong received and by way of punishment, that is, in revenge, to mulct the enemy of a part of his territory in proportion to the character of the wrong, or even on this ground to seize a fortress or town. This, however, must be done within due limits, as already said, and not as utterly far as our strength and armed force enable us to go in seizing and storming. And if necessity and the principle of war require the seizure of the larger part of the enemy's land, and the capture of numerous cities, they ought to be restored when the strife is adjusted and the war is over, only so much being retained as is just, in way of compensation for damages caused and expenses incurred and of vengeance for wrongs done, and with due regard for equity and humanity, seeing that punishment ought to be proportionate to the fault.[150]

(4)   *Post Bellum Tribute*

Distinctly *post bellum* is the question of a lawful tribute imposed on conquered enemies. Vitoria thinks this is decidedly lawful, stating: "Whether it is lawful to impose a tribute on conquered enemies. My answer is that it is undoubtedly lawful, not only in order to recoup damages, but also as a punishment and by way of revenge."[151]

(5)   *Post Bellum Regime Change*

Also distinctly *post bellum* is the question of deposing the princes of conquered enemies. Vitoria thinks this can be lawful, but it must be proportionate.

> Whether it is lawful to depose the princes of the enemy and appoint new ones or keep the princedom for oneself. First proposition: This is not unqualifiedly permissible, nor for any and every cause of just war, as appears from what has been said. For punishment should not exceed the degree and nature of the offense. Nay, punishments should be awarded restrictively, and rewards extensively. This is not a rule of human law only, but also of natural and divine law. Therefore, even assuming that the enemy's offense is a sufficient cause of war, it will not always suffice to justify the overthrow of the enemy's sovereignty and the deposition of

---

150   Ibid 185.
151   Ibid.

lawful and natural princes; for these would be utterly savage and inhumane measures.[152]

When is it acceptable to change the enemy regime? It can be due to the power of the just cause (*jus ad bellum*) of the war, but it is especially true when it is necessary to achieve a sustainable peace (a *jus post bellum* concern).

> It is undeniable that there may sometimes arise sufficient and lawful causes for effecting a change of princes or for seizing a sovereignty; and this may be either because of the number and aggravated quality of the damages and wrongs which have been wrought or, especially, when security and peace can not otherwise be had of the enemy and grave danger from them would threaten the State if this were not done. This is obvious, for if the seizure of a city is lawful for good cause, as has been said, it follows that the removal of its prince is also lawful. And the same holds good of a province and the prince of a province, if proportionately graver cause arise.
>
> Note, however, with regard to Doubts VI to IX, that sometimes, nay, frequently, not only subjects, but princes, too, who in reality have no just cause of war, may nevertheless be waging war in good faith, with such good faith, I say, as to free them from fault; as, for instance, if the war is made after a careful examination and in accordance with the opinion of learned and upright men. And since no one who has not committed a fault should be punished, in that case, although the victor may recoup himself for things that have been taken from him and for any expenses of the war, yet, just as it is unlawful to go on killing after victory in the war has been won, so the victor ought not to make seizures or exactions in temporal matters beyond the limits of just satisfaction, seeing that anything beyond these limits could only be justified as a punishment, such as could not be visited on the innocent.[153]

Vitoria summarizes his canons of warfare as follows:

> 60. All this can be summarized in a few canons or rules of warfare. First canon: Assuming that a prince has authority to make war, he should first of all not go seeking occasions and causes of war, but should, if possible,

---

152 Ibid 185–187.
153 Ibid 185–187.

live in peace with all men, as St. Paul enjoins on us (Romans, Ch. 12). Moreover, he should reflect that others are his neighbors, whom we are bound to love as ourselves, and that we all have one common Lord, before whose tribunal we shall have to render our account. For it is the extreme of savagery to seek for and rejoice in grounds for killing and destroying men whom God has created and for whom Christ died. But only under compulsion and reluctantly should he come to the necessity of war.

Second canon: When war for a just cause has broken out, it must not be waged so as to ruin the people against whom it is directed, but only so as to obtain one's rights and the defense of one's country and in order that from that war peace and security may in time result."[154]

In short, avoid war when possible and only with proper authority, and wage war so as to achieve lasting peace and security. Vitoria again takes an integrated approach to *jus ad bellum, jus in bello,* and *jus post bellum*.

c) Conclusion

Vitoria covers a wide field of material that relates to *jus post bellum*. Critical subject areas include: first, peace as the aim of armed conflict; second, post-conflict justice; third, an integrated view of *jus ad bellum, jus in bello,* and *jus post bellum*; and fourth, post bellum regime change. Together, Vitoria's writings amount to a new foundation for *jus post bellum*.

7 *Francisco Suarez (1548–1617)*

a) Introduction

As mentioned previously, Since the pioneering work of James Brown Scott in the 1920s[155] and 1930s,[156] the Spanish neo-scholastics of Francisco de Vitoria and Francisco Suarez have been recognized as the principal point of origin for the modern doctrine of the law of nations.[157] These theologians are the best known members of the "School of Salamanca" or the "second scholastic,"

---

154 Ibid 185–187.
155 James Brown Scott, *The Spanish Origin of International Law: Lectures on Francisco de Vitoria (1480–1546) and Francisco Suarez (1548–16717)*, Washington, 1928.
156 James Brown Scott, *The Catholic Conception of International Law: Francisco de Vitoria, founder of the modern law of nations; Francisco Suarez, founder of the modern philosophy of law in general and in particular of the law of nations; A critical examination and a justified appreciation*, Washington, 1934.
157 Randall Lesaffer (2002) An Early Treatise on Peace Treaties: Petrus Gudelinus between Roman Law and Modern Practice, The Journal of Legal History, 23:3, 223–252, DOI: 10.1080/01440362308539651, p. 224.

building on Aquinas to address new issues.[158] Like Vitoria, Francisco Suarez emphasized the positive law nature of *ius gentium*, based not on natural law but on custom.[159]

b) Writings and Relation to *Jus Post Bellum*

If James Brown Scott was correct that Francisco de Vitoria was the founder of international law, Francisco Suarez was the philosopher, and Hugo Grotius was the organizer[160]—what did the philosopher have to say about the transition from armed conflict to peace? Suarez is noteworthy in large part due to his systematic commentary on the writings of Aquinas.[161]

Scholars often cite the primary contribution of Suarez to the just war tradition is the emphasis on what would now be called *jus in bello*, the importance of the means of warfare.[162] To understand Suarez's approach to the transition to peace, one must focus first on *jus ad bellum* factors, specifically on just cause. Suarez did not consider aggressive war to be necessarily evil, rather he argued that it might be right and necessary if punishment was merited.[163] He did not consider it a problem that sovereigns would be judges in their own case, both at the outset, during, and after war—because there is no other option.[164]

Suarez also emphasizes the role of charity with regards to the pursuing a just cause with an eye towards the post-conflict situation.[165] Even if a war is just, or a demand for payment is just, if "the debtor incurs very serious losses in consequence, while the property in question is not in great degree necessary to

---

158 Annabel Brett, *Francisco De Vitoria (1483–1546) and Francisco Suárez (1548–1617)*, The Oxford Handbook of the History of International Law, Edited by Bardo Fassbender and Anne Peters (Oxford University Press, 2012).
159 Ibid.
160 James Brown Scott, *The Catholic Conception of International Law: Francisco de Vitoria, founder of the modern law of nations; Francisco Suarez, founder of the modern philosophy of law in general and in particular of the law of nations; A critical examination and a justified appreciation*, Washington, 1934, pp. 183–184.
161 Ibid.
162 May, Larry. "Grotius and Contingent Pacifism." *Studies in the History of Ethics* (2006): 1–24.
163 *Selections from Three Works of Francisco Suárez, S.J.* Prepared by Gwladys L. Williams, Ammi Brown, and John Waldron. Oxford: Clarendon Press, 1944, *Disputatio de Bello* (disp. 13), Is War Intrinsically Evil, pp. 803, 818. Available at http://www.heinonline.org/HOL/Page?handle=hein.beal/sftw0002&id=901&collection=beal&index=beal/sftw.
164 *Selections from Three Works of Francisco Suárez, S.J.* Prepared by Gwladys L. Williams, Ammi Brown, and John Waldron. Oxford: Clarendon Press, 1944, *Disputatio de Bello* (disp. 13), Is War Intrinsically Evil, p. 819.
165 Ibid 820–821.

the creditor."[166] Suarez also condemns disproportionate risk of post-war loss and peril for the realm of a justly aggrieved prince:

> [I]f one prince begins a war upon another, even with just cause, while exposing his own realm to disproportionate loss and peril, then he will be sinning not only against charity, but also against the justice due to his own state. The reason for this assertion is as follows: a prince is bound in justice to have greater regard for the common good of his state than for his own good; otherwise, he will become a tyrant.[167]

Suarez was also interested in the probability of a successful *post bellum* result as a condition of starting a war.[168] He disagreed with Cardinal Thomas de Vio (known as Cajetan) that "for a war to be just, the sovereign ought to be so sure of the degree of his power, that he is morally certain of victory."[169] Suarez does not think this condition of certitude is absolutely essential, because it is almost impossible to realize, because it can lead to undue hesitancy, and also because it effectively discriminates against weaker sovereigns (*vis a vis* stronger sovereigns).[170]

c)   Conclusion

Suarez's view of the law of war necessarily informed his writings dealing with the transition to peace. He does not condemn aggressive war necessarily[171] but insists on the role of charity with regards to pursuing a just cause, due to the need for a sustainable post-conflict peace.[172] The likelihood of a just peace must be evaluated before beginning a war,[173] but certainty of outcome is not required.[174]

8   *Alberico Gentili (1552–1608)*
a)   Introduction

It is not unreasonable to trace the key origins of modern international legal thought to Alberico Gentili.[175] His application of the concept of sovereignty is

---

166   Ibid 821.
167   Ibid.
168   Ibid 822.
169   Ibid 822.
170   Ibid 822.
171   Ibid 803, 818.
172   Ibid 820–821.
173   Ibid 821.
174   Ibid 822.
175   For a concise introduction to Gentili and his historiography, see Scattola, Merio Fassbender, "Alberico Gentili (1552–1608)" in Bardo, et al. *The Oxford handbook of the history of*

strikingly modern, and his development of jurisprudence separate from the church was a pivotal contribution.[176] Working shortly before Hugo Grotius, he was a Professor of Civil Law in Oxford, bringing a history-infused Italian outlook to his efforts to describe the law. Nonetheless, he draws heavily on earlier scholars for authority and understanding, again demonstrating the deep conceptual roots of his subject matter.[177]

b)   Writings and Relation to *Jus Post Bellum*

Gentili's most famous work, and his most important work with respect to *jus post bellum* and the just war tradition in general, is *De Iure Belli Libri Tres*.[178] Gentili first published his thoughts on the law of war in 1589 under the title *De Jure Belli Commentationes Tres*. *De Iure Belli Libri Tres* (three books on the law of war), an expanded version of *De Jure Belli Commentationes Tres* was first published in 1598. The third of the three books that make up this work is of particular interest. The three books roughly match the contemporary *jus ad bellum, jus in bello, jus post bellum* framework in widespread use today. Before reviewing that third book, however, some initial stops in the first and the end of the second book are warranted.

Book I, Chapter XXIV deals with "Whether war is handed on to future generations."[179] This is framed as a question of what would now be called *jus ad bellum*, the transmissibility of just cause against "successors and posterity" or as Gentili puts it: "is it lawful to make against successors and posterity a war which it would have been lawful to make against their predecessors?"[180] In modern conceptions of armed conflict as an interaction between socially and

---

international law. Oxford University Press, 2012.

176 See T.E. Holland, An inaugural lecture on Albericus Gentilis (1874); Haggenmacher, 'Grotius and Gentili: A Reassessment of Thomas E. Holland's Inaugural Lecture,' in H. Bull, B. Kingsbury, and A. Roberts (eds), Hugo Grotius and International Relations (1990), at 133; G. van der Molen, Alberico Gentili and the Development of International Law: His Life, Work and Times (1937).

177 For contextualization of Alberico Gentili as a predecessor to later scholars, see Lesaffer, Randall. "A Schoolmaster Abolishing Homework? Vattel on Peacemaking and Peace Treaties." *Vattel's International Law from a XXI st Century Perspective/Le Droit International de Vattel vu du XXI e Siècle*. Brill, 2011. 353–384, 356–357.

178 The best treatment of Gentili and his relevance for *jus post bellum* is Lesaffer, Randall. "Alberico Gentili's just post bellum and Early Modern Peace Treaties." in Kingsbury, Benedict, and Benjamin Straumann. *The Roman foundations of the law of nations: Alberico Gentili and the justice of empire*. Oxford University Press, 2010.

179 2 Alberico Gentili, De Iure Belli Libri Tres (John C. Rolfe trans.), p. 120 (1933). Whether War is Handed on the Future Generations, available at http://heinonline.org/HOL/Page?handle=hein.beal/cilnaa0002&id=180&collection=unaudvis&index=beal/cilnaa#180.

180 Ibid 120.

legally constructed entities, not natural persons, this question is not normally asked. The idea of the natural persons inheriting the sins of their predecessors is not the framework a modern public international lawyer normally asks, and indeed for the secular-oriented Gentili shows the pressure of religious thinking at the time. If the answer given was no, then this would serve as a structural check on war's recurrence. Unfortunately, perhaps, the answer given by Gentili (and, in a sense, by current law) is that biological succession from one generation to the next is not itself a check on grievances between sovereigns. Gentili rationalizes this on normative and legal terms by pointing out that positive inheritances may also be undeserved, but are nonetheless not seen as immoral or unlawful.[181] On the other hand, he stands against those who would not make binding agreements been sovereigns on public matters endure past the deaths of those who made the oaths—the framework for lasting peace and enduring treaties.[182] Again, this question would not arise today, but that is because Gentili and others established the framework that is now (usually) used without question or reflection.

In Book II, Chapter XII "Of Truces" strongly argues that the mere cessation of violence caused by truces does not amount to peace.[183] While truces may be long (he cites truces lasting 100 years) and the land can seem at peace during truces, they are not permanent. Truces "do not interrupt hostility, but only bring hostile acts to an end."[184] The subject of the nature of truces, whether they amount to a third state between peace and war, is hotly debated, and Gentili notes this debate without being overly committed to any side.[185]

In Book III, Chapter I "On Peace and the End of War," Gentili enters into what could be called *jus post bellum* proper. The opening paragraph is worth noting in full:

> Up to this point we have discussed the laws of both of beginning and of carrying on war. Hence but one point still remains; namely, to tell of the rules for bringing war to an end. And indeed the end of war for which all ought to strive is peace. 'War should be entered upon in such a way,' says Cicero, 'that its aim should seem to be nothing else than peace.' Augustine also and the Canons declare that 'peace should be one's desire, war a necessity. For peace is not sought in order to arouse war; but war is waged

---

181 Ibid.
182 Ibid 121.
183 Ibid 186 (Of Truces).
184 Ibid 187.
185 Ibid.

in order to win peace.' Therefore victory is the end of the general's art, says Aristotle, when the victory is characterized by honour and by justice, which is peace.[186]

Gentili is integrating the transition from war as part of the overall law of war. He cites Cicero, Aristotle, Augustine, and Canon Law to insist that this transition to peace infuses the entire enterprise of armed conflict, from its overall goals to the general's art of achieving victory with honour and justice.

Gentili is interested in the definition of *pax*, citing Festus and Ulpian for the etymology deriving the term from agreement (*pactio*), and Isidore who derives compact (*pactum*) from peace (*pax*).[187] Peace agreements put an end to war, or prevent its occurrence.[188] Gentili ultimately defines peace as follows:

> But peace is define in a general way of Augustine as 'ordered harmony'; and order is the proper distribution of things, which in the opinion of our own jurists and others is the nature of justice. We therefore define peace here as the orderly settlement of war. Baldus calls it a complete cessation of discord, declaring that peace cannot exist while war remains. This is true, and we shall maintain that view later at some length. But our definition also contains this point, and besides has the provision about justice, which is what we seek in this cessation of war, along with order and the assignment of his own to each man.[189]

This definition of peace, insisting on not only justice but distributional justice, and that the goal is not only to end a conflict but to prevent its occurrence, seems strikingly contemporary. Here is a foundation for an insistence on not just "negative" peace but a just and sustainable peace as the goal of the third part of the just war tradition, *jus post bellum*.

Our current English word "peace" derives from the Latin *pax*, meaning an agreement — a pact — to refrain from hostilities.[190] Thus, the root of concept of peace is a *constructed* peace, not simply a natural

Gentili continues:

---

186 Ibid 289 (On Peace and the End of War).
187 Ibid 290.
188 Ibid.
189 Ibid.
190 S.C. Neff, *War and the Law of Nations: A General History* (CUP 2005), 29–38.

> And as to this order or right distribution we shall now speak, saying that it is brought about by the victor alone, or by both sides together; and that both sides commonly consider, not only the past, but also the future, and indeed ought to do so. This is taught by Homer, that father of all wisdom, and is observed by the great authority Plutarch. Also our own omniscient and all-defining Baldus set it forth in his *Responses*. The past has an eye to vengeance, the future to a permanent establishment of peace; nay, the past also has regard to this permanence, as will appear from what follows. But the two topics must be considered separately.[191]

The future-oriented nature of the function of *jus post bellum* has ancient roots. It is not, however, free to ignore the past, but must resolve past grievances to secure a just peace.

This leads Gentili to Book III, Chapter II "Of the Vengeance of the Victor."[192] This chapter is not actually celebrating vengeance,[193] but rather is a treatment of post-conflict justice. Citing Baldus, Gentili states:

> [I]t is not fitting for a judge to give his attention to establishing peace until the faults which led to war are punished; so in this subject we must first provide for a just penalty, in order that when all the roots of war have, so to say, been cut away, peace may acquire greater firmness.[194]

Gentili here connects the *justice* of a peace to its *sustainability*. The promise of post-conflict justice is necessary for war's cessation: "There would never be peace, and war would be to the death and contrary to nature, if the will of the victor controlled everything and the vanquished could lose everything."[195]

Gentili is not only considered about negative repercussions for the vanquished in war, but to the potentially pernicious effects of victory on the victor. Following Augustine, he is concerned with the effect of war on internal character, not only external results:

> [O]ne should ask the question, not what the victor is able to do and what victory may demand, but what befits the character of the victor, as well as

---

191   2 Alberico Gentili, De Iure Belli Libri Tres (John C. Rolfe trans.), p. 290 (1933).
192   Ibid 291 (Of the Vengeance of the Victor).
193   Gentili defines vengeance as the other side of the coin to punishment, where "punishment is one thing, which has regard to the one who suffers it; and vengeance is another, which relates to him who inflicts it[.]" Ibid 295.
194   Ibid 291.
195   Ibid.

that of the vanquished; but in the case of the victor in particular, it should be considered what becomes him and also the nature of the war which is being carried on. But everything must be directed towards the true purpose of victory, which is the blessing of peace. 'Lead those whom you defeat to the advantages of the peace brought about by their defeat,' says Augustine.[196]

Gentili does not think post-conflict justice requires an equal approach to "cultivated peoples" and "barbarians" or "uncivilized nations," holding that "with barbarians violence is more potent that kindness."[197] Similarly, haughty or proud defeated peoples should be treated with harshness, according to Gentili.[198] That said, Gentili insists that "the penalty ought never to exceed the deserts of the offender, but it ought to be determined according to the measure of each offence. The punishment, too, ought to fall upon the one by whom the crime is committed."[199] Here is the seed of principles dear to modern post-conflict justice: proportionality of punishment and individual criminal responsibility. He continues arguing for a bar on unnatural punishment:

> Punishments which any respect for Nature would forbid should have no place here. We leave to others the special discussion of those penalties which are forbidden by the civil law, and which seem to me to be forbidden by respect for Nature, such as the cutting off of both hands and feet.[200]

He continues barring cruel punishment, citing Baldus for the idea that "nothing which is cruel is just."[201] He ties these restrictions on punishment to the goal of achieving a sustainable peace: "It is such conduct [cruel or disfiguring punishment] which keeps a war which is finished from being permanently at an end, and this conduct Augustine censures at great length."[202]

In Book III, Chapter III "Of the Expenses and Losses Due to War," Gentili analyses the difficult issue of war reparations. He compares the issue to legal disputes in which:

---

196 Ibid 293.
197 Ibid.
198 Ibid 294.
199 Ibid 295.
200 Ibid.
201 Ibid.
202 Ibid 296.

> [T]he loser must refund the costs to the victor, not only in civil but also in criminal cases, if he did not have a just cause; this is especially true in case the plaintiff is defeated [...] But if the loser appears to have had ground for litigation, he is not condemned.[203]

Gentili argues that the law regarding the transition to peace is "subject to a special law"—specifically including:

> [T]hat the goods of private individuals, for the sake of peace, may be given away by the state or the sovereign. And it is common doctrine that the wrongs and losses of subjects may for the reason be remitted by their sovereign, and that the subjects in their turn may never make complaint, either in a civil or a criminal suit.[204]

The sovereign in turn is bound to restore goods taken from his or her subjects in accordance with the law of nations and the demands of peace, but unjustly according to domestic law.[205] Citing Baldus, Gentili raises the issue of waiving public rights before individuals, and the idea that agreements between sovereigns should not disadvantage particular private individuals, but be general[206]—but in the end comes out against pursuing reparation for violations of the law of war after the peace is made and the terms of peace agreed upon.[207]

Gentili's remarks "On Exacting Tribute and Lands from the Vanquished"[208] are part reasonable justification for taxation, part apology for empire. While Gentili endorses the right of conquest and *jus victoriae*, including exacting tribute and lands, the right of the victor is not unlimited. He states "property may be taken from the enemy, provided that in so doing justice and equity are observed. The victor will not make everything his own which force and his victory make it possible to seize."[209] In "Of Despoiling the Conquered of Their Ornaments"[210] Gentili limits looting religious objects "only if the gods themselves were destroyed when their statues were lost. For it is not permitted the

---

203   Ibid 298 (Of the Expenses and Losses Due to War).
204   Ibid 300.
205   Ibid.
206   Ibid.
207   Ibid 302.
208   Ibid 303 (On Exacting Tribute and Lands from the Vanquished).
209   Ibid 305.
210   Ibid 310, Of Despoiling the Conquered of Their Ornaments (Book III, Chapter VI).

victors in dealing with the conquered to violate the laws of God or of Nature."[211] His preference to the general looting he finds the laws permits is "to show respect to moderation and honour, and to refrain from doing what is permitted by the laws."[212] But while "it is always proper to consider the reason for making war and to bring all the actions of the war into harmony with it, so far as possible"[213] things which are not sacred may undoubtedly be seized by the victor, according to Gentili.[214] After much debate, Gentili comes out against executing captive leaders of the enemy, and restricts perpetual imprisonment of enemy leaders if the victor has other means to achieve a sustainable peace.[215] In a chapter likely to be abhorrent to the modern reader but reflective of state practice at the time, he comes out forcefully in favour of the legality of slavery in the law of nations[216] but points out the custom of *postliminium* in which a slave, including those captured in war, one may be freed by escaping and returning home during wartime. He generally treats the capture of slaves as a matter of chattel, but holds that "an enemy may not be held captive perpetually and must not be sold."[217] He dismisses religious arguments against slavery with this strikingly secular analysis: "For in divine affairs man is nothing; and in establishing the law between God and man, which is religion, he has no weight; but it is not so in human affairs nor in establishing human law."[218] While much of Gentili's writings evince a much greater concern with religious teachings and history than would be the norm in later years or today, it is this clear effort to divide religion from human law that is so striking for Gentili at the time, compared to the religious scholars opining on the law of war before him.

Book III, Chapter X "On Changing One's Condition"[219] regards what Immanuel Kant might have called changing the constitution of a people, or what might be called today "transformative occupation" or perhaps just the form of local government in an empire. Gentili has no compunction about the right of the victor to change local governments: "[I]t is just for the vanquished to be forced to adopt the government of the conquerors; or if they do not yield, it is

---

211   Ibid 311.
212   Ibid 313.
213   Ibid 315, Of the Destruction and Sacking of Cities (Book III, Chapter VII).
214   Ibid.
215   Ibid 327, Of the Captive Leaders of the Enemy (Book III, Chapter VIII).
216   Ibid 328, Of Slaves (Book III, Chapter IX).
217   Ibid.
218   Ibid 332, Of Slaves (Book III, Chapter IX).
219   Ibid 336, On Changing One's Condition.

right to crush them."²²⁰ For forced changes in religion, however, Gentili is sceptical except for "those who are enslaved to a perverse religion" when "their religion made the conquest less decisive."²²¹ Generally, Gentili finds forcible changes to religious practice not to be helpful to consolidate the peace.²²²

Nor should unnecessary changes to custom be imposed. Gentili states there are many instances:

> [I]in which natural justice is offended and with respect to which the victor has no rights. These are all things which furnish a natural cause for war, and the purpose is, that the victor may not propose to the vanquished to undertake things which offer a natural cause for making war.²²³

He gives the example of forced prostitution as a condition of peace that would lead to future war, as it violated honour and natural law.²²⁴ Disarmament of the conquered, however, is legal and routine.²²⁵ While the victor may set up memorials of his victory, it is inexpedient to do so as they may prompt rebellion.²²⁶

Perhaps the most crucial series of chapters in *De Iure Belli Libri Tres* with respect to *jus post bellum* begins with Book III, Chapter XIII: "On Insuring Peace for the Future."²²⁷ Gentili begins by reiterating the importance of future orientation, saying that punishment (*ultio*) fulfils both the desire for solace for injury and also for security for the future.²²⁸ He states that "the victor should grant a peace of such a kind as to be lasting, since it is the nature of peace to be permanent."²²⁹ What specifically makes a peace lasting? Citing Augustine, Gentili notes compassion and restraint on anger in punishment as critical.²³⁰ From Epictetus's definition of peace as "liberty combined with tranquillity"²³¹ Gentili derives the "one enduring principle, namely justice"²³² for creating a

---

220   Ibid 338.
221   Ibid 342, On Change of Religion and Other Conditions.
222   Ibid.
223   Ibid 346.
224   Ibid.
225   Ibid 347 On Change of Religion and Other Conditions.
226   Ibid 350 When There Is a Conflict between What Is Honourable and What Is Expedient.
227   Ibid 353, On Insuring Peace for the Future.
228   Ibid 353.
229   Ibid.
230   Ibid.
231   Ibid 354.
232   Ibid.

lasting peace. He discounts marriage,[233] oaths,[234] and temporary strength over the conquered[235] as unreliable foundations for peace if justice is absent. That said, in the peace which the victors grant to the conquered, "[e]verything is in the hands of the victor, save for such exceptions as are suggested by the laws of nature"[236] including keeping women hostages.[237]

Gentili makes a distinction between peace granted to the conquered and the settling of war by both belligerents, a subject he takes up in Chapter XIV, "On the Law of Agreements."[238] Citing Baldus, Gentili emphasizes the aim of a permanent quiet, and more colourfully citing Hippocrates, compares injustice in the peace agreement and its effect on peace to what remains after a crisis "since in diseases it is what remains after the crisis that usually causes death."[239] Echoing Baldus, Gentili asks:

> But shall we also say that a war which springs from a former one is the same war, as if it came from a root which has been left in the ground? That certainly is not peace which does not do away with all controversy; a disease is not cured unless the root is destroyed.[240]

Gentili inveighs against subtlety, deception, and exceptions in peace treaties, saying that fine points of law are not suited for trustworthiness.[241] No exception is made to the binding nature of a peace treaty due to fear or duress, since (citing Baldus) Gentili points out that fear is natural after victory, and "hence one must keep his agreement who makes one because he is conquered in war; and the same thing applies to the agreements of prisoners of war."[242] That said, Gentili carves out exception for those subject to unjust force and fear while imprisoned,[243] fraud,[244] or unforeseeable change of circumstances.[245] He argues for a framework in which to evaluate potentially conflicting obligations from multiple peace treaties and treaties of alliance, starting with feudal

---

233 Ibid 355.
234 Ibid 356.
235 Ibid 358.
236 Ibid 359.
237 Ibid.
238 Ibid 360.
239 Ibid.
240 Ibid.
241 Ibid.
242 Ibid 363, On the Law of Agreements.
243 Ibid 363–364.
244 Ibid 365.
245 Ibid.

obligations,[246] restricting aiding both sides in a conflict,[247] aiding just causes,[248] aiding the party with the prior claim,[249] to avoid providing aid when in doubt as to conflicting claims,[250] and to favour an ally waging defensive war over one waging offensive war.[251] Gentili argues for making peace treaties (but not alliances) with non-Christian sovereigns[252] and places arms control squarely into his Book III analysis regarding the transition to peace.[253]

c) Conclusion

In *De Iure Belli Libri Tres* we find a tri-partite hybrid functional approach to the just war tradition that is in many respects strikingly contemporary. The first of three books covers not the start of war, but the overall justice and theory of entering into war.[254] The second book covers the more detailed practice of fighting war.[255] The third book covers not the period after war, but the ending

---

[246] Ibid 390, Of Friendship and Alliance.
[247] Ibid 390, 393.
[248] Ibid 391.
[249] Ibid 392.
[250] Ibid.
[251] Ibid.
[252] Ibid 397, Whether It Is Right to Make a Treaty with Men of a Different Religion.
[253] Ibid. 404 Of Arms and Armies; Ibid 407, Of Citadels and Garrisons.
[254] The subjects in the first book include the following chapter titles, allowing the reader to make a relatively speedy evaluation of the contents of the volume: I. Of International Law as applied to War; II. The Definition of War; III. War is waged by Sovereigns; IV. Brigands do not wage War; V. It is Just to wage War; VI. That War may be waged Justly by Both Sides; VII. Of the Causes of War; VIII. Of Divine Causes for making War; IX. Whether it is Just to wage War for the sake of Religion; X. Whether a Sovereign may justly resort to War to maintain Religion; among his Subjects; XI. Should Subjects war against their Sovereign because of Religion?; XII. Whether there are Natural Causes for making War; XIII. Of Necessary Defence; XIV. Of Defence on Grounds of Expediency; XV. Of Defence for the sake of Honour; XVI. On Defending the Subjects of Another against their Sovereign; XVII. Those who make War of Necessity; XVIII. Those who make War from Motives of Expediency; XIX. Of Natural Reasons for making War; XX. Of Human Reasons for making War; XXI. Of the Misdeeds of Private Individuals; XXII. On not Reviving Old Causes for War; XXIII. Of the Overthrow of Kingdoms; XXIV. Whether War is handed on to Future Generations; XXV. Of an Honourable Reason for waging War.
[255] The subjects in the second book include the following chapter titles, allowing the reader to make a relatively speedy evaluation of the contents of the volume: I. Of Declaring War; II. When War is Not Declared; III. Of Craft and Strategy; IV. Of Deception by Words; V. Of Falsehoods; VI. Of Poisoning; VII. Of Arms and Counterfeit Arms; VIII. Of Scaevola, Judith, and Similar Cases; IX. Of Zopyrus and other Deserters; X. Of the Compacts of Leaders; XI. Of Agreements by the Soldiers; XII. Of Truces; XIII. When a Truce is Violated; XIV. Of Safe-conduct; XV. Of the Exchange and Liberation of Prisoners; XVI. Of Captives: that they are not to be Slain; XVII. Of Those who Surrender to the Enemy; XVIII. Of Cruelty

of war and the practice of crafting a new era of peace.²⁵⁶ For skeptics of the pedigree of this hybrid functional approach to *jus ad bellum, jus in bello,* and *jus post bellum* (re-)reading Gentili may be useful.

9 Petrus Gudelinus (1550–1619)

a) Introduction

Petrus Gudelinus's work *De jure pacis commentaris,*²⁵⁷ was published posthumously in 1620.²⁵⁸ He builds on Baldus de Ubaldis and Bartolus of Sassoferrato, and likely influenced Hugo Grotius.²⁵⁹ Like Baldus de Ubaldis, he was not interested in parsing the peace treaty he was analysing, the Peace of Constanz, article by article—rather he would comment on the phenomenon of peace treaties in general.²⁶⁰

b) Writings and Relation to *Jus Post Bellum*

De jure pacis commentaris is only 14 pages in the *Opera omnia*²⁶¹ and has twelve sections or *capita*. The first section includes a section on methods and a

---

towards Prisoners and Captives; XIX. Of Hostages; XX. Of Suppliants; XXI. Of Women and Children; XXII. Of Farmers, Traders, Pilgrims, and the Like; XXIII. Of Devastation and Fires; XXIV. Of the Burial of the Slain.

256   See *supra.*

257   Petrus Gudelinus, *De jure pacis commentarius, in quo praecipuae de hoc jure quaestionis distinctis capitibus eleganter pertractantur,* Louvain, 1620. References initially from Randall Lesaffer (2002) An Early Treatise on Peace Treaties: Petrus Gudelinus between Roman Law and Modern Practice, The Journal of Legal History, 23:3, 223–252, DOI: 10.1080/01440362308539651. The 1628 Louvain edition was titled *De jure pacis commentaries ad constitutionem Frederici de pace Constantiense.* References here are from the edition in *Opera Omnia* (Collected works), Antwerp, 1685.

258   Randall Lesaffer (2002) An Early Treatise on Peace Treaties: Petrus Gudelinus between Roman Law and Modern Practice, The Journal of Legal History, 23:3, 223–252, DOI: 10.1080/01440362308539651, p. 223.

259   Ibid 224.

260   Ibid 228. For contextualization of Petrus Gudelinus as a predecessor to later scholars, see Lesaffer, Randall. "A Schoolmaster Abolishing Homework? Vattel on Peacemaking and Peace Treaties." *Vattel's International Law from a XXI st Century Perspective/Le Droit International de Vattel vu du XXI e Siècle.* Brill, 2011. 353–384, 356–357.

261   Petrus Gudelinus, *De jure pacis commentarius, in quo praecipuae de hoc jure quaestionis distinctis capitibus eleganter pertractantur,* Louvain, 1620. References initially from Randall Lesaffer (2002) An Early Treatise on Peace Treaties: Petrus Gudelinus between Roman Law and Modern Practice, The Journal of Legal History, 23:3, 223–252, DOI: 10.1080/01440362308539651. The 1628 Louvain edition was titled *De jure pacis commentarius ad constitutionem Frederici de pace Constantiense.* References here are from the edition in *Opera Omnia* (Collected works), Antwerp, 1685.

definition of peace (*description Pacis*).[262] He recognizes peace as having many definitions,[263] but defines it specifically in contrast with war[264] and as freedom in tranquillity.[265] Peace was created by a treaty and was intended to be permanent, like a marriage.[266]

The second section describes the right authority to make peace treaties, mirroring the classic requirement under Aquinas for proper authority and public declaration to make war, which would later be echoed by Grotius.[267] Appealing to the authority of Bartolus but ultimately disagreeing with him in substance, Gudelinus distinguishes between military truces (that could be made by generals) and proper peace treaties.[268]

Section three discussed the contents of peace treaties going back as far as Livy and Athenian history, analogizing them with contracts between private parties that could have explicit and implicit sections.[269] Two substantive components were always part of such peace treaties that would guide the transition to peace—the cessation of hostilities and agreements regarding conquered and seized objects.[270] Gudelinus also describes amnesty as a standard part of treaties, including the Peace of Constanz, but does not include actions in compensation as part of the general practice of amnesty.[271]

Section four discusses the *post bellum* restitution of goods and rights.[272] Gudelinus is concerned not only with the need for peace treaties to specifically

---

262 Petrus Gudelinus, *Opera Omnia*, p. 551.
263 "*Ut pluribus verbis Pacem definiam*" Petrus Gudelinus, *De jure pacis commentarius* in *Opera Omnia*, (Collected works), Antwerp, 1685, p. 551.
264 "*bello contraria*" Ibid. 551.
265 "*pax est tranquilla libertas*" Ibid.
266 Ibid.
267 Ibid 552–553.
268 Ibid 552.
269 Ibid 553–554. Randall Lesaffer (2002) An Early Treatise on Peace Treaties: Petrus Gudelinus between Roman Law and Modern Practice, The Journal of Legal History, 23:3, 223–252, DOI: 10.1080/01440362308539651, p. 232.
270 Randall Lesaffer (2002) An Early Treatise on Peace Treaties: Petrus Gudelinus between Roman Law and Modern Practice, The Journal of Legal History, 23:3, 223–252, DOI: 10.1080/0144036230853965, pp. 232–233.
271 Petrus Gudelinus, *De jure pacis commentarius* in *Opera Omnia*, (Collected works), Antwerp, 1685, pp. 553–554. Randall Lesaffer (2002) An Early Treatise on Peace Treaties: Petrus Gudelinus between Roman Law and Modern Practice, The Journal of Legal History, 23:3, 223–252, DOI: 10.1080/01440362308539651, p. 233.
272 Petrus Gudelinus, *De jure pacis commentarius* in *Opera Omnia*, (Collected works), Antwerp, 1685, pp. 554–555. Randall Lesaffer (2002) An Early Treatise on Peace Treaties: Petrus Gudelinus between Roman Law and Modern Practice, The Journal of Legal History, 23:3, 223–252, DOI: 10.1080/01440362308539651, p. 234.

address the restitution of property, but also to explicitly address the release of prisoners of war. By the second paragraph, Gudelinus is addressing the ancient Roman doctrine of *postliminium*, whereby Roman soldiers captured by the enemy (*intra praesidia*) are regarded as legally dead, but that liberated soldiers reassumed their suspended civil and property rights.[273] (*Postliminium* is now used to refer to the right under international law, post-belligerent occupation, to invalidate acts such as transfers of property performed by the occupying belligerent in the occupied state's territory. *Postliminium* can be translated to mean "a return to one's threshold." It is a critical element of the Institutes of Justinian's treatment of the transition to peace.)[274] Gudelinus's stance on this issue meant that the release of prisoners of war could not be assumed *post bellum*. Rather, the solution to the problem of prisoners of war had to be specifically addressed after every conflict. Prisoners of war held by a legitimate authority could be held for ransom, and other war booty could be legitimately held—but those that could not legitimately gain under the law of war (*jure belli*) could not legitimately gain in the transition to peace.[275] The transition to peace did not operate identically with sovereigns and with pirates (*piratis*), robbers, (*latronibus*) or rebels (*rebellibus*).[276] What would now be called non-international armed conflict (with rebels) was to some degree consigned to the realm of criminality (robbers and pirates), leaving the transition from international armed conflict in its own category. That said, loot and territories taken from rebels were considered legitimate prizes of war, and through peace treaties rebels could have property returned to them.[277]

Section five builds upon section four, providing general rules for restitution clauses in peace treaties, while noting that treaties could provide for specific situations. Private individuals could also be covered by restitution clauses, not just states. Armed conflict was not a license for states to gain property—the rights of private parties could survive war. Gudelinus distinguishes profits gained from estates during wartime and the goods themselves—during armed

---

273 Aaron X. Fellmeth and Maurice Horwitz, *Guide to Latin in International Law*, 2009, Oxford University Press.
274 Ibid.
275 Petrus Gudelinus, *De jure pacis commentarius* in *Opera Omnia*, (Collected works), Antwerp, 1685, p. 555.
276 Ibid 555.
277 Petrus Gudelinus, *De jure pacis commentarius* in *Opera Omnia*, (Collected works), Antwerp, 1685, p. 555; Randall Lesaffer (2002) An Early Treatise on Peace Treaties: Petrus Gudelinus between Roman Law and Modern Practice, The Journal of Legal History, 23:3, 223–252, DOI: 10.1080/01440362308539651, p. 235.

conflict an occupier could enjoy the profits of occupied goods. Rebels had no right to enjoy such profits, however.[278]

Sections six and seven deal further with the difficult questions of costs, restitution, and indemnification with regards to private property in order to achieve the public good of peace.[279] Gudelinus applies the equitable principle whereby all owners of cargo on a ship would compensate the owner of cargo that had been thrown overboard to save the ship to the problem of an individual who loses private property as part of a treaty. Peace treaties may, in effect, violate the normal natural law protecting property rights for the greater collective good of building a lasting peace, but if the private party losing property is blameless, they should be compensated to the extent possible. Section eight serves as a brief precursor to the limitations on occupying powers that now exist—limiting occupying powers from making enduring one-sided legal acts.[280]

Section nine and ten are somewhat in tension with each other, with section nine minimizing the amount religious principles may be diminished by agreements with heretics (only in necessity) but emphasizing the sanctity and binding power of peace treaties in section ten.[281] Of particular interest to *jus post bellum* scholars, Gudelinus links the laws of war to the rationale for obeying peace treaties—arguing that if it is required to keep faith with an enemy in wartime, this requirement of oath-keeping was even stronger in peacetime. In section eleven, Gudelinus extends this requirement of fidelity to peace treaties to include not only treaties with other sovereigns, but to rebels.

Section twelve emphasizes that peace treaties bind not only the individual, mortal sovereign, but also their successors. Like Baldus, Gudelinus argues that

---

278   Petrus Gudelinus, *De jure pacis commentarius* in *Opera Omnia*, (Collected works), Antwerp, 1685, pp. 555–557; Randall Lesaffer (2002) An Early Treatise on Peace Treaties: Petrus Gudelinus between Roman Law and Modern Practice, The Journal of Legal History, 23:3, 223–252, DOI: 10.1080/01440362308539651, pp. 235–236.

279   Petrus Gudelinus, *De jure pacis commentarius* in *Opera Omnia*, (Collected works), Antwerp, 1685, pp. 557–559; Randall Lesaffer (2002) An Early Treatise on Peace Treaties: Petrus Gudelinus between Roman Law and Modern Practice, The Journal of Legal History, 23:3, 223–252, DOI: 10.1080/01440362308539651, pp. 236–238.

280   Randall Lesaffer (2002) An Early Treatise on Peace Treaties: Petrus Gudelinus between Roman Law and Modern Practice, The Journal of Legal History, 23:3, 223–252, DOI: 10.1080/01440362308539651, p. 238.

281   Petrus Gudelinus, *De jure pacis commentarius* in *Opera Omnia*, (Collected works), Antwerp, 1685, pp. 560–562; Randall Lesaffer (2002) An Early Treatise on Peace Treaties: Petrus Gudelinus between Roman Law and Modern Practice, The Journal of Legal History, 23:3, 223–252, DOI: 10.1080/01440362308539651, pp. 238–240.

treaties are not private, temporary affairs. Gudelinus asserts that it is not the oath of the sovereign that binds the successor sovereign (which would be questionable) but the *conventio*, the agreement itself. This is a step from inter-sovereign agreements resembling temporary, private contracts to autonomous, permanent inter-state treaties and peace agreements more generally that is a foundation of the modern *jus post bellum*.[282]

c) Conclusion

In *De jure pacis commentaris*, Gudelinus takes peace seriously, not merely as a simple natural state but as a creation and an institution—something to be built and treasured, like marriage.[283] He recognized important constituent parts of a constructed peace, including the cessation of hostilities,[284] the distribution of[285] and restitution[286] for goods and rights, amnesty,[287] and exchange of captives.[288] He noted the difference between conflicts between sovereigns and those involving rebels.[289] This short work is important, not least due to its likely influence on Hugo Grotius.

---

282 Petrus Gudelinus, *De jure pacis commentarius* in *Opera Omnia*, (Collected works), Antwerp, 1685, pp. 563–564; Randall Lesaffer (2002) An Early Treatise on Peace Treaties: Petrus Gudelinus between Roman Law and Modern Practice, The Journal of Legal History, 23:3, 223–252, DOI: 10.1080/01440362308539651, pp. 241–242.

283 Petrus Gudelinus, *De jure pacis commentarius* in *Opera Omnia*, (Collected works), Antwerp, 1685, p. 551.

284 Randall Lesaffer (2002) An Early Treatise on Peace Treaties: Petrus Gudelinus between Roman Law and Modern Practice, The Journal of Legal History, 23:3, 223–252, DOI: 10.1080/0144036230853965, pp. 232–233.

285 Randall Lesaffer (2002) An Early Treatise on Peace Treaties: Petrus Gudelinus between Roman Law and Modern Practice, The Journal of Legal History, 23:3, 223–252, DOI: 10.1080/0144036230853965, pp. 232–233.

286 Petrus Gudelinus, *De jure pacis commentarius* in *Opera Omnia*, (Collected works), Antwerp, 1685, pp. 554–555. Randall Lesaffer (2002) An Early Treatise on Peace Treaties: Petrus Gudelinus between Roman Law and Modern Practice, The Journal of Legal History, 23:3, 223–252, DOI: 10.1080/01440362308539651, p. 234.

287 Petrus Gudelinus, *De jure pacis commentarius* in *Opera Omnia*, (Collected works), Antwerp, 1685, pp. 553–554. Randall Lesaffer (2002) An Early Treatise on Peace Treaties: Petrus Gudelinus between Roman Law and Modern Practice, The Journal of Legal History, 23:3, 223–252, DOI: 10.1080/01440362308539651, p. 233.

288 Aaron X. Fellmeth and Maurice Horwitz, *Guide to Latin in International Law*, 2009, Oxford University Press.

289 Petrus Gudelinus, *De jure pacis commentarius* in *Opera Omnia*, (Collected works), Antwerp, 1685, p. 555.

10 Hugo Grotius (1583–1645)

a) Introduction

Hugo Grotius was a wunderkind, writing Latin poetry as a child, entering university at eleven, receiving his doctorate in law at fifteen, publishing his first book[290] and beginning practice as a lawyer in sixteen. He received international acclaim in his lifetime. He counted the Dutch East India Company as a client, which lead to his treatise *De Iure Praedae*, a chapter of which (*Mare Liberum*) was first published anonymously with a view to influencing the truce negotiations with Spain.[291] His *Inleidinge tot de Hollandsche Rechts-geleerdheid* (Introduction to Dutch Legal Learning)[292] published in 1620, proved influential in The Netherlands. In 1625 he published his most famous work, *De Iure Belli ac Pacis* (On the Law of War and Peace).[293] Peter Haggenmacher claimed that *De jure belli ac pacis libre tres* was not a general study on the law of nations but specifically focused on the laws of war.[294] That said, it was a work that would prove influential in legal philosophy, private law,[295] and international law. If James Brown Scott was correct that Francisco de Vitoria was the founder of international law, Francisco Suarez was the philosopher, and Hugo Grotius was the organizer[296]—what did the organizer have to say about the transition from armed conflict to peace?[297]

---

290 *Parallelon Rerum Publicarum de Moribus Ingenioque Populorum Atheniensium, Romanorum, Batavorum* (1601–1603).

291 Laurens Winkel, *Grotius, Hugo* in The Oxford International Encyclopedia of Legal History (Stanley N Katz ed. Oxford University Press 2009).

292 Grotius, Hugo. *Inleidinge tot de Hollandsche rechts-geleerdheid*. 1st ed. 1631. Latin version: J. van der Linden, *Institutiones juris hollandici et belgici*, 1835, edited by H.F.W.D. Fischer. Haarlem, Netherlands: H.D. Tjeenk Willink, 1962. English translation: R.W. Lee, *An Introduction to Roman-Dutch Law* (Oxford, U.K.: Clarendon Press, 1915 [5th ed. 1953]). Standard edition: Eduard M. Meijers, Folke Dovring, and H.F.W.D. Fischer (Leiden, Netherlands: Universitaire Pers Leiden, 1952 [2d ed. 1965]).

293 Grotius, Hugo, *Libri tres de jure belli ac pacis, in quibus ius naturae et gentium, item iuris publici praecipua explicantur*, 1st ed. (Paris, 1625). English translation: Francis W. Kelsey, et al. (Oxford, U.K.: Clarendon Press, 1925). Recent standard edition: Hugo Grotius, *Libri tres de jure belli ac pacis, in quibus ius naturae et gentium, item iuris publici praecipua explicantur*, edited by B.J.A. de Kanter-van Hettinga Tromp, (Aalen, Germany: Scientia Verlag, 1993).

294 Peter Haggenmacher, *Grotius et la doctrine de la guerre juste*, Paris, 1983.

295 Lauterpacht, Hersch. *Private Law Sources and Analogies of International Law*. London: Longmans, 1927. Reprints, Hamden, Conn.: Archon Books, 1970, and Union, N.J.: Lawbook Exchange, 2002.

296 James Brown Scott, *The Catholic Conception of International Law: Francisco de Vitoria, founder of the modern law of nations; Francisco Suarez, founder of the modern philosophy of law in general and in particular of the law of nations; A critical examination and a justified appreciation*, Washington, 1934, pp. 183–184.

297 For contextualization of Hugo Grotius as a predecessor to later scholars, see Lesaffer, Randall. "A Schoolmaster Abolishing Homework? Vattel on Peacemaking and Peace Treaties."

b) Writings and Relation to *Jus Post Bellum*

When describing the structure of *De jure belli ac pacis libre tres*, Grotius summarizes the third book as follows:

> The third Book treats first of what is lawful in War; and then, having distinguished that which is done with bare Impunity, or which is even defended as lawful among foreign Nations, from that which is really blameless, descends to the several Kinds of Peace, and all Agreements made in war.[298]

To use contemporary terminology, Book III addresses not only *jus in bello*, but also *jus post bellum*.

Of particular interest is Book III, Chapter XX. "Concerning the publick Faith whereby War is finished; of Treaties of Peace, Lots, set Combats, Arbitrations, Surrenders, Hostages, and Pledges."[299] Early on in this chapter, Grotius describes the authority needed for peace treaties: "They who have Power to begin a War, have likewise Power to enter upon a Treaty to finish it[.]"[300]

Grotius places limits on what may be agreed to in a peace treaty:

> Now let us see what Things are subject to such an Agreement. Most Kings in our Days, holding their Kingdoms not as patrimonial, but as usufructuary, have no Power by any Treaty to alienate the Sovereignty in Whole, or in Part: Yea, and before they come to the Government, at what Time the People are their Superiors; such Acts may [by] a fundamental Law, for the future be rendered absolutely void and null; so that even as to Damages and Interest, they shall be no ways binding. For it is probable, that Nations thought fit to ordain that in that Case, the other Party should have no Action against the King for Damages and Interest, since, if that took Place, the Goods of the Subjects might be seized, as answerable for the King's Debt; and so the Precaution that might have been taken to hinder the Alienation of the Sovereignty, would become entirely useless.[301]

      Vattel's International Law from a XXI st Century Perspective/Le Droit International de Vattel vu du XXI e Siècle. Brill, 2011. 353–384, 354–358.
298 Hugo Grotius, The Rights of War and Peace, edited and with an Introduction by Richard Tuck, from the Edition by Jean Barbeyrac (Indianapolis: Liberty Fund, 2005). Vol. 1.
299 Ibid Vol. 3.
300 Ibid Vol. 3., p. 1551.
301 Ibid Vol. 3, pp. 1553–1554.

Grotius is limiting the scope of the treaty-making authority of government in most cases[302] particularly in the case of alienating the goods of the country. While the State may use the goods of private men to procure a peace, it must restore its subjects when it is able.[303] The State is not obliged to make its nationals whole if they suffer damage from the war itself, however.[304]

Grotius argues that peace treaties should be read in light of the stated reasons for going to war, and not for further gain or punishment:

> Wherefore where the Meaning of the Articles is ambiguous, it should be taken in this Sense, that he that has the Justice of the War on his Side, should obtain what he took up Arms for, and also recover his Costs and Damages, but not that he should get any Thing farther by way of Punishment, for that is odious.[305]

Grotius is generally conservative in his approach to changing the facts on the ground with peace treaties. He cites Thucydides for the general principle "ἔχοντες ἃ ἔχουσι, That Things should remain as they are"[306] unless specifically agreed to, including returning captives,[307] restoring fugitives,[308] or claiming property.[309] If there is no clause dealing with damages from war, those damages should be considered forgiven.[310] Similarly, the right to punishment for grievances that might make the peace incomplete should be considered forgiven.[311] He sums up the overall function of peace agreements saying "it is humane to believe that those who make Peace intend sincerely to stifle the Seeds of War."[312]

Grotius places particular duties on a conqueror, forbidding unjust action (especially extrajudicial execution and expropriation) and commending clemency, liberality, and a general pardon:

---

302 He notes the possibility of absolute rulers to go beyond the power of sovereignty if they have property rights over the goods in their lands, as in the case of the Pharoah.
303 Ibid Vol. 3, p. 1556.
304 Ibid Vol. 3, p. 1557.
305 Ibid Vol. 3, p. 1558.
306 Ibid.
307 Ibid.
308 Ibid.
309 Ibid Vol. 3, p. 1559.
310 Ibid Vol. 3, pp. 1561–1562.
311 Ibid Vol. 3, p. 1563.
312 Ibid Vol. 3, p. 1564.

But the Conqueror, that he may do nothing unjustly, ought first to take Care that no Man be killed, unless for some capital Crime; so also, that no Man's Goods be taken away, unless by Way of just Punishment. And even by keeping within these Bounds, as far as his own Security will permit it, it is honourable (to a Conqueror) to shew Clemency and Liberality, and sometimes even necessary, by the Rules of Virtue, according as Circumstances shall require. Admirable are the Conclusions of those Wars which are finished with a general Pardon[.][313]

c) Conclusion

Grotius is not silent on the issue of the transition to peace. Indeed, his ideas of transitions to peace that could build a pacific order were reflected in the Peace of Westphalia, and while not all that was in the Westphalia treaties matched Grotius' ideas,[314] in general Grotius' theory and Westphalian practice matched.[315] Give Grotius' long fame, there is an overwhelming surfeit of secondary material on Grotius' writing, yet his contribution to *jus post bellum*, when *jus post bellum* is conceived of as playing a particular function in the international community, to manage the transition to a just and sustainable peace, is under-recognized.

11 *Christian Wolff (1679–1754)*

a) Introduction

Christian Wolff[316] was trained both as a mathematician and philosopher.[317] A prolific author, his works shifted over time from pure mathematics[318] to

---

313 Ibid Vol. 3, p. 1586.
314 Hedley Bull, "The Importance of Grotius in the Study of International Relations," Bull, Hedley, Benedict Kingsbury, and Adam Roberts, eds. *Hugo Grotius and international relations*. Oxford University Press, 1992, p. 75.
315 Ibid 77.
316 Sometimes referenced as "Christian von Wolff" or in the Latin e.g. *Instiutiones Juris Naturae et Gentium* "Christiano L.B. de Wolffo See Wolff , Christian. *Jus naturae methodo scientifico pertractatum*. 8 vols. Leipzig, Germany: Prostat in Officina Libraria Rengeriana, 1741–1748. This is Wolff 's main work, abridged as *Institutiones juris naturae et gentium: In quibus ex ipsa hominis natura continuo nexu omnes obligationes et jura omnia deducuntur* (Halle and Magdeburg, Germany, 1750). Wolff saw *Jus naturae* as complimentary to his *Jus gentium* Wolff, Christian, *Jus gentium methodo scientifica pertractatum*, Clarendon press (1934) Volume Two, p. 426. Translation by Francis J. Hemelt.
317 Katz, Stanley N. *The Oxford International Encyclopedia of Legal History,* Wolff, Christian von. Oxford University Press, 2009.
318 See e.g. Wolff, Christian. "Dissertatio algebraica de algorithmo infinitesimali differentiali quam gratioso indultu amplissimi philosophorum ordinis." (1704).

ethical philosophy, never leaving his insistence on the application of logic to deduce natural laws through syllogisms.[319] Wolff wrote *Jus Gentium Methodo Scientifica Pertractatum*[320] at the end of his career—the name of the work (roughly *The Law of Nations According to the Scientific Method*) is revealing both of his mathematical training and his faith that there was agreement between ethical duty, natural laws based on human behaviour, and positive laws.[321]

b) Writings and Relation to *Jus Ad Bellum* and *Jus In Bello*

Before discussing Wolff and *jus post bellum*, it may be worth noting his discussion of *jus ad bellum* and *jus in bello*. As noted previously, Robert Kolb tentatively credited Josef Kunz with coining the terms *jus ad bellum* and *jus in bellum* in their contemporary sense in 1934.[322] Stahn has identified the emergence of the terms in the 1920s,[323] with Guiliano Enriques using the term *jus ad bellum* in 1928.[324] That said, it is perhaps worth noting that the *terms jus ad bellum* and *jus in bello* had been used before, even in relatively close proximity to each other. For example, Christian Wolff, in the 1764 edition of his *Jus Gentium Methodo Scientifica Pertractatum* states:

> Since hostilities in war are due to the force by which we pursue our right in war, which consists either in collecting a debt or imposing a penalty, and therefore all our right in war is to be determined thereby, the right to destroy the property of an enemy is not to be determined otherwise, unless you should wish to assume a thing which can be assumed only in contravention of the law of nature, that there is absolutely no place left in

---

319 Katz, Stanley N. *The Oxford International Encyclopedia of Legal History*, Wolff, Christian von. Oxford University Press, 2009.
320 Wolff, Christian, *Jus gentium methodo scientifica pertractatum*, Clarendon press (1934) Volume Two, p. 426. Translation by Francis J. Hemelt.
321 For an interesting review of Wolff's approach to mathematical method in areas outside mathematics, see Frängsmyr, Tore. "Christian Wolff's mathematical method and its impact on the eighteenth century." *Journal of the History of Ideas* 36.4 (1975): 653–668.
322 Kolb, Robert, *Origin of the twin terms jus ad bellum/jus in bello*, International Review of the Red Cross (1997), 561.
323 Stahn, Carsten, *Jus Post Bellum*: Mapping the Discipline(s), 23 Am. U. Int'l L. Rev., 311, 2007–2008, 312.
324 See Enriques, Giuliano, *Considerazioni sulla teoria della Guerra nel diritto Internazionale* (Considerations on the Theory of War in International Law), 7 Rivista Di Diritto Internazionale (Journal of International Law) 172 (1928).

war for justice, which orders us to give each one his right, and that *right in war* disappears in mere licence, to which none can be entitled.[325]

The italicized text, "right in war" corresponds to the term *"jus in bello"* on page 300 of the original Latin text. On the next page of the original text, Wolff asserts:

> The law of nature, which gives us a *right to war*, gives also a right against the property of enemies, as far as that is necessary in waging war; for otherwise the former right would be useless, if it were not allowable to claim the latter.[326]

The translated text "right to war" is in the original text: *"jus ad bellum."*

What does this tell us about the contemporary usage of the term? Nothing definite, to be sure. Reviewing the terms as they were used does not indicate any clear link to the current usage. Nor is there any evidence that these terms, as used by Wolff, were identified by subsequent scholars. It is unsurprising that those particular words should come together in a long book in Latin about international law.

That said, this usage is still interesting with respect to the question of the normative and historical foundations of *jus ad bellum, jus in bello*, and their sister term, *jus post bellum*. Wolff, in these passages seeking to determine the natural law pertaining to the right to destroy enemy property, appears to distinguish between justice during war[327] and the right to go to war.[328] He may not have meant exactly what contemporary scholars mean by these terms or concepts—again, hardly surprising given the development of international law over almost 250 years. But it is also relatively clear that the general questions of right to war and right in war, whatever term was used, have a long genealogy.

c) Writings and Relation to *Jus Post Bellum*

As for Wolff's approach to *jus post bellum*, his main contribution is to build upon Grotius (see *supra*) and inspire Vattel (see *infra*), particularly on the matter of

---

325 Wolff, Christian, *Jus gentium methodo scientifica pertractatum*, Clarendon press (1934) Volume Two, p. 426. Translation by Joseph H. Drake and Francis J. Hemelt. (Emphasis supplied.)
326 Ibid 427. (Emphasis supplied.)
327 Ibid 426.
328 Ibid 427.

peace agreements. Chapter VIII of *Jus gentium methodo scientifica pertractatum*[329] "Of Peace and the Treaty of Peace" spends two introductory paragraphs on the nature of peace[330] before stating the duty "Of cultivating peace": "Nations are bound by nature to cultivate peace with each other."[331] From this general precept and others, Wolff derives "How long a just war may be continued"[332] ("until the enemy no longer opposes your righteous force"[333]). This bold prescription for potentially endless war is softened by his analysis of the length of war "How long in a doubtful case" (until compromise is accepted).[334] While Wolff discusses the possibility of war continuing until the other party has been completely conquered[335] (what Lesaffer, following Gentili, references as *ius victoriae*)[336] most of Wolff's chapter considers peace established through treaty (what Lesaffer, following Gentili, references as *ius ad pacem*).[337]

The link between what we now might call *jus ad bellum* and *jus post bellum* is referenced, arguing in this chapter "Of Peace and the Treaty of Peace" that there is no right to continue an unjust war[338] and that even a war that begins on a justifiable basis should be ended if the belligerent has "acquired his right" or if "in a doubtful case he should be unwilling to accept fair terms of peace."[339] Wolff emphasises the need for compromise if every right is insisted upon, stating "Peace, then, cannot be made in such a way that the one to whom a right is due can acquire it completely. [...] [P]eace can be made only through a compromise."[340] Wolff prefigures May's valuable contributions on Meionexia (detailed elsewhere),[341] making much the same point but without reference to Aristotle.

---

329   Ibid 486.
330   Ibid 486, paras. 959, 960.
331   Ibid 487, para. 961.
332   Ibid 490, para. 969.
333   Ibid.
334   Ibid 491, para. 970.
335   Ibid. 492, para. 972.
336   Lesaffer, Randall. "A Schoolmaster Abolishing Homework? Vattel on Peacemaking and Peace Treaties." *Vattel's International Law from a XXI st Century Perspective/Le Droit International de Vattel vu du XXI e Siècle*. Brill, 2011. 353–384, 357.
337   Ibid.
338   Wolff, Christian, *Jus gentium methodo scientifica pertractatum*, Clarendon press (1934) Volume Two, p. 493. Translation by Joseph H. Drake and Francis J. Hemelt, para. 973.
339   Ibid 493, para. 974.
340   Ibid. 500, para. 986.
341   See e.g., *Jus Post Bellum*, Grotius, and *Meionexia*, in Jus Post Bellum: Mapping the Normative Foundations, edited by Carsten Stahn, Jennifer S. Easterday, Jens Iverson (Oxford University Press 2014); Larry May, *After War Ends: A Philosophical Approach* (Cambridge University Press 2012).

Alongside proportionality, Wolff mentions the uses of an amnesty as part of a peace treaty (as understood at the time) whereby "all deeds are consigned to perpetual oblivion and everlasting silence."[342] The point of a treaty of peace is not to convict the other of wrong, he asserts that in every such treaty there is such an amnesty, "even if there should be no agreement for it."[343] His approach to such amnesty is consistent with his overall approach towards a peace agreement serving as a final settlement on the injustices of an armed conflict, whereby "things captured in war may not be declared to have been wrongfully seized, but a compromise must be made on the terms which can be agreed upon; that which has been agreed upon is to be considered as law."[344] Similarly, losses in war are not recoverable unless there has been an agreement otherwise,[345] nor debts or obligations unrelated to the war discharged.[346]

Wolff is primarily concerned in this chapter with laws and principles concerning peace treaties between sovereigns, what would now be called International Armed Conflicts. Wolff does note, however, the possibility of what might now be called non-international armed conflicts, including rebellion (where subjects have an unjust cause)[347] and civil war (where subjects have a just cause).[348] Of particular interest in terms of modern peace treaty law is Wolff's practical assertion that "A treaty of peace is not invalid because it has been extorted by warlike force or by fear" because otherwise "it will always be possible to renew war[.]"[349]

d) Conclusion

Wolff continues the genealogy of *jus post bellum avant la letter* from Grotius to Vattel. He demonstrates how the general obligation of nations to cultivate peace with each other[350] Like others before him, he notes that the absolute demands that might be expected from the justifications for war must be tempered with compromise and admit the possibility of error and doubt in order to create the possibility of a successful peace treaty, and a sustainable peace.[351]

---

342 Wolff, Christian, *Jus gentium methodo scientifica pertractatum*, Clarendon press (1934) Volume Two, p. 502. Translation by Joseph H. Drake and Francis J. Hemelt, para. 989.
343 Ibid 502, para. 990.
344 Ibid 503, para. 991. See also para. 996 on movable property.
345 Ibid 504, para. 993.
346 Ibid 504, para. 994.
347 Ibid 513, para. 1010.
348 Ibid 514, para. 1011.
349 Ibid 522–523, para. 1035.
350 Ibid 487, para. 961.
351 Ibid 500, para. 986.

He applies his analysis not only to what would now be called international armed conflicts, but recognizes that laws and principles apply to the resolution of what would now be called non-international armed conflicts as well.[352] Finally, Wolff's emphasis on the desired sustainability of peace is shown by his emphasis that even "A treaty of [...] extorted by warlike force or by fear" is valid and binding.[353]

12 Emer de Vattel (1714–1767)

a) Introduction

Vattel's[354] *Le Droit des Gens, ou Principes de la Loi Naturelle, appliqués à la Conduite et aux Affaires des Nations et des Souverains*[355] is a classic of international law. Emmanuelle Jouannet has gone so far as to consider Vattel a principal founder of modern international law.[356] A follower of Christian Wolff, Vattel has had a profound and continuing impact on public international law. With respect to *jus post bellum*, as in many areas, he took Wolff's work and expanded it into a more comprehensive treatise on the transition to peace, paying particular attention to the law applicable to the formation and results of peace treaties.

b) Writings and Relation to *Jus Post Bellum*

Out of four books in *Le Droit des Gens,* Vattel devotes an entire volume to largely to the subject of the transition to peace: "Of the Restoration of Peace; and of Embassies." This ultimate book in *Le Droit des Gens* begins with a definition of peace as the natural state of mankind, *contra* Hobbes.[357] Sovereigns were not

---

352　Ibid 513-514, para. 1010–1011.
353　Ibid 522–523, para. 1035.
354　Vattel was christened "Emer." Some authors have mistakenly given him a German name, "Emerich." See the Introduction for Emer de Vattel, *The Law of Nations, Or, Principles of the Law of Nature, Applied to the Conduct and Affairs of nations and Sovereigns, with Three Early Essays on the Origin and Nature of Natural Law and on Luxury,* edited and with an Introduction by Béla Kapossy and Richard Whitmore (Indianapolis: Liberty Fund, 2008).
355　E. de Vattel, Le Droit des Gens, ou Principes de la Loi Naturelle, appliqués à la Conduite et aux Affaires des Nations et des Souverains (1758), The Law of Nations, Or, Principles of the Law of Nature, Applied to the Conduct and Affairs of Nations and Sovereigns, with Three Early Essays on the Origin and Nature of Natural Law and on Luxury, edited and with an Introduction by Béla Kapossy and Richard Whitmore (Indianapolis: Liberty Fund, 2008).
356　Jouannet, Emmanuelle. *Emer de Vattel et l' émergence doctrinale du droit international classique.* Paris: A Pedone, 1998.
357　Book IV, Chapter I: Of Peace, and the Obligation to cultivate it, in E. de Vattel, Le Droit des Gens, ou Principes de la Loi Naturelle, appliqués à la Conduite et aux Affaires des Nations et des Souverains (1758), The Law of Nations, Or, Principles of the Law of Nature, Applied to the Conduct and Affairs of Nations and Sovereigns, with Three Early Essays on the

free to take the obligation of cultivating peace lightly, but were bound to it by a "double tie"—as an obligation both to the people and to foreign nations.[358] This restricts the sovereign not only from "embarking in a war without necessity," but also "persevering in it after the necessity has ceased to exist."[359]

Vattel is applying his law "Of the Restoration of Peace" functionally, before peace starts and during war, not limited by time. Many of the themes sounded by Vattel are, unsurprisingly, along the same lines of Wolff. A sovereign "may carry on the operations of war till he has attained its lawful end, which is, to procure justice and safety"[360]—showing that the object in mind is a peace both just and safe (and thus not unsustainable). The power to determine the conditions of peace, and "regulate the manner in which it is to be restored and supported," is the same power to make war.[361] The power of the king to alienate that which belongs to the state is limited, but if made with the nation's consent cannot be invalidated.[362] The sovereign may dispose of the property of individuals if necessary via eminent domain, but the state is bound to indemnify those who suffer as a result.[363]

A treaty of peace is inevitably a compromise, in which the rules of strict and rigid justice are not observed; otherwise it would be impossible to ever make peace.[364] A peace treaty extinguishes any grievance that gave rise to war, and creates a reciprocal obligation to preserve perpetual peace (at least with regards to that subject).[365] Amnesty is implied in all peace treaties, as peace should extinguish all subjects of discord.[366] Peace treaties take effect as soon as possible.[367] In case of doubt, any interpretation of the peace treaty should be read against the party who prescribed the terms of the treaty.[368]

The best scholarship on Vattel with respect to the transition from armed conflict to peace was written by Randall Lesaffer in his contributions to two edited volumes (*Vattel's International Law from a XXIst Century Perspective/Le Droit International de Vattel vu du XXIe Siècle* and *The Oxford Handbook of the*

Origin and Nature of Natural Law and on Luxury, edited and with an Introduction by Béla Kapossy and Richard Whitmore (Indianapolis: Liberty Fund, 2008).

358 Ibid, Book IV, Chapter I, Section 3.
359 Ibid, Book IV, Chapter I, Section 6.
360 Ibid.
361 Ibid, Book IV, Chapter II, Section 9.
362 Ibid, Book IV, Chapter II, Section 11.
363 Ibid, Book IV, Chapter II, Section 12.
364 Ibid, Book IV, Chapter II, Section 18.
365 Ibid, Book IV, Chapter II, Section 19.
366 Ibid, Book IV, Chapter II, Section 20.
367 Ibid, Book IV, Chapter II, Section 26.
368 Ibid, Book IV, Chapter II, Section 32.

History of International Law).³⁶⁹ The author has no wish to be repetitive of Lessafer's excellent summation, but would like to draw out certain highlights. For a more comprehensive synopsis of the work of Vattel, including Wolff's impact on Vattel, with respect to *jus post bellum*, the aforementioned works are recommended.

First, in *A Schoolmaster Abolishing Homework? Vattel on Peacemaking and Peace Treaties*,³⁷⁰ Lessafer places Vattel (along with his intellectual muse Christian Wolff) as the leading voice on the law of peace treaties in the 17th and 18th centuries.³⁷¹ Lesaffer notes that Wolff and Vattel both emphasised the need for compromise and a less-than-maximalist approach to just claims in order to achieve peace.³⁷² Vattel emphasizes from the outset that there is an obligation on all nations to cultivate peace.³⁷³ Lessafer notes the underlying issues that Vattel identifies must be resolved by a peace treaty: disputes that led to war, the termination of the state of war, and the organization of and preservation of the peace.³⁷⁴ Like Wolff,³⁷⁵ Vattel considered an amnesty for all claims, civil and criminal, for actions during and because of the war to be an implicit part of every peace treaty—a common feature of peace treaties since the 15th century.³⁷⁶ In Vattel's commentary on *postliminium* (see discussion on the Institutes of Justinian, Gentili, and Gudelinus *supra*) is limited, but he does insist that prisoners had to be released, even if not mandated by a peace treaty.³⁷⁷

Like Wolff, Vattel argues that duress does not invalidate peace treaties, but he blurs the issues somewhat by claiming that in the case of an extremely oppressive peace imposed by a victor, the exception of duress did apply.³⁷⁸ Vattel

---

369   For more on peace treaties in general, see e.g. Lesaffer, Randall. "The Westphalia peace treaties and the development of the tradition of great European peace settlements prior to 1648." *Grotiana* 18 (1997); Lesaffer, Randall, ed. *Peace treaties and international law in European history: from the late Middle Ages to World War One*. Cambridge University Press, 2004.
370   Lesaffer, Randall. "A Schoolmaster Abolishing Homework? Vattel on Peacemaking and Peace Treaties." *Vattel's International Law from a XXI st Century Perspective/Le Droit International de Vattel vu du XXI e Siècle*. Brill, 2011. 353–384.
371   Ibid 358.
372   Ibid 363.
373   Ibid 366.
374   Ibid 369.
375   Wolff, Christian, *Jus gentium methodo scientifica pertractatum*, Clarendon press (1934) Volume Two, p. 502. Translation by Joseph H. Drake and Francis J. Hemelt, para. 989.
376   Lesaffer, Randall. "A Schoolmaster Abolishing Homework? Vattel on Peacemaking and Peace Treaties." *Vattel's International Law from a XXI st Century Perspective/Le Droit International de Vattel vu du XXI e Siècle*. Brill, 2011. 353–384, 373.
377   Ibid 375.
378   Ibid 377.

was aware of the tension and possibility of abuse of this uncertain argument. Should the peace treaty be breached, the injured party had the right to annul the treaty, ask for compensation, and if compensation was refused, resort to war.[379]

Second, Lesaffer also integrates his analysis of Wolff and Vattel's emphasis on the practical need to compromise in his concise overview of the impact of peace treaties on international law in *Peace Treaties and the Formation of International Law*.[380] Lesaffer emphasizes that Wolff and Vattel both found that basing the resolution of an armed conflict on the *jus ad bellum* question alone was impracticable, because determining *jus ad bellum* claims was usually impossible and because sovereigns would not subject themselves to other sovereign's judgment on this matter.[381] Lesaffer points to the overall effect of this approach and of state practice in Europe at the time, peace treaties from the 1500s to the early 1900s did not demand compensation for the act of fighting an unjust war or restrictions on the military capacity of the unjust belligerent.[382]

c) Conclusion

Vattel not only provided specific content to the law applicable to the transition to peace, but also made it the foundation of diplomacy and further relations between states. He considered this law necessary,[383] immutable,[384] and obligatory.[385] Vattel was interested in making a profound and lasting contribution to analyzing the possibilities available to secure liberty against constant interruption by war.[386] Like many of the authors listed above, he was a product of his time and circumstances—writing mostly in absolute monarchies, taking the feelings of their patrons into account. Some of his views would be considered retrograde by modern standards, but his interest in establishing a means to achieve a just and sustainable peace addresses a problem that remains current, and pressing.

---

379 Ibid, 379.
380 Lesaffer, Randall. "Peace treaties and the formation of international law." *The Oxford Handbook of the History of International Law* (2012): 71–94.
381 Ibid 88.
382 Ibid.
383 E. de Vattel, Le Droit des Gens, Preface, Section 7.
384 Ibid, Preface, Section 8.
385 Ibid, Preface, Section 9.
386 See the Introduction for Emer de Vattel, *The Law of Nations, Or, Principles of the Law of Nature, Applied to the Conduct and Affairs of nations and Sovereigns, with Three Early Essays on the Origin and Nature of Natural Law and on Luxury*, edited and with an Introduction by Béla Kapossy and Richard Whitmore (Indianapolis: Liberty Fund, 2008).

13 Immanuel Kant (1724–1804)

a) Introduction

Immanuel Kant's contributions to thinking on the transition to peace and the tripartite conception of the law of armed conflict are relatively well known. In Carsten Stahn's foundational essay on *jus post bellum*, he cites Kant as a conceptual founder of the idea.[387] Like all of the authors above, Kant did not use the term "jus post bellum" but for modern purposes can be seen to be outlining the concept *avant la lettre*. Kant was building on an Enlightenment tradition of an optimistic view of mankind that could construct a peaceful order for Europe. This tradition includes William Penn's suggestion of a European confederation in his *Essay towards the Present and Future Peace of Europe* (1693).[388] Abbé de Saint-Pierre's *Projet pour rendre la Paix perpétuelle en Europe* (Fayard Utrecht 1713)[389] imagined a federation of Christian states. Kant builds on this tradition without positing a supranational entity as such.

b) Writings and Relation to *Jus Post Bellum*

Kant's vision of the possibility of perpetual peace was based partially on states sharing "republican" constitutions. By "republican," Kant was referring to certain basic elements core to what is thought of as "democratic today: liberty, equal treatment under the law, representative government, and separation of powers.[390] Kant's vision was thus very much a precursor of our modern conception of a democratic peace. Kant's ultimate hope was not merely that single states be made free or peaceful, but that there could be a systematic effect on the international plane, what he called a "federation of free states."[391]

Preliminary Articles for Perpetual Peace Among States[392] is an essay filled with relevance to *jus post bellum*. His goal was, as far as feasible, to propose a system that would have a particular function: to make a *permanent* transition

---

387 Stahn, Carsten. "Jus ad bellum,' 'jus in bello'…'jus post bellum'?–Rethinking the Conception of the Law of Armed Force." *European Journal of International Law* 17.5 (2006): 921–943.

388 William Penn, The Political Writings of William Penn, introduction and annotations by Andrew R. Murphy (Indianapolis: Liberty Fund, 2002).

389 See Perkins, Merle L. *The moral and political philosophy of the Abbé de Saint-Pierre*. Vol. 24. Librairie Droz, 1959.

390 See Immanuel Kant, Toward Perpetual Peace, 1932, U.S. Library Association, Westwood Hills Press, Los Angeles, California, U.S.A; Russett, Bruce. Grasping the democratic peace: Principles for a post-Cold War world. Princeton University Press, 1994, p. 4.

391 Ibid.

392 Ibid 67–109.

to peace—and because he was first and foremost a moral philosopher, Kant would only support such a peace that was just. He lists six preliminary articles for perpetual peace among states and three definitive articles for perpetual peace among states. Each article will be addressed in turn.

Kant's first preliminary article was "No treaty of peace shall be esteemed valid, on which is tacitly reserved matter for future war."[393] Kant connects *jus post bellum* to *lex pacificatoria* – connecting the validity of peace treaties to whether they comprehensively address the issues needed to establish a sustainable peace. His second article stated "Any state, of whatever extent, shall never pass under the dominion of another state, whether by inheritance, exchange, purchase, or donation."[394] Here, Kant connects *jus post bellum* to the law of occupation and the prohibition against aggression. His third article reads "Standing armies (*miles perpetuus*) shall in time be "totally abolished."[395] Kant is connecting armed control and military expenditure to *jus post bellum*. The fourth preliminary article holds that "National debts shall not be contracted with a view of maintaining the interest of the state abroad."[396] Kant here connects the internal dynamics of empire and national finance to *jus post bellum*. The fifth article states that "No state shall by force interfere with either the constitution or government of another state."[397] This principle connects *jus post bellum* to occupation law, the prohibition against aggression, and the need for self-determination. Article six proclaims "A state shall not, during war, admit of hostilities of a nature that would render reciprocal confidence in a succeeding peace impossible: such as employing assassins (percussores), poisoners (venefici), violation of capitulations, secret instigation to rebellion (perduellio), etc."[398] This principle connects what would now be termed *jus in bello* norms (no unnecessary suffering/heinous means) to *jus post bellum* ends (permanent peace).

In addition to the six preliminary articles listed above, Kant suggests three definitive articles. Firstly, "The civil constitution of every state ought to be republican." Given his definition of republican, Kant was referring to certain basic elements core to what is thought of as "democratic" today: liberty, equal treatment under the law, representative government, and separation of

---

393 Ibid.
394 Ibid.
395 Ibid.
396 Ibid.
397 Ibid.
398 Ibid.

powers.³⁹⁹ Secondly, "The public right ought to be founded upon a federation of free states." Kant here connects municipal law to the structure of the international system (including sovereignty) to *jus post bellum*. Thirdly, "The cosmopolitical right shall be limited to conditions of universal hospitality." Kant is underlining the importance of the rights of foreigners to receive diplomatic protection.

c) Conclusion

Kant's ideas of perpetual peace still haunt the international system. While not yet achieved, they informed the creation of the League of Nations and the United Nations, and served as a precursor for the idea of a Democratic Peace. While limited, admitting the validity at the time of the idea of conquest,⁴⁰⁰ he repudiated the flexibility of earlier thinkers such as Hugo Grotius, Puffendorf, and Vattel as "miserable comforters,"⁴⁰¹ in reality he built upon a long tradition, reinforced it with new ethical imagination, and laid the foundation for future efforts.

C Conclusion

While not encyclopaedic, it is worth emphasizing some of the highlights of the material reviewed above. From Augustine we know that war has purposes that may or may not be fulfilled by the transition to peace that the transition to peace is not always normatively better than continued war—and that, mercy must guide war and allow a successful transition to a just and sustainable peace. From Aquinas we know that Right authority is important, not merely for its own sake, but because it is conducive to peace; that peace should be a just peace, where the poor are rescued and the needy delivered; that the right intent should be securing peace, punishing evil-doers, and uplifting the good; and that that the ultimate goal of a prosperous peace controls not only post-conflict behaviour but the warring itself. Baldus de Ubaldis plays an important part in establishing that peace treaties and peace agreements could and should

---

399   Ibid; Russett, Bruce. Grasping the democratic peace: Principles for a post-Cold War world. Princeton University Press, 1994, p. 4.
400   Immanuel Kant, *Metaphysische Anfangsgründe der Rechtslehre* (The Philosophy of Law: An Exposition of the Fundamental Principles of Jurisprudence as the Science of Right, originally published 1887, tr W. Hastie, The Lawbook Exchange 2002).
401   Kant, Immanuel, The Advocate of Peace (1894–1920), Vol. 59, No. 5 (May 1897), pp. 111–116, p. 114.

endure. Without the idea that such agreements could be permanent, outlasting the king, a key foundation of *jus post bellum* would be lacking. Baldus manages to lay this foundation without sacrificing the idea that kings should be individually responsible for their personal crimes.

Francisco de Vitoria covers a wide field of material that relates to *jus post bellum*, including: first, peace as the aim of armed conflict; second, post-conflict justice; third, an integrated view of *jus ad bellum, jus in bello*, and *jus post bellum*; and fourth, post bellum regime change. Together, Vitoria's writings amount to a new foundation for *jus post bellum*. Francisco Suarez insists on the role of charity with regards to pursuing a just cause, due to the need for sustainable post-conflict peace, and it is from Suarez we have the idea that the likelihood of a just peace must be evaluated before beginning a war.

In Albericio Gentili's *De Iure Belli Libri Tres* we find a tri-partite hybrid functional approach to the just war tradition that is in many respects strikingly contemporary. Petrus Gudelinus likely influenced Grotius with his writings on important constituent parts of a constructed peace, including the cessation of hostilities, the distribution of and restitution for goods and rights, amnesty, and exchange of captives; and he noted the difference between conflicts between sovereigns and those involving rebels. When describing the structure of *De jure belli ac pacis libre tres*, Grotius says that, in part, book III describes "the several Kinds of Peace, and all Agreements made in war." To use contemporary terminology, Book III addresses not only *jus in bello*, but also *jus post bellum*.

Christian Wolff and Emer de Vattel not only provided specific content to the law applicable to the transition to peace, but also made it the foundation of diplomacy and further relations between states. Vattel considered this law necessary, immutable, and obligatory. Immanuel Kant's ideas of perpetual peace still haunt the international system. While not yet achieved, they informed the creation of the League of Nations and the United Nations, and served as a precursor for the idea of a Democratic Peace.

To critics of *jus post bellum* who would state that "*il n'existe pas dans cette tradition de droit de la transition du conflit à la paix*"[402] the above summary should serve as an adequate response. For others, such as Robert Cryer, the note of caution regarding using venerable authors who "were working in a very different tradition," it has merit as far as it goes in terms of making a legal

---

402 Lewkowicz, Grégory. "Jus Post Bellum: vieille antienne ou nouvelle branche du droit? Sur le mythe de l'origine vénérable du Jus Post Bellum." *Revue belge de droit international* 1 (2011).

argument in a court, for example.[403] Unlike Lewkowicz, Cryer is not arguing that *jus post bellum (avant la lettre)* is not part of the just war tradition.

Cryer is, of course, correct in his implication that if one were to simplistically assert that writings of past scholars constituted binding law today, one would be mistaken. However, neither Orend nor Stahn does so. It is far from useless to discuss the ancient traditions of normative and legal thinking on the justice of war and peace, and indeed failure to reevaluate and consider the traditions that gave rise to contemporary international law is to doom oneself to a curious form of self-imposed blindness—not only to the beneficial analysis of past authors, but also to their errors (such as using *jus post bellum* as a general license to violate other norms). Contemporary international law theorists and practitioners would be well served to be better grounded in the tradition they have inherited and may be invoking without even knowing it. Cryer's overall approach of caution, on the other hand, is well placed. This should not be a call to reject the utility of historical legal scholarship, but rather to expand and clarify the intellectual traditions that underpin the way lawyers approach their work. While this chapter could be expanded into its own volume, there is current added value in taking a fresh look at classic works with the particular, coherent perspective of a hybrid functional approach to *jus post bellum*.

Various approaches to the transition to peace are considered so natural as to be invisible today—that one needs a certain amount of authority to conclude a peace treaty or peace agreement, that a peace treaty has binding effect even after the natural person who agreed to it has died, that the victorious power should not be utterly unfettered in his treatment of those who lose a conflict. One today may nod and say "of course"—but why does this seem natural today, whereas it required careful explanation earlier? Precisely because a tradition so powerful as to become the intellectual water in which we swim has been developed by the very authors some would disregard.

The preceding review of the deep roots of *jus post bellum* is inevitably incomplete. Examinations of the writings of Grotius analyzed elsewhere in this work are not repeated here. The ambition of this chapter is less an encyclopaedic recitation of the evolution of the concept than an exploration of the particular tradition from which *jus ad bellum* and *jus in bello* also derived. There is a temptation to naturalize these terms: to assume they represent

---

403 Cryer, Robert. "Law and the Jus Post Bellum," *Morality, Jus Post Bellum, and International Law*. Ed. Larry May and Andrew Forcehimes. 1st ed. Cambridge: Cambridge University Press, 2012. pp. 223–249, p. 226 ff (see generally the section *Jus Post Bellum: Historically Defensible?*).

something unchanging and inherent. Upon realization that they are of relatively recent coinage, one might have an overreaction in the other direction, assuming that the fundamental issues addressed are purely contemporary. The powerful legal and normative tradition that informs the development of these ideas is best approached carefully. Contemporary *jus post bellum* is best addressed with an awareness of its history, respect for experience and past scholarship, but without a false presumption of being bound by past moral or legal precepts if they do not meet contemporary standards of positive legal authority or the needs of those attempting the difficult task of constructing a positive peace.

CHAPTER 2

Exploration of Sister Terms

Only with a basic understanding of the *jus ad bellum/jus in bello* dichotomy can an exploration of a *jus ad bellum/jus in bello/jus post bellum* trichotomy properly begin. Before examining the suggestion that the *jus ad bellum/jus in bello* dichotomy be replaced with a *jus ad bellum/jus in bello/jus post bellum* trichotomy, this section will further introduce and critically explore *jus post bellum*'s more established "sister terms," *jus in bello* and *jus ad bellum*. Each term will be described in more detail, and then the import for *jus post bellum* and the *jus ad bellum/jus in bello/jus post bellum* trichotomy will be explored.

A   *Jus In Bello*

Jus in bello addresses many issues. *Jus in bello* now includes, *inter alia*, regulations protecting and regulating civilians, civilian objects, refugees,[1] women,[2] children,[3] military medical personnel, military religious personnel, military prisoners, civilian prisoners, surrendering combatants, incapacitated combatants, and members of the International Committee of the Red Cross. It requires collecting and caring for the wounded and sick.[4] Modern *jus in bello* regulates armed conflicts between states ("International Armed Conflicts") and other conflicts ("Non-International Armed Conflicts"). *Jus in bello* regulates active combat,[5] and also law-making and administration during and after

---

1   E.g., Fourth Geneva Convention and Additional Protocol I.
2   E.g., GCIII, Arts 14, 16; GCIII, Art 25; GCIV, Art 27; API, Art 76(2); APII, Art 4(2).
3   E.g., Geneva Conventions; The Optional Protocol on the Involvement of Children in Armed Conflict (2000), UN General Assembly, Optional Protocol to the Convention on the Rights of the Child on the Involvement of Children in Armed Conflict, 25 May 2000 (UN General Assembly, Optional Protocol to the Convention on the Rights of the Child on the Involvement of Children in Armed Conflict, 25 May 2000), an amendment to the Convention on the Rights of the Child (1989) UN General Assembly, Convention on the Rights of the Child, 20 November 1989, United Nations, Treaty Series, vol. 1577, p. 3 (The Convention on the Rights of the Child was adopted and opened for signature, ratification and accession by General Assembly resolution 44/25 of 20 November 1989. It entered into force on 2 September 1990, in accordance with article 49.).
4   E.g., Common Article III.
5   E.g., GC I/II, AP I/II.

belligerent occupation.[6] (Belligerent occupation occurs during an International Armed Conflict when a territory is no longer under the control of the sovereign territorial state and is not part of the front line of active combat).[7] It includes certain protections for armed forces on land,[8] in the air,[9] and at sea.[10] It includes certain duties that may occur during peacetime, such as the duty to disseminate the texts of the Geneva Convention and educate the military and civilian populations in the principles of *jus in bello*[11] and the duty to determine whether a new weapon, means or method of warfare violates Additional Protocol I or any other applicable rule of International Law.[12]

Jus in bello restricts not only the general conduct of combatants but also the specific means and methods of warfare, including weapons. The use of exploding projectiles weighing less than 400 grams was prohibited in 1868,[13] and bullets that flatten upon entering the human body were prohibited in 1899.[14] Poison and poisoned weapons were banned in the 1907 Hague Regulations.[15] The use of chemical weapons and bacteriological methods were banned in the 1925 Geneva Protocol,[16] a ban updated by the 1972 Biological Weapons Convention[17]

---

6   E.g., GC IV.
7   See generally, Benvenisti, The International Law of Occupation (2nd ed 2012 OUP); Yoram Dinstein, The International Law of Belligerent Occupation (CUP 2009).
8   E.g., GC I.
9   E.g., AP I Article 42.
10 E.g., GC II.
11 E.g., GC I/II/III/IV, Arts. 47/48/127/144):
    The High Contracting Parties undertake, in time of peace as in time of war, to disseminate the text of the present Convention as widely as possible in their respective countries, and, in particular, to include the study thereof in their programmes of military and, if possible, civil instruction, so that the principles thereof may become known to all their armed forces and to the entire population.
12 Art. 36 AP I.
13 Short title: Declaration of Saint Petersburg (1868); Declaration Renouncing the Use, in Time of War, of Explosive Projectiles Under 400 Grammes Weight. Saint Petersburg, adopted 11 December 1868, D.Schindler and J.Toman, The Laws of Armed Conflicts, Martinus Nihjoff Publisher, 1988, p.102.
14 Short title: Hague Declaration (1899); International Peace Conference 1899, Declaration (IV,3) concerning Expanding Bullets. The Hague, adopted 29 July 1899, (entry into force 4 September 1900).
15 Short title: Hague Regulations (1907); International Conferences (The Hague), Hague Convention (IV) Respecting the Laws and Customs of War on Land and Its Annex: Regulations Concerning the Laws and Customs of War on Land, 18 October 1907.
16 Short title: Geneva Protocol (1925); United Nations, Protocol for the Prohibition of the Use in War of Asphyxiating, Poisonous or other Gases, and of Bacteriological Methods of Warfare, 17 June 1925 (Entry into force: 8 February 1928).
17 Short title: 1972 Biological Weapons Convention; 1972 Convention on the Prohibition of the Development, Production and Stockpiling of Bacteriological (Biological) and Toxin

and the 1993 Chemical Weapons Convention[18] (extending the prohibition beyond use to development, production, acquisition, stockpiling, retention, and transfer of biological and chemical weapons). The 1980 Convention on Certain Conventional Weapons (CCW)[19] and its Protocols regulate a number of weapons, including incendiary weapons,[20] mines,[21] booby traps,[22] blinding laser weapons,[23] explosive remnants of war,[24] and munitions that create fragments not detectable by X-ray.[25] Interestingly, the CCW is the first treaty to address the post-conflict dangers of the explosive remnants of war. The 1997 Convention on the Prohibition of the Use, Stockpiling, Production and Transfer of Anti-Personnel Mines and on their Destruction[26] describes itself well, and was

---

Weapons and on their Destruction, 1015 UNTS 163 / [1977] ATS 23 / 11 ILM 309 (1972) , 10 April 1972 (Entry into force: 26 March 1975).

18   Short title: Convention on the prohibition of chemical weapons (1993); Convention on the Prohibition of the Development, Production, Stockpiling and Use of Chemical Weapons and on their Destruction, 3 September 1992 (Entry into force: 29 April 1997); *see also* UN General Assembly, Implementation of the Convention on the Prohibition of the Development, Production, Stockpiling and Use of Chemical Weapons and on Their Destruction: Resolution adopted by the General Assembly, 17 December 2003, A/RES/58/52.

19   Short title: Convention on Certain Conventional Weapons; United Nations, Convention on Prohibitions or Restrictions on the Use of Certain Conventional Weapons Which May be Deemed to be Excessively Injurious or to Have Indiscriminate Effects (and Protocols) (As Amended on 21 December 2001), 10 October 1980, 1342 UNTS 137 (Entry into force: 2 December 1983; Registered No. 22495).

20   Short title: Protocol III (1980) to the Convention on Certain Conventional Weapons; Protocol on Prohibitions or Restrictions on the Use of Incendiary Weapons (Protocol III). Geneva, 10 October 1980 (Entry into force: 2 December 1983).

21   Short title: Protocol II, as amended (1996), to the Convention on Certain Conventional Weapons; Protocol (II) on Prohibitions or Restrictions on the Use of Mines, Booby-Traps and Other Devices. Geneva, 10 October 1980 (Entry into force: 2 December 1983).

22   Ibid.

23   Short title: Protocol IV (1995) to the Convention on Certain Conventional Weapons; Protocol on Blinding Laser Weapons (Protocol IV to the 1980 Convention), 13 October 1995 (Entry into force: 30 July 1998).

24   Short title: Protocol V (2003) to the Convention on Certain Conventional Weapons; Protocol on Explosive Remnants of War (Protocol V to the 1980 CCW Convention), 28 November 2003 (Entry into force: 12 November.2006).

25   Short title: Protocol I (1980) to the Convention on Certain Conventional Weapons; Protocol on Non-Detectable Fragments (Protocol I). Geneva, 10 October 1980 (Entry into force: 2 December 1983).

26   Short title: Convention on the Prohibition of Anti-Personnel Mines (Ottawa Treaty) (1997); The 1997 Convention on the Prohibition of the Use, Stockpiling, Production and transfer of Anti-Personnel Mines and on their Destruction (Entry into force: 1 March 1999).

followed up logically by the 2008 Convention on Cluster Munitions.[27] The 2013 Arms Trade Treaty[28] regulating the international trade in conventional weapons entered into force 24 December 2014.

These types of treaties, focused on weapons, are considered to be in the domain of *jus in bello* or, to use the more modern term (discussed *infra*) International Humanitarian Law. But not all regulations of weaponry are considered to be *jus in bello*. The regulation of nuclear weapons in terms of disarmament, non-proliferation, testing restriction, and nuclear-free zones are generally considered to be in a category of its own (or series of categories), with such nuclear weapons treaties not considered primarily as a subset of International Humanitarian Law,[29] even though the International Court of Justice has concluded that their use would generally be contrary to the rules of International Humanitarian Law.[30] The ICRC finds it difficult to envisage how nuclear weapons use could be compatible with International Humanitarian Law.[31] Nonetheless, bilateral treaties such as Strategic Arms Limitation Treaty (I and II) or multilateral treaties such as the Convention on the Physical Protection of Nuclear Material[32] are often considered outside of *jus in bello*. Similarly, United Nations Security Council Resolutions on arms control[33] or domestic restrictions on arms or defence[34] (let alone small arms) are not generally considered part of *jus in bello*. From expanding bullets to nuclear weapons, *jus in bello* serves a regulatory role with regards to weapons, but as shown with respect to nuclear weapons, United Nations Security Council Resolutions or

---

27 Convention on Cluster Munitions, Dublin Diplomatic Conference on Cluster Munitions, 30 May 2008 (Entry into force: 1 August 2010).
28 United Nations, Arms Trade Treaty, 2 April 2013 (Entry into force: 24 December 2014).
29 Nystuen, Gro, Stuart Casey-Maslen, and Annie Golden Bersagel, eds. Nuclear Weapons Under International Law. Cambridge University Press, 2014, particularly Part V "International Disarmament Law."
30 Legality of the Threat or Use of Nuclear Weapons, Advisory Opinion, I.C.J. Reports 1996, p. 226, International Court of Justice (ICJ), 8 July 1996.
31 See *Who will assist the victims of nuclear weapons?* Statement by Peter Maurer, President of the ICRC, International conference on the humanitarian impact of nuclear weapons, Oslo, 4–5 March 2013, available at http://www.icrc.org/eng/resources/documents/statement/2013/13-03-04-nuclear-weapons.htm, last visited 18 August 2014.
32 UN General Assembly, Convention on the Physical Protection of Nuclear Material, 26 October 1979, No. 24631, (Entry into force: 8 February 1987).
33 For example, the restrictions on Iraq, Iran (July 2006 (1696), December 2006 (1737), March 2007 (1747), March 2008 (1803), September 2008 (1835) and June 2010 (1929)), North Korea, or Syria.
34 For example, the restrictions in Germany or Japan after the First World War, or domestically in Nicaragua or at times in Haiti.

domestic restrictions, *jus in bello* does not occupy the field with regard to weapons regulation.

Does this broad body of law, *jus in bello*, cohere? To the degree it does, why does it cohere? The answer to this may be found in the terms used somewhat interchangeably to refer to the same body of law. The term *jus in bello* is often used interchangeably in an English-language context with "the law of armed conflict," "International Humanitarian Law" and analogous terms in other languages. "Laws of war" is also sometimes used. While these non-Latin phrases have the considerable advantage for those not fluent in Latin of being comprehensible in a common tongue, but they have their own drawbacks. The term "International Humanitarian Law" emphasizes a particular normative value that can provide coherence to the many strands of *jus in bello*: humanitarianism, or the saving of lives and reducing of suffering.

Before continuing further, a brief note on methodology and tools for the analysis of *jus post bellum* and related terms might be helpful. This volume includes both very traditional methods such as literature review and close readings of important legal and historical texts, but also what is increasingly called in the Humanities the varied methodology and tools of the "Digital Humanities."[35] Each general category of methodology has its strengths and weaknesses, and may be most effective in combination. A strength of using the tool of a digitized collection of millions of books and constructing a visual representation of the quantitative data derived from that collection (namely the frequency of works using a phrase as a percentage of the works published in that year) is the comprehensiveness of this approach. While surely imperfect, it is also far more comprehensive an approach than could ever be attempted by a single researcher, or indeed by any team of researchers not using the tools of digitalization, optical character recognition, and automated linguistic analysis. It also reduces questions of objectivity that might be present with traditional approaches. That said, traditional approaches are far superior with respect to actually reading and comprehending key works, deriving the meaning and influence of those works, and providing the historical and intellectual context for the ideas expressed.

These terms, "*jus in bello*," "the law of armed conflict" and "International Humanitarian Law," are all largely 20th century terms. This is perhaps not surprising with respect to the use of the term "humanitarian," which during the 19th

---

35   Patrik Svensson, The Landscape of Digital Humanities, Digital Humanities Quarterly, 2010 Volume 4 Number 1, available at http://digitalhumanities.org/dhq/vol/4/1/000080/000080.html last visited 16 July 2014.

century was often used contemptuously in the sense of sentimentality.[36] Figure 1 shows the usage of the terms as a percentage of all terms in an extremely large body of scanned work since 1500.[37]

Concentrating on usage since 1900, one gets a picture as shown in Figure 2.

Similarly, if one were to focus on a more limited dataset that might reveal popular usage rather than all published materials, one sees a similar pattern. Figure 3 shows the number of articles in the New York Times mentioning "law of war," "law of armed conflict," and "humanitarian law" since 1850.

In this New York Times dataset, there is almost no usage of *jus ad bellum*, *jus in bello*, or *jus post bellum*, but there are spikes in the usage of "law of war" during the US Civil War, World War I, World War II, and since 2001. There is a tremendous increase in usage of the phrase "humanitarian law" in the post-Cold War era, and particularly since 2010.

A more telling picture in terms of interest in the subject as a whole may be found if the y-axis is the percentage of articles published instead of the absolute number, see Figure 4.

This shows, again, the great interest in the subject in the pages of the New York Times during the U.S. Civil War, World War I, World War II, and

---

36   Shorter Oxford English Dictionary, Vol. 1, (Oxford University Press 1973), p. 995.
37   The author recognizes that the graphical representations of historical data is not universally appreciated, but hopes for those who find it illuminating these graphs are of some use. This data uses the unequalled dataset of millions of books digitized by Google. A digitized book is usually a physical book that has been scanned, including the identification of characters through optical character recognition. Words are identified, and from those words two-word phrases ("bigrams") three-word phrases ("trigrams") and other phrases are identified and made viewable through Google's "NGram viewer." The results are normalized by year, so the y axis represents a percentage of the books published in that year that have include the searched-for phrase. If this were not done, the acceleration in the rate of publication would make the results more difficult to interpret meaningfully. More information can be found at https://books.google.com/ngrams/info [last visited 27 June 2014] and http://googleresearch.blogspot.nl/2012/10/ngram-viewer-20.html [last visited 27 June 2014]. Unless otherwise noted, the 2012 English language dataset is used, comprising over 20 million works. The original paper explaining the dataset used for these graphs is Jean-Baptiste Michel*, Yuan Kui Shen, Aviva Presser Aiden, Adrian Veres, Matthew K. Gray, William Brockman, The Google Books Team, Joseph P. Pickett, Dale Hoiberg, Dan Clancy, Peter Norvig, Jon Orwant, Steven Pinker, Martin A. Nowak, and Erez Lieberman Aiden*. Quantitative Analysis of Culture Using Millions of Digitized Books. Science (Published online ahead of print: 12/16/2010). Regarding point of speech tagging, see Yuri Lin, Jean-Baptiste Michel, Erez Lieberman Aiden, Jon Orwant, William Brockman, Slav Petrov. Syntactic Annotations for the Google Books Ngram Corpus. Proceedings of the 50th Annual Meeting of the Association for Computational Linguistics Volume 2: Demo Papers (ACL '12) (2012).

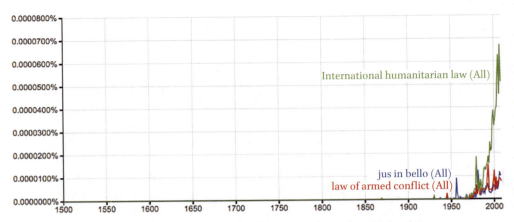

FIGURE 1 Frequency of the use of "*jus in bello*," "the law of armed conflict" and "International Humanitarian Law" in millions of volumes published in English since 1500.

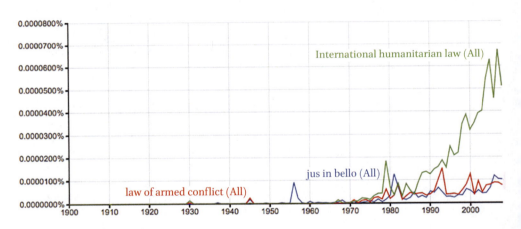

FIGURE 2 Frequency of the use of "*jus in bello*," "the law of armed conflict" and "International Humanitarian Law" in millions of volumes published in English since 1900.

in the post-Cold War era, with the interest now (expressed now more as "humanitarian law" than "law of war") exceeding any period since the U.S. Civil War.

Figures 1–4 show a few interesting trends. First, the dominant term at present is clearly "international humanitarian law."[38] "International humanitarian

---

38 In the present discussion, all references to the terms "international humanitarian law," "jus in bello," and "law of armed conflict" are referring to their usage with major forms of

FIGURE 3   Number of articles in the New York Times mentioning "law of war," "law of armed conflict," and "humanitarian law."

FIGURE 4   Percent of total articles published by the New York Times in a given year mentioning "law of war," "law of armed conflict," and "humanitarian law."

law" is used approximately five times as much as "*jus in bello*" or "law of armed conflict." This seems to have happened due to a large increase in the use of the term since the mid-1980s. There seems to have been spikes in the use of "*jus in bello*" in the mid-1950s and early 1980s. It is interesting to note

capitalization combined into a single set of statistics, combining for example uncapitalized (e.g." jus in bello,") first letter of each word capitalized (e.g. "Jus In Bello"), and all-caps (e.g. "JUS IN BELLO").

this happened approximately five years after the Geneva Conventions of 1949 and Additional Protocols of 1977. There was a general increase in the use of the term "law of armed conflict" since the 1990s. This is a term more frequently preferred by the military and is also the term favored in the Geneva Conventions of 1949.[39] "*Jus in bello*" and the "law of armed conflict" are not in disuse; rather published references to "international humanitarian law" have shot upwards without necessarily being at the expense of these related terms.

Of potential note in the development and conceptualization of this terminology are the major initiatives in the late 1960s and 1970s by the International Commission of Jurists and other NGOs.[40] These launched a process that ultimately led to the rebranding of the law of war as international humanitarian law, and indeed the negotiation and adoption of the 1977 additional protocols.[41] Twenty years after the Universal Declaration of Human Rights was promulgated, in 1968, the International Conference on Human Rights adopted Resolution XXIII on Human Rights in Armed Conflicts.[42] This Resolution invited the General Assembly of the UN to invite the Secretary-General of the UN to study "The need for additional humanitarian international conventions or for possible revision of existing Conventions."[43] As a result, the Secretary-General produced two reports,[44] the second of which dealt extensively with the derogation clauses of human rights treaties and the *travaux* of the ICCPR, and concluded that killing that is lawful under International Humanitarian Law would not be considered an arbitrary deprivation of life under Article 6 of the ICCPR. This effort to integrate human rights law and international humanitarian law must be seen as a historically bounded and contingent process, not an absolute, ahistorical legal truth. As Marko Milanovic puts it "The whole point of the integrationist project was that the newly rebranded IHL was

---

39 *See*, Gary D. Solis, The Law of Armed Conflict: International Humanitarian Law in War, p. 26; also personal communications with military lawyers.

40 Milanovic, Marko, The Lost Origins of Lex Specialis: Rethinking the Relationship between Human Rights and International Humanitarian Law (July 9, 2014). Theoretical Boundaries of Armed Conflict and Human Rights, Jens David Ohlin ed., Cambridge University Press, Forthcoming, at 15. Available at SSRN: http://ssrn.com/abstract=2463957.

41 Ibid.

42 Proclamation of Teheran, Final Act of the International Conference on Human Rights, Teheran, 22 April to 13 May 1968, U.N. Doc. A/CONF. 32/41 at 3 (1968).

43 Ibid, para. 1.b.

44 Respect for Human Rights in Armed Conflicts, UN Doc. A/7 720, 20 November 1969; Respect for Human Rights in Armed Conflict, UN Doc. A/8052, 18 September 1970.

somehow an extension of human rights to armed conflict, or an exceptional, specialized part of IHRL."[45]

While they may be synonyms or near-synonyms, the terms evoke differing responses and allude to differing organizing principles. If *jus post bellum* is to be understood in part in relation to *jus in bello*, *jus in bello* must also be understood in relation and to some degree in distinction from similar terms. Why might one term be used over another? What does the relative triumph of "international humanitarian law" say about differing organizing principles and their weight in the discourse about the regulation of armed conflict? What is *jus post bellum* in an age of "international humanitarian law" (rather than *"jus in bello"*)?

The main point of *jus in bello* can be said to be its distinction from *jus ad bellum*, underlining the argument that regardless of the merits (or lack thereof) of the *jus ad bellum* justification for the resort to the use of armed force, the laws and principles known as *jus in bello* still apply. Thus, discussions of *jus in bello* can be said to be inherently reinforcing the importance of neutral application of the laws between the parties (particularly in International Armed Conflicts, the traditional area of application for this field).

The organizing principle of "international humanitarian law" is humanitarianism, or the saving of lives and reducing suffering. It did not emerge from the struggle of rights-claimants, but from a sense of charity – *inter arma caritas*.[46] The Martens Clause, in the Preamble to the Hague Conventions on the Laws and Customs of War on Land, is sometimes given credit as the point of entry into international law of the concept of humanitarian law.[47] As formulated in 1899, the Marten clause stated:

> Until a more complete code of the laws of war is issued, the High Contracting Parties think it right to declare that in cases not included in the

---

[45] Milanovic, Marko, The Lost Origins of Lex Specialis: Rethinking the Relationship between Human Rights and International Humanitarian Law (July 9, 2014). Theoretical Boundaries of Armed Conflict and Human Rights, Jens David Ohlin ed., Cambridge University Press, Forthcoming, at 24. Available at SSRN: http://ssrn.com/abstract=2463957.

[46] "In war, charity." Now the motto of the International Committee of the Red Cross. See 40 Isr. L. Rev. 313 (2007) Interplay between International Humanitarian Law and International Human Rights Law in Situations of Armed Conflict, The; Droege, Cordula.

[47] Meron, Theodor. "The Martens Clause, principles of humanity, and dictates of public conscience." American Journal of International Law (2000): 78–89; Johnson, James Turner, *Ideology, Reason, and the Limitation of War: Religious and Secular Concepts 1200–1740*, (Princeton University Press 1975), p. 262.

Regulations adopted by them, populations and belligerents remain under the protection and empire of the principles of international law, as they result from the usages established between civilized nations, from the laws of humanity, and the requirements of the public conscience.[48]

The influence of the Martens Clause is broad and deep.[49] "Humanitarian" groups such as national Red Cross/Red Crescent societies provide humanitarian services during natural and man-made catastrophes, during war and peace. They are the first responders, and are given a central place in the narrative of the Geneva Conventions of 1949 and additional protocols of 1977. The International Committee of the Red Cross has developed the "egg model" which emerged from interagency discussions on protection.[50] It posits three spheres of protective action from the point of violation: responsive action, remedial

---

48 Hague Convention No. II of 1899 with Respect to the Laws and Customs of War on Land, with annex of regulations, July 29, 1899, 32 Stat. 1803, 1 Bevans 247.

49 The Martens Clause was restated in slightly different versions in the Hague Convention of 1907, (International Conferences (The Hague), Hague Convention (IV) Respecting the Laws and Customs of War on Land and Its Annex: Regulations Concerning the Laws and Customs of War on Land, 18 October 1907), the Geneva Conventions of 1949 (Convention for the Amelioration of the Condition of the Wounded and Sick in Armed Forces in the Field, Aug. 12, 1949, Art. 63, 6 UST 3114, 75 UNTS 31; Convention for the Amelioration of the Wounded, Sick, and Shipwrecked Members of Armed Forces at Sea, Aug. 12, 1949, Art. 62, 6 UST 3217, 75 UNTS 85; Convention Relative to the Treatment of Prisoners of War, Aug. 12, 1949, Art. 142, 6 UST 3316, 75 UNTS 135; Convention Relative to the Protection of Civilian Persons in Time of War, Aug. 12, 1949, Art. 158, 6 UST 3516, 75 UNTS 287), the 1977 Additional Protocols to the Geneva Conventions (Protocol Additional to the Geneva Conventions of 12 August 1949, and Relating to the Protection of Victims of International Armed Conflicts, *opened for signature* Dec. 12, 1977, Art. 1(2), 1125 UNTS 3; Protocol Additional to the Geneva Conventions of 12 August 1949, and Relating to the Protections of Victims of Non-International Armed Conflicts, *opened for signature* Dec. 12, 1977, pmbl., para. 4, 1125 UNTS 609), and the Preamble to the Convention on Prohibitions or Restrictions on the Use of Certain Conventional Weapons Which May be Deemed to Be Excessively Injurious or to Have Indiscriminate Effects, Oct. 10, 1980, pmbl., para. 5, 1342 UNTS 137. It is paraphrased in Resolution XXIII of the of the Tehran Conference on Human Rights of 1968, and is cited or referred to in various military manuals such as the US (Dep't of the Army, the Law of Land Warfare, para. 6 (Field Manual No. 27-10, 1956); U.S. Dept of the Air Force, International Law—The Conduct of Armed Conflict and Air Operations 1-7(b) (AFP No. 110-31, 1976)), the United Kingdom (United Kingdom War Office, The Law of War on Land, Being Part III of the Manual of Military Law, paras. 2, 3, 5 (1958)), and Germany (Federal Ministry of Defense, Humanitarian Law in Armed Conflict-Manual, para. 129 (ZAv 15/2, 1992).

50 Giossi Caverzasio, Sylvie (2001) Strengthening Protection in War: a Search for Professional Standards. Geneva: ICRC.

action, and environment-building action.[51] Responsive action is closest to the victims of a violation—action that aims to stop, prevent, or alleviate the worst and most immediate effects of abuse.[52] Remedial action is more restorative and is aimed at helping people recover and live with subsequent effects.[53] Environment-building action focuses more on societal structures and norms that will prevent or limit current and future violations and abuses; it aims to consolidate political, social, cultural and institutional norms conducive to protection.[54] This model recognizes that deprivation through impoverishment, dispossession, destitution, disease and sheer exhaustion are responsible for the majority of civilian deaths in war—that throughout the 1990s, "most civilians died *from war* rather than violently *in war*."[55] Humanitarian action tends to focus on responsive action. Remedial action is the traditional sphere of human rights work, although part of the expanding sphere of humanitarian groups. Environment-building tends to be associated more with development and "rule of law" work. It all centers on the victim and the pattern of abuse of that victim. This pattern of abuse is not necessarily identical to the action of the organized armed group. For such groups, fighting in an armed conflict is in a sense "normal" and legitimate as long as within regulated limits.

The bulk of what is commonly referred to as "international humanitarian law" is codified in six treaties, namely the four Geneva Conventions of 1949 and the two additional protocols of 1977. The most authoritative contemporary definition of the term comes from the Commentary on the Additional Protocols of 8 June 1977 to the Geneva Conventions of 12 August 1949:

> International humanitarian law applicable in armed conflict means international rules, established by treaties or custom, which are specifically intended to solve humanitarian problems directly arising from international or non-international armed conflicts and which, for humanitarian reasons, limit the right of Parties to a conflict to use the methods and means of warfare of their choice or protect persons and property that are, or may be, affected by conflict[.][56]

---

51 Hugo Slim Andrew Bonwick, Protection: An ALNAP guide for humanitarian agencies (Overseas Development Institute, London, 2005), p. 42.
52 Ibid.
53 Ibid.
54 Ibid.
55 Ibid 25.
56 Commentary on the Additional Protocols of 8 June 1977 to the Geneva Conventions of 12 August 1949, Yves Sandoz, Christophe Swinarski and Bruno Zimmermann, eds., International Committee of the Red Cross, Martinus Nijhoff Publishers, Geneva, 1987, p. xxvii.

FIGURE 5   "Egg model" of humanitarian response
Note: Ibid. 43.

This definition emphasizes the unifying telos of humanitarianism around international humanitarian law. It does not emphasize the distinction with *jus ad bellum*. Again, it is the dominant term used for this area of law, showing a great increase in usage in recent decades.

As mentioned previously, the "law of armed conflict" is the term that tends to be favoured by the armed forces themselves. In contrast with "international humanitarian law," it evokes more the image of military manuals than manuals for groups working hand in glove (or yolk in egg-white) with human rights and development groups. While it recognizes that there is law that applies to armed conflict (armed conflict is not *beyond* the law), it also implicitly recognizes that armed conflict can be legal (armed conflict is not inherently *against* the law). It lacks the automatic emphasis on the distinction between *jus ad bellum* and *jus in bello* that "*jus in bello*" has within it. While "international humanitarian law" is clearly a term of art with a relatively specific meaning for a specialist

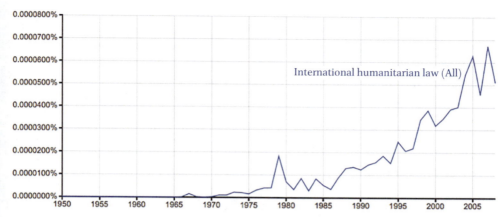

FIGURE 6   Graph of all works published in English from 1950 to 2008 using the phrase "international humanitarian law" regardless of capitalization

community, the "law of armed conflict" may be more immediately understood as a general matter by the general community. It could, however, cause more confusion if it tends to blur the *jus ad bellum*/*jus in bello* distinction. This might happen particularly if the "law of armed conflict" is used synonymously with the "law of war"[57]—a term even more apparently plain but possibly confusing. The "law of war" has historically and currently been used to refer both to *jus ad bellum* and *jus in bello* concerns. Since "armed conflict" is often thought of as synonymous with "war" among non-specialists, and there is a long history of trying to divide the application of the law into periods of "war" and "peace,"[58] it may make sense for non-specialists to conflate the "law of armed conflict" with both *jus ad bellum* and *jus in bello* concerns.

Jus in bello or international humanitarian law is not merely what Sir Hersch Lauterpacht has called "the rules of warfare *pendent bello*,"[59] that is, "during war" or more formally (1) While engaged in a formal war or (2) During the

---

[57] *See*, Gary D. Solis, The Law of Armed Conflict: International Humanitarian Law in War, p. 26; also personal communications with military lawyers.

[58] *See e.g.* Grotius, Hugo, and Jean Barbeyrac. *The Rights of War and Peace, in Three Books: Wherein are Explained, the Law of Nature and Nations, and the Principal Points Relating to Government.* The Lawbook Exchange, Ltd., 1738.

[59] 'The Limits Of The Operation Of The Law Of War,' H. Lauterpacht, 30 Brit. Y.B. Int'l L. 206 1953, p. 211. See also, "The dispossession of the lawful government by the invader pendente bello is no more than an incident of military occupation." Hersch Lauterpacht, Recognition of States in International Law, 53 Yale L.J. 385, 412 n.63 (1944).

course of an armed conflict.[60] It covers peacetime obligations as well, such as the duty to disseminate the texts of the Geneva Convention and educate the military and civilian populations in the principles of *jus in bello*[61] and the duty to determine whether a new weapon, means or method of warfare violates Additional Protocol I or any other applicable rule of International Law.[62] The principal characteristic of *jus in bello*, historically, is the contrast it makes with *jus ad bellum*.

B   *Jus Ad Bellum*

What of *jus ad bellum*? The term "*jus ad bellum*" does not have the same competition for conceptual dominance as "*jus in bello*" does with "law of armed conflict" or "international humanitarian law." Many would say that the *jus ad bellum* became largely *jus contra bellum* on or before the establishment of the U.N. Charter (with self-defence and action under Chapter 7 of the U.N. Charter as notable exceptions to the general rule).[63] Generally, as a matter of international law, resort to armed force is forbidden[64] unless it falls within two narrow exceptions, self-defence (individual or collective)[65] or authorization by the Security Council pursuant to a resolution under Chapter 7 authority. War is no

---

60   Guide to Latin in International Law, (OUP 2009 (print edition) 2011 (online edition) Aaron X. Fellmeth and Maurice Horwitz, available at http://www.oxfordreference.com/view/10.1093/acref/9780195369380.001.0001/acref-9780195369380-e-1581 last visited 5 August 2014.

61   E.g., GC I/II/III/IV, Arts. 47/48/127/144):
"The High Contracting Parties undertake, in time of peace as in time of war, to disseminate the text of the present Convention as widely as possible in their respective countries, and, in particular, to include the study thereof in their programmes of military and, if possible, civil instruction, so that the principles thereof may become known to all their armed forces and to the entire population."

62   Art. 36 AP I.

63   *See e.g.* Kolb, Robert. "Origin of the twin terms jus ad bellum/jus in bello."*International Review of the Red Cross* 37.320 (1997): 553–562; Sharma, Serena K. "The Legacy of Jus Contra Bellum: Echoes of Pacifism in Contemporary Just War Thought." *Journal of Military Ethics* 8.3 (2009): 217–230; Dinstein, Yoram. "Comments on War." *Harv. JL & Pub. Pol'y* 27 (2003): 877.

64   *See* Article 2 UN Charter, signed 26 June 1945, 59 Stat. 1031, T.S. No. 993, 3 Bevans 1 153 (entered into force 24 October 1945).

65   *See* ibid, Article 51.

longer a legal regime in the way it was before the restrictions of the 20th century were developed. Instead of war representing a separate legal regime diametrically opposed to and hermetically sealed from the regime of peace,[66] war was described as a factual reality—armed conflict—regulated by various bodies of law.

One landmark academic source on this change in the nature of war is the article by Hersch Lauterpacht entitled *The Limits of the Operation of the Law of War*.[67] Published in 1953 and building upon "Rules of War in an Unlawful War,"[68] Lauterpacht reviews the effect that the change in the legal nature of war has on other areas of law. He notes the "basic international obligation prohibiting recourse to war as an instrument of national policy"[69] making some wars, wars of aggression, illegal. He explains that:

> [A]s the result of some general international treaties of a legislative character adopted after the First and Second World Wars, the place of war in the system of international law has undergone a fundamental change. This is so for the reason that, in consequence of the successive renunciation and prohibition of war in such instruments as the Covenant of the League of Nations and, in particular, the Pact of Paris and the Charter of the United Nations, war has ceased to be a right which sovereign States are entitled to exercise at their unfettered discretion. War undertaken in violation of these enactments is an unlawful and criminal—and not only an immoral—act. The true nature of that change has been obscured, in the popular estimation by the repeated violations of these undertakings in the past and the widely felt danger of their being disregarded in the future.[70]

Lauterpacht asserts that, before the Covenant of the League of Nations, the General Treaty for the Renunciation of War, and the Charter of the United Nations, the justice or legality of a war was separate from the applicability of

---

66   See Stephen Neff, War and the Law of Nations (2005), at 177–196.
67   Hersch Lauterpacht, *The Limits of the Operation of the Law of War*, 30 Brit. Y.B. Int'l L. 206 (1953).
68   Hersch Lauterpacht, "Rules of War in an Unlawful War," *Law and Politics in the World Community* 89 (Lipsky, ed., 1953).
69   Hersch Lauterpacht, *The Limits of the Operation of the Law of War*, 30 Brit. Y.B. Int'l L. 206 (1953), at 206.
70   Ibid 208.

the rules of warfare.[71] He cites Johann Kaspar Blutschli's *Das modern kriegsrecht der zivilisierten Staaten*[72] for this preposition, quoting the following assertion: "The law of war civilizes on a fully equal footing both the legal and illegal war. It is only because it ignores that distinction that it is in the position to secure its general application"[73] This quote does establish that the distinction between *jus ad bellum* and *jus in bello* was present *avant la lettre*. Blutschli was an influential scholar and co-founder of the Institute of International Law who sought to replace religion and ethics with positive legal norms as sources of law.[74] His introduction to *Das moderne Völkerrecht der civilisirten Staten als Rechtsbuch dargestellt*,[75] addressed to Francis Lieber, stated "[m]y codification can gain authority to the extent that today's civilized world recognizes in it a timely and genuine expression of its legal consciousness, and to the extent that the powers that be heed public opinion."[76] Blutschli's writings were ahead of his time, dealing in part with *lex lata*[77] and in part with *lex ferenda*.[78]

Is *jus ad bellum* a coherent body of law? *Jus ad bellum* is often referenced with various translations into English, from a right to wage war or right to war, to justification for use of force, reasons for war, prevention of war, or simply "just war theory." In practice, as with *jus in bello*, some rules dealing with the legality and justifications for entering into and participating in armed conflict that could theoretically be considered part of *jus ad bellum* are not generally considered to be part of *jus ad bellum*. While United Nations Security Council resolutions that authorize the use of force may be considered part of the

---

71 Ibid 210.
72 Johann Kaspar Blutschli, *Das modern kriegsrecht der zivilisierten Staaten als Rechtsbuch dargestellt* (1866).
73 Johann Kaspar Blutschli, *Das modern kriegsrecht der zivilisierten Staaten als Rechtsbuch dargestellt* (1866) at 519, as cited by Hersch Lauterpacht, The Limits of the Operation of the Law of War, 30 Brit. Y.B. Int'l L. 206 (1953), at 210.
74 For more on Blutschli, see e.g. Betsy Baker, The 'Civilized Nation' in the work of Johann Caspar Blutschli, in Kremer, Markus, and Hans-Richard Reuter, eds. Macht und Moral: politisches Denken im 17. und 18. Jahrhundert. Vol. 31. W. Kohlhammer Verlag, 2007 at 342.
75 Johann Kaspar Blutschli, *Das modern Völkerrecht der civilisirten Staten als Rechtsbuch dargestellt* (1868).
76 Johann Kaspar Blutschli, *Das modern Völkerrecht der civilisirten Staten als Rechtsbuch dargestellt* (1868), as cited in Betsy Baker, The 'Civilized Nation' in the work of Johann Caspar Blutschli, in Kremer, Markus, and Hans-Richard Reuter, eds. Macht und Moral: politisches Denken im 17. und 18. Jahrhundert. Vol. 31. W. Kohlhammer Verlag, 2007 at 342.
77 Law as it exists.
78 Law as it should be.

modern *jus ad bellum* calculus (in evaluating whether there has been a violation of Article 2 of the United Nations Charter), restrictions on action, such as resolutions demanding a ceasefire,[79] demanding withdrawal of forces,[80] or otherwise forbidding the use of force[81] are *not* generally considered to be part of *jus ad bellum*.[82] Nor are General Assembly resolutions condemning or restricting participation in armed conflict generally considered part of *jus ad bellum*, although arguably the "Uniting for Peace" Resolution(s)[83] have been considered part of *jus ad bellum*. Treaty obligations may be considered as part of the *jus ad bellum* calculations (in order to determine what qualifies as collective self-defence) but those treaties themselves[84] are not generally considered to be part of *jus ad bellum*. Domestic law, even domestic law imposed as a result of international armed conflict with the objective of preventing further international armed conflict such as German and Japanese law, is not generally considered part of *jus ad bellum*. While United Nations Security Council or General Assembly authorization for the use of armed force may be considered part of the *jus ad bellum* calculus, domestic judicial, parliamentary, and administrative decisions authorizing participation in an armed conflict are generally not considered part of *jus ad bellum*.

The historical background of *jus ad bellum* as a normative, natural law, perhaps more so than *jus in bello*, retains a clear and resounding connection between positive law and normative principles. Nowhere is this truer than with the controversial subject of humanitarian intervention, recently reframed as the "responsibility to protect." *Jus ad bellum*'s historical emphasis on such factors as just cause, right intention, final resort, legitimate authority, proportional means, and reasonable prospect are directly replicated in legal and normative debates regarding humanitarian intervention. For those advocating humanitarian intervention, lawyers ought to lead towards a world order that can prevent atrocity crimes—with the U.N. Security Council if possible,

---

79   E.g. UNSC Res. 1701 (2006).
80   E.g. UNSC Res. 1559 (2004).
81   E.g. UNSC Res. 688 (1991).
82   See generally, Moore, John Norton. "Jus Ad Bellum Before the International Court of Justice."*Va. J. Int'l L.* 52 (2011): 903.
83   'Uniting for Peace' UNGA Res 377 (V) (3 November 1950) UN Doc A/1775, 10. Since 1950, ten emergency special sessions have been convened in accordance with the conditions stipulated in UNGA Resolution 377 (V). Christina Binder, Uniting for Peace Resolution (1950), Max Planck Encyclopedia of Public International Law, last accessed 19 August 2014.
84   E.g. North Atlantic Treaty (signed 4 April 1949, entered into force 24 August 1949) 34 UNTS 243.

non-violently if possible, but without such authorization and with force if necessary. This is not necessarily calling for radical change, but rather reflects frustration with the likely impossibility of any profound structural change under the current U.N. Charter without reinterpretation, perhaps echoing Edmund Burke's maxim—"A state without the means of change is without the means of its conservation."[85] If international lawyers do not discover a way to change the international system to prevent atrocity crimes, it is a threat to the conservation of the international system itself, and an abdication of duty. If the law of war is at the vanishing point of international law,[86] unresolved issues of preventing atrocity crime and the massive loss of life, using force if necessary, is at the normative center of international relations and foreign policy. *Jus ad bellum* has not, historically, been purely a legal domain. Rather, it contains a strong normative component as part of its basic functioning. This remains the case with current *jus ad bellum* debates.

C Import for *Jus Post Bellum* and the Trichotomy

What are the implications for *jus post bellum* in this analysis? The use of the term *"jus post bellum"* inherently references *jus ad bellum* and *jus in bello*. On a surface level, this might reinforce the distinction between *jus in bello* and *jus ad bellum* and the importance of equal application of the laws of armed conflict. On a deeper level, however, the term *"jus post bellum"* may create tension with that organizing principle. Some influential *jus post bellum* scholars such as Brian Orend have come out directly against the normative distinction between *jus ad bellum* and *jus in bello*, holding that all is lost for a side, normatively, that is waging war wrongly in terms of *jus ad bellum*.[87] Brian Orend remains in a small minority on this point. Nonetheless, *jus post bellum* will often need to address *both* the legality and norms of each side fighting at all, as well as questions regarding how they fought. Peace agreements imposed by a victorious party may accuse the losing party both of aggression and war crimes. While it is possible to address issues of *jus ad bellum* and *jus in bello* while strictly maintaining the distinction between the

---

85 Edmund Burke, Reflections on the Revolution in France, 1790.
86 See Lauterpacht, H, The Problem of the Revision of the Law of War, *British Year Book of International Law* 29 (1952) 360, 381–382.
87 *See e.g.* Orend, Brian. War and international justice: A Kantian perspective. Wilfrid Laurier Univ. Press, 2000; Orend, Brian. The morality of war. Broadview Press, 2013.

two during the transition to peace, doing so will not always be straightforward or simple.

As discussed *infra* in Chapter 3 (*Three Theories of Jus Post Bellum*), a hybrid functional theory of *jus post bellum* includes both peacemaking and post-conflict justice. Post-conflict justice is broader than criminal justice, resolving group and institutional claims and responsibilities, and many of the issues often dealt with under the rubric of "transitional justice." (Differentiating transitional justice and *jus post bellum* is the subject of much of Chapter 4.B.) The process of peacemaking, what Christine Bell calls the *lex pacificatoria*,[88] inherently has to choose whether and how to address issues of *jus ad bellum* and *jus in bello*. The question of whether the *res*, the thing that is being fought over, has been achieved, might be both part of the peacemaking process and post-conflict justice. Questions regarding amnesty are vital for a successful transition to peace, but the underlying substance of alleged violations are not *jus post bellum* but either *jus ad bellum* or *jus in bello*: for violations of the law of armed conflict, (*jus in bello*) for the crime of aggression in international armed conflicts (*jus ad bellum*) or for treason in a non-international armed conflict. Amnesties may be given recognizing that there were violations of *jus in bello* but that accountability for those violations may not be judged to be worth pursuing given the wish to resolve issues that drove the war (*jus ad bellum*) and thus build a just and lasting peace (*jus post bellum*, although some would question the justice of such an arrangement). Questions of right authority, a *jus ad bellum* concept, might come in to play with early negotiations as to who can sit around the peacemaking table, or whether peace negotiations happen at all.

Even without the application of international criminal law during the transition to peace, the questions of why the war was fought and how the war was fought will almost inevitably be part of the transition to peace. While in *jus in bello* analysis it is possible to both temporally and functionally separate the analysis from *jus ad bello* questions, in *jus post bellum* the analysis may overlap with *jus in bello* temporally and connect with *jus ad bellum* and *jus in bello* functionally.

While these issues can be interrelated in practice, as described in the paragraphs *supra*, this makes conceptual clarity all the more important. That does not mean that each concept cannot be somewhat complicated, problematic, or historically contingent, as discussed in the sections *supra*. The history of *jus*

---

88 See e.g. Christine Bell, *On the Law of Peace: Peace Agreements and the Lex Pacificatoria* (Oxford University Press 2008).

in bello would seem to include the prohibition of dum dum bullets[89] and efforts to ban explosives dropped from hot air balloons, but not necessarily efforts to limit nuclear weapons. Modern *jus ad bellum* is generally recognized to cover the United Nations Charter prohibition on the resort to armed force without Security Council authorization (excepting self-defence until that authorization is obtained) but is not generally discussed in terms of additional restrictions on the use of force, whether under international or domestic law. *Jus post bellum* in practice is even more complicated, but that does not mean that it is not coherent or conceptually sound.

---

89 The language of the 1899 Hague Declaration is "bullets which expand or flatten easily in the human body, such as bullets with a hard envelope which does not entirely cover the core or is pierced with incisions." Short title: Hague Declaration (1899); International Peace Conference 1899, Declaration (IV,3) concerning Expanding Bullets. The Hague, adopted 29 July 1899, (entry into force 4 September 1900).

CHAPTER 3

Three Approaches to *Jus Post Bellum*

A   Introduction

The distinction between the overall choice to use force (*jus ad bellum*) and the choice of conduct within armed conflict (*jus in bellum*) is important, but that distinction does not contain the entire universe of questions on the principles and law governing armed conflict. In Parts B, C, and D, this chapter will outline the fundamental difference between taking a temporal approach or a functional approach to *jus post bellum*, and emphasizes the potential of taking a hybrid functional approach that emphasizes the functional aspects of *jus post bellum* while nonetheless rooting it in a general timeline of transition from armed conflict to peace. In Part E, it will discuss the functioning of *jus post bellum* as a *lex specialis*, and in Part F will examine the intermingling of different aspects of *jus ad bellum*, *jus in bello*, and *jus post bellum*, as well as the co-existence of these concepts with other bodies of law. Part G will map the internal workings of a hybrid approach to *jus post bellum*.

B   Temporal Approach

The simplest explanation of the *jus ad bellum/jus in bello/jus post bellum* tripartite division is that these areas cover the beginning, middle, and end of armed conflict. This might be called a "temporal" tripartite division. It might be thought of as a "horizontal" approach, where *jus ad bellum* covers the moment of entry into armed conflict, the *jus in bello* covers the period during armed conflict, and *jus post bellum* covers the period after armed conflict.

This conception of *jus post bellum* needs little theorization, only a set of assumptions—most strikingly that the temporal boundaries of armed conflict can be clearly defined in all cases. It harkens back to the older conception of armed conflict as its own domain of law. Linguistically, it takes its cue not from "ad bellum" or really "in bello" but from "post bellum" with the "post" tied to the time of application of the law, not the desired end result. The logical extension of this "post bellum" approach might be to rename *jus ad bellum* to *"jus ante bello"* and *jus in bello* to *"jus durante bello,"* and indeed to rename *jus ad bellum* to *"jus ad bello."* The author does not recommend this renaming, or this approach.

TABLE 1 Temporal/horizontal conception of the tripartite *ad bellum/in bello/post bellum* division

Moment of entry into armed conflict	Armed conflict	Post-armed conflict
Jus ad bellum (*laws/principles that apply at the start*)	Jus in bello (*laws/principles that apply in the middle/during*)	Jus post bellum (*laws/principles that apply at the end/after*)

C Functional Approach

An alternative approach might emphasize the function each division played in addressing armed conflict.

With the functional conception, *jus ad bellum, jus in bello*, and *jus post bellum* can overlap temporally. They are not fundamentally sequential concepts. Rather, as indicated in the illustration above, they are defined by what they do, not when they do it. It is supported by recognition by the International Criminal Tribunal for the former Yugoslavia that once the existence of an armed conflict has been established, international humanitarian law continues to apply beyond the cessation of hostilities.[1] The UN Security Council has made similar findings regarding the territories occupied by Israel.[2] Linguistically, this focuses on the "ad bellum" and "in bello" language and sees "post bellum" as the *telos* or desired end of the law, not a description of its time of application.

D Hybrid Approach

After introducing a purely temporal and purely functional approach, one can also readily describe a hybrid approach, one that takes into account both time and function. This approach is most helpfully framed with respect to the concept pioneered by Johan Galtung,[3] central to Peace Studies, of "positive peace"

---

[1] *Kunarac*, IT-96-23-T, Judgment of 22 Feb. 2001, at para. 414.
[2] See, e.g., U.N. Security Council Resolution 592 (1986). *See* Alexander Orakhelashvili, The Interaction between Human Rights and Humanitarian Law: Fragmentation, Conflict, Parallelism, or Convergence? Eur J Int Law (2008) 19 (1): 161–182 at 164 doi:10.1093/ejil/chm055.
[3] See e.g. Johan Galtung, "Violence, Peace, and Peace Research" (1969) 6(3) *Journal of Peace Research* 167–91.

TABLE 2   Functional/vertical conception of the tripartite *ad bellum/in bello/post bellum* division.

Function	Jus ad bellum (*whether force may be used at all*)
	Jus in bello (*how to fight humanely*)
	Jus post bellum (*how to transition to a just and sustainablve peace*)

(as opposed to "negative peace"). This approach would be temporally limited. It would likely tend to begin with negative peace and ends with positive peace. This approach would also be functionally specific. It is focussed on the construction of positive peace within the context of a negative peace. Negative Peace, in this understanding, is the mere absence of armed conflict, or as Galtung puts it "personal violence."[4] Positive Peace, in contrast, is the absence of what Galtung calls "structural violence."[5] This imagines that the end of armed conflict is neat, and that attempts to address "structural violence" are necessarily subsequent to the end of armed conflict.

The idea of "density of application" referenced in the caption of Table 3 (functional/vertical conception of the tripartite *ad bellum/in bello/post bellum* division), is intended to indicate the likely force and dominance of application of each area of law at any particular point in time. It also is meant as a reminder of the often chaotic, partial, contingent, and reversible nature of the modern transition to peace. Rather than a moment akin to the "eleventh hour of the eleventh day of the eleventh month" that almost mythologically ended the First World War,[6] modern transitions to peace may involve splintering non-governmental actors with varying approaches, relapses to organized armed violence, and variations over territory—that is, the answer to the existence of an armed conflict may vary over time, identity of the groups, and territory. This is not to say that the divisions between the existence of armed conflict and peace are not relevant. All three operate differently depending on whether there is a state of armed conflict or not, and many actions that can be legal during armed conflict are forbidden during peacetime (types of killing,

---

4 Ibid 183.
5 Ibid.
6 For more on the final period of the First World War, see Persico, Joseph E. Eleventh Month, Eleventh Day, Eleventh Hour. Random House, 2005.

TABLE 3   Hybrid conception of the tripartite *ad bellum/in bello/post bellum* division, with the density of application changing over time but not fundamentally defined by time period.

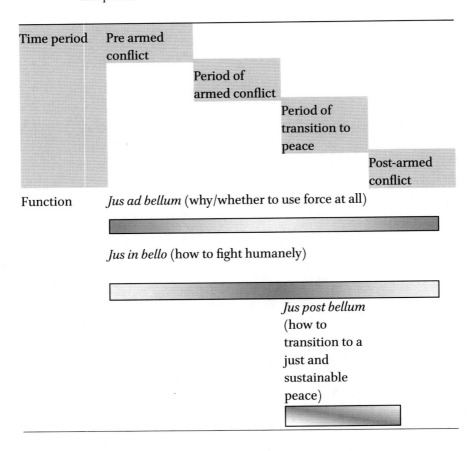

detention) and there are protections that exist during armed conflict and occupation, for example, that may not exist post-armed conflict and occupation. The point of Table 3 is to serve as a reminder that there are aspects of each that apply at various points.

E   Lex Specialis and Lex Generalis

The hybrid approach referenced above works well with the idea of clarifying and prioritizing legal claims through the idea that *lex specialis* will be applied in lieu of or to differently interpret *lex generalis*. For example, under a hybrid approach, most battlefield decisions will be governed by *jus in bello*, but there may be situations where *jus post bellum* would constitute *lex specialis*. This could occur for example when the possibility of the return to a just and sustainable peace may be radically changed by what might be otherwise legitimate conduct under *jus in bello*.

Milanovic describes three conceptions of *lex specialis*: "as a rule of *total displacement*; as a rule of *partial displacement* or norm conflict resolution; and as a mere *interpretive tool* or rule of norm conflict avoidance.[7] This mechanism helps to resolve potential fragmentation and conflict between different areas of law. *Lex specialis* as total displacement is a functional repetition of the classical divide between the law of war and the law of peace—a divide that applied to *all* of international law.[8] This position has been rejected since the Second World War.[9] *Lex specialis* as partial displacement indicates that where a norm conflict is unavoidable, the conflict would be resolved by displacing or qualifying the *lex generalis* to the extent required to resolve the conflict.[10] This rests on the premise that states, when authoring laws, could not have intended to legislate hierarchically equal laws that are contradictory. *Lex specialis* as interpretation does not try to resolve a norm conflict so much as avoid it, essentially an articulation of the principle that that in interpreting

---

7   Milanovic, Marko, The Lost Origins of Lex Specialis: Rethinking the Relationship between Human Rights and International Humanitarian Law (July 9, 2014). Theoretical Boundaries of Armed Conflict and Human Rights, Jens David Ohlin ed., Cambridge University Press, Forthcoming, at 24. Available at SSRN: http://ssrn.com/abstract=2463957; *see generally* Marko Milanovic, Extraterritorial Application Of Human Rights Treaties: Law, Principles, And Policy (2011).

8   Milanovic, Marko, The Lost Origins of Lex Specialis: Rethinking the Relationship between Human Rights and International Humanitarian Law (July 9, 2014). Theoretical Boundaries of Armed Conflict and Human Rights, Jens David Ohlin ed., Cambridge University Press, Forthcoming, at 24. Available at SSRN: http://ssrn.com/abstract=2463957; *see* Stephen Neff, War and the Law of Nations: A General History (2005), at 178.

9   Art 3. ILC Draft Articles on the Effects of Armed Conflict on Treaties, UN Doc. A/66/10, para. 100 (the "existence of an armed conflict does not *ipso facto* terminate or suspend the operation of treaties: (a) as between States parties to the conflict; (b) as between a State party to the conflict and a State that is not."); *ibid* para 101.

10 Milanovic, Marko, The Lost Origins of Lex Specialis: Rethinking the Relationship between Human Rights and International Humanitarian Law (July 9, 2014). THEORETICAL BOUNDARIES OF ARMED CONFLICT AND HUMAN RIGHTS, Jens David Ohlin ed., Cambridge University Press, Forthcoming, at 27. Available at SSRN: http://ssrn.com/abstract=2463957.

treaties one takes into account other relevant rules of international law between parties.[11]

F   Interplay

This interplay of what are normally seen as different bodies of law within specialist legal texts (on children, international criminal law, victims, persons with disabilities) should not threaten the coherence of international humanitarian law and international human rights law, rather it extends and clarifies both bodies of law on specific subjects (children, victims, persons with disabilities) and functionalities (the determination of international criminal responsibility before the International Criminal Court). Hopefully, the determination that aspects of *jus post bellum* can be found not within a discrete corpus of *jus post bellum* treaties but rather within existing legal thinking about the transition to peace will also not be seen as fatal for the legitimacy of *jus post bellum* as an intellectually coherent body of laws and principles. *Jus post bellum* must not only be distinguished from *jus in bello* and *jus ad bellum*, it must also find its place alongside other coherent but related bodies of law such as human rights law, refugee/asylum law, environmental law, investment law, and property law.

It might be helpful to imagine an act that implicated *jus ad bellum, jus in bello*, and *jus post bellum* at once, in order to explain the difference in the application of each area of law and normative principles. Imagine that the first act that began an armed conflict was a bombing campaign that used cluster munitions that left high levels of unexploded ordinance. The question of whether resort to the use of force was legal at all is a *jus ad bellum* question, answerable by reference to the United Nations Charter, any relevant Security Council resolutions, and perhaps customary law regarding self-defence against an imminent attack. In order to determine whether (or which) violations of *jus in bello* occurred, one would have to consider classic questions of targeting, proportionality, and military necessity, the applicability of both treaty (e.g. Geneva Convention IV, the relevant Additional Protocol, as well as potentially 1980 Convention on Certain Conventional Weapons (CCW) and its Protocol on explosive remnants of war,[12] and the 2008 Convention on Cluster

---

11 Art. 31(3)(c) of the Vienna Convention on the Law of Treaties.
12 Protocol V (2003) to the Convention on Certain Conventional Weapons.

Munitions[13]) and customary law. The question of whether the act could also be restricted on the basis that it would make the transition to peace unjustifiably difficult pursuant to the 1980 Convention on Certain Conventional Weapons may also be considered a *jus post bellum* question,[14] and the resolution of the *jus ad bellum* and *jus in bello* violations may require *jus post bellum* practice in order to determine accountability for the act, and build a just and sustainable peace.

The example above could be extended further to see how a single act could implicate multiple areas of law without necessarily confusing their application or resulting in legal fragmentation. Environmental damage might violate environmental law. The treatment of refugees created from the attack would be governed by refugee/asylum law. The human rights of those affected by the attack, now and in the future, would implicate international human rights law under the approach taken by the Human Rights Committee with respect to human rights during armed conflict.[15]

G Hybrid Approach to *Jus Post Bellum*

What does the hybrid approach to *jus post bellum* mean for *jus post bellum* itself, as opposed to how *jus post bellum* relates to *jus ad bellum* and *jus in bello*? What would a hybrid *jus post bellum* look like, particularly in comparison with a temporal *jus post bellum*? It helps to think of at least two large subcategories of *jus post bellum*: the law of ending the armed conflict (which may be termed

---

13 Convention on Cluster Munitions (2008).
14 The CCW is the first treaty to address the post-conflict dangers of the explosive remnants of war. http://www.icrc.org/eng/war-and-law/weapons/overview-weapons.htm.
15 See e.g., Schabas, William A. "Lex Specialis-Belt and Suspenders-the Parallel Operation of Human Rights Law and the Law of Armed Conflict, and the Conundrum of Jus Ad Bellum." Isr. L. Rev. 40 (2007): 592; Droege, Cordula. "Interplay between International Humanitarian Law and International Human Rights Law in Situations of Armed Conflict, The." Isr. L. Rev. 40 (2007): 310; Orakhelashvili, Alexander. "The interaction between human rights and humanitarian law: fragmentation, conflict, parallelism, or convergence?." European Journal of International Law 19.1 (2008): 161–182; Cassimatis, Anthony E. "International humanitarian law, international human rights law, and fragmentation of international law." International and Comparative Law Quarterly 56.03 (2007): 623–639.

TABLE 4   Temporal/horizontal conception of the tripartite division of *jus post bellum*

Armed conflict	Post-armed conflict/ early peace	Stabilized peace
Jus terminatio/lex pacificatoria (*laws/principles that apply before the armed conflict ends to the termination of armed conflict*)	Post-conflict justice and peacebuilding (*laws/principles that apply after the armed conflict ends during early peace. Many of the practices included under the rubric of "Transitional Justice" may happen here, primarily*)	"Normal law"/jus pacis (*law that applies after the transition to peace is stabilized*)

jus terminatio[16] or, following Christine Bell, *lex pacificatoria*[17]) and post-conflict justice and post-conflict peacebuilding.

Under a temporal framework, these two would be neatly divided, as neatly as a hypothesized divide between war and peace. Graphically, it might be depicted as shown in Table 4.

A more sophisticated hybrid approach might emphasize the function each subcomponent within *jus post bellum* played in addressing the transition to a just and sustainable peace.

It is worth noting the change in language as well as the change in structure in Tables 4–5. Under the temporal conception, *jus terminatio/lex pacificatoria* could be described as the "law and principles that apply before the armed conflict ends to the termination of armed conflict." Under the hybrid conception, *jus terminatio/lex pacificatoria* could be described as the "law and principles

---

16   The primary contemporary promoter and theorizer of this term is David Rodin. See Rodin, David. "Two Emerging Issues of Jus Post Bellum: War Termination and the Liability of Soldiers for Crimes of Aggression." *Jus Post Bellum: Towards a Law of Transition from Conflict to Peace*. Ed. Carsten Stahn and Jann K. Kleffner (The Hague: T.M.C. Asser Press, 2008), 53–62; Rodin, David. "Ending war." *Ethics & International Affairs* 25.03 (2011): 359–367; Rodin, David. "The War Trap: Dilemmas of jus terminatio." *Ethics* 125.3 (2015): 674–695. (N.b. he does not use the term *"jus terminationis"*).

17   See e.g. Christine Bell, *On the Law of Peace: Peace Agreements and the Lex Pacificatoria* (Oxford University Press 2008).

TABLE 5   Hybrid conception of the *jus post bellum*, with the density of application likely to change over time but not fundamentally defined by time period.

Armed conflict	Post-armed conflict/ early peace	Stabilized peace

Jus terminatio/lex pacificatoria

(*laws/principles that apply primarily to the termination of armed conflict and laying the initial foundation of a just and sustainable peace.*)

Post-conflict justice and peacebuilding

(*laws/principles that apply primarily to the building of peace and resolving justice issues from the armed conflict. Many of the practices included under the rubric of "Transitional Justice" may happen here, primarily.*)

"Normal law"

(*law that applies to matters primarily unrelated to war*)

that apply primarily to the termination of armed conflict and laying the initial foundation of a just and sustainable peace." The title is the same, but the definition switches from a temporal focus (defined by when it applies) to a functional focus (defined by what it does) applied with sensitivity as to the timeline of armed conflict (thus hybrid). Under the hybrid approach, *jus terminatio/lex pacificatoria* applies to all stages of the negotiation and implementation of peace agreements, including initial framework discussions before any peace agreement is reached and implementation agreements after the armed conflict has technically ended.

Under the temporal conception, post-conflict justice and peacebuilding could be described as the "law and principles that apply after the armed conflict ends and during early peace." Under the hybrid conception, post-conflict justice and peacebuilding could be described as the "law and principles that

TABLE 6   Schematic depiction of law and norms regarding the transition to peace.

General/Global	
– Vienna Convention on the Law of Treaties as applied to Peace Treaties/Customary Law of Treaties – Customary international law of state recognition – Customary international law of government recognition – Treaty and customary international law regarding amnesty and the responsibility to prosecute alleged perpetration of certain crimes – Recognition of states and governments by global international organizations	– UNSC Resolution 1325 – Customary international law on post-conflict administration – Global judicial bodies jurisprudence relating to *jus post bellum*	– Customary international law of occupation – Customary international law of state responsibility, particularly with regards to new states – Customary international law on reparations – Global peacekeeping norms

	Procedural	Mixed	Substantive
Midrange/Regional	– Recognition of states and governments by regional international organizations – Multilateral negotiations regarding issues related to *jus post bellum* – Regional positions regarding amnesty and individual criminal responsibility (e.g. African Union positions on al Bashir)	– Regional judicial bodies jurisprudence relating to *jus post bellum* – Multilateral disarmament treaties, including verification	– Regional peacekeeping efforts – Atypical "wars" (e.g. war on terror)
Specific/Local	– Bilateral regarding issues related to *jus post bellum* Specific amnesties – Specific state recognition – Specific government recognition – Intrastate/domestic negotiations	– Specific disarmament/ demobilization/ reintegration efforts, including verification – Domestic judicial bodies jurisprudence relating to *jus post bellum*	– Particular reparation – State practice regarding state responsibility – State practice regarding occupation – Particular occupation – Specific peacekeeping

apply primarily to the building of peace and resolving justice issues from the armed conflict." Under either conception, many of the practices sometimes included under the rubric of "Transitional Justice" may happen as part of post-conflict justice, including criminal prosecutions, truth commissions, reparations programs, gender justice programs, security system reform, "DDR" (disarmament, demobilization, and reintegration), memorialization,[18] vetting (also known as "lustration," "screening," "administrative justice," and "purging")[19] and education.[20] (For more explaining the difference between Transitional Justice and *jus post bellum*, properly conceived, see Chapter 4.B, *infra*.)

The hybrid approach to *jus post bellum* allows an exploration of the interaction between temporally overlapping *jus terminatio/lex pacificatoria* and post-conflict justice/peacebuilding efforts. While criminal prosecutions, for example, typically happen after armed conflict has terminated, there is no requirement for that to occur,[21] and indeed criminal prosecutions are sometimes justified on the basis that they will serve to build the peace through incapacitation and deterrence.[22] Disarmament, demobilization, and reintegration may happen after the conflict has ended, but in certain countries such as Uganda, may be an ongoing effort even before the conflict is ended or pushed into other countries. This hybrid approach allows the concept of *jus post bellum* to have a much greater utility, encouraging an exploration of the entire transformation from armed conflict to peace, in all its variety and complexity.

It is important to note that this hybrid approach works whether *jus post bellum* is operating as a body of laws and principles, an interpretive tool, or as a framework. As a body of laws and principles, *jus post bellum* includes all of the items evaluated in the chart of relevant laws and norms.

This schematic will be used as a useful guide, connective tissue, and leitmotif at various points throughout the volume. It is not intended to be an exhaustive

---

18   International Center for Transitional Justice (ICTJ), "What is Transitional Justice" available at http://ictj.org/about/transitional-justice (accessed 27 May 2016).

19   Alexander Mayer-Rieckh and Pablo de Greiff (eds), *Justice as Prevention: Vetting Public Employees in Transitional Societies* (Social Science Research Council 2007).

20   See e.g. Elizabeth A. Cole and Judy Barsalou, "Unite or Divide? The Challenges of Teaching History in Societies emerging from Violent Conflict" (United States Institute for Peace 2006) 2 ("History education should be understood as an integral but underutilized part of Transitional Justice and social reconstruction").

21   See, for example, the initial prosecutions at the International Criminal Tribunal for the former Yugoslavia.

22   For an interesting compilation of material on the question of the effect of criminal prosecutions on peace, *see* Human Rights Watch, *Selling Justice Short: Why Accountability Matters for Peace* (2009) http://www.hrw.org/sites/default/files/reports/ijo709webwcover_3.pdf last visited 15 July 2014.

inventory, but rather to guide the reader through the diverse contents of *jus post bellum* as the issue is approached through a variety of perspectives. As an interpretive tool, current laws can be interpreted with the goal of achieving a just and sustainable peace in mind. As a framework, it can help order competing norms and laws to prioritize the successful transition to *jus post bellum*.

CHAPTER 4

Present – An Exploration of Contemporary Usage

A   The Existing Matrix of Definitions: A Review of Contemporary Scholarship

1   *Introduction*
What is *"jus post bellum"*? *Jus post bellum* is often described in shorthand as "law after war" or "the law of transition from war to peace." This chapter addresses the question of *jus post bellum*'s meaning in scholarship. Supplementing this empirical analysis, this chapter takes a comparative look specifically at the temporal dimension of *jus post bellum*, Transitional Justice, and International Criminal Law. Together, these analyses provide a clearer picture of what "jus post bellum" means for those who use the term. The picture is not simple. But without oversimplifying, it can be made more comprehensible. This chapter clarifies not only current usage, but also identifies the problems that scholars and practitioners are addressing when identifying laws and principles under the rubric of *jus post bellum*.

In many respects, the definition of *jus post bellum* is clear. To those familiar with the terms, *jus post bellum* is obviously tied to *jus ad bellum* and *jus in bello*, traditional categories of international law dealing with armed force and more broadly the norms of the just war tradition. *Jus ad bellum*[1] seeks to limit resort to the use of force between states. *Jus in bello* seeks to limit the suffering caused by war.[2] Again, *jus post bellum* is often described in shorthand as "law after war" or "the law of transition from war to peace." It is seen as completing the effort, begun with *jus ad bellum* and *jus in bello*, to apply law and norms to the difficult area of armed conflict. *Jus post bellum* can be clearly distinguished on a number of levels from similar terms such as "Transitional Justice." Transitional Justice can be usefully defined as "the conception of justice associated with periods of political change, characterized by legal responses to confront the wrongdoings of repressive predecessor regimes."[3] The concept of Transitional

---

[1] Some prefer (or use as an equivalent) the term *jus contra bellum*, law against war/armed conflict.
[2] See e.g. IHL and other legal regimes – jus ad bellum and jus in bello available at http://www.icrc.org/eng/war-and-law/ihl-other-legal-regmies/jus-in-bello-jus-ad-bellum/overview-jus-ad-bellum-jus-in-bello.htm last viewed 17 October 2012.
[3] Ruti Teitel, Transitional Justice Geneology, 16 Harvard Human Rights J., Spring 2003, p. 69 (internal citations omitted).

Justice emerged organically from the intense focus on transitions to democracy from the 1970s through the 1990s. The post-Cold War questions of transformative occupation, peacebuilding, and international territorial administration set the frame for *jus post bellum*. The content of *jus post bellum* can be usefully plotted in a matrix, ranging from laws and norms that are more substantive to more procedural in nature, and from more local to more global. This matrix has already been employed in Chapter 3.H. to orient the reader, and should provide continuity in this section as well.

In at least one key aspect, however, the definition of *jus post bellum* is unsettled. That respect has to do with the relative importance or unimportance of fixing the definition by using a timeline with sharp divisions marking the end of armed conflict, which this chapter refers to as the "temporal aspect" or "temporal dimension" of *jus post bellum*. The temporal aspect of *jus post bellum* is not a mere technical concern. When analyzed properly, the question "what is '*jus post bellum*'" ultimately brings us to the question: "Why use the term '*jus post bellum*?'" It brings those interested in the subject of *jus post bellum* to the question of what, if anything, we are trying to accomplish.

This work responds to these questions, albeit in a manner that seeks to open further avenues for research rather than close the questions with a "definitive" answer. The short definitions given above, "law after war" or "the laws of transition from war to peace" turn out to contain important differences. "Law after war" implies a timeline with a sharp division marking the end of war (or to use the more commonly used and more useful term for modern practitioners, armed conflict). In contrast, the "laws of transition from armed conflict to peace" language does not depend on any clean division between periods of armed conflict and peace, sitting more comfortably with a *status mixtus*,[4] or a period in which armed conflict starts and stops before resolving into a sustainable peace. Without clarifying this divide, the status of critical subject areas (such as peace negotiations and agreements that can occur before peace is established, belligerent occupation, counter-insurgency, and laws applying to non-state actors) remains unclear, as they may or may not fall under *jus post bellum*.

Identifying that *jus post bellum* does not have a single, consolidated definition but rather a matrix of definitions that have changed over time is a critical step if that matrix of definitions is to be properly analyzed. What follows is an assessment of this matrix. The empirical section focuses on the temporal-functional

---

4 See Schwarzenberger, Georg, *Jus pacis ac belli? Prolegomena to a sociology of International Law*, 37 Am. J. Int'l L. 460 (1943), 470.

dichotomy *within* the body of work addressing *jus post bellum*. In addition to looking at usage from *within* the limited corpus of work using one phrase (*"jus post bellum"*), it is helpful to look at usage from *without*—that is, in comparative perspective. By looking at the scholarship on *jus post bellum* from the "inside" and the "outside," empirically and comparatively, the definition of *jus post bellum* is clarified.

2   *Identifying the Definitional Dichotomy — Functional vs. Temporal*

This subject has been treated in more detail on a theoretical level *supra*. Here, the methodology of evaluating contemporary scholarship is reviewed. Emphasis on the functional-temporal dichotomy was not something arrived at *a priori*, as it were, but rather through observations of the literature by the author. It appeared that there was a divide emerging without any clear awareness by legal scholars of that split. The divide is between those who placed their primary definitional emphasis on the body of laws and norms bounded by time (a temporal emphasis) and those who placed their primary definitional emphasis on the body of laws and norms oriented around the function of transitioning from armed conflict to peace (a functional emphasis). The author hoped to verify the existence of and clarify the nature of that divide. The hybrid functional approach outlined in this work *supra*, namely, one that emphasizes the *functional* aspects of *jus post bellum* (establishing a just and lasting peace) while nonetheless rooting it in a general timeline of transition from armed conflict to peace, is an attempt to recognize this dichotomy and to the degree possible achieve synthesis.

An example may be helpful to dramatize the difference between the two approaches. Imagine a targeting decision during an armed conflict. A military target is within or proximate to an important cultural site in a manner such that attacking the target would destroy the cultural site. There is existing law on the legality of such an attack, but it is unclear whether *jus post bellum* would have anything to say about the question. A temporal emphasis would clearly rule out *jus post bellum* playing a role. Under a temporal emphasis, the armed conflict is ongoing, so *jus post bellum* has not begun. A hybrid functional emphasis may allow *jus post bellum* to speak, even (or especially) if the temporal context is taken into account. Specifically, if avoiding the destruction of the cultural site is particularly important for the process of eventually establishing a sustainable peace, then the norms of a functionally-focused *jus post bellum* are implicated. While the normal application of *jus in bello* principles of proportionality and distinction might permit destruction of a cultural site in some instances, the simultaneous application of *jus post bellum* principles, either as a second-order method of interpretation (giving more substantive meaning to the principle of proportionality) or as a first-order application of discrete rules, might forbid the destruction of the site.

Proportionality in targeting is actually a notoriously difficult area to operationalize given that it involves a comparison between military advantage and the inherent value of protected persons and objects. By emphasizing the weight given to protected objects if their preservation increases the likelihood of the eventual construction of a just and sustainable peace, legal certainty may be increased in targeting decisions that are of colorable illegality. This does not necessarily create more legal uncertainty, given that it may move a marginal targeting decision from uncertain legality (given the amorphousness of *jus in bello* proportionality calculations) to fairly certain illegality, but it does potentially make the process of evaluating a target more complex.

The unclear definition of *jus post bellum* might be described as its original sin. Take the following quote from Brian Orend's foundational essay, *Jus Post Bellum*.

> It seems, then, that just war theorists must consider the justice not only of the resort to war in the first place, and not only of the conduct within war, once it has begun, but also of the termination phase of the war, in terms of the cessation of hostilities and the move back from war to peace. It seems, in short, that we also need to detail a set of just war norms or rules for what we might call *jus post bellum*: justice after war.[5]

On one hand, Orend refers to the termination phase of the war and the move back from war to peace. On the other hand, he speaks of "justice after war," which taken literally, would not obviously include the termination of phase of the war and the move back from war to peace. This ambiguity has been there from the beginning.

Many of the works analyzed for this chapter are only ambiguously categorizable as using a temporal or functional definition of *jus post bellum*. Some are not categorizable one way or another. No work represents a Weberian "ideal type" of self-consciously using a temporal or functional definition of *jus post bellum*. Thus, it might be helpful to provide an ideal type of an article that exemplifies adopting one definition and rejecting another.

The "ideal type" of a work adopting a temporal definition of *jus post bellum* would have the following characteristics. It would discuss *jus post bellum* as "law after war" or something similar. It would indicate that the term applied when, *and only when*, armed conflict had ceased. It would effectively be

---

5 Orend, Brian, *Jus Post Bellum*, Journal of Social Philosophy, Vol. 31 No. 1, Spring 2000, 117–137.

discussing the law that applied during "early peace." There would be little or no emphasis on the function of the area of law. The focus would be on what happens "after war/armed conflict," or "in the aftermath of war/armed conflict." The areas of law and practice focused on in such an article would deal with implementing peace treaties and agreements[6] during peacetime, but not the negotiation of peace agreements or the peace agreements themselves. Peacetime peacebuilding would be emphasized, but not peacekeeping amidst intermittent conflict. Environmental law would not be subject to *jus post bellum* principles until after armed conflict had ended. The law regarding belligerent occupation would not be subject to *jus post bellum* principles until after the armed conflict had ended. Similarly, concerns regarding counter-insurgency in a *status mixtus* or intermittent conflict would not be addressed. Law relating to non-state actors would only apply if the armed conflict had ceased. Such an article would not envisage *jus post bellum* dealing with the entire transition from armed conflict to a sustainable peace.

The "ideal type" of a work adopting a functional definition of *jus post bellum* would have the following characteristics. It would discuss *jus post bellum* as the body of law applying to the "transition to peace" or something similar. It would focus on whether the law was intended to or had an important role in transitioning from armed conflict to a sustainable peace. It would include laws that applied during armed conflict if they played that function. It may not include laws that happen to occur shortly after armed conflict ends if they do not focus on or contribute to the transition to a sustainable peace. It would conceive of *jus post bellum* as including the entire process of negotiating, agreeing to, implementing, and modifying peace agreements. Peacekeeping and peacebuilding would be included. Environmental law and the protection of cultural goods could apply during armed conflict if they substantially related to the transition to a sustainable peace. The questions of belligerent occupation and the question of transformative occupation would be squarely addressed. The work would explicitly consider *jus post bellum* in a *status mixtus* or a situation of intermittent conflict. It could apply to law addressed to non-state actors if it was part of the law of transition to a just and sustainable peace. It would not place primary emphasis on the moment of ending armed conflict.

Both the temporal and functional approaches involve an analysis very cognizant of the passage of time. While the functional approach is not as focused on fixing the moment when war ends, it is still very focused on the forward

---

6 Hereinafter, this chapter will merely reference "peace agreements" instead of "peace treaties and peace agreements" under the rationale that peace treaties can be thought of as a specific subset of peace agreements, specifically those that relate to agreements between states.

progression of events—a transition towards a sustainable peace. With the functional approach, the focus is forward-looking, as with the *post bellum* being an aspiration of the *jus*, rather than a description of it. The purpose or *telos* of the law—post bellum—is embedded in the name, under the functional approach. It is unclear if the temporal approach has the same sort of internal purpose, although perhaps simply establishing the law during early peace is purpose enough.

The works analyzed in this chapter provides real-world examples of what these definitions look like in practice. They do not resemble exhaustive checklists, but they will provide meat for the theoretical bones provided by the above ideal types. For example, take *Obligations of the New Occupier: The Contours of a Jus Post Bellum* by Kristen E. Boon (2009).[7] This work indicates that there is no clear temporal division between war and peace. Boon states "Yet with the exception of the law of belligerent occupation, neither jus ad bellum nor jus in bello provide much guidance on temporary interventions after war and before peace."[8] This understanding pushes against a simple temporal definition, starting with the end of armed conflict. The focus is on the process of transitioning out of armed conflict into peace.

The reason for the focus on the temporal-functional dichotomy is because it is not only one of the most important divides in the conception of *jus post bellum*, but also because it is one of the least well understood. There is no published literature squarely addressing the dichotomy, although it is hinted at through much of the literature, as evidenced by the empirical analysis below. By addressing the dichotomy, the author addresses a number of problems: the problem the dichotomy holds to the discourse/interpretive community concerned with *jus post bellum*; the problem the dichotomy holds as a matter of law; and the problem the dichotomy holds for research.

3   *Problems of the Dichotomy*
a   The Problem as a Discourse Community or Interpretive
            Community

Erik Borg contrasted the terms "discourse community" and "interpretive community" as follows:

---

7   Boon, Kristen E., Obligations of the New Occupier: The Contours of a Jus Post Bellum (June, 29 2009). Loyola of Los Angeles International and Comparative Law Review, Vol. 31, No. 2, 2008.
8   Ibid 102.

We do not generally use language to communicate with the world at large, but with individuals or groups of individuals. As in life, for discussion and analysis in applied linguistics these groups are gathered into communities. One such grouping that is widely used to analyse written communication is *discourse community*. John Swales, an influential analyst of written communication, described discourse communities as groups that have goals or purposes, and use communication to achieve these goals. [...] 'Interpretive community' (Fish 1980), on the other hand, refers not to a gathering of individuals, but to an open network of people who share ways of reading texts[...] [U]nlike an interpretive community, members of a discourse community actively share goals and communicate with other members to pursue those goals.[9]

If people use multiple definitions of the same term, particularly without realizing it, the clarity of their communications lessens. This is true in an interpretive community or a discourse community. If asked (and the terms were defined), some groups scholars and practitioners using the term *jus post bellum* might categorize themselves as part of the interpretive community, others might call themselves part of a discourse community. The functional-temporal dichotomy is a particular problem for a discourse community. If a discourse community cannot agree on fundamental aspects of the central concept of their community, not only will they be unable to communicate clearly, but they will also be unable to agree on the goals they should actively share.

b   The Problem as Law

Ambiguity in definitions can be a problem with any interpretive community or discourse community. The author suggests it is a particular problem when the community centers on legal issues. From a normative point of view, legal ambiguity can mean an arbitrary and counter-normative application of law.[10] From an analytical point of view, the ambiguity with respect to an area of law may prevent particular potentially legal rules from being recognized as law and thus objectively fail to be, objectively, law.[11]

---

9   Borg, Erik, *Discourse Community*, ELT Journal, Volume 57/4, October 2003, Oxford University Press, p. 398.
10   *See generally e.g.*, Schauer, Frederick F., *Playing by the rules: a philosophical examination of rule-based decision-making in law and in life* (1991) Oxford University Press.
11   On the idea of the "rule of recognition," *see* Hart, H.L.A., *The Concept of Law*, 1961, Oxford University Press.

c   The Problem for Research

What would be helpful for a researcher trying to map this definitional dichotomy would be a database containing sample sets of available research on the issue that have been analyzed to see how the term *jus post bellum* is used in contemporary literature. As no such database existed, the author has created such a database. The database contains both the actual research literature (the text of the articles) and metadata describing that literature. The database was developed with the assistance of the Living Lab Project at Leiden University and is hosted online using a Virtual Research Environment platform.[12] More about the database will be explained in Chapter 5.

There are, of course, potential opportunities for the practitioners or experts in a term with an amorphous definition. One can look to the term "Transitional Justice" as an example of this phenomenon. Transitional Justice practitioners have arguably been able to expand the portfolio of their work over time as their underlying concept became broader and less defined. In fact, "Transitional Justice" has been redefined by some to include not only "the conception of justice associated with periods of political change, characterized by legal responses to confront the wrongdoings of repressive predecessor regimes,"[13] but also "transitions from war to peace," which is a fundamentally different concept—one which threatens to confuse Transitional Justice with *jus post bellum*, particularly if the contrast in temporal aspects remain unexamined. There is as yet no published systematic analysis of the temporal aspect of Transitional Justice or *jus post bellum*, so clarifying this critical aspect remains crucial. Accordingly, Part IV provides a systematic analysis of the temporal aspect of these two concepts, and tries to draw overall conclusions for the better understanding when two possible understandings are proffered.

4   *Importance*

As stated before, when analyzed properly, the question "what is 'jus post bellum'" ultimately brings us to the question: "Why use the term 'jus post bellum?'" It brings those interested in the subject of *jus post bellum* to the question of what, if anything, we are trying to accomplish.

It may be that we are merely attempting to describe what law applies at a certain time period during early peace. An alternative effort would be to describe both the *lex lata* and the *lex ferenda* with respect to the function of

---

12   The database is currently hosted at https://vre.leidenuniv.nl/vre/jpb/definitions/default.aspx. For full access, please see the author.

13   Ruti Teitel, Transitional Justice Geneology, 16 Harvard Human Rights J., Spring 2003, p. 69 (internal citations omitted).

establishing a sustainable peace. If the underlying goal is to establish a sustainable peace after armed conflict, then ignoring or diminishing the laws that apply to efforts to establish a sustainable peace *during* armed conflict will leave an incomplete area of law. It is possible, however, that in searching for completeness, clarity (or at least simplicity) will suffer.

5 *Empirical Analysis*

For a granular analysis of the works analysed, please see Chapter 5. The summary results are as follows. There has been a steady expansion of references *to jus post bellum* in a variety of journals. With the expansion of references, there has been an increase of ambiguity, not a consolidation around a consensus definition. The trend in the less-legally focused dataset (SSRN articles) is away from an emphasis on functional aspects and towards temporal aspects. The overall trend is hard to discern, but for articles with more than a glancing reference to *jus post bellum* there seems to be an arc that went from a functional definition, towards, a temporal definition, and with a renewed legal interest back towards a more functional definition. Whether a consensus will be achieved, and what that consensus might be, is as yet unclear. Again, for a full analysis of the empirical data gathered, please see Chapter 5.

The question asked influences the truth found. By emphasizing the question of the *goal* of the discourse around the term *"jus post bellum,"* a functional definition may already be framed in a more flattering light. A functional definition, giving *jus post bellum* a *telos* or ultimate object, naturally answers the question of the goal of *jus post bellum* discourse more clearly than a temporal definition.

Another way to phrase the question is whether *jus post bellum* is essentially a *nominal* idea. That is, is *jus post bellum* simply old wine in a new bottle, a new collection of old concepts, or a branding exercise?[14] None of these ways of describing a nominal idea is inherently negative, but neither are they particularly inspiring. Fundamentally, if the transition from armed conflict to a sustainable peace is a worthwhile goal, then there is an opportunity cost if *jus post bellum* could focus explicitly on that goal but does not.

There are a great number of terms used by scholars and practitioners that mean something along the lines of *jus post bellum*: including "post-conflict justice," peacekeeping, or an (in the author's opinion) overly broad definition of Transitional Justice. The relatively obvious virtue of using the term *jus post bellum* is that it brings *jus ad bellum* and *jus in bello* to mind. It invites those

---

14 Österdahl, Inger, and Esther Van Zadel. "What will jus post bellum mean? Of new wine and old bottles." *Journal of Conflict and Security Law* 14.2 (2009): 175–207.

grappling with the difficulties of establishing a sustainable peace to integrate their conceptual framework into the larger just war tradition. It invites those familiar with the law of armed conflict and norms on aggression to consider the return to peace from the beginning.

It is worth responding to the suggestion that the entire body of law applying to the transition from armed conflict to sustainable peace *in parts*, with for example the part during armed conflict discussed under one rubric and the part in early peace under the rubric of *jus post bellum*. This, for example, is the approach of David Rodin, who suggests the term *jus terminatio* (or Termination Law) for the law of ending armed conflict and suggests limiting the term of *jus post bellum* to the obligations of combatants after war.[15] With respect, the author finds this approach lacking. While it may be useful to discuss *jus terminatio* as part of a broader *jus post bellum*, dividing the law into the law of ending armed conflict and the law of obligations of combatants after war does not cover the entire process of transition to a sustainable peace. It does not work well with Christine Bell's conception of a *lex pacificatoria*[16] or law of peacemakers, which bridges the various types of peace agreements, including post-conflict implementation agreements. Rodin's *lex terminatio* would presumably stop in the midst of the *lex pacificatoria*, with a different framework for different peace agreements. Rodin's *jus post bellum* would not cover any law dealing with non-combatant obligations, for example. It certainly would not help to inform the question of choices during armed conflict that would make a sustainable peace more difficult to achieve—as in the example of bombing a cultural monument occupied by an enemy force given earlier in this article.

It is also worth responding to the argument that a hybrid functional approach lessens the clarity of the concept. The temporal approach may appear at first glance to be clearer conceptually, a binary application—either on or off—depending on whether the armed conflict has ended or not. In reality, because the reality of a *status mixtus* is messy, the apparent conceptual clarity of the temporal approach is likely to be illusory in practice. Particularly in the context of counterinsurgency, non-state actors, factions, and low-level conflicts, evaluating whether armed conflict has ended or not is neither simple, nor final—the transition to a sustainable peace can be uncertain and uneven

---

15   See Rodin, David. "Two Emerging Issues of Jus Post Bellum: War Termination and the Liability of Soldiers for Crimes of Aggression." *Jus Post Bellum: Towards a Law of Transition from Conflict to Peace*. Ed. Carsten Stahn and Jann K. Kleffner (The Hague: T.M.C. Asser Press, 2008), 53–62; Rodin, David. "Ending war." *Ethics & International Affairs* 25.03 (2011): 359–367; Rodin, David. "The War Trap: Dilemmas of jus terminatio." *Ethics* 125.3 (2015): 674–695.

16   Bell, Christine, *Peace Agreements: Their Nature and Legal Status*, p. 407.

over time and geography and across groups. In addition to not necessarily being clearer to apply in practice, the temporal approach lessens the power of the concept and limits the problems it can address. The hybrid functional approach, focusing on the full process of transition to a sustainable peace, is more likely to comprehensively and successfully address the problems of that transition.

B   Contrasting *Jus Post Bellum* and Transitional Justice

1   *Introduction*

In the Introduction to this work and in Chapter 3 (Three Theories of *Jus Post Bellum*) supra, a hybrid functional approach to *jus post bellum* is propounded that serves the function of organizing the effort to transition from armed conflict to a just and sustainable peace while retaining an awareness of temporal context.[17] Functional subcomponents of this effort were identified as peacemaking or *lex pacificatoria* and post-conflict justice. A major component of post-conflict justice is international criminal law, but there are also aspects to post-conflict justice that are often described under the rubric of transitional justice. Yet *jus post bellum*, and transitional justice are separate concepts. For the benefit of both ideas, it is extremely important to clarify the distinctions and interactions between them.

Ninety years ago, even amongst the invisible college of international law scholars, the phrases "Transitional Justice" and "*jus post bellum*" would have been met with uncertainty. The terms were unknown. Perhaps more surprisingly, *jus post bellum*'s sister terms "*jus ad bellum*" and "*jus in bello*," now enshrined as central and seemingly immovable pillars of the law of armed conflict, would also have prompted few knowing nods of recognition, only blank stares.[18] Academic neoterisms—innovations in language such as a new word or term—can tell us something about the historical moment of their origin, and the tradition within which they emerge. The focus on *jus ad bellum* and *jus*

---

17   This sub-chapter builds upon Iverson, Jens. "Contrasting the Normative and Historical Foundations of Transitional Justice and Jus Post Bellum: Outlining the Matrix of Definitions in Comparative Perspective": 80–101." *Jus Post Bellum: Mapping the Normative Foundations*. New York: OUP (2014); and Iverson, Jens. "Transitional Justice, Jus Post Bellum and International Criminal Law: Differentiating the Usages, History and Dynamics. "*International Journal of Transitional Justice* 7.3 (2013): 413–433.

18   Robert Kolb, "Origin of the Twin Terms Jus Ad Bellum/Jus In Bello" (1997) 37 *International Review of the Red Cross* 553; Carsten Stahn, "Jus Post Bellum: Mapping the Discipline(s)" (2008) 23 *American University International Law Review* 311, 312.

in bello after the horrors of the First World War is hardly surprising. The concept of Transitional Justice emerged organically from the intense focus on transitions to democracy from the 1970s through the 1990s. The post-Cold War questions of transformative occupation, peacebuilding, and international territorial administration set the frame for *jus post bellum*.

It is impossible to tell whether Transitional Justice and *jus post bellum* will seize the collective imagination of those who concern themselves with international law in an enduring manner, or whether these concepts will quickly fade. The longevity of a term depends largely on how that term may be used in unknowable, future contexts. But it also may depend at least in part on the internal coherence of the body of concepts referenced by the term, and whether this coherence is maintained over time by its practitioners and advocates. Those invested in the success of a philosophy underlying a term have the most to gain from an effort to closely analyze the meanings of a term, and where necessary draw distinctions between related concepts.

2   The Grotian Tradition

Both Transitional Justice and *jus post bellum* are products not only of the decades in which they emerged, but also part of what Hersch Lauterpacht identified as "the Grotian tradition."[19] Both the specific historical moments and the wider tradition are examined below.

In 1933, Hersch Lauterpacht famously described "The Function of Law in the International Community." This work, which Martti Koskenniemi has described as the most important book in English in the twentieth century,[20] concerned itself, *inter alia*, with whether international law was a comprehensive system, capable of settling disputes brought to international judicial fora. Lauterpacht forcefully argued for a conception of international law as a complete system, with the function and duty of international legal practitioners to settle disputes. For Lauterpacht, there existed a prohibition of judicial *non liquet* (in essence, a ruling that there was no law to apply to determine a dispute), admitting no exception.[21] In the same way that a court, faced with a claim of property ownership, would have to make a determination as to that property claim regardless of the uncertainty surrounding the claim, the history

---

19   Hersch Lauterpacht, "The Grotian Tradition in International Law" (1946) 23 *British Year Book of International Law* 1.
20   Martti Koskenniemi, "The Function of Law in the International Community: 75 Years After" (2008) 79 *British Year Book of International Law* 353.
21   Hersch Lauterpacht, *The Function of Law in the International Community* (Oxford University Press 1933) 134.

of international judicial settlement provided "continuous proof"[22] of the capacity of international law to address "so-called gaps."[23]

Lauterpacht's argument is in contrast with, for example, Hans Morgenthau, from the perspective of international relations, with his contrast between political "tensions" not amenable to legal resolution and "disputes" that were amenable to legal resolution.[24] Lauterpacht's perspective is also in contrast with the "Vienna School" of Hans Kelsen who essentially advocated a positivist model that limited the role of law in the international community.[25] Lauterpacht's work was both a conception of what international law was and a project to define what law should do—to extend the process of dispute settlement through law. The issue of whether gaps exist in the fabric of international law, and what approach should be taken if apparent lacunae are highlighted, remains an enduring problem.

What was Lauterpacht's goal in enshrining these goals as part of the Grotian tradition? The article *The Grotian Tradition in International Law* seeks to selectively praise Hugo Grotius,[26] not to bury him—it suggests that despite the flaws in argument and substance of *De jure belli ac pacis* (1625), Grotius' enduring fame and influence is deserved because of the tradition he established. The tradition, as framed by Lauterpacht, appears to be a series of goals for international law. Unsurprisingly, these goals appear to be largely shared by Lauterpacht, although Lauterpacht may not have used the term "goals" but insisted that they were an accurate description of international law. Lauterpacht's insistence on a complete system of international law, one that would broach no judicial *non liquet*, is strengthened by the idea that there is a tradition insisting on *The Subjection of the Totality of International Relations to the Rule of Law*[27] and *The Rejection of "Reason of State."*[28] Should there have been areas of International Relations to which no laws could apply, perhaps due to an assertion of *Raison d'État*, the system of international law would clearly be incomplete, and rulings based on a finding of *non liquet* would clearly be expected.

In a sense, both Transitional Justice and *jus post bellum* represent attempts to fill apparent lacunae. Transitional Justice practitioners, as a general rule, are

---

22 Ibid.
23 Ibid.
24 Koskenniemi, "The Function of Law in the International Community: 75 Years After."
25 See e.g. Joseph Kunz, "The 'Vienna School' and International Law" (1933–34) 11 *New York University Law Quarterly Review* 370.
26 As Hugo de Groot is generally referred to by his Latin eponym, I will follow that practice in this chapter.
27 Lauterpacht, "The Grotian Tradition in International Law" 19.
28 Ibid 30.

committed to the "fight against impunity." This impunity is seen as an unwanted gap. Transitional Justice seeks primarily to respond to the real-world gap in the universality of human rights as applied—a universality that is fundamental to the project of human rights. These rights are not derived from an individual's status *vis-à-vis* a state but solely due to being human, as a result of shared humanity. An apparent gap in the universality of international human rights protections caused by a change in regime (perhaps with amnesties for previous regime officials) or by the mere existence of unpunished systematic or widespread human rights abuses may cry out to be addressed by Transitional Justice practitioners. Additionally, uncovering and establishing the truth of past human rights abuses may be seen as filling a historical lacuna, which itself may serve as a form of reparation for victims. The idea that there should always be a purposeful (legal and otherwise) response to human rights abuses is very much in line with Lauterpacht's vision of the Grotian Tradition.

Jus post bellum, on its face, appears to be responding to the need to complete the temporal story of the law of armed conflict—with *jus ad bellum* governing the beginning of armed conflict, *just in bello* governing the conflict itself, and *jus post bellum* governing its aftermath. While there is certainly power behind this simple depiction, a deeper understanding of the history of international law as it applies to law and peace reveals a more fundamental gap that *jus post bellum* can help to fill. Filling these lacunae is best understood with reference to what Lauterpacht called "The Grotian Tradition in International Law."[29] Lauterpacht identifies several features of the Grotian tradition that are potentially pertinent. He suggests that the Grotian tradition includes *The Subjection of the Totality of International Relations to the Rule of Law*;[30] *The Rejection of "Reason of State"*;[31] *The Distinction between Just and Unjust Wars*;[32] *The Fundamental Rights and Freedoms of the Individual*;[33] and *The Idea of Peace*.[34] By *The Idea of Peace*, Lauterpacht means Grotius's strong preference for peace, and the lack of praise for war as somehow beneficial or strengthening in character.[35] In particular, *The Subjection of the Totality of International Relations to the Rule of Law* and *The Rejection of "Reason of State"*; is relevant to the creation

---

29 Ibid.
30 Ibid 19.
31 Ibid 30.
32 Ibid 35.
33 Ibid 43.
34 Ibid 46.
35 Ibid.

of *jus ad bellum*, *jus in bello*, and eventually *jus post bellum*. These themes certainly echo Lauterpacht's split from his teacher Hans Kelsen.[36]

To use the term "*jus post bellum*" is itself to make an assertion, namely that a set of laws exists that applies to the transition to peace. Because the term is a recent arrival in contemporary legal discourse (see Chapter 4.B.8 below), the claim may seem controversial. One might ask how a body of law could have been constructed without, until recently, a name. Further, one might ask whether those using the term are really advocating restraints upon the peacemakers and erecting barriers to peace.[37] After all, if this chapter claims that *jus post bellum* is a continuance and completion of the Grotian Tradition, and embedded in the Grotian Tradition is a strong preference for peace, then how can barriers to peace be appropriate?

With respect to the first concern about the implausibility of a heretofore "nameless" body of law, the history of the terms *jus ad bellum* and *jus in bello* stand as an answer. The concerns and laws of *jus post bellum*, like those of *jus ad bellum* and *jus in bello*, predate the terms themselves. For example, Brian Orend argues that the concept of *jus post bellum* should be credited to Immanuel Kant.[38] Regardless of its provenance, it is important to note the relative humility of the concept. The term "*jus post bellum*" does not seek to displace *jus ad bellum* or *jus in bello*, but rather to complement them. It does not seek to supplant the separate frameworks of humanitarian law, human rights law, or international criminal law,[39] and indeed to challenge the entire notion of public international law as traditionally understood,[40] but simply to integrate the law applicable to a particular phenomenon, the transition to a sustainable peace, into a more coherent whole.

With respect to the second concern regarding the possible drawbacks of clarifying and even extending the law applicable to the transition to a sustainable peace, one need only look to the atrocities that have historically followed military victory to understand the *prima facie* need for *jus post bellum*. No longer is it acceptable and commonplace to exterminate or enslave the defeated population. The prohibition on the annexation of territory is central not only

---

36   See Martti Koskenniemi, "Lauterpacht: The Victorian Tradition in International Law" (1997) 8 *European Journal of International Law* 215, 217–18.

37   Eric De Brabandere, "The Responsibility for Post-Conflict Reforms: A Critical Assessment of Jus Post Bellum as a Legal Concept" (2010) 43 *Vanderbilt Journal of Transnational Law* 119.

38   Brian Orend, *War And International Justice: A Kantian Perspective* (Wilfrid Laurier University Press 2000) 57.

39   See e.g. Ruti Teitel, *Humanity's Law* (Oxford University Press 2011).

40   Ibid.

in determining the legality of particular post-conflict settlement, but also in underpinning the entire order of stable and pacific interstate relations. An abhorrence of regulation and insistence on the "freedom" from law of those involved in the transition to a sustainable peace is effectively an application of the rationale of *Raison d'État* to the ending of conflict and the reestablishment of peace—to assert that a dispute regarding the legality of actions taken in the transition to a sustainable peace would be met with a judicial *non liquet*. This is not to say that there is a tight constraint in all circumstances or no role for discretion. There are many choices between equally legal options during the transition to sustainable peace. Regardless of one's view as to the function of law in the international community, a vision of the reestablishment of peace as a law-free or law-poor zone is likely to result in an impoverished peace that does not tend to acceptably resolve the problems underlying the conflict or lay the foundation for a robust, positive peace.

Perhaps more directly relevant for analysis of Lauterpacht's claim of a Grotian Tradition are the works of Grotius himself. In Grotius's 1604 work, *De iure praedae commentarius* (*Commentary on the law of prize and booty*), Grotius plainly asks in the first sentence of Chapter 3: "*De praeda igitur dicturis primum belli quaestio expedienda est, possitne scilicet bellum aliquod justum esse.*"[41] ("Accordingly, before we enter into a discussion of prize and booty, we must dispose of a certain question regarding war, namely: Can any war be just?")[42] Grotius asks four questions:

1) Is any war just?
2) Is any war just for Christians?
3) Is any war just for Christians, against Christians?
4) Is any war just for Christians, against Christians, from the standpoint of all law?

The first question helps to connection Grotius's work to the contemporary questions of the legality of resorting to armed force, that is, *jus ad bellum*. The remaining, Christianity-focused questions help to illustrate the difference between the context in which Grotius worked and the more secular world of contemporary law.

The colorful history of this work, *De iure praedae commentarius*, in some ways echoes the "lost and found" nature of just war theory being downplayed

---

41 Grotius, Hugo, *De iure praedae commentarius*, Martinum Nijhoff, (written 1604–1608, published 1868), p. 31.

42 Hugo Grotius, Commentary on the Law of Prize and Booty (*De Jure Praedae Commentarius*), eds. Gwladys L. Williams and W.H. Zeydel (Oxford: Clarendon Press, 1950), vol. 1: A Translation of the Original Manuscript of 1604 by Gwladys L. Williams, with the collaboration of Walter H. Zeydel, p. 51.

by positivists who emphasized *Raison d'État,* only to be restored and translated into a modern context by those who wished to outlaw (or at least minimize) war in the late 19th and 20th centuries. *De iure praedae commentarius* was not published during Grotius' lifetime, or indeed for the two subsequent centuries, only reemerging in 1864, published in Latin in 1868 by Martinus Nijhoff, and finally being translated and published in English in 1950.[43]

Grotius' fame and influence were not, of course, based on a work misplaced for so long but rather on the work that was well known even during his lifetime, particularly *De iure belli ac pacis* ("The Rights of War and Peace"). In *De iure belli ac pacis*, Book I, Chapter 2, Grotius asks the same question: "Whether it is ever lawful to make War."[44] This question is the starting point of the contemporary *jus ad bellum* discourse. Similarly, in *De iure belli ac pacis*, Book III, Grotius considers "what is allowable in War, and how far, and in what Circumstances it is so."[45] While his conception is far removed from contemporary law, perhaps exemplified most notoriously in his declaration in the title of Book III, Chapter 1, Section 2 that "In War all Things necessary to the End are lawful."[46] Notwithstanding this difference, the fact that these subjects were central to Grotius' thinking and reputation shows their importance in the Grotian tradition.

3 Basic Definitions
a Transitional Justice

In *Transitional Justice Genealogy*,[47] Ruti Teitel begins with a definition, stating, "Transitional justice can be defined as the conception of justice associated with periods of political change, characterized by legal responses to confront the wrongdoings of repressive predecessor regimes."[48] This definition, adopted

---

43 Grotius, Hugo, *Commentary on the Law of Prize and Booty,* Martine Julia van Ittersum (ed.), Liberty Fund (2006), p. xxiii; *See also* Van Ittersum, Martine Julia, *Dating the manuscript of De Jure Praedae (1604–1608): What watermarks, foliation and quire divisions can tell us about Hugo Grotius' development as a natural rights and natural law theorist,* History of European Ideas, Vol. 35, Issue 2, June 2009, p. 125–193, ISSN 0191-6599, 10.1016/j.histeuroideas.2009.01.004, available at http://www.sciencedirect.com/science/article/pii/S0191659909000175.
44 Grotius, Hugo, *The Rights of War and Peace,* Richard Tuck (ed.), Indianapolis: Liberty Fund (2005). Vol. 1, p. 180 (emphasis removed).
45 Ibid 1185.
46 Ibid 1186 (emphasis removed).
47 Ruti Teitel, "Transitional Justice Genealogy" (2003) 16 *Harvard Human Rights Journal* 69; see also Ruti Teitel, *Transitional Justice* (Oxford University Press 2000) 3.
48 Ruti Teitel, "Transitional Justice Genealogy."

very carefully in a self-reflective article by the individual often credited with coining the term, is a good place to start.

The substantive emphasis of Transitional Justice is on justice for human rights violations.[49] Temporally, the emphasis is on subjecting the acts that occurred during the predecessor regime to a toolbox of responses within the time period of the successor regime. The term contains an aspirational element—that a transition toward justice is possible in line with the political change in the wake of a change in regime. There is no assumption of armed conflict, nor is there a denial of the possibility of armed conflict. Armed conflict has only a potential, secondary importance in Transitional Justice—an importance derived not from the effects of armed conflict, nor the thing itself. These potential effects, human rights violations, and regime change may each occur with or without armed conflict. The goals of Transitional Justice are fundamentally tied to the aspiration of transition, both toward justice for past violations and toward a cementing of a new political order that will prevent the old order, with its attendant human rights violations, from returning.

b   *Jus Post Bellum*

There is, as yet, no authoritative definition for *jus post bellum*, although many have been proffered. For the purposes of this chapter, for reasons that are explained *supra*, the term *jus post bellum* is defined as the body of legal norms that apply to the entire process of the transition from armed conflict to a just and sustainable peace.[50]

Jus post bellum must be understood in the context of its sister terms, *jus ad bellum* and *jus in bello*. None of these terms make sense without armed conflict. They are concerned with the use of armed force as a matter of primary, central importance. Collectively, they seek to describe the constraints and rights regarding whether armed force may be used at all, the constraints and

---

49   Sections of this chapter draw partly from Jens Iverson, "Transitional Justice, Jus Post Bellum, and International Criminal Law: Differentiating the Usages, History, and Dynamics" (2013) *International Journal of Transitional Justice*.

50   See e.g. Immanuel Kant, *Metaphysische Anfangsgründe der Rechtslehre* (*The Philosophy of Law: An Exposition of the Fundamental Principles of Jurisprudence as the Science of Right*, originally published 1887, tr. W. Hastie, The Lawbook Exchange 2002) (emphasis added) 214 ("The Right of Nations in relation to the State of War may be divided into: 1. The Right of *going to* War; 2. Right *during* War; and 3. Right *after* War, the object of which is to constrain the nations mutually *to pass from this state of war, and to found a common Constitution establishing Perpetual Peace.*") The definition of a "just and sustainable peace" is itself an extremely interesting research topic, involving what many have termed "positive peace" vs. "negative peace," and definitions of sustainable peace not in terms of the relations of two states but in terms of the international system as a whole.

rights related to the use of armed force during armed conflict (how it may be used), and the constraints and rights related to the transition from armed conflict to a sustainable peace.

The substantive emphasis of *jus post bellum* is broader than human rights violations. It also clearly includes, *inter alia*, violations of the laws of armed conflict, the rights and privileges that spring from the laws of armed conflict, environmental law (including legal access to natural resources and regulating the toxic remnants of war), state responsibility outside of the realm of human rights, recognition of states and governments, laws and norms applicable to peace treaties and peace agreements, peacekeeping, occupation, and post-conflict peacebuilding—laws that directly or through interpretation regulate and enable the transition to a just and sustainable peace.

The conceptual foundations for *jus post bellum* (the third component of the just war tradition that, unlike *jus ad bellum* and *jus in bello*, applies to the transition from armed conflict to peace), like International Criminal Law, have deep historical roots, reaching back to the ancient just war tradition, but has re-emerged as a contemporary neoterism in recent decades in the context of peacebuilding and the end of the Cold War. It represents an approach most likely to push conduct at the crucial period of transitioning from armed conflict to peace in the direction of a just and sustainable solution to the underlying problems that caused the conflict.

4　*Contrasting the Content of Transitional Justice and* Jus Post Bellum
a　General Contrast

The basic definition of Transitional Justice provided in the Basic Definitions section above is not the only definition worth considering. Again, in *Transitional Justice Genealogy*,[51] Teitel states, "Transitional justice can be defined as the conception of justice associated with periods of political change, characterized by legal responses to confront the wrongdoings of repressive predecessor regimes."[52] In contrast, the *Report of the Secretary-General on the Rule of Law and Transitional Justice in Conflict and Post-Conflict Societies* (2004) defines Transitional Justice as:

> [...] the full range of processes and mechanisms associated with a society's attempts to come to terms with a legacy of large-scale past abuses, in order to ensure accountability, serve justice and achieve reconciliation. These may include both judicial and non-judicial mechanisms, with

---

51　Teitel, "Transitional Justice Genealogy" 3.
52　Ibid 69.

differing levels of international involvement (or none at all) and individual prosecutions, reparations, truth-seeking, institutional reform, vetting and dismissals, or a combination thereof.[53]

Similarly, the stocktaking report of the same name *Report of the Secretary-General on the Rule of Law and Transitional Justice in Conflict and Post-Conflict Societies* (2011) describes Transitional Justice as follows:

> Transitional justice initiatives promote accountability, reinforce respect for human rights and are critical to fostering the strong levels of civic trust required to bolster rule of law reform, economic development and democratic governance. Transitional justice initiatives may encompass both judicial and non-judicial mechanisms, including individual prosecutions, reparations, truth-seeking, institutional reform, vetting and dismissals.[54]

Transitional Justice practitioners may know about and concern themselves with issues outside of human rights violations, such as violations of the laws of armed conflict, the rights and privileges that spring from the laws of armed conflict, state responsibility outside of the realm of human rights, recognition of states and governments, laws and norms applicable to peace treaties and peace agreements, occupation, and particularly post-conflict peacebuilding. That said, these subjects are not the fundamental concern of Transitional Justice properly speaking. They are the fundamental concern of *jus post bellum*.

While *jus post bellum* is substantively broader than Transitional Justice in many respects, *jus post bellum* is also clearly inapplicable in certain scenarios where Transitional Justice is applicable. Following a peaceful, non-violent revolution or regime change, the principles of *jus post bellum* may apply by analogy, but not directly.

Similarly, one can imagine a change in regime in which no significant human rights violations were perpetrated by the previous regime, deposed by armed conflict. Armed conflicts happen without massive human rights violations. (The 1982 conflict in the Falkland/Malvinas Islands might provide such an example, the involvement of two 17-year-old armed service members

---

53 UN Security Council, "The Rule of Law and Transitional Justice in Conflict and Post-conflict Societies: Report of the Secretary-General" (23 August 2004) UN Doc. S/2004/616, 4.
54 Ibid 6.

notwithstanding.)⁵⁵ Additionally, armed conflicts occur without regime change. In these instances, Transitional Justice would tend not to apply, but *jus post bellum* would.

Just as *jus post bellum* is necessarily connected to an armed conflict, to the degree that *jus post bellum* has an aspirational character, it must relate in part to questions of war and peace. One would think that *jus post bellum* is tied to the contemporary aspirational character of *jus ad bellum* and *jus in bello*: to constrain the use of armed force. In addition to that negative goal of reducing the effects of unfettered armed force, practitioners of *jus post bellum* generally seek to build a "positive peace."⁵⁶ This builds upon Lauterpacht's idea that part of the Grotian Tradition is *The Idea of Peace*.⁵⁷ Again, by *The Idea of Peace*, Lauterpacht is invoking Grotius's strong preference for peace, and the lack of praise for war as somehow beneficial or strengthening in character.⁵⁸ Sustainable peace is a central aspirational norm of *jus post bellum*, following a long but not uncontested tradition in international law.

This is not to say that human rights are not central to *jus post bellum*—they are. As ably demonstrated in such works as *Transitional Justice in the Twenty-first Century: Beyond Truth Versus Justice*⁵⁹ and *Selling Justice Short: Why Accountability Matters for Peace*⁶⁰ the supposed tension between different maximands such as peace and justice or truth and justice is frequently overblown. Discovering the truth about human rights violations and achieving justice for those violations is widely recognized as important in building a positive peace. But there will be responses to human rights violations that are not properly the concern of *jus post bellum*.

b   Substance of Transitional Justice

Transitional Justice practitioners are interested in the application of a collection of responses to human rights violations (sometimes referred to as a

---

55 Amnesty International, "United Kingdom: Summary of Concerns Raised with the Human Rights Committee" (1 November 2001) available at https://www.amnesty.org/download/Documents/128000/eur450242001en.pdf (last accessed 2 June 2016).

56 See e.g. Johan Galtung, "Violence, Peace, and Peace Research" (1969) 6(3) *Journal of Peace Research* 167–91.

57 Lauterpacht, "Grotian Tradition in International Law" 46.

58 Ibid.

59 Naomi Roht-Arriaza and Javier Mariezcurrena (eds), *Transitional Justice in the Twenty-first Century: Beyond Truth Versus Justice* (Cambridge University Press 2006).

60 Human Rights Watch, *Selling Justice Short: Why Accountability Matters for Peace* (July 2009) available at http://www.hrw.org/sites/default/files/reports/ijo709webwcover_3.pdf (accessed 20 August 2014).

"toolbox" or "package" of mechanisms)[61] including criminal prosecutions, truth commissions, reparations programs, gender justice programs, security system reform, memorialization,[62] vetting (also known as "lustration," "screening," "administrative justice," and "purging")[63] and education.[64] These responses will also likely be of interest to scholars and practitioners of *jus post bellum*, particularly during the period after the cessation of armed conflict. The emphasis, however, may be different. Those coming from the Transitional Justice perspective may share the natural primary concern of responding to human rights violations, while those coming from the tradition of emphasizing the importance of transitioning to a stable peace may highlight other areas, albeit often through responding to human rights violations. The content of what is called Transitional Justice has expanded as practitioners have looked for pragmatic problems to the difficult challenges inherent in the aftermath of human rights violations by a previous regime. The question of what qualifies as "Transitional Justice" is a pragmatic, and in some ways inherently political question, as it depends at least in part on what is considered useful in making a successful political transition.

It is not particularly useful to apply the term "Transitional Justice" to efforts that use the tools or approaches used in Transitional Justice but which bear no relationship to a distinct transition in political regime. If, at the present moment, there was a truth commission or memorialization effort for the deaths of more than 12,000 prisoners of war housed at the Confederate Andersonville Prisoner of War Camp during the US Civil War, it is hard to see how it is helpful to call these "Transitional Justice," even in light of the political changes that occurred as a result of the armed conflict. A truth commission or memorial to victims does not necessarily imply a "transition" in the sense that is normally implicated by the term "Transitional Justice." Applying the term to the post-conflict trial and execution of Henry Wirz, commander of the Andersonville Prison, as well as the 1908 monument to Wirz by the United Daughters of the

---

61   See e.g. Naomi Roht-Arriaza, "Transitional Justice and Peace Agreements" (2005) *Working Paper, International Council on Human Rights Policy* 3, 5 available at http://www.ichrp.org/files/papers/63/128_-_Transitional_Justice_and_Peace_Agreements_Roht-Arriaza__Naomi__2005.pdf (accessed 20 August 2014).

62   International Center for Transitional Justice (ICTJ), "What is Transitional Justice" available at http://ictj.org/about/transitional-justice (accessed 27 May 2016).

63   Alexander Mayer-Rieckh and Pablo de Greiff (eds), *Justice as Prevention: Vetting Public Employees in Transitional Societies* (Social Science Research Council 2007).

64   See e.g. Elizabeth A. Cole and Judy Barsalou, "Unite or Divide? The Challenges of Teaching History in Societies emerging from Violent Conflict" (United States Institute for Peace 2006) 2 ("History education should be understood as an integral but underutilized part of Transitional Justice and social reconstruction").

Confederacy and continuing memorialization[65] would also constitute an unjustified enlargement of the term "Transitional Justice." While both the trial and the monument may have had (conflicting) political implications or intents, the trial was hardly looking towards any sort of regime change in the US federal government, and the misplaced valorization of Wirz has more to do with denial of Confederate crimes than establishment of accountability for human rights violation of a previous regime. While some may feel that stretching the term is somehow innovative or exciting, overstretching the term tends to lead to the term lacking specific meaning and force. As Seneca the Younger noted: *Nusquam est qui ubique est* (roughly translated, "Nowhere is the one who is everywhere" or "to be everywhere is to be nowhere").[66]

To take perhaps a more controversial example, it seems unhelpful to use the term "Transitional Justice" in application to the serial truth commissions in Uganda, including the Commission of Inquiry into the Disappearances of People in Uganda since 25 January 1971 established by Idi Amin Dada and the 1986 Commission of Inquiry into Violations of Human Rights.[67] While these Truth Commissions, along with various efforts at memorialization and even the International Crimes Division within the High Court of Uganda technically fit with the type of broad definition such as "a response to systematic or widespread violations of human rights"[68] they should not be considered to be Transitional Justice mechanisms, properly conceived. These are not the type of "conception of justice associated with periods of political change"[69] traditionally and properly associated with the term Transitional Justice. Discussing these institutions as "Transitional Justice" should at a minimum be done critically and cautiously, noting that they are not clearly part of a transition to a more democratic and accountable regime. They are, in each instance, a one-sided exercise of a regime not clearly moving toward ongoing accountability for their own human rights abuses. If the term "Transitional Justice" simply means an institutionalized allegation of abuse by the losing party in a conflict, even an allegation by a regime not in the process of transitioning to a superior approach toward human rights, it is unclear why "Transitional Justice" should retain its widespread support, or why the term would endure.

---

65 Glen W. LaForce, "The Trial of Major Henry Wirz—A National Disgrace" (1988) *1988 Army Law* 3.
66 Seneca the Younger, *Epistula Ad Lucilium 11*, Book 1, Letter 2, line 2.
67 Joanna R. Quinn, "Chicken and Egg? Sequencing in Transitional Justice: The Case of Uganda" (Autumn/Winter 2009) 14(2) *International Journal of Peace Studies* 35–53.
68 International Center for Transitional Justice (ICTJ), "What is Transitional Justice" available at http://ictj.org/about/transitional-justice (accessed 27 May 2016).
69 Teitel, "Transitional Justice Genealogy" 69.

This is not to say that Transitional Justice efforts have to be without flaw or criticism to merit the title of "Transitional Justice." As a phenomenon associated with political change, carried out by fallible humans, any instance of Transitional Justice will inevitably be flawed. Rather, calling an effort "Transitional Justice" should necessarily be an assertion that the substance of that effort contains the aspiration of transition to a new regime of accountability for human rights abuses.

Noémie Turgis in *What is Transitional Justice?* begins and ends with a warning regarding broadening the scope of transitional justice.[70] As she puts it:

> The risk of broadening the meaning of the concept is to dilute it and turning it into something meaningless. [...] The core element of transitional justice is here: offering a "toolbox" filled with elements designed to deal with the violations of human rights from a predecessor regime to form the basis of an order to prevent their reoccurrence.[71]

This is well put, although some might object to the "toolbox" metaphor given that it may tend to reduce complex problems to simpler plumbing analogues. The content of Transitional Justice is rooted in a transformative response to a predecessor regime's human rights violations in order to prevent further violations.

c   More Substantive in Nature

Contemporary international law specifically outlaws many acts that may be (and historically have been) carried out during the transition from armed conflict to peace. Christine Bell provides a helpful table in *Peace Agreements and Human Rights*[72] with respect to "political strategies for dealing with minorities." The table can usefully be generalized with application to the international law prescription for a variety of acts that are regulated by *jus post bellum*.

A party to the conflict may frame the conflict as caused by the existence or power of another group, and wish to act upon that second group in prohibited ways. For instance, a party to the conflict may adopt a strategy of eliminating the second group, through genocide, expulsion, or voluntary expatriation. The first two are specifically outlawed under international law,[73] the third is unclear

---

70   Noémie Turgis, "What is Transitional Justice?" (2010) 1 *International Journal of Law, Transitional Justice and Human Rights* 9, 14.
71   Turgis, "What is Transitional Justice?" 14.
72   Christine Bell, *Peace Agreements and Human Rights* (Oxford University Press 2000) 17.
73   Christine Bell, *Peace Agreements and Human Rights* (Oxford University Press 2000) 17; Convention on the Prevention and Punishment of the Crime of Genocide (adopted 9

but likely suspect if attached to the goal of elimination, as the "voluntary" nature will be in doubt in light of the potential crime of persecution. If the strategy of domination is adopted, the likely method of implementing that strategy discrimination against a minority is specifically outlawed. This, of course, includes the prohibition of slavery.

A party to the conflict may also frame the cause of the conflict as caused by the relationship of another group to others, and choose to act upon that second group in ways that are regulated but not necessarily prohibited by international law. If the strategy of assimilation is adopted, the increased recognition of minority rights in international law[74] may constrain any attempt to eliminate communal differences. Separate treatment may depend upon the particular provisions and the balance between individual rights and collective rights, including whether the treatment is more in the form of recognition and accommodation for vulnerable minorities or discrimination against minority groups.[75] Many conflicts are framed in terms of self-determination, whether it is a demand for internal autonomy or outright secession. The question of the legality of self-determination is inextricably tied to the rights of territorial integrity and the rights of minorities and individuals within the new framework.[76]

All of the substantive legal norms listed thus far are binding directly as part of non-derogable international human rights regimes that apply in times of peace, armed conflict, and periods that could be described as *status mixtus*,[77] but may have special and distinctive characteristics during the transition from armed conflict to peace. Most particularly, these norms bind those crafting peace agreements and those who enjoy transitional governmental authority. Bell suggests that international law applying to peace processes (including the crafting of peace agreements) should reflect the distinctive nature of these acts, including: a distinctive self-determination role bound to questions of state legitimacy and human rights protections; hybrid international/domestic legal status based on a distinctive mix of state and non-state categories; obligations that may need to be interpreted from both a treaty or contract law

---

December 1948, entered into force 12 January 1951) 78 UNTS 277; Jean-Marie Henckaerts, *Mass Expulsion in Modern International Law and Practice* (Martinus Nijhoff 1995).

74   Christine Bell, *Peace Agreements and Human Rights* (Oxford University Press 2000) 17; see also Nātān Lerner, *Group Rights and Discrimination in International Law* (Martinus Nijhoff 2003).

75   Christine Bell, *Peace Agreements and Human Rights* (Oxford University Press 2000) 17.

76   Ibid.

77   See Georg Schwarzenberger, "Jus Pacis Ac Belli? Prolegomena to a Sociology of International Law" (1943) 37 *American Journal of International Law* 460, 470.

framework and a constitutional law framework; and distinctive types of third-party delegation.[78]

Certain areas of *jus ad bellum* and *jus in bello* are also heavily implicated in a body of law governing the transition from armed conflict to peace. The prohibition of annexation as the result of armed conflict is tied to the prohibition of acts of aggression, a clear *jus ad bellum* concern. Acts of aggression also raise the question of response in the transition to peace, including the question of reparations—an issue that implicates the law of state responsibility. United Nations Security Council resolutions under Chapter VII authority frequently provide specific binding law that applies to particular transitions from armed conflict to peace.

All of the limits of the law of armed conflict applying to belligerent occupation under the law of armed conflict are traditionally classified as *jus in bello* (including Geneva Convention IV, Additional Protocol I, and Article 42 of the 1907 Hague Regulations[79]). The reality and legal restraints of "transformative occupation" requires a complementary understanding of *jus post bellum* to reconcile current practice (including the endorsement of some practitioners of transitional justice) and the Conservation Principle of *jus in bello* (prohibiting major changes in the institutions of the occupied territory). The tradition of *jus post bellum* covering occupation goes back to Immanuel Kant's exception to the Conservation Principle when it comes to the constitution of warlike states.[80] Arguably, if a *legitimate* new government is established and widely recognized, belligerent occupation (where a foreign state exercises effective control over another state's territory without the latter state's consent) may become pacific occupation (occupation with the latter state's consent) or international territorial administration,[81] such as the United Nations Transitional

---

78 Christine Bell, *Peace Agreements and Human Rights* (Oxford University Press 2000) 407; see also Christine Bell, *On the Law of Peace: Peace Agreements and the Lex Pacificatoria* (Oxford University Press 2008).
79 Convention (IV) respecting the Laws and Customs of War on Land and its annex: Regulations concerning the Laws and Customs of War on Land (adopted 18 October 1907, entered into force 26 January 1910), 36 Stat. 2277, 1 Bevans 631, 205 Consol TS 277, Art. 42.
80 See e.g. Immanuel Kant, Metaphysische Anfangsgründe der Rechtslehre (The Philosophy of Law: An Exposition of the Fundamental Principles of Jurisprudence as the Science of Right, originally published 1887, tr. W. Hastie, The Lawbook Exchange 2002).
81 See e.g. Carsten Stahn, *The Law and Practice of International Territorial Administration: Versailles to Iraq and Beyond* (Cambridge University Press 2008); Ralph Wilde, *International Territorial Administration: How Trusteeship and the Civilizing Mission Never Went Away* (Oxford University Press 2010).

Authority in Cambodia.[82] This is, of course, a highly problematic, charged, and contested issue, but one that cannot be ignored. Merely placing a compliant puppet or satellite state should not remove the obligations of the occupier under *jus in bello*. The legitimacy of post-belligerent occupation is clearly tied to the validity of consent free from the threat of use of force as guaranteed by Article 52 of the Vienna Convention on the Law of Treaties—*jus post bellum* law that is more procedural in nature, to which we shall turn shortly.

The international law applicable to state responsibility,[83] particularly with regards to new states created through conflict, is also an area of law that must be referenced by a body of law applicable to the transition from armed conflict to peace. State responsibilities also can provide the framework for considering the responsibility of international organizations and institutions.

The international law applicable to peacekeeping operations in the aftermath of armed conflict must also be considered in a comprehensive body of law applicable to the transition to peace. Similarly, status of armed forces on foreign territory agreements (SOFAs) are implicated by a *jus post bellum* regime.

Criminal law, both international and domestic, as well as laws regarding reparations (whether included as part of a criminal law regime or not) are also an important part of *jus post bellum*, if those laws have application to the transition from armed conflict to peace. The important criterion for their inclusion is not the venue (international or domestic) nor the source, but their applicability to the transition to peace.

Environmental law, particularly with respect to the rights and obligations relating to repairing and rebuilding the environmental damage from the conflict, but also resolving any resource disputes related to the conflict, may be implicated in the transition to a sustainable peace.

The Responsibility to Protect doctrine[84] includes the Responsibility to Prevent, Responsibility to Respond, and the Responsibility to Rebuild. Of the three

---

82   See e.g. Steven R. Ratner, "The Cambodia Settlement Agreements" (1993) 87 *American Journal of International Law* 1.

83   See International Law Commission (ILC), "Draft Articles on Responsibility of States for Internationally Wrongful Acts" in ILC, "Report of the International Law Commission on the Work of its Fifty-third Session" (2001) UN GAOR 56th Session Supplement 10, 43; UN Doc. A/56/10.

84   See International Commission on Intervention and State Sovereignty, *The Responsibility to Protect: Report of the International Commission on Intervention and State Sovereignty* (International Development Research Centre 2001) 39–45; see also United Nations Secretary General's High-Level Panel on Threats, Challenges and Change, *A More Secure World: Our Shared Responsibility, Report of the High-level Panel on Threats, Challenges and Change* (2004) 65–7; United Nations General Assembly, *2005 World Summit Outcome*, UN Doc.

norms within the Responsibility to Protection doctrine, the Responsibility to Respond has received the most attention and has the most bearing on questions related to *jus ad bellum* and *jus in bello*, as it seeks to replace the rhetoric of humanitarian intervention with guidelines of responses short of the use of armed force and constraints on the resort to armed force and how it is used. The Responsibility to Prevent and the Responsibility to Rebuild are more tightly tied to *jus post bellum*.

d   More Procedural in Nature

Article 52 of the Vienna Convention on the Law of Treaties states in full: "A treaty is void if its conclusion has been procured by the threat or use of force in violation of the principles of international law embodied in the Charter of the United Nations."[85] This is a particular area of concern for *jus post bellum*. First a note on terminology: use of the term "peace treaty" indicates an agreement exclusively between states, unlike the term "peace agreement," which is used for agreements not exclusively between states. Consider a generic, hypothetical peace treaty. Article 52 of the Vienna Convention on the Law of Treaties implies that the validity of that peace treaty, the foundation of a transition from interstate armed conflict to peace, depends on whether there has been an illegal threat or use of force to procure that treaty. In other words, the legal validity of the foundation of the transition to peace depends on what is typically considered a question of *jus ad bellum*, the legality of the use or threat of force. This connection between *jus ad bellum* and *jus post bellum* emerges not through an analysis of *substantive* rights and restrictions during the transition to peace, but through an analysis of the legitimate procedure for creating a peace treaty.

Recognition is also a critical question in *jus post bellum*. In order to apply *jus post bellum*, practitioners must be able to identify states and governments. This can be a contested issue, particularly for states in the case of secession (e.g. Bangladesh) and for governments in the case of contested legitimacy of a new regime (e.g. post-Democratic Kampuchea Cambodia). The law regarding recognition of states and recognition of governments is clearly implicated in the transition to peace.

A/60/L.1 (15 September 2005) paras 138–9; United Nations General Assembly, *Implementing the Responsibility to Protect: Report of the Secretary-General*, UN Doc. A/63/677 (12 January 2009) para. 48.

85 Vienna Convention on the Law of Treaties (adopted 23 May 1969, entered into force 27 January 1980) 1155 UNTS 331, Art. 52.

The procedural laws applicable to substantive criminal and civil law are also part of the transition to peace. This is not only with respect to the high profile, highly contested issues such as amnesties for the perpetration of alleged crimes related to the armed conflict. It includes questions of jurisdiction, immunities, statutes of limitation, and other questions of admissibility.

e   Mixed Substantive and Procedural in Nature

Some subjects are very difficult to characterize as mostly substantive or procedural, or at least require further analysis to distinguish particular aspects that are more substantive or procedural. For example, the United Nations Security Council Resolution 1325[86] enunciates both procedural norms for the resolution of armed conflict[87] and norms for the substance of peace agreements.[88]

f   Summarizing the Contrast in Content

Transitional Justice has evolved into a robust body of law and practice involving a wide variety of tools to respond to the challenges of responding to widespread or systematic human rights abuses in the context of a political transition to a new regime. *Jus post bellum* implicates a rich variety of legal traditions and regimes, applied to the particular situation of the transition from an armed conflict to a sustainable peace.

5   *Temporal Contrast – The Dynamics*
a   Introduction: Time within the Concepts

This section analyses the dynamics of Transitional Justice, *jus post bellum*, and International Criminal Law, that is, how each concept operates over time. As stated earlier, "Transitional Justice" has been redefined by some to include not only "the conception of justice associated with periods of political change, characterized by legal responses to confront the wrongdoings of repressive

---

86   UNSC Res. 1325 (31 October 2000) UN Doc. S/RES/1325.
87   "1. Urges Member States to ensure increased representation of women at all decision-making levels in national, regional and international institutions and mechanisms for the prevention, management, and resolution of conflict[.]."
88   "8. Calls on all actors involved, when negotiating and implementing peace agreements, to adopt a gender perspective, including, inter alia: (a) The special needs of women and girls during repatriation and resettlement and for rehabilitation, reintegration and post-conflict reconstruction; (b) Measures that support local women's peace initiatives and indigenous processes for conflict resolution, and that involve women in all of the implementation mechanisms of the peace agreements; (c) Measures that ensure the protection of and respect for human rights of women and girls, particularly as they relate to the constitution, the electoral system, the police and the judiciary[.]"

predecessor regimes"[89] but also "transition from conflict," which is a fundamentally different concept. This threatens to confuse Transitional Justice with *jus post bellum*, particularly if the contrast in temporal aspects remains unexamined. Discussing how time operates within a concept provides a more granular approach than a broad historical analysis—allowing for a discussion of the internal functioning of a concept.

What role each concept can play depends in part on *when* one asks the question. Transitional Justice comes to the fore in consolidating a transition to a new, human-rights-centered regime or political order. *Jus post bellum* applies throughout the transition to peace, but will focus on different questions at different times. International Criminal Law on principle takes an unchanging stance with respect to determining criminal culpability regardless of domestic regime or a state of war—but is particularly constrained with respect to *ex post facto* application of the law. Understanding the dynamics of each concept, how it works and orients itself over time, provides a more comprehensive guide to the role each concept can play and how they can be integrated into particular situations.

b   Dynamics of Transitional Justice
i   *The Double Beginning of Transitional Justice*

Due to the emphasis on responding to human rights violations of repressive predecessor regimes, Transitional Justice in practice largely begins after a change in regime and responds to the actions of a previous regime, which may or may not correspond to a period of armed conflict. That is, the practice of Transitional Justice tends to begin after a change in regime, or at least a dramatic political shift. The subject of that practice, however, is largely focused on responding to the acts taken in the previous regime. Transitional Justice thus tends to have a double beginning – the subject matter (or referent) and the response to the subject matter. The first beginning occurs during the repressive predecessor regime, the second begins during the succeeding, presumably non-repressive, regime.

There are, of course, potential complications with the working guideline above. One critical complication is the ever-present, heated question of amnesty for violations of human rights committed before the peace agreement is signed. Transitional Justice practitioners, whether they are external or domestic, are certainly interested in whether such amnesties are included in these peace agreements. Whether or not that interest makes the negotiation of peace agreements part of an intellectually coherent phenomenon called "Transitional

---

89   Teitel, *Transitional Justice Genealogy*, p. 69 (internal citations omitted).

Justice" is somewhat doubtful, however. Including this within the ambit of "Transitional Justice" deviates from the definition given by its practitioners "conception of justice associated with periods of political change, characterized by legal responses to confront the wrongdoings of repressive predecessor regimes."[90]

It is important to emphasize that despite the blanketing rhetoric against "amnesty" and a "culture of impunity," rhetoric driven by valid human rights concerns, certain amnesties are not only permitted, but also suggested by the laws of armed conflict. The most obvious case is when someone has participated in the conflict as a legal combatant under international humanitarian law, but his or her participation is considered illegal under domestic law (either directly or through criminalizing activities such as carrying arms.) Article 10.1 of Additional Protocol II of the Geneva Conventions, to take a more specific example, forbids punishment of ethical medical care even if it supports an insurgency: "Under no circumstances shall any person be punished for having carried out medical activities compatible with medical ethics, regardless of the person benefiting therefrom." An amnesty provision covering such activities may well be necessary, given the increasingly overbroad domestic legislation covering aiding or abetting administratively determined terrorist groups, for example. The virtues of certain forms of amnesty are perhaps more likely to be emphasized by those focusing on *jus post bellum* than those focusing on Transitional Justice, again underlining the need for both terms to be focused and both areas of practice to be further developed.

One might inquire if peace agreement negotiation was part of Transitional Justice despite the "predecessor regime" not yet being a predecessor regime, whether all human rights activism during a repressive regime is also part of Transitional Justice. In fact, it may become difficult to differentiate Transitional Justice from anything touching upon human rights once the definition begins to expand. That is not to say that such concerns are not of interest, in the same way that someone interested in human rights might not also be interested in the specific rights flowing from an individual's nationality.

Similarly, one might point to international criminal law efforts that begin before a change in regime, and are not necessarily predicated on a regime change. The International Criminal Tribunal for the former Yugoslavia and the International Criminal Court have not necessarily waited for a change in regime to proceed, although such regime changes or at changes in government have proven helpful. One might ask if this does not complicate the temporal

---

90 Ruti Teitel, Transitional Justice Geneology, 16 Harvard Human Rights J., Spring 2003, p. 69 (internal citations omitted).

definition of Transitional Justice. But again, if one does not provide a clear definition that follows coherently from the definition given by practitioners, Transitional Justice may end up including all of International Criminal Law. This is, at a minimum, not helpful.

When determining the temporal limits of Transitional Justice in terms of when it begins, it is important to specify whether the human rights violations or the reactions to those violations are being discussed. The human rights violations of the preceding regime may (or may not) stretch to the beginning of that regime. The reactions, as part of Transitional Justice, may begin with the new succeeding regime, or they may begin substantially later.

ii *Immediacy and Sequencing*

Once an iniquitous regime has fallen, one would expect that the subject matter of Transitional Justice (the human rights violations of the previous regime) would be over. There is, however, a complication to the idea of a double beginning of Transitional Justice that deserves mention, one that highlights the questions of immediacy and sequencing. Some patterns of human rights violations are considered ongoing as long as the information about the crime is withheld. This complicates the analysis of transitional justice because the work of Transitional Justice is entangled in the subject matter of Transitional Justice—disclosing the truth about the initial act becomes a matter of immediate and pressing obligation for the successor regime to avoid participating in an ongoing human rights violation. In general, a successor regime using a model of Transitional Justice premised on political change will wish to maximize the perceived distance between it and the previous regime, but with a "composite act" such as forced disappearance, the successor regime may be considered responsible even if it did not initiate the wrongful act.[91]

Some crimes themselves are not concluded until the disclosure of certain information is complete.[92] The crime most often referenced in this context is

---

91 See Art. 15.1 of International Law Commission, Draft *Articles on Responsibility of States for Internationally Wrongful Acts*, November 2001, Supplement No. 10 (A/56/10), Chp.IV.E.1, Adopted by the General Assembly in resolution 56/83 of 12 December 2001, corrected by a/56/49(Vol. I)/Corr. 4.): "The breach of an international obligation by a State through a series of actions or omissions defined in aggregate as wrongful occurs when the action or omission occurs which, taken with the other actions or omissions, is sufficient to constitute the wrongful act."

92 See La Fontaine, Fannie, *No Amnesty or Statute of Limitation for Enforced Disappearances: the Sandoval Case before the Supreme Court of Chile*, 3 J. Int'l Crim. Just. 469 (2005).

the crime of "forced" or "enforced"[93] disappearance.[94] The basic idea is that as long as the fate or whereabouts of the victim has not been established, the crime has a continuous character.[95] This temporal framing may allow procedural or jurisdictional limits (such as statutes of limitations, amnesties tied to a time period, or the entry into force of the Rome Statute) to be circumvented. More generally, it points to the difficulty of drawing clean temporal lines when applying a variety of laws to a variety of factual situations.

Sequencing is often discussed more prospectively than historically, with specialists suggesting, for example, that a country might try a truth commission, followed by criminal prosecution, followed by memorialisation efforts. What may be recommended for one situation may differ for another. The critical theoretical point when analyzing the temporal dimension of Transitional Justice is that different tools may have different timelines, both by design and because of historical and social forces. Because of the various "tools in the toolbox," determining the *overall* timeline in any particular instance of Transitional Justice can be very difficult. In practice, the timeline may not be a one-direction narrative of progress, but instead involve reversals and pauses, sometimes repeatedly.

The question of the timeline in Transitional Justice is inherently tied to the question of political change, as is appropriate for a field focused on responses to past abuses in the context of political change. In *The Law and Politics of Contemporary Transitional Justice*,[96] Teitel discusses the sequencing and immediacy in situations of diminished legitimacy, such as the responses to the Saddam Hussein regime after the change of regime in Iraq.[97] She characterizes the

---

93 See ibid., p. 470. La Fontaine reports that the Supreme Court of Chile has said that the domestic crime of "aggravated abduction" (*secuestro calificado*) is the equivalent of forced disappearance.

94 The definition of "Enforced disappearance of persons" given by Art. 7(2)(i) of the Rome Statute is "the arrest, detention or abduction of persons by, or with the authorization, support or acquiescence of, a State or a political organization, followed by a refusal to acknowledge that deprivation of freedom or to give information on the fate or whereabouts of those persons, with the intention of removing them from the protection of the law for a prolonged period of time." Rome Statute of the International Criminal Court art. 7(2)(i), July 17, 1998, 2187 U.N.T.S. 90. See also e.g. *Inter-American Convention On Forced Disappearance Of Persons* available at http://www.oas.org/juridico/english/treaties/a-60.html . For more on the historical basis of the crime, *see* Finucane, Brian, *Enforced Disappearance as a Crime Under International Law: A Neglected Origin in the Laws of War* Yale Journal of International Law, Vol. 35, 171, 2010.

95 Ibid.

96 Teitel, Ruti, *The Law and Politics of Contemporary Transitional Justice*, Cornell Int. Law Journal 38 (2005), 837.

97 Ibid 846.

application of criminal law as aimed at promoting political transition,[98] a process complicated by certain deficiencies of both the trials[99] and the political transition itself.[100] She suggests that the International Criminal Tribunal for the Former Yugoslavia (ICTY) offers a cautionary tale of Transitional Justice causing a nationalist backlash, which may have hindered, in her view, political change.[101] While Teitel's evaluation of the ICTY may be qualified in light of subsequent political change, the fundamental point of linking the understanding of the timeline of Transitional Justice, particularly with respect to sequencing and immediacy, must be viewed in light of the political realities at the heart of the conception of Transitional Justice.

One phenomenon that also must be noted in order to understand the dynamics of Transitional Justice is what has been called a "justice cascade."[102] A justice cascade refers more generally to how one legal proceeding, often abroad, can trigger subsequent domestic proceedings, and how the creation of a critical mass of efforts to prosecute can reach a tipping point so that prosecution is the norm, rather than impunity.[103]

Regardless of whether some of the crimes allegedly perpetrated under the previous regime are of an ongoing nature, the practice of Transitional Justice may not begin immediately. The mode of transition matters. An overthrow or complete military victory over the previous regime (*e.g.* Post-World War II France) may create the possibility for unfettered and immediate criminal prosecutions.[104] In other circumstances those who had power within the previous regime may retain significant power even after the transition to a new regime is well underway[105] or pressure for Transitional Justice mechanisms may be weak.[106] It can take years, even decades, for the practice of Transitional Justice to begin. One contemporary example is the controversy rather regarding the response to human rights violations during the 1936–1975 Francisco Franco dictatorship in Spain. Decades later, it is unclear whether the proper beginning of Transitional Justice in Spain is still effectively in the future.

---

98   Ibid.
99   Ibid 848.
100 Ibid 849.
101 Ibid 846.
102 See Lutz, Ellen and Sikkink, Kathryn, *The Justice Cascade: The Evolution and Impact of Foreign Human Rights Trials in Latin America*, 2 Chi. J. Int'l L. 1 (2001); Sikkink, Kathryn, The Justice Cascade: How Human Rights Prosecutions Are Changing World Politics (2011).
103 Ibid 2.
104 See Kritz, Neil J., *Transitional Justice: How Emerging Democracies Reckon With Former Regimes*, US Institute of Peace Press (1995), p. 114.
105 Ibid.
106 Ibid.

Another, arguably more complex example is in post-Khmer Rouge Cambodia. Between 1975 and 1979, the Democratic Kampuchea regime murdered millions through forced labor, starvation and execution. Among many others, the jurists of Cambodia were killed. An estimated six to ten legal professionals survived.[107] The Democratic Kampuchea regime's crimes eradicated the institutions and people who could normally attempt to address those injustices through criminal law. In 1979 Vietnam reacted to a pattern of atrocities by the Khmer Rouge in Vietnam along the border and occupied the country. The new regime held a trial in absentia for the top Khmer Rouge leaders, Pol Pot and Ieng Sary. A new government was set up by 1981, but the international community largely refused to recognize it. Cambodia remained plagued by guerrilla warfare. Hundreds of thousands of people became refugees. The mass movement represented by the "National Front" ("Renakse") included mass membership organizations of Buddhist monks, nuns, women, youth, workers, and other categories. Renakse organized the "petitions" or "Million Documents" which remains the only nationwide opportunity for survivors of the Khmer Rouge regime to describe atrocities they suffered. The Million Documents were the result of the Renakse research committee that interviewed survivors throughout the country. Various efforts at memorialisation occurred, including famously at Tuol Sleng, Choeung Ek, and the annual May 20th activities often known as the "Day of Hatred." In 1990, Vietnam left and the United Nations entered. The Paris Peace Accords were signed between the government and Khmer Rouge, amongst others, in 1991. In 1993 the United Nations mandate ended with first general elections.

Where does the timeline for Transitional Justice begin for Cambodia? In 1979, with the occupation of the country? The Khmer Rouge had been driven from Phnom Penh, but the Khmer Rouge endured on the Thai border, and the conflict continued through the 1980s. In 1979, with the trial in absentia, and various efforts at memorialization? The years 1981, 1991, 1993, also present themselves, as well as the 2003 agreement between the United Nations and the Cambodian government to establish the Extraordinary Chambers in the Courts of Cambodia to try Khmer Rouge officials. Analyzing the question of where the timeline for Transitional Justice begins highlights the need to keep in mind the dual beginnings of Transitional Justice, as described above. Clearly, the referent or substance of Transitional Justice has a different beginning than the practice of Transitional Justice. Analyzing the timeline also highlights the issues of immediacy and sequencing. Does the occupying forces' show trial in

---

107   Rebuilding Cambodia: human resources, human rights, and law: three essays by Dolores A. Donovan, Sidney Jones and Dinah PoKempner, Robert J. Muscat; editor, (1993), p. 69.

absentia qualify as an immediate response, or was Cambodia an instance where efforts were made too late, allowing most alleged perpetrators to die of old age? Did the sequencing of memorialisation help to make the Extraordinary Chambers in the Courts of Cambodia possible, or did it make the evidence unreliable, or both?

iii   *The Unclear Ending of the Transition in Transitional Justice*
Even in the case of seemingly immediate and unfettered instances of Transitional Justice, such as in post-World War II France, determining when Transitional Justice ends can be difficult. France has long wrestled with the issue of collaboration, producing an early wave of executions and humiliations, stretching and repeating through the relatively recent trial (1995–1998) of Maurice Papon.[108] Given Papon's alleged crimes in Algeria, was a trial for Vichy era crimes Transitional Justice for Vichy or a proxy for Transitional Justice for the Fourth Republic? As with Cambodia, when the practice of Transitional Justice has a referent of arguably more than one regime in the past (*e.g.*, the post-United Nations Transitional Authority in Cambodia (UNTAC) Cambodian government holding trials not with respect to what happened under the current regime, nor UNTAC, nor the period of post-occupation, nor the period of occupation, but for the Democratic Kampuchea regime before the occupation), the question of what political change is involved gets considerably more complex. In Cambodia, given that the current Prime Minister Hun Sen has retained power through multiple putative regime changes, the particular political goal of a transition to democracy is made more problematic.

Whether the Extraordinary Chambers in the Courts of Cambodia or trials for crimes under the Vichy regime in the 1990s count as Transitional Justice or not depend in part on whether the political change *implicated* in the referent material is complete, or at least complete enough that there is a consensus that the new political system is seen as normal. As this a matter of debate and political self-definition within each polity, the temporal dimension of Transitional Justice is once again as much a political determination as a legal one. Unlike International Criminal Law, Transitional Justice must look to an analysis of the society and political system in transition to determine if Transitional Justice must look to an analysis of the society and political system in transition to determine if Transitional Justice is "over"—to see if the needed transition has actually occurred.

---

108   *See e.g.* Curran, Vivian, *The Politics of Memory/Errinerungspolitik and the Use and Propriety of Law in the Process of Memory Construction*, Law and Critique, 19 October 2003, Springer, 316.

c   *Dynamics of* Jus Post Bellum
i   *Beginning with the Effort to End Conflict, not the End of Conflict*

Despite the most facile reading of its name, *jus post bellum* should not be overly defined by reference to the time a conflict ends. The term *jus post bellum* may naturally lead to an emphasis on the temporal boundaries of the armed conflict—as though the question of whether the norms of *jus post bellum* can be applied can always be clearly demarcated by an event.[109] The proper study of *jus post bellum* should complicate and enrich this overly-neat temporal picture by emphasising the links between the areas of *jus post bellum* and *jus ad bellum* as well as between *jus post bellum* and *jus in bello*.

The question of whether demands for unconditional surrender are permissible,[110] for example, is a query asked of a period well before the guns are silenced—and is an issue that links the traditional criteria of *jus ad bellum* (*e.g.* just cause) to traditional concerns of *jus post bellum* or *jus victoriae*[111] as to the rights and responsibilities of the victors. Increased attention to *jus post bellum* should highlight that demarcating when a conflict terminates is frequently difficult, particularly when non-state actors may splinter, transform, or lie temporarily dormant. *Jus post bellum* should not be marked off and isolated from other bodies of legal norms on the basis of time, but rather seen as part of a comprehensive framework for managing an interconnected set of problems related to armed conflict.[112]

Not all contemporary scholars agree on the definition. David Rodin, for example, defines *jus post bellum* narrowly (limited to the obligations of combatants after war) as a separate subject from what he describes as *termination* law or *jus terminatio* (covering the transition from war to peace).[113] Rodin's

---

109   See e.g. Österdahl, Inger and Esther van Zadel, *What Will Jus Post Bellum Mean? Of New Wine and Old Bottles,* Journal of Conflict & Security Law (2009), Vol. 14 No. 2, 185, 176.

110   See Brian Orend, "*Jus Post Bellum*: A Just War Theory Perspective" in *Jus Post Bellum: Towards a Law of Transition from Conflict to Peace*, ed. Carsten Stahn and Jann K. Kleffner (The Hague: T.M.C. Asser Press, 2008), 39–40. See also Orend, Brian, *Jus Post Bellum*: The Perspective of a Just-War Theorist, Leiden Journal of International Law, 20 (2007), 579–580. Orend suggests that demands for surrender and the terms of those demands must be linked to the original just cause of those making the demand.

111   See Stephen C. Neff, "Conflict Termination and Peace-Making in the Law of Nations: A Historical Perspective" in *Jus Post Bellum: Towards a Law of Transition from Conflict to Peace*, ed. Carsten Stahn and Jann K. Kleffner (The Hague: T.M.C. Asser Press, 2008), 77–91.

112   See Brian Orend, "*Jus Post Bellum*: A Just War Theory Perspective" in *Jus Post Bellum: Towards a Law of Transition from Conflict to Peace*, ed. Carsten Stahn and Jann K. Kleffner (The Hague: T.M.C. Asser Press, 2008), 36.

113   See David Rodin, "Two Emerging Issues of *Jus Post Bellum*: War Termination and the Liability of Soldiers for Crimes of Aggression" in *Jus Post Bellum: Towards a Law of Transition*

terminology conflicts with the definition previously adopted for this Chapter, where *jus post bellum* legitimately defines norms applicable to the transition from armed conflict to a just and sustainable peace. The more comprehensive approach with respect to terminology is more similar to Carsten Stahn's, who suggests that *jus post bellum* must be understood in a holistic sense.[114] He decries the frequent fragmented approach in which practitioners of international humanitarian law, criminal law, human rights law, and those supporting specific agendas such as the "responsibility to protect" speak past each other.[115] Christine Bell's conception of a *lex pacificatoria*[116] or law of peacemakers (echoing *lex mercatoria* for merchants) which bridges the various types of peace agreements, including post-conflict implementation agreements, clashes with Rodin's *lex terminatio*, which would presumably stop in the midst of the *lex pacificatoria*, with a different framework for different peace agreements. While the definition used in this Chapter may differ from Rodin's, the division between norms focusing on the process of termination of conflict and the norms involved focusing on the process of building a sustainable peace is useful.

ii   Peace Agreement as a Process

A peace agreement is usually seen as a noun, a document created at a specific point that marks the temporal division between "wartime" and "peacetime."[117]

---

from Conflict to Peace, ed. Carsten Stahn and Jann K. Kleffner (The Hague: T.M.C. Asser Press, 2008), 53–62.

114   See Carsten Stahn, "*Jus Post Bellum*, Mapping the Discipline(s)" in *Jus Post Bellum: Towards a Law of Transition from Conflict to Peace*, ed. Carsten Stahn and Jann K. Kleffner (The Hague: T.M.C. Asser Press, 2008), 105. *See also* Stahn, Carsten, *Jus Post Bellum*: Mapping the Discipline(s), 23 Am. U. Int'l L. Rev., 332, 2007–2008; Stahn, Carsten "*Jus Ad Bellum*," "*Jus In Bello*," "*Jus Post Bellum*?" Rethinking the Conception of the Law of Armed Force, ASIL Proceedings, 2006, 159; Österdahl, Inger and Esther van Zadel, *What Will Jus Post Bellum Mean? Of New Wine and Old Bottles*, Journal of Conflict & Security Law (2009), Vol. 14 No. 2, 178.

115   See Carsten Stahn, "*Jus Post Bellum*, Mapping the Discipline(s)" in *Jus Post Bellum: Towards a Law of Transition from Conflict to Peace*, ed. Carsten Stahn and Jann K. Kleffner (The Hague: T.M.C. Asser Press, 2008), 105. *See also* Stahn, Carsten, *Jus Post Bellum*: Mapping the Discipline(s), 23 Am. U. Int'l L. Rev., 332, 2007–2008; Stahn, Carsten "*Jus Ad Bellum*," "*Jus In Bello*," "*Jus Post Bellum*?" Rethinking the Conception of the Law of Armed Force, ASIL Proceedings, 2006, 159.

116   Bell, Christine, *Peace Agreements: Their Nature and Legal Status*, p. 407.

117   For a fascinating, in-depth analysis of the idea of "wartime" as a legal and cultural construct, particularly with respect to the United States, *see* Dudziak, Mary L. *War time: An idea, its history, its* consequences, (2013) Oxford University Press. *See also* Dudziak, Mary L., *Law, War, and the History of Time*, 98 Cal. L. Rev. 1669 (2010).

This division between periods of war and peace is extremely important, but it can be overstated. There are often periods that could be described as *status mixtus*,[118] where the status and durability of a hoped for peace is uncertain, particularly without at the benefit of hindsight. What is of increased interest at those moments from a *jus post bellum* perspective is not whether or not a status of *post bellum* has technically been achieved, but rather whether legal norms are being applied with *post bellum* as the goal. It is this orientation towards the creation of a just and sustainable peace that separates *jus post bellum* from other strands of just war theory. The law of making peace agreements or "law of peacemakers," what Christine Bell has called *lex pacificatoria*[119] is a crucial part of *jus post bellum*. In operation it often spans periods of armed conflict and peace, because modern peace agreements often come in series, with preliminary agreements paving the way for "comprehensive" peace agreements that often need to be followed by implementing steps. Other crucial subject areas of *jus post bellum*, including environmental law and resource allocation issues during the transition to peace, regulation of state responsibility, recognition of states and governments, and occupation law are often tightly tied to the successful coming to the agreements necessary to build a just and sustainable peace. Coming to lasting agreements about peace is better understood as a dynamic process rather than an equation that is solved a particular moment.

iii *Temporal Relation to* Jus Ad Bellum *and* Jus In Bello: *Two Examples of Complications*

It may be helpful, when confronting the temporal expectations surrounding the terms *jus ad bellum, jus in bello*, and *jus post bellum* to reflect further on the perhaps surprisingly complex temporal dimensions of *jus ad bellum* and *jus in bello* in certain instances. These examples are not intended to be exhaustive, merely illustrative.

The contemporary difference between an armistice and a peace treaty supplies an example of an apparent oddity in the neat timeline of *jus ad bellum* followed by *jus in bello*, and concluded by *jus post bellum*. The simple narrative puts *jus ad bellum* at the beginning of the story of a state of peace turning to a state of war. An armistice, under contemporary usage, ends a conflict between belligerent states, but does not establish peace in the sense that a full peace

---

118 *See* Schwarzenberger, Georg, *Jus pacis ac belli? Prolegomena to a sociology of International Law*, 37 Am. J. Int'l L. 460 (1943), 470.
119 *See inter alia*, Bell, Christine, 'Peace Agreements: Their Nature and Legal Status,' (2006) 100 American Journal of International Law 373.

treaty provides—a full normalization of relations.[120] Once an armistice has been agreed to, the author would suggest that considerations of *jus ad bellum* come into play when considering whether there is any restriction in international law or just war theory on either side breaking the armistice. This means that in every instance where an armistice leads to a peace treaty, *jus ad bellum* considerations apply both at the beginning and the end of the full story of the conflict, stretching from peace to peace. *Jus ad bellum* considerations, in these instances, are intimately connected to the transition to peace. One cannot understand a body of law that covers the transition from armed conflict to peace without understanding *jus ad bellum*. One cannot understand *jus post bellum* without *jus ad bellum*.

Belligerent occupation provides another example of a situation where the overly neat timeline of temporally self-contained areas of *ad bellum, in bello, post bellum* must be reconsidered. Belligerent occupation does not require active resistance, and may lead to a sustained peace without shots being fired. Nonetheless, at least since the Geneva Conventions of 1949 belligerent occupation is included as a time period and circumstance in which what has been termed *jus in bello* applies. Geneva Convention IV and Additional Protocol I are particularly important for determining the law of armed conflict in a belligerent occupation. (While the term *jus in bello* may not have been applied at the time, the modern understanding of occupation is rooted in Article 42 of the 1907 Hague Regulations[121] and the identical text in the 1874 Brussels Declaration.[122]) Should the transition to peace via preliminary peace negotiations occur during belligerent occupation, should this period be considered *jus in bello* or *jus post bellum*? It makes more sense to consider that both regimes apply during the same time period than to try to determine a fine line between the two.

iv   The Endpoint of Jus Post Bellum

As with Transitional Justice, the endpoint of *jus post bellum* defined as regulating a transition to a *just and sustainable* peace can be difficult to identify. While a situation may be analysed retrospectively to determine whether a peace is sustained, the law must be applied without the benefit of future hindsight. The

---

120   Dinstein, Yoram, *War, Aggression and Self-Defence* (3rd ed.) Cambridge (2001), pp. 39–43.
121   Hague Convention (Date signed: 18th October 1907), IV (Convention Relating to the Laws and Customs of War on Land), Annex (Regulations respecting the Laws and Customs of War on Land), Section III (Military Authority over the Territory of the Hostile State), Art. 42.
122   Project of an International Declaration concerning the Laws and Customs of War ((signed 27 August 1874) (1873–74) 65 BFSP 1005 (1907) 1 AJIL 96).

question of whether the current situation is *sustainable* at a particular moment (as opposed to sustained as a matter of historical fact) is a matter of political science and other areas of social science besides law. The question of whether a peace is *just* may lie more in an normative analysis, likely grounded in human rights and the Just War Tradition, as much as positive law. While the focus of Transitional Justice is on the accomplishment of a particular conception of justice more than the realization of a sustainable peace, the experience of Transitional Justice practitioners may be helpful in using various social sciences to analyse the result of applying an area of law or legal approach to a particular instance.

d   Summarizing the Contrast in Temporal Aspects

Many of the differences in the temporal aspects of each concept have been highlighted above. International Criminal Law may in general serve the purposes of Transitional Justice and *jus post bellum*, but because of the inherent importance of the human rights of the accused and the fallibility of state power, the actual practice of International Criminal Law should as far as possible not be instrumentalized to secure a new domestic human rights-protective regime or sustainable peace.

The importance placed by Transitional Justice practitioners on looking to the past and establishing the historical truth of past human rights abuses provides a useful reminder that those applying *jus post bellum* should keep in mind the perceived causes of the armed conflict. Resource conflicts may require particular concern for environmental law, context-specific reparation including access to natural resources, and environmental remediation and concern for the environment in post-conflict rebuilding. Conflicts based primarily on perceptions of human rights violations may require an extra emphasis on the application of human rights norms during the closing of the armed conflict and during the post-conflict phase. Successful application of *jus post bellum* norms requires specific understanding of the local views of history.

The need to pay attention to the sequence of responses in Transitional Justice and sometimes not-so-immediate application of the law also holds lessons for *jus post bellum*. Application of the law regarding to the recognition of states or governments may need to precede the application of laws regarding foreign or international efforts in post-conflict rebuilding, for the very practical reason and evident need of identifying legitimate local authorities to work with. Bell's framework[123] for identifying different stages of peace making including the

---

123   Bell, Christine, Peace Settlements and International Law: From Lex Pacificatoria to Jus Post Bellum (May 17, 2012). Edinburgh School of Law Research Paper No. 2012/16. Available

implementation of peace agreements also emphasises the sequencing of agreements in order for the peace-making process to work.

6   *Specific to Global Contrast*

a   The National and International Dimensions of Transitional Justice

One phenomenon that must be addressed with respect to the national and international dimensions of Transitional Justice is what has been called a "justice cascade."[124] This term was coined to describe the dynamics behind the transnational effort to try Augusto Pinochet for alleged crimes under his regime, specifically "what changed between 1982 and 1999 that made Pinochet's arrest in Britain possible,"[125] and refers more generally to how one legal proceeding, often abroad, can trigger domestic proceedings. It is clear that to understand how and why Transitional Justice works, one must keep in mind the sequence of Transitional Justice efforts, not only in terms of domestic application of Transitional Justice tools, but in terms of steps taken internationally and in domestic fora.

While there are *international* tools of transitional justice, notably international fact-finding missions and particular investigations and criminal prosecutions in international fora, there could also be international criminal prosecutions that should not be considered transitional justice. Such prosecutions could take place in a time that had effectively no particular reference to the transition in regime, such as a prosecution for crimes that happened several regimes ago, as well as international criminal prosecutions that do not implicate human rights violations (for example a prosecution purely for the crime of aggression or a war crime that did not implicate a human rights violation) or a change in political regime (such as a failed coup or election-related violence).

To return to the "justice cascade" phenomenon, it is clear that while transitional justice has historically been largely focused on *domestic* responses to crimes of previous regimes, the picture of modern transitional justice is not complete without awareness of how the geographic scope of Transitional Justice may cross national borders. Tightly linked to the idea of a "justice cascade" in which judicial action in one (foreign) forum can result in judicial action in

---

at SSRN: http://ssrn.com/abstract=2061706 or http://dx.doi.org/10.2139/ssrn.2061706.

124   See Ellen Lutz and Kathryn Sikkink, "The Justice Cascade: The Evolution and Impact of Foreign Human Rights Trials in Latin America" (2001) 2 *Chicago Journal of International Law* 1; see also Kathryn Sikkink, *The Justice Cascade: How Human Rights Prosecutions Are Changing World Politics* (W.W. Norton & Co. 2011).

125   Lutz and Sikkink, "The Justice Cascade" 2.

another forum is the idea of the "Pinochet Effect."[126] The Pinochet Effect emphasizes the transnational change in tone across Latin America and the world due to the effective fight against impunity by leaders of previous regimes. This idea of the international climate or zeitgeist influencing transitional justice is helpful in order to understand the interplay between the domestic, regional, and international arenas.

b   Plotting the Content of *Jus Post Bellum*: Specific to Global

The idea of *jus post bellum* as international law may lead one to believe that local context is largely irrelevant to the law; that it is a universal standard that applies to varied local and specific facts, but that the law itself does not change. In other words, while the assumption of Transitional Justice may be local actors working locally, the assumption with respect to *jus post bellum* may be that international norms, international fora, and the international perspective is all that fundamentally matters. This is not the case. In addition to the global or international level, it is also helpful to consider regional or mid-range level and local or specific levels of analysis.

On the regional or mid-range level, a few examples may be helpful. Substantively, in addition to UN peacekeeping efforts, there exist regional peacekeeping efforts that may be subject to specific regional guidelines and governance. To take an example of what may be a mid-level rather than a regional set of *jus post bellum* problems, the particular problems of resolving such atypical and contested armed conflicts such as the so-called "war on terror" (spanning multiple, non-contiguous countries) or the "war on drugs" (involving massive loss of life in northern Mexico, civil wars in Colombia and Afghanistan, etc.)— conflicts which often cross national borders or exist transnationally in disparate networks with little reference to national borders. Of course, traditional conflicts also have important specific regional contexts, whether in the great lakes region of Africa or the central-south Asian context of Afghanistan and Pakistan. Procedurally, regional international organizations are also faced with the question of recognition of states and governments after conflicts. Multilateral negotiations to end armed conflict and build a sustainable peace are often regional (rather than global or bilateral) in scope. Regional positions regarding procedural issues such as immunity, for example, the African Union positions on Sudanese President al Bashir, are obviously neither global nor local in scope. Mixed procedural and substantive regional or mid-level applications of *jus*

---

126 See Naomi Roht-Arriaza, *The Pinochet Effect: Transnational Justice in the Age of Human Rights* (University of Pennsylvania Press 2006).

post bellum include the jurisprudence of regional judicial bodies and multilateral treaties regarding disarmament, including procedures for verification. On the specific or local level, more substantive examples of *jus post bellum* in practice might include particular instances of reparation; post-conflict resolution of a particular *res* or just cause under just war theory; particular instances of state practice regarding state responsibility, occupation, and peacekeeping. Instances of local more procedural *jus post bellum* might include bilateral or purely domestic/intrastate agreements, specific amnesties, and specific state and government recognition. Mixed substantive and procedural local *jus post bellum* can be found in specific disarmament, demobilization, or reintegration efforts, including verification; and jurisprudence from domestic judicial bodies relating to *jus post bellum*. The astute reader will note that this analysis of geographic scope builds upon the dimension of "more substantive" or "more procedural" used in the analysis of the content of *jus post bellum*. Together, these analyses allow a two-dimensional plotting of *jus post bellum*.

7   Legal Contrast

Jus post bellum, like *jus gentium* or *jus civile*, is best understood as *by definition* primarily a system or body of law and related principles. The term "*jus*," used in this context, dates back to Roman law. A *jus* is "one particular system or body of particular law."[127] While *jus post bellum* in practice always exists in a particular political context, the thing in itself is fundamentally legal in nature, not political. It is a primarily legal concept (of the existence of a body of law) with political implications. *Jus post bellum* can also legitimately be used to reference the aspects of just war theory that apply to the transition from armed conflict to peace that are philosophical in nature, as is the case with its sister terms *jus ad bellum* and *jus in bello*.

Transitional Justice weds a legal idea—human rights—to the political change that makes human rights enforcement possible and necessary. Transitional Justice is tied to the change in regime and a change in enforcement. For Transitional Justice to work, it is necessary to create a distinction between the old culture of impunity and the new norms of justice. Transitional Justice is political in the sense of bringing a full political awareness to the project of securing a political-legal system that respects and enforces human rights norms. The International Center for Transitional Justice takes pains to emphasize that

---

127   *Black's Law Dictionary* (6th edn, West Group, 1991). The alternative definition of *jus* as "a right," that is, "a power, privilege, faculty, or demand inherent in one person and incident upon another" is not applicable in this instance.

Transitional Justice "is not a 'special' kind of justice, but an approach to achieving justice in times of transition from conflict and/or state repression."[128]

Contrasting *jus post bellum* and Transitional Justice with respect to how political or legal in nature each concept is may suggest—*contra* Lauterpacht—that some actions, from a political perspective, are impossible to call legal or illegal, but are instead out of the realm of law and into the realm of politics, in the manner espoused by Morgenthau and Kelsen. This suggestion is not the intent of the author. Identifying the political nature or political implications of a concept should not imply that any act cannot be analyzed from a legal perspective. Transitional Justice practitioners are rooted in a specific legal regime—International Human Rights Law.

One concept that deserves mention in this context is the idea of "meta-conflict,"[129] or "the conflict about what the conflict is about." Different narrative frames to understand an armed conflict will often be political in nature. This has implications for the politicization of *jus post bellum*. Because the true causes of the conflict are almost inevitably contested, the steps that need to be taken to resolve those causes and create a sustainable peace are also likely to be contested.

8   *Historical Foundations*

The value of placing an idea within a specific historical context is at least twofold. First, knowing the environment in which a concept emerged helps understand the idea. Second, the fact that an idea crystallized and grew at a particular time allows reasonable inferences to be made about the wider international system at that time. For *jus post bellum* and Transitional Justice particularly, these are concepts with time and a dynamic view of events at their core. Their relatively recent emergence and popularity allow the inference that recent periods are more receptive to the idea of dynamic change. The emergence and development in content of these concepts should change how the international system is regarded, from a more static to a more dynamic entity. That dynamism, with inherent emphasis on change over time, means that time has become a more critical factor in understanding how the international system works.

A comparative analysis of the historical foundations of Transitional Justice, *jus post bellum*, and International Criminal Law demonstrates the particularities

---

128   International Center for Transitional Justice (ICTJ), "What is Transitional Justice" available at http://ictj.org/about/transitional-justice (accessed 27 May 2016).
129   Christine Bell, *Peace Agreements and Human Rights* (Oxford University Press 2000) 15.

of each concept—how each concept is separately rooted in a particular context. International Criminal Law is helpful to include in a comparative study because the concept of post-conflict criminal justice is often confused with *jus post bellum*. The fact that International Criminal Law *strictu sensu* was not institutionalized from the Treaties of Westphalia to World War II, but has flowered since the end of the Cold War, suggests an incompatibility between a conception of International Law that directly addresses the criminal culpability of natural persons and the dominant conception of International Law during the aforementioned period. The idea that International Law can reach down to the individual, potentially including governmental officials, did not reach a receptive audience until the period after World War II.

Similarly, the historical foundation of Transitional Justice in contemporary transitions to democracy reveals why the concept did not take root earlier. The idea of bias towards transitions to democracy or at least human rights protective regimes would have been anathema to an international order that was protective of the status quo and dominated by non-democracies.

Finally, it is true that particularly in the aftermath of the conflicts of the late 19th Century and World War I, sovereign states could consent to limitations to the resort to armed force and the methods of warfare encapsulated in the concepts of *jus ad bellum* and *jus in bello*. That said, the idea of restricting a victorious state with normatively-grounded law as an armed conflict concludes, a moment typically left entirely to politics and the facts on the ground, meant that the normative teachings of the Just War Tradition regarding the transition from armed conflict to peace were not fully developed into international law.

An analysis of the temporal dimensions of each concept assists in understanding the systematic effect of the concepts on the international system as a whole. Transitional Justice, with its framework assuming a new political-legal system that can evaluate a previous political-legal system, embraces a normative vision that rejects a status quo of sovereign supremacy at the expense of accountability for human rights violations. Regimes in charge of sovereign states that do not protect human rights are not likely to embrace a concept that suggests that there should be a transition to a new regime that would hold previous regime actors accountable for mass human rights violations.

Jus post bellum seeks to constrain armed groups at the moment they are most difficult to constrain—emerging victorious, with potential opposition exhausted. The idea that agreements are void "if its conclusion has been procured by the threat or use of force in violation of the principles of international law"[130] would have invalidated many peace agreements if taken literally during the Westphalian era, and certainly would have posed problems with agreements that formed the legal cover for much of the colonial era.

The systemic effects of International Criminal Law may reach beyond the purposes of Transitional Justice and *jus post bellum* by focusing International Law more on natural persons and less on states. Like Transitional Justice, International Criminal Law can be retrospective in its evaluation of past events, and prospective in terms of improving the future through deterrence, incapacitation, rehabilitation, education, and reconciliation. Where the purpose of International Criminal Law is not future-oriented, it strikes directly at a model of international law that leaves sovereign states as the sole subjects and objects, with criminal law reserved for municipal law. The supremacy of sovereignty is left subtly challenged on multiple levels—no longer is a regime expected to go unchallenged by internal challenges to its political-legal system, challenges as it concludes a conflict and sets up a new legal system to govern the peace, or challenges over its monopoly on penal law.

These challenges to the supremacy of sovereignty may not continue. International Criminal Law may fail to meet its promise if institutional budgets are throttled back by the states that the institutions rely upon. Transitional Justice may lose its focus and become in part a tool of abusive regimes. *Jus post bellum* may fail to establish itself with its sister terms, be depreciated and lose currency. But the tide of history since World War II seems to be flowing towards concepts that reconfigure sovereignty, while still depending on sovereign states for operation. A proper understanding of the historic and current role of each concept, and how they work together to change the international system, is essential for those who wish these concepts to endure.

Transitional Justice challenges the bias towards the status quo and against regime change arguably inherent in the international system—instead seeking to end a climate of impunity and secure durable political and legal systems that protect human rights.

International Criminal Law challenges a jealous view of sovereignty by suggesting that international law directly criminalizes individual conduct. *Jus post bellum* challenges sovereign authority even up to the supreme moment of sovereignty when one state has emerged as victorious in a conflict with another state.

---

130   Article 52, Vienna Convention on the Law of Treaties, May 23, 1969, 1155 U.N.T.S. 331.

a   Transitional Justice

The term is rooted in political transitions of Latin American and Eastern Europe in the late 1980s and early 1990s, with the term "transition" emphasizing the change from authoritarian rule to democracy.[131] Teitel links the withdrawal of support from the USSR to guerilla forces in the late 1970s to the eventual end of military rule in South America.[132] The transitions in Eastern Europe after 1989 were obviously tied to the collapse of the Soviet Union. Transitional Justice, as a concept, cannot be understood without reference to the domestic political transition. As a historical phenomenon, it cannot be understood without reference to international power politics and foreign relations. Teitel suggests that the phase of post-Cold War Transitional Justice has been replaced with a new phase associated with globalization and heightened political instability.[133] A full exposition of the history of Transitional Justice is outside the scope of this chapter, but even a brief look at its history emphasizes the point emphasized by the International Center for Transitional Justice that Transitional Justice "is not a special form of justice but justice adapted to societies transforming themselves after a period of pervasive human rights abuse."[134]

b   *Jus Post Bellum*

Understanding the historical foundations of *jus post bellum* requires an analysis of the contemporary division between *jus ad bellum* and *jus in bello*, as well as looking at the treatment of the concept of law applying to the transition to peace as well. Robert Kolb tentatively credited Josef Kunz with coining the terms *jus ad bellum* and *jus in bello* in their contemporary sense in 1934.[135] Stahn has identified the emergence of the terms in the 1920s,[136] with Guiliano Enriques using the term *jus ad bellum* in 1928.[137]

---

131   International Center for Transitional Justice (ICTJ), "What is Transitional Justice" available at http://ictj.org/about/transitional-justice (accessed 27 May 2016); see also Juan Linz, *Problems of Democratic Transition and Consolidation: Southern Europe, South America, and Post-Communist Europe* (Johns Hopkins University Press 1996); Guilermo O'Donnell, Philippe C. Schmitter, and Laurence Whitehead, *Transitions from Authoritarian Rule: Tentative Conclusions about Uncertain Democracies* Vol. 4 (Johns Hopkins University Press 1986).
132   Teitel, "Transitional Justice Genealogy" 71.
133   Teitel, "Transitional Justice Genealogy" 71.
134   International Center for Transitional Justice (ICTJ), "What is Transitional Justice" available at http://ictj.org/about/transitional-justice (accessed 27 May 2016).
135   Kolb, "Origin of the Twin Terms Jus Ad Bellum/Jus In Bello" 561.
136   Stahn, "*Jus Post Bellum*: Mapping the Discipline(s)" 312.
137   See Giuliano Enriques, "*Considerazioni sulla teoria della Guerra nel diritto Internazionale*" (Considerations on the Theory of War in International Law) (1928) 7 *Rivista Di Diritto Internazionale* (*Journal of International Law*) 172.

The interwar period was hardly the first time concepts of *jus ad bellum* and *jus in bello* were in play. Indeed, the reason for the success of these terms was not only because of their usefulness in discussing the law as it was at the time, but to discuss the history of international law on these issues.

The traditional division in classical international law between the law of war and the law of peace was a sharp one. War, generally speaking, discontinued the application of what might be called the "ordinary" international law that occurred during periods of peace. Treaties, formed in peacetime between non-belligerents, were abrogated when states became belligerents. During the classical positivist era, even the naturalist constraints on the power to wage war were downplayed. The pre-First World War Hague Conventions of 1899 and 1907 and the post-First World War efforts such as the League of Nations and the Kellogg-Briand pact can be seen as part of an effort to lessen (and ultimately eradicate) the possibility of war ceasing the application of the international law of peace. Of particular interest is the Pacific Settlement of International Disputes (Hague I) of 18 October 1907.

The terms *jus ad bellum* and *jus in bello* arose in the context framed by the pre- and post-First World War efforts to address the question of the power to wage war, and indeed on Lauterpacht's framing of the function of law in the international community as a comprehensive system. Those using the terms built on a rich tradition, and in many ways surpassed the classical naturalists in establishing rules to constrain armed conflict. Armed conflict, regardless of whether it was adorned with the trappings of formal declarations or recognitions of a state of war, was increasingly going to be considered less of a reason for a suspension of the "ordinary" functions of law in the international community, the functions that pertain during peace.

Robert Kolb, in the "Origin of the twin terms jus ad bellum/jus in bello," leads one to an irony in the origins of the creation of a fundamental aspect of *jus in bello*—that it applies regardless of the justness of the cause of either side, generally applying to all belligerents. The strength of the idea of the *Reason of State* depreciated the question of the justness of war during the nineteenth century.[138] Kolb suggests, following Peter Haggenmacher,[139] that the idea of the *Reason of State* allowed a focus on the *de facto* and *de jure* conduct of hostilities, regardless of the justness of the resort to armed force. A critical function of the emergence of these two terms is the emphasis on the separate

---

138 Kolb, "Origin of the Twin Terms Jus Ad Bellum/Jus In Bello" 556.
139 Peter Haggenmacher, *Grotius et la doctrine de la guerre juste* (Presses Universitaires de France 1983) 599.

operation of these two terms—underlining the idea that one can (and should) objectively evaluate the rights and duties pertaining to the conduct of armed force separately from the legality of resorting to armed force, and *vice versa*.

In the context of the Grotian tradition as identified by Lauterpacht, there is an irony that the apparent failure of one aspect of the Grotian tradition enabled the success of another aspect of the Grotian tradition. Namely, the failure of the *Rejection of "Reason of State"*[140] with respect to the resort to armed force enabled *The Subjection of the Totality of International Relations to the Rule of Law*[141] with respect to what might be seen as one of the most difficult areas to apply the Rule of Law—the rights and duties *durante bello*, when international relations between the belligerents has been reduced to armed conflict. This, in a sense, is an important part of the story Kolb tells about the emergence of the terms *jus ad bellum* and *jus in bello*.

It is also the story that needs to be told of *jus post bellum*—the subjection of the totality of international relations to the rule of law, even at the moment when a victorious state would be expected to leave law and normative principles behind and follow only the mandates of politics and force. Seen historically, *jus post bellum* represents the last frontier of subjecting relations between states to the rule of law, not only in times of established peace or established armed conflict but during the difficult *status mixtus* periods when new states and new political-legal structures are born.

As Randall Lesaffer notes, interest in the history of international law has waxed and waned, with an increase during the First and Second World Wars followed by a subsequent decline.[142] This last peak in interest generally coincides with the coining of *jus ad bellum* and *jus in bello*, in addition to Lauterpacht's framing of the Grotian Tradition. Lesaffer suggests that we are in the midst of a new surge of interest in international history, perhaps preparing the ground for adoption and development of a new term, *jus post bellum*.

9   *Going Forward – Continuing the Grotian Tradition*

Those interested in *jus post bellum* would be well served to pay attention to Transitional Justice for a variety of reasons. Transitional Justice will often be applied simultaneously with *jus post bellum*. The area of law at the heart of Transitional Justice, International Human Rights Law, is critical to understanding the law

---

140   Lauterpacht, "The Grotian Tradition in International Law" 30.
141   Ibid 19.
142   Randall Lesaffer, *Peace Treaties and International Law in European History: From the Late Middle Ages to World War One* (Cambridge University Press 2004) 2.

applicable to the ending of conflict and the building of peace—from the treatment of amnesties in peace agreements to the protection of human rights in constitutional documents. The success of Transitional Justice advocates in placing human rights and the fight against impunity at the centre of global governance should be lauded and emulated. At the same time, those interested in *jus post bellum* may wish to take note of the danger in definitional creep, particularly using a relatively new term such as "Transitional Justice" and applying it without a change in regime, particularly in a one-sided manner by a human rights-abusing regime.

Whether Transitional Justice and *jus post bellum* continue to grow and endure as useful concepts depends in part on whether these terms are defined with sufficient rigour. Because both terms deal with complex phenomena and benefit from scholarly interest from disparate fields and traditions, coming closer to a consensus on the definition of these terms is difficult. Since Transitional Justice and *jus post bellum* will often (but not always) apply simultaneously, it is all the more important to attempt this difficult task—to define both terms clearly and develop them in accordance with contemporary realities. It is important to recognize that multiple maximands will co-exist, rooted in the separate but related traditions, sometimes in tension, but hopefully almost always carried forward with goodwill.

The observant reader may have noted that, in contrast with other scholars, the definition of Transitional Justice embraced by this chapter is *narrower* than the increasingly broad definitions commonly used, while the definition of *jus post bellum* is broader. I do not see this as a contradiction, but rather a reflection of the separate problems each concept is designed to address.

Transitional Justice, as a specific conception of justice responding to the particular problems of political change and confronting the wrongdoings of repressive predecessor regimes, allows for establishing a new political compact that pledges an end to impunity for human rights abuses, including by new elites. Focusing on that specific problem and specific concept makes the term more useful than a general euphemism for anything alleging human rights abuses, regardless of political circumstance.

Jus post bellum recognizes the problem of systematically applying international law to the difficult area of transitioning from armed conflict to a sustainable peace. A narrow focus on one aspect of the transition to a sustainable peace misses the challenge implied by the term *"jus,"* that the effort of those involved must be to find the connections between various legal obligations and discover what is systematic about the law that applies to the process of achieving a sustainable peace.

There is, perhaps, an irony in suggesting that the Grotian Tradition as identified by Lauterpacht is "continuing" with the development of *jus post bellum* as a system of law pertaining to the transition from armed conflict to a sustainable peace. Lauterpacht did not portray international law as an inkspot that had spread to some areas but not others. Should disputes have arisen in his era as to the legality of acts taken during the transition to a sustainable peace, he surely would have felt those disputes could have arisen.

Yet embracing the concept that there should be no judicial *non liquet* in international law permits the idea that international law changes and develops, clarifies and matures. In a sense, uncovering the normative and historical foundations of *jus post bellum* is a project of construction as much as genealogy or archaeology. Application of international law in the transition to sustainable peace may be more or less part of a coherent and integrated system. The vision of Transitional Justice practitioners of their field as not a "special" field of law but a "holistic" practice of judicial and non-judicial approaches to a particular circumstance[143] surely provides some guidance and reassurance to those approaching the definitional questions of *jus post bellum*.

While I maintain that *jus post bellum* is best viewed primarily as a system of law, it is not yet as tightly internally integrated as its sister systems of law, *jus ad bellum*, and *jus in bello*. Conversely, *jus post bellum* is probably more tightly connected to diverse fields of law that operate during times of transition from armed conflict and during other circumstances. This is not a threat to the legitimacy of the concept of studying the international law that exists during the circumstance of transition to a sustainable peace, rather it is an opportunity and a challenge to discern the operations of law in this complex and varied environment.

---

143   International Center for Transitional Justice (ICTJ), "What is Transitional Justice" available at http://ictj.org/about/transitional-justice (accessed 27 May 2016).

CHAPTER 5

An Empirical Analysis of the Literature

A   Introduction

This chapter expands upon the empirical analysis of research on *jus post bellum* analysed in Chapter 4.A. *supra*. No publicly available database of *jus post bellum* scholarship existed when the author began his research. The database of *jus post bellum* scholarship created by the author serves as the basis of the following findings.

B   Method

Datasets were created in stages. The initial, proof-of-concept data set was created by finding all articles available on the Social Science Research Network (SSRN) that mention *jus post bellum*. The Social Science Research Network has over 207,000 authors and more than 1.3 million users.[1]

The database was created with one record for each article. The Microsoft Word or Portable Document Format (PDF) version of the article was uploaded into the database, and the available metadata regarding each article was entered in the appropriate field. The fields were created from the Document Center template in the Microsoft SharePoint Server 2010, with the addition of customized fields where appropriate. This was hosted and supported by the Living Lab at the Grotius Centre for International Legal Studies, University of Leiden and the Jus Post Bellum Project under the Virtual Research Environment framework.[2]

---

1   See *Social Science Research Network Frequently Asked Questions*, available at http://www.ssrn.com/update/general/ssrn_faq.html#what_is. (Last accessed 5 October 2012.)

2   The relevant fields describing each article are as follows: Name, Title, Rating (0-5), Number of Ratings, WorkCitation, PublicationYear, Volume, Issue, Pages, JPBDefinition, Abstract, Tags, Keywords, ArXiv ID, DOI, JPBDefinitionPointCite, ScholarlyField, Author, Publisher, DefinitionQuote, Collection, Date, JournalName, Language, Note, Westlaw Subjects, and MinimalJusPostBellumReference. Some fields, like Rating and Number of Ratings, are reserved for future use. Most fields are text fields, although some have restricted inputs such as a checkbox for indicating that the ScholarlyField is "law." The Collection field indicates the dataset, such as SSRN or Westlaw. MinimalJusPostBellumReference is a Boolean variable indicating whether the reference to *jus post bellum* is truly a mere passing reference. Of particular note are the JPBDefinitionPointCite and DefinitionQuote fields. Together, they allow an export of

Once the database was created and populated with this initial dataset of 13 articles from SSRN, a series of potential datasets was evaluated. Westlaw, being a leading, widely available and widely used legal search engine, was one potential source for an additional data set. Of the potential searches within Westlaw, the best option seemed to be a collection of all articles from Westlaw, specifically all articles that were received from a "terms and connectors" search in the world-jlr database (Combined World Journals and Law Reviews) for the term "jus post bellum." This search would yield 89 documents at the time of the search. Google Scholar was additional option, widely available but arguably less widely accepted. A general Google Scholar search for the term would return 819 hits, which could be further narrowed to 759 hits if the "no citations" option was used. Further narrowing the Google Scholar search to filter for only what Google Scholar considered "legal documents" narrowed the search to 95 results. Searching in the same catalogue with "jus post bellum" in any field revealed 126 results, with 111 peer-reviewed articles and 124 with the full text online. These search results were re-verified on 15 August 2012.

Many other possible datasets are possible—for example, HeinOnline or WestLaw for international researchers. The current point of this research, however, is not to be comprehensive but instead to be reasonably representative while still functional. Additional research options are addressed in the sections in the Conclusion that deal with further avenues of research and implementing further research.

Of these candidate datasets, the Westlaw dataset was picked for the main body of the empirical analysis presented here. In part, this was a matter of a reasonable sample size and the scope of research, as a full evaluation of 819 references from Google Scholar might prove difficult on a practical level, particularly when providing a consistent evaluation of each article throughout. In addition, Google Scholar has unique problems as a primary data set for analysis. Google Scholar is broad, but unreliable, relying on automated entry without human checks. This required the author to make an additional level of subjective evaluations as to the suitability of the results, which in turn potentially undermines the reliability of the empirical results derived from the dataset. These limitations of existing datasets are discussed in "Areas for Further Research" in the conclusion of this section.

In an effort to increase transparency, it is important to note that the author leans towards the functional approach. When evaluating the articles as more functional or temporal the author tried to be objective as possible, with no

---

the metadata allowing external evaluation of the analysis of definitions, specifically into a linked Microsoft Excel file.

known expectations as to the trends in scholarship. The main point of this chapter is not to argue for one approach or the other (although the comparative analysis should demonstrate the coherence of the functional approach). Rather, this article seeks to highlight that these two separate approaches exist and that consolidating around one approach would be useful.

Once the articles were analyzed and the data entered, the metadata was exported to Microsoft Excel format and further analyzed, including the creation of the graphs included below.

C   Findings

i   *Introduction*

The findings below will be presented first according to the analysis of the SSRN dataset, then the analysis of the contemporary scholarship as analyzed overall (including disaggregation when appropriate). The overall findings could legitimately be summarized as follows: There has been a steady expansion of references to *jus post bellum* in a variety of journals. (See *figs. 7, 8*) With the expansion of references, there has been an increase of ambiguity, not a consolidation around a consensus definition. The trend is generally an increase in trivial references to *jus post bellum*, in addition to a trend towards a simple, literal temporal definition. Whether a consensus focus will be achieved, and what that consensus might be, is as yet unclear.

The overall year-by-year pattern of publication mentioning *jus post bellum* in the analyzed datasets can be visualized using Figure 7.

The data in Figure 7 above is explained in more detail in the Westlaw and SSRN Analysis section, see Figure 8.

The widespread nature of the published works can be seen here. While there are a few noteworthy leading journals on the subject, overall the scholarship is spread over a large number of journals.

With this overall picture established, we can turn to the particular subject of interest, trends with respect to the temporal-functional dichotomy.

ii   *SSRN Analysis*
1   Summary Findings

For articles in SSRN, the general trend is towards a generally temporal definition and away from a generally functional definition of *jus post bellum*. This is summarized in Figure 9 which covers the period in which articles mentioning *jus post bellum* (2002–2012). Please note that in all of the Figures in this article, there are overlaps in data points, but the line shows the general trend.

The SSRN articles are described below, first with respect two unclassifiable articles, then with respect to articles with a primarily functional definition and

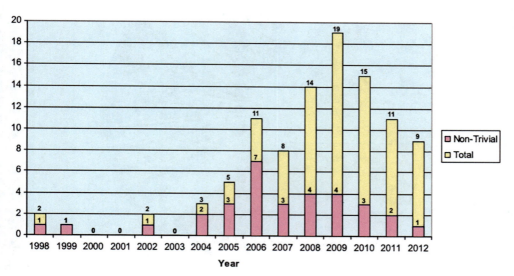

FIGURE 7   Total v. non-trivial *jus post bellum* articles

then with respect to articles with a primarily temporal definition. This close analysis, article by article, is intended to help evaluate not only the articles in question, but also the meaning of "primarily functional definition" and "primarily temporal definition" in practice.

2   Unclassifiable

Two SSRN articles discussing *jus post bellum* have proved quite difficult to reasonably classify: *Grandeur et déclin de l'idée de résistance à l'occupation : Réflexions à propos de la légitimité des « insurgés »* by Frederic Megret[3] and *Legislative*

---

3   Megret, Frederic, *On the Legitimacy of 'Insurgency': Rise and Fall of the Idea of Resistance to Occupation* (*Grandeur Et Declin De L'Idee De Resistance a L'Occupation: Reflexions a Propos de la Legitimite des 'Insurges'*) (November 5, 2008). Revue Belge de Droit International, 2009. Available at SSRN: http://ssrn.com/abstract=1296060 or http://dx.doi.org/10.2139/ssrn.1296060.

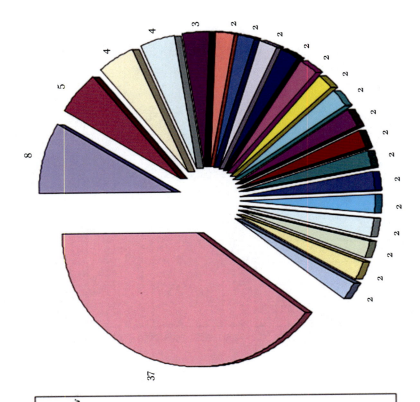

FIGURE 8   Widespread publishing on *jus post bellum*

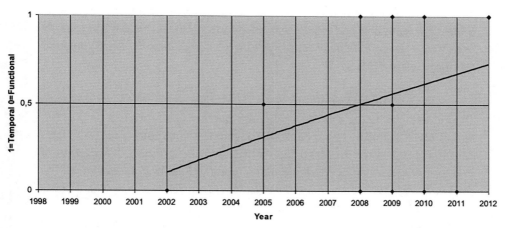

FIGURE 9   Functional or temporal definitions over time from SSRN

Reform in Post-Conflict Zones: Jus Post Bellum and the Contemporary Occupant's Law-Making Powers by Kristen Boon.[4]

Legislative Reform in Post-Conflict Zones: Jus Post Bellum and the Contemporary Occupant's Law-Making Powers by Kristen Boon[5] defines *jus post bellum* as follows: "Jus post bellum, or the justice of post-war settlements and reconstruction, is assumed to draw on similar principles as *jus ad bellum* (law of war) and *jus in bello* (law in war)."[6] This could be read with an emphasis on the clear "post-war" temporal definition, but it is also clearly tied to particular goals and qualities (settlement and reconstruction). It is interesting to note that Boon's subsequent work on *jus post bellum* in SSRN emphasise the functional aspects more clearly.

One SSRN article, *Grandeur et déclin de l'idée de résistance à l'occupation : Réflexions à propos de la légitimité des « insurgés »*[7] by Frederic Megret did not

---

4   Boon, Kristen E., Legislative Reform in Post-Conflict Zones: Jus Post Bellum and the Contemporary Occupant's Law-Making Powers. McGill Law Journal, Vol. 50, 2005; Seton Hall Public Law Research Paper No. 962094. Available at SSRN: http://ssrn.com/abstract=962094.
5   Ibid.
6   Ibid 7.
7   Megret, Frederic, *On the Legitimacy of 'Insurgency': Rise and Fall of the Idea of Resistance to Occupation (Grandeur Et Declin De L'Idee De Resistance a L'Occupation: Reflexions a Propos de la Legitimite des 'Insurges')* (November 5, 2008). Revue Belge de Droit International, 2009. Available at SSRN: http://ssrn.com/abstract=1296060 or http://dx.doi.org/10.2139/ssrn.1296060.

have a definition of *jus post bellum* that could clearly be categorized as functional or temporal. It recognizes that the definition of the term is not entirely fixed ("*Bien entendu, la définition exacte du jus post bellum demeure une question amplement débattue.*")⁸

3 Functional Definitions

The following SSRN articles use a generally functional definition of *jus post bellum*: *On War as Hell* by Roger Paul Alford (2002),⁹ *Obligations of the New Occupier: The Contours of a Jus Post Bellum* by Kristen E. Boon (2009),¹⁰ *The Future of the Law of Occupation* by Kristen E. Boon (2009),¹¹ *New Modes and Orders: The Difficulties of a Jus Post Bellum of Constitutional Transformation* by Nehal Bhuta (2010)¹² and *Corporate Legitimacy* by Laszlo Zasolnai (2011).¹³

On War as Hell by Roger Paul Alford (2002)¹⁴ indicates clearly that *jus post bellum* includes principles not only for the period after war ends, but for the process of war termination and the transition to peace. Alford states: "International relations scholars have recently begun articulating principles of *jus post bellum*, modernizing and expanding just war theory to address principles for the termination of war and the transition to peace."¹⁵ The focus of the article is

---

8 Roughly translated: "Of course, the exact definition of jus post bellum remains a widely debated question." Megret, Frederic, *On the Legitimacy of 'Insurgency': Rise and Fall of the Idea of Resistance to Occupation (Grandeur Et Declin De L'Idee De Resistance a L'Occupation: Reflexions a Propos de la Legitimite des 'Insurges')* (November 5, 2008). Revue Belge de Droit International, 2009, p. 18.

9 Alford, Roger Paul, On War as Hell. Chicago Journal of International Law, Vol. 3, No. 1, Spring 2002. Available at SSRN: http://ssrn.com/abstract=867208.

10 Boon, Kristen E., Obligations of the New Occupier: The Contours of a Jus Post Bellum (June, 29 2009). Loyola of Los Angeles International and Comparative Law Review, Vol. 31, No. 2, 2008. Available at SSRN: http://ssrn.com/abstract=1427355.

11 Boon, Kristen E., The Future of the Law of Occupation (June 30, 2009). Kristen E. Boon, The Future of the Law of Occupation, Canadian Yearbook of International Law, 2009. Available at SSRN: http://ssrn.com/abstract=1464443.

12 Bhuta, Nehal, New Modes and Orders: The Difficulties of a Jus Post Bellum of Constitutional Transformation (March 1, 2010). New York University International Law and Justice Working Paper No. 2010/1. Available at SSRN: http://ssrn.com/abstract=1574329 or http://dx.doi.org/10.2139/ssrn.1574329.

13 Zsolnai, Laszlo, Corporate Legitimacy (March 18, 2011). Available at SSRN: http://ssrn.com/abstract=1789884 or http://dx.doi.org/10.2139/ssrn.1789884.

14 Alford, Roger Paul, On War as Hell. Chicago Journal of International Law, Vol. 3, No. 1, Spring 2002. Available at SSRN: http://ssrn.com/abstract=867208.

15 Ibid 217, fn. 29.

on war reparations. This subject, perhaps, lends itself to the terms and processes of peace negotiations that occur as part of war termination and the implementation of the peace agreements in the transition to peace.

Obligations of the New Occupier: The Contours of a Jus Post Bellum by Kristen E. Boon (2009)[16] indicates that there is no clear temporal division between war and peace. Boon states "Yet with the exception of the law of belligerent occupation, neither jus ad bellum nor jus in bello provide much guidance on temporary interventions after war and before peace."[17] This understanding pushes against a simple temporal definition, starting with the end of armed conflict. The focus is on the process of transitioning out of armed conflict into peace. One could argue that this is simply a different temporal definition, starting earlier and covering the period of "transition." This argument, however, misses the principal point of the distinction—that a functional definition emphasizes whether a process is going on (the termination of armed conflict and transition to peace) rather than whether an event has happened (war ending). This article falls into the former category, and was thus classified as "functional."

The Future of the Law of Occupation by Kristen E. Boon (2009)[18] clearly emphasizes the function of transition from law to peace. Boon states, "While the scope and content of jus post bellum are only developing, a significant contribution of a jus post bellum would be to fill existing gaps and establish a uniform legal regime applicable to the exercise of public authority during transitions."[19] Again, like in *Obligations of the New Occupier: The Contours of a Jus Post Bellum*, Boon is emphasizing the action of transition (particularly the action of the exercise of public authority) rather than a temporal definition.

Corporate Legitimacy by Laszlo Zsolnai (2011),[20] which mirrors a chapter in *Business Ethics and Corporate Sustainability* edited by Antonio Tencati and

---

16   Boon, Kristen E., Obligations of the New Occupier: The Contours of a Jus Post Bellum (June, 29 2009). Loyola of Los Angeles International and Comparative Law Review, Vol. 31, No. 2, 2008.
17   Ibid. 102.
18   Boon, Kristen E., The Future of the Law of Occupation (June 30, 2009). Kristen E. Boon, The Future of the Law of Occupation, Canadian Yearbook of International Law, 2009.
19   Ibid 23.
20   Zsolnai, Laszlo, Corporate Legitimacy (March 18, 2011). Available at SSRN: http://ssrn.com/abstract=1789884 or http://dx.doi.org/10.2139/ssrn.1789884.

Francesco Perrini.[21] Zsolnai defines *jus post bellum* as follows: "In more recent years, a third category — "jus post bellum" — has been added, which governs the justice of war termination and peace agreements, as well as the trying of war criminals." This definition is largely functional in nature. It is perhaps not the most legally precise definition, but that may be expected in a work that is using just war theory as an analogy for business ethics. Including this work raises the question of the "interpretive community" or "discourse community" of *jus post bellum*. It clearly extends beyond law, and may extend in surprising ways. This may be an instance where an idea is spreading out (to business ethics in this instance) rather than true dialogue across disciplines. In any case, for methodological consistency, as this was article appears in a search for *jus post bellum* in SSRN, this article must be included.

In *New Modes and Orders: The Difficulties of a Jus Post Bellum of Constitutional Transformation*,[22] Nehal Bhuta defines *jus post bellum* as a project of legal codification "that would provide a set of standards governing the relationship between occupier or administrator and the population of a territory, in order to ensure that constitutional change is indeed a product of the internal sovereignty of the people."[23] This does not necessarily include the norms that are included in many functional definitions, including peace negotiations and peace agreements, but it does not exclude them either. The emphasis is clearly on function, in any case, not time, even if the function specified is narrower than many definitions.

4   Temporal Definitions

The following SSRN articles use a generally temporal definition of *jus post bellum*: *Putting an End to Human Rights Violations by Proxy: Accountability of International Organizations and Member States in the Framework of Jus Post*

---

21   Tencati, Antonio and Francesco Perrini, *Business Ethics and Corporate Sustainability*, 2011, Edward Elgar Publishing Limited.
22   Bhuta, Nehal, New Modes and Orders: The Difficulties of a Jus Post Bellum of Constitutional Transformation (March 1, 2010). New York University International Law and Justice Working Paper No. 2010/1. Available at SSRN: http://ssrn.com/abstract=1574329 or http://dx.doi.org/10.2139/ssrn.1574329.
23   Bhuta, Nehal, New Modes and Orders: The Difficulties of a Jus Post Bellum of Constitutional Transformation (March 1, 2010). New York University International Law and Justice Working Paper No. 2010/1, p. 5.

Bellum by Matteo Tondini (2008),[24] *Post-Conflict Peacebuilding – Ambiguity and Identity* by Vincent Chetail (2009),[25] *Post-Conflict Peacebuilding*, by Vincent Chetail in Lexique de la Consolidation de la Paix[26] (2009), *The Responsibility for Post-Conflict Reforms: A Critical Assessment of Jus Post Bellum as a Legal Concept* by Eric de Brabandere (2009),[27] *Jus Post Bellum in Iraq: The Development of Emerging Norms for Economic Reform in Post Conflict Countries* by Christina Benson (2012),[28] and *Peace Settlements and International Law: From Lex Pacificatoria to Jus Post Bellum* by Christine Bell (2012).[29]

Putting an End to Human Rights Violations by Proxy: Accountability of International Organizations and Member States in the Framework of Jus Post Bellum by Matteo Tondini (2008) was a chapter in *Jus Post Bellum: Towards a Law of Transition From Conflict to Peace* edited by Carsten Stahn and Jann Kleffner.[30] Tondini defines *jus post bellum* as peace-making "Moreover, the call for accountability in post-conflict situations coincides with a broader systemic challenge which is at the heart of *jus post bellum*, namely a 'normative gap' in the law governing peace-making after conflict."[31]

---

24 Tondini, Matteo, Putting an End to Human Rights Violations by Proxy: Accountability of International Organizations and Member States in the Framework of Jus Post Bellum (2008). C. Stahn and J. Kleffner (eds.), Jus Post Bellum: Towards a Law of Transition From Conflict to Peace, The Hague: TMC Asser Press, 2008, pp. 187–212. Available at SSRN: http://ssrn.com/abstract=2100944.

25 Chetail, Vincent, Post-Conflict Peacebuilding – Ambiguity and Identity (March 16, 2009). Post-Conflict Peace-Building: A Lexicon, pp. 1–33, Vincent Chetail, ed., Oxford University Press, 2009. Available at SSRN: http://ssrn.com/abstract=1641243.

26 Chetail, Vincent, Post-Conflict Peacebuilding (July 19, 2009). Lexique De La Consolidation De La Paix, Vincent Chetail, ed., Bruylant, pp. 29–70, 2009. Available at SSRN: http://ssrn.com/abstract=1645183.

27 De Brabandere, Eric, The Responsibility for Post-Conflict Reforms: A Critical Assessment of Jus Post Bellum as a Legal Concept (October 1, 2009). Vanderbilt Journal of Transnational Law, Vol. 43, No. 1, 2010. Available at SSRN: http://ssrn.com/abstract=1569990.

28 Benson, Christina C., Jus Post Bellum in Iraq: The Development of Emerging Norms for Economic Reform in Post Conflict Countries (April 10, 2012). Forthcoming in: Richmond Journal of Global Law and Business, Issue 4, Vol. 11 (Fall 2012). Available at SSRN: http://ssrn.com/abstract=2037561.

29 Bell, Christine, Peace Settlements and International Law: From Lex Pacificatoria to Jus Post Bellum (May 17, 2012). Edinburgh School of Law Research Paper No. 2012/16. Available at SSRN: http://ssrn.com/abstract=2061706 or http://dx.doi.org/10.2139/ssrn.2061706.

30 Tondini, Matteo, Putting an End to Human Rights Violations by Proxy: Accountability of International Organizations and Member States in the Framework of Jus Post Bellum (2008). C. Stahn and J. Kleffner (eds.), Jus Post Bellum: Towards a Law of Transition From Conflict to Peace, The Hague: TMC Asser Press, 2008, pp. 187–212. Available at SSRN: http://ssrn.com/abstract=2100944.

31 Ibid 188.

Post-Conflict Peacebuilding – Ambiguity and Identity by Vincent Chetail is a chapter in *Post-Conflict Peace-Building: A Lexicon* edited by the same Vincent Chetail.32 It states: "Following this perspective, jus post bellum can be generally defined as the set of norms applicable at the end of an armed conflict—whether internal or international—with a view to establishing a sustainable peace."33 This is arguably a mixed temporal and functional definition, because the clear temporal definition—norms applicable at a particular time, at the end of an armed conflict—is qualified with a particular goal for the norms in question—establishing a sustainable peace. It could have been coded as a .5 (as a midpoint between a "0" coding for "functional" definitions and a "1" coding for "temporal" definitions), between temporal and functional. But a natural reading of the sentence, as well as the article as a whole, indicates that peace agreements are not included in the definition. The function of transition from armed conflict to peace is thus incomplete. Accordingly, it has been coded as temporal, rather than functional.

Post-Conflict Peacebuilding, by Vincent Chetail in Lexique de la Consolidation de la Paix34 is similar, and likely identical, to *Post-Conflict Peacebuilding – Ambiguity and Identity* described *supra*.35 The definition, "*Suivant cette, optique, le jus post bellum peut etre defini dans un sens large comme l'ensemble des regles applicables a la sortie d'un conflit arme – interne ou international – en vue d'instaurer une paix durable*" is functionally identical. One might exclude it from the coding, but as it is published twice and presumably reaches a different audience, it was coded as two separate works.

The Responsibility for Post-Conflict Reforms: A Critical Assessment of Jus Post Bellum as a Legal Concept by Eric de Brabandere36 defines *jus post bellum* in the following sentence: "Several scholars have drawn attention to the need to move toward a distinct discipline on the law after conflict—jus post bellum—a systemic adaptation of the current division between the 'law of war' and the 'law

---

32 Chetail, Vincent, Post-Conflict Peacebuilding – Ambiguity and Identity (March 16, 2009). Post-Conflict Peace-Building: A Lexicon, pp. 1–33, Vincent Chetail, ed., Oxford University Press, 2009. Available at SSRN: http://ssrn.com/abstract=1641243.

33 Ibid 18.

34 Chetail, Vincent, Post-Conflict Peacebuilding (July 19, 2009). Lexique De La Consolidation De La Paix, Vincent Chetail, ed., Bruylant, pp. 29–70, 2009. Available at SSRN: http://ssrn.com/abstract=1645183.

35 Chetail, Vincent, Post-Conflict Peacebuilding – Ambiguity and Identity (March 16, 2009). Post-Conflict Peace-Building: A Lexicon, pp. 1–33, Vincent Chetail, ed., Oxford University Press, 2009. Available at SSRN: http://ssrn.com/abstract=1641243.

36 De Brabandere, Eric, The Responsibility for Post-Conflict Reforms: A Critical Assessment of Jus Post Bellum as a Legal Concept (October 1, 2009). Vanderbilt Journal of Transnational Law, Vol. 43, No. 1, 2010. Available at SSRN: http://ssrn.com/abstract=1569990.

of peace.'"[37] The emphasis is on the temporal—law after conflict. The substantive emphasis in the article is rather limited, mostly to reconstruction and occupation.

Jus Post Bellum in Iraq: The Development of Emerging Norms for Economic Reform in Post Conflict Countries by Christina Benson[38] defines *jus post bellum* using temporal markers: "Rather, the focus of this paper is on the justice of developments during the post-war period of occupation ("jus post bellum"), after the CPA took control of the country and up until such time as a nominally representative sovereign government could be elected."[39] *Jus post bellum* as the justice that applies from one point to another, specifically during occupation, is clearly a temporal definition.

Peace Settlements and International Law: From Lex Pacificatoria to Jus Post Bellum by Christine Bell[40] appears to define *jus post bellum* temporally. Bell states "From this dislike derives an instinct to codify a jus post bellum that would regulate post-conflict dilemmas more clearly and more appropriately. If international law is now a law of regimes, and the post-conflict environment has no specific or appropriate regime, then, the argument runs, it now needs one."[41] The emphasis seems to be on the post-conflict period, rather than any particular function. This contrasts with Bell's *lex pacificatoria*, which emerges from peace settlements and is alternatively called the "law of the peacemakers."[42] The research paper is self-reflective with respect to definitions and quite nuanced, but is best coded as classifying *jus post bellum* through a temporal lens.

iii   Westlaw and SSRN Analysis

Adding the SSRN and Westlaw searches together, overall the references look like Figure 10.

---

37   De Brabandere, Eric, The Responsibility for Post-Conflict Reforms: A Critical Assessment of Jus Post Bellum as a Legal Concept (October 1, 2009). Vanderbilt Journal of Transnational Law, Vol. 43, No. 1, 2010, 121.
38   Benson, Christina C., Jus Post Bellum in Iraq: The Development of Emerging Norms for Economic Reform in Post Conflict Countries (April 10, 2012). Forthcoming in: Richmond Journal of Global Law and Business, Issue 4, Vol. 11 (Fall 2012). Available at SSRN: http://ssrn.com/abstract=2037561.
39   Benson, Christina C., Jus Post Bellum in Iraq: The Development of Emerging Norms for Economic Reform in Post Conflict Countries (April 10, 2012). Forthcoming in: Richmond Journal of Global Law and Business, Issue 4, Vol. 11 (Fall 2012), p. 5.
40   Bell, Christine, Peace Settlements and International Law: From Lex Pacificatoria to Jus Post Bellum (May 17, 2012). Edinburgh School of Law Research Paper No. 2012/16. Available at SSRN: http://ssrn.com/abstract=2061706 or http://dx.doi.org/10.2139/ssrn.2061706.
41   Bell, Christine, Peace Settlements and International Law: From Lex Pacificatoria to Jus Post Bellum (May 17, 2012). Edinburgh School of Law Research Paper No. 2012/16, p. 51.
42   Ibid 1.

Many of the references, however, are trivial. Graphing only the non-trivial references to *jus post bellum* looks like Figure 11.

Putting the two together, one can visualize the data as shown in Figure 12.

This dataset simplifies works that give two-year spans as their publication year as the first publication year, so for example, if there were 6 articles with 2006 as the publication year, 2 articles (etc.) with 2007 as the publication year, and 1 work with 2006–2007 as the publication year, the totals used would be 7 works with 2006 as the publication year and 2 works with 2007 as the publication year.

It is interesting to note the high percentage (32%) of works with only trivial reference to *jus post bellum*.

All works with essentially trivial references to *jus post bellum* were coded as "Non-Defined" in the JPBDefinition variable. The JPBDefinition variable can thus only be meaningfully analyzed with non-trivial references.

One way to visualize this data is shown in Figure 13.

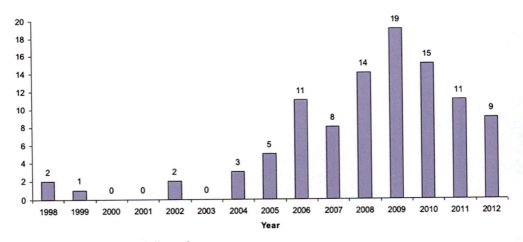

FIGURE 10   *Jus post bellum* references

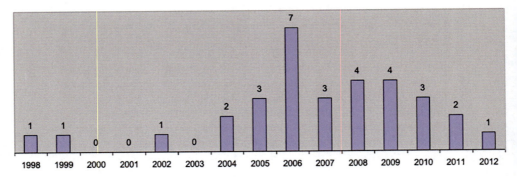

FIGURE 11   Non-trivial *jus post bellum* references

AN EMPIRICAL ANALYSIS OF THE LITERATURE

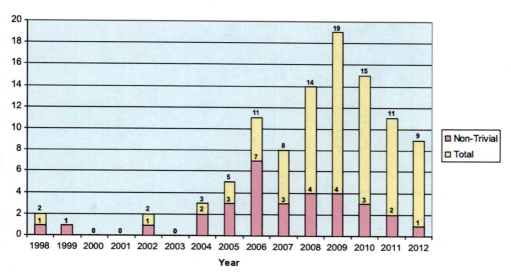

FIGURE 12   Trivial and non-trivial *jus post bellum* references

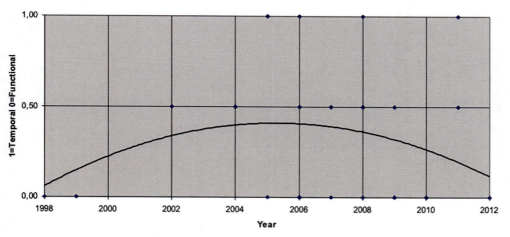

FIGURE 13   Functional or temporal definitions over time from Westlaw

This indicates, using a second-degree polynomial trend line, that there was an uptick in ambiguous or temporal definitions of *jus post bellum* in works listed in Westlaw during the mid-2000s, but that the understanding is returning to the original functional understanding of the phrase.

As indicated above, the SSRN data can be visualized as shown in Figure 14.

As above, this is a second-degree polynomial trend line, indicating a steady trend towards a more temporal framework in the more general social science audience of SSRN.

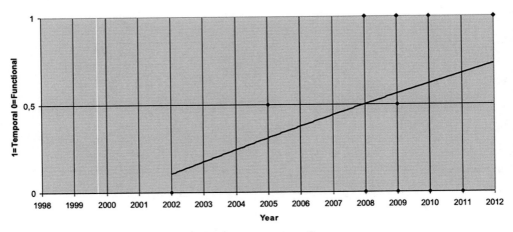

FIGURE 14   Functional or temporal definitions over time from SSRN

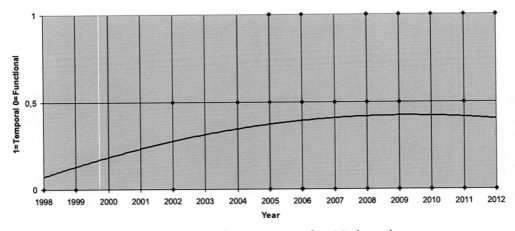

FIGURE 15   Functional or temporal definitions over time from Westlaw and SSRN

Adding the SSRN information back in, the overall trend line looks like Figure 15.

However, forcing a trend line is possibly unjustified given the limits of the dataset. A clearer visualization might be the following summation of the combined SSRN and Westlaw data, excluding trivial references, see Figure 16.

This Figure shows the early use of functional definition, an intermediate period of indeterminate definition, and increasing use of temporal references compared to functional approaches in 2012. In absolute terms, the publications can be represented as seen in Figure 17.

One interpretation of this data could be that the term "*jus post bellum*" is gaining at least a superficial currency and "mindshare," as seen by the number of glancing references to the term. There has been an increasing number of

AN EMPIRICAL ANALYSIS OF THE LITERATURE   195

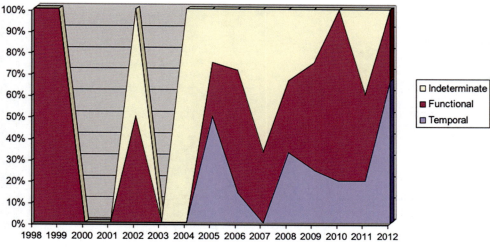

FIGURE 16   Number of non-trivial publications – proportional

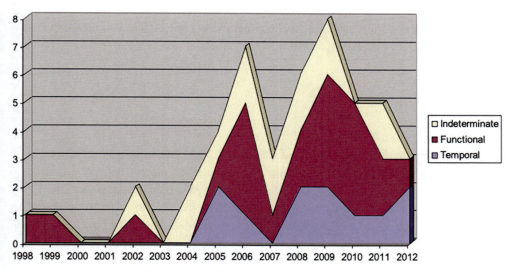

FIGURE 17   Number of non-trivial publications – absolute

references overall. This can be illustrated in the following chart showing usage of each phrase in a large corpus of printed work.[43]

---

43   Source: Google Books Ngram Viewer, dataset 20090715, available at: http://books.google.com/ngrams/graph?content=jus+post+bellum&year_start=1990&year_end=2008&corpus=0&smoothing=0 last visited 10 October 2012. This represents the usage of "*jus post bellum*" over time within millions of printed books.
     For more on the use of bigram analysis of a large corpus of scanned materials, see Michel, Jean-Baptiste, et al., Quantitative Analysis of Culture Using Millions of Digitized

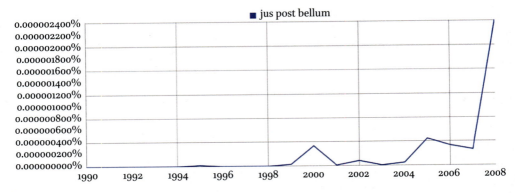

FIGURE 18 Increasing number of references to *jus post bellum*.

Indeed, the increasing number of references overall as well as the increasing number of substantive references indicate that *jus post bellum*'s utility for legal scholars is more than superficial. There is a risk, however, that with increased usage there will be an increased lack of clarity and consistency as to the meaning of the term. There are a number of works which are at least ambiguous as to the nature of the phrase.

D   Conclusion

There has been a steady expansion of references to *jus post bellum* in a variety of journals. With the expansion of references, there has been an increase of ambiguity, not a consolidation around a consensus definition. The trend in the less-legally focused dataset (SSRN articles) is away from an emphasis on functional aspects and towards temporal aspects. The overall trend is hard to discern, but for articles with more than a glancing reference to *jus post bellum* there seems to be an arc that went from a functional definition, towards, a temporal definition, and with a renewed legal interest back towards a more functional definition. Whether a consensus will be achieved, and what that consensus might be, is as yet unclear.

i   *Areas for Further Research*
The body of scholarship analyzed in this work does not cover all existing works, nor of course future works. There are, of course, various options for further research available now, and in the future.

Books, Science, 16 December 2010, available at http://www.sciencemag.org/content/331/6014/176.

For a researcher wishing to pursue a similar methodology but use a more comprehensive analysis, the datasets identified, researched, and evaluated but not uploaded into the database from Google Scholar could be gathered, included in the same database used for this work or a similar work, and further analyzed. Broadening the data analyzed would result in a more reliable analysis and allow the researcher to draw more robust conclusions. The Google Scholar material would broaden the amount of material considerably. Greater analysis of material within monographs, edited volumes, and other published work would be valuable. On the other end, analysis of material outside the scholarly sphere, such as news reports or communications for practitioners attempting to apply the law to guide a situation from armed conflict to peace would also be extremely interesting. The material analyzed could also be expanded by following the relevant citations within the materials already analyzed.

To keep the data fresh, the existing datasets or additional datasets could be updated, either periodically or an ongoing basis. Many research tools allow the automatic notification of new works which match a particular search. It will be valuable to see if current trends continue.

In addition, it would be very interesting to get a better map of the importance of different works, and weight the empirical analysis accordingly. For example, the number of times an SSRN article is viewed or downloaded could be incorporated. The impact of particular journals could be evaluated.[44] Alternatively, the weight given to various articles could be qualitatively (if perhaps subjectively) analyzed, either by a single scholar or through an open model with online input.

The Jus Post Bellum Virtual Research Environment[45] (hereinafter "Jus Post Bellum VRE,") is the online database which served as a central research tool and scholarship repository for this work. The Jus Post Bellum VRE could be the foundation of a published critical bibliography of *jus post bellum*, as well as an ongoing, interactive *jus post bellum* critical bibliography—continually updated for the use of scholars.

Finally, more generally, similar research (on terms other than *jus post bellum*) could build upon the research recorded in this work, potentially even using the

---

[44] *See e.g.* the Impact Factor of the Washington and Lee University School of Law Most-Cited Legal Periodicals, available at http://law.wlu.edu/library/mostcited/method.asp (last visited 10 October 2012) or the Journal Citation Reports, available at http://thomsonreuters.com/products_services/science/science_products/a-z/journal_citation_reports/ (last visited 10 October 2012).

[45] This online database or "virtual research environment" is currently hosted at https://vre.leidenuniv.nl/vre/jpb/definitions/default.aspx.

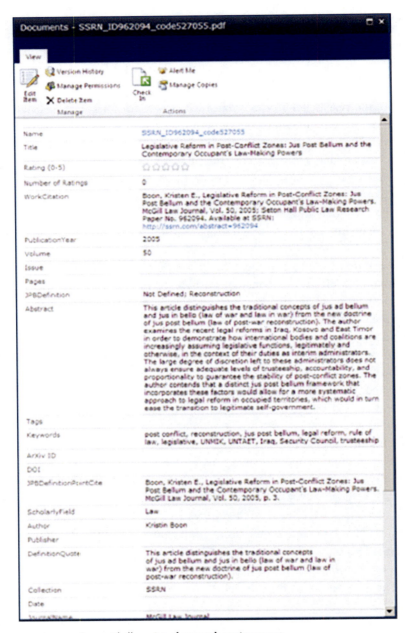

FIGURE 19 *Jus post bellum* virtual research environment

Jus Post Bellum VRE as a template. Research on *jus post bellum* would be furthered by doing an analysis of the contemporary literature on related terms. More generally, this sort of empirical analysis of contemporary literature could be used more frequently in scholarship to evaluate definitional ambiguity.

ii *Implementing Further Research*

Many of the areas for further research described above could be implemented through extending the Jus Post Bellum VRE. As can be seen in the screenshot above, articles can be checked in and checked out for the purposes of editing the associated metadata. Additionally, it is possible for multiple users to rate individual articles.

The author hopes that others will find the Jus Post Bellum VRE useful. He would greatly welcome the collaboration of scholars and practitioners interested in *jus post bellum*, with feedback on the research thus far, with respect to the Jus Post Bellum VRE's design for research going forward, and with respect to extending and repurposing the Jus Post Bellum VRE for additional research projects.

This work has posed answers to the questions "what is *'jus post bellum'*" and "why use the term *'jus post bellum'*" in a manner that opens further avenues for research rather than close the questions with a "definitive" answer. There is no consensus definition for *jus post bellum* with respect to the emphasis on functional or temporal aspects. Accordingly, the reasons why scholars and practitioners use the term *'jus post bellum'* varies.

The author suggests that a *jus post bellum* solution that explicitly focuses on the goal of the transition to sustainable peace is preferable going forward, given the opportunity cost of not focusing on that goal and adopting what might be called a simply nominal approach to categorizing law. Regardless of whether those using the term agree with this suggestion, it is imperative for the term to be explicitly defined with respect to functional or temporal emphasis. This should clarify the debate going forward, and assist the community using the term arrive at a consensus.

PART 2

Substance and Promise: The Utility and Potential of Focusing on the Goal of Just and Sustainable Peace

CHAPTER 6

Jus Post Bellum in the Context of International and Non-International Armed Conflict

A   Introduction

One important dimension that needs explicit exploration is the differences and commonalities between *jus post bellum* in two types of armed conflict: international armed conflict and non-international armed conflict. "Armed conflict" as a standard replacement for the term "war" originates with the Geneva Conventions of 1949. The Pictet Commentary to the First Geneva Convention of 1949 is clear that substituting "armed conflict" in place of "war" was intentionally done to ensure that States do not attempt to deny the applicability of the law by, for example, claiming that they are engaged only in a police action, rather than a war.[1]

These two categories, international armed conflict and non-international armed conflict, are the two dominant concepts that structure thinking about armed conflict. The concepts are well-understood in the field of international humanitarian law, but can cause confusion without precise definition. The clearest term used in the Geneva Conventions of 1949 is, for non-international armed conflicts: "armed conflict not of an international character."[2] The explanation of armed conflicts of an international character (that is, international armed conflict) is as follows:

> [a]ll cases of declared war or of any other armed conflict which may arise between two or more of the High Contracting Parties, even if the state of war is not recognized by one of them. The Convention shall also apply to all cases of partial or total occupation of the territory of a High Contracting Party, even if the said occupation meets with no armed resistance.[3]

---

[1] The Geneva Conventions of 12 August 1949: Commentary (Vol.I) – Geneva Convention For the Amelioration of the Condition of the Wounded and Sick in Armed Forces in the Field by Pictet, Jean S. (1952), Chapter I General Provisions, p.27 Article 2 – Application of the Convention, p.32.
[2] See, e.g., Common Article 3 of each of the Geneva Conventions of 1949.
[3] Common Article 2 of each of the Geneva Conventions of 1949.

The actual wording of above suggests a distinction not normally drawn between international armed conflict ("[a]ll cases of declared war or of any other armed conflict which may arise between two or more of the High Contracting Parties, even if the state of war is not recognized by one of them") and occupation ("shall also apply"). It is clear that the Geneva Conventions, and thus International Humanitarian Law, apply to declared war or any other armed conflict as well as occupation. Further, Additional Protocol II explains that what is normally described as "International Armed Conflict" "include[s] armed conflicts in which peoples are fighting against colonial domination and alien occupation and against racist régimes in the exercise of their right of self-determination[.]"[4] The following sections will first discuss the traditional area of distinguishing International Armed Conflict from Non-International Armed Conflict for *jus in bello*, then for *jus ad bellum*, before turning to *jus post bellum*.

B   *Jus In Bello* in IAC and NIAC

This section does not intend to outline international humanitarian law/*jus in bello* in general—this has been done in an introductory manner in Chapter 2.A. The focus of this section is to emphasize that in contemporary law, it is clear that both International Armed Conflicts and Non-International Armed Conflicts are regulated by *jus in bello*.

The purported origins of *jus in bello* purely in International Armed Conflict, as opposed to Non-International Armed Conflict, is based in the early positivist stance that international law regulates only states. The longer Just War Tradition was not so limited. One need merely look at the writings of Francisco de Victoria's *De Indis et De Jure Belli*[5] regarding the law of nations or the trial of King Charles I of England for violations of the law of war during the two civil wars during his reign to complicate the overly-neat picture of progression from *jus in bello* only applying to International Armed Conflict before it was purportedly extended for the first time to Non-International Armed Conflict in Common Article 3 of the Geneva Conventions of 1949. Hugo Grotius discusses the idea of private and mercenary wars. Emer de Vattel argued that a sovereign must observe the laws of war in the case of open rebellion. Francis Lieber's codification of the laws of war occurred during the U.S. Civil War. Nonetheless,

---

4   APII, Article 1.
5   De Vitoria, Francisco. Francisci de Victoria De Indis et De ivre belli relectiones. No. 7. Carnegie Institution of Washington, 1917.

given the dominant positivist stance of international law and the primitive state of human rights law, Common Article 3 is rightly celebrated as a turning point in the formalization and universalization of the regulation of the conduct of Non-International Armed Conflict (i.e., NIAC *jus in bello*).

Common Article 3 is often described as a mini-convention, meant to provide a baseline standard for all armed conflict.[6] Literally read, it applies only to "armed conflict not of an international character occurring in the territory of one of the High Contracting Parties" not all armed conflict, but given the universal ratification of the Geneva Conventions of 1949 there is no real territorial bar and it has been generally recognized as customary international law for all armed conflicts. It protects "Persons taking no active part in the hostilities" and obliges each party to the conflict to treat such persons humanely, specifically prohibiting a short list of inhumane conduct.[7]

In order to establish the existence of an International Armed Conflict, the threshold of violence is thus very low—the first shot fired downrange can suffice, or no shots at all in the case of occupation or declared war.[8] The critical element is that the armed conflict must be between two or more states. For a Non-International Armed Conflict, differing thresholds apply depending upon whether Common Article 3 or Additional Protocol II applies. Common Article 3 has a lower threshold, requiring a minimum level of intensity, and requiring the non-state armed groups to possess organized armed forces, for example, command structure and ability to sustain military operations.[9] The protections of Common Article 3 were substantially extended for a certain set of Non-International Armed Conflicts with Additional Protocol II. Additional

---

6 For more on the history leading to the creation of Common Article 3, see Elder, David A. "Historical Background of Common Article 3 of the Geneva Convention of 1949, The." Case W. Res. J. Int'l L. 11 (1979): 37.
7 (a) violence to life and person, in particular murder of all kinds, mutilation, cruel treatment and torture;
(b) taking of hostages;
(c) outrages upon personal dignity, in particular humiliating and degrading treatment;
(d) the passing of sentences and the carrying out of executions without previous judgment pronounced by a regularly constituted court affording all the judicial guarantees which are recognized as indispensable by civilized peoples.
8 But see *Nicaragua v. United States of America* [1986] ICJ Rep 14, [195] regarding "mere frontier incidents": ("The Court sees no reason to deny that, in customary law, the prohibition of armed attacks may apply to the sending by a State of armed bands to the territory of another State, if such an operation, because of its scale and effects, would have been classified as an armed attack rather than as a mere frontier incident had it been carried out by regular armed forces.")
9 ICTY, Appeals Chamber, *Tadic*, 2 October 1995.

Protocol II requires the thresholds of intensity and organization required by Common Article 3, and additionally:

> shall apply to all armed conflicts which are not covered by Article 1 of the Protocol Additional to the Geneva Conventions of 12 August 1949, and relating to the Protection of Victims of International Armed Conflicts (Protocol I) and which take place in the territory of a High Contracting Party between its armed forces and dissident armed forces or other organized armed groups which, under responsible command, exercise such control over a part of its territory as to enable them to carry out sustained and concerted military operations and to implement this Protocol.[10]

Unlike Common Article 3, the threshold for Additional Protocol II also requires that it is not of the character of the armed conflicts described in Article 1 Additional Protocol I, that a state's armed forces are party to the conflict, and that the non-state party's armed group exercise control over territory in a manner that enables them to carry out sustained and concerted military operations and to implement Additional Protocol II.

In addition to the four Geneva Conventions of 1949 and the two Additional Protocols of 1977, there are a host of additional treaties, many detailed in Section *Introduction, Exploration of Sister Terms, Jus in bello* above. The two Additional Protocols of 1977 continue not only the Geneva Conventions of 1949 but the Hague Conventions of 1899 and 1907 in restricting the means and methods of warfare, including specific rules that apply to demilitarized zones and non-defended areas.

There are also treaties that restrict weapons that are part of *jus in bello* both with respect to non-international armed conflict and international armed conflict. These treaties have already also been examined to some extent in Section *Introduction, Exploration of Sister Terms, Jus in bello* above. The trend is to make clear or provide means by which these treaties apply to non-international armed conflicts as well as international armed conflicts. Protocol on Prohibitions or Restrictions on the Use of Mines, Booby-Traps and Other Devices (Protocol II), adopted 10 October 1980, explicitly applied to non-international armed conflicts:

> 2. This Protocol shall apply, in addition to situations referred to in Article 1 of this Convention, to situations referred to in Article 3 common to the Geneva Conventions of 12 August 1949. This Protocol shall not apply to

---

10   AP I, Art. 1.1.

situations of internal disturbances and tensions, such as riots, isolated and sporadic acts of violence and other acts of a similar nature, as not being armed conflicts.

3. In case of armed conflicts not of an international character occurring in the territory of one of the High Contracting Parties, each party to the conflict shall be bound to apply the prohibitions and restrictions of this Protocol.[11]

Similarly, under the 1995 Protocol on Blinding Laser Weapons (Protocol IV)[12] non-international armed conflict was covered, and ultimately the 1980 Convention on Prohibitions or Restrictions on the Use of Certain Conventional Weapons which may be Deemed to be Excessively Injurious or to have Indiscriminate Effects[13] was amended in 2001 to cover non-international armed conflicts.[14]

In addition, the Convention for the Protection of Cultural Property in the Event of Armed Conflict specifically applies to non-international armed conflict with regards to "respect for cultural property."[15] This means the bulk of the convention on its own terms is applicable in non-international armed conflicts. The Second Protocol to the Hague Convention of 1954 for the Protection of Cultural Property in the Event of Armed Conflict extends the entire Convention to non-international armed conflicts.[16]

---

11 Convention on Prohibitions or Restrictions on the Use of Certain Conventional Weapons which may be Deemed to be Excessively Injurious or to have Indiscriminate Effect (United Nations [UN]) 1342 UNTS 137, UN Reg No I-22495, Protocol II Protocol on Prohibitions or Restrictions on the Use of Mines, Booby-Traps and Other Devices.
12 1995 Protocol on Blinding Laser Weapons (Protocol IV; adopted 13 October 1995, entered into force 30 July 1998; 2024 UNTS 163).
13 Convention on Prohibitions or Restrictions on the Use of Certain Conventional Weapons which may be Deemed to be Excessively Injurious or to have Indiscriminate Effect (United Nations [UN]) 1342 UNTS 137, UN Reg No I-22495, Art.1.
14 Second Review Conference of the States Parties to the Convention on Prohibitions or Restrictions on the Use of Certain Conventional Weapons which may be Deemed to be Excessively Injurious or to have Indiscriminate Effects – Final Document, Part II Final Declaration.
15 Convention for the Protection of Cultural Property in the Event of Armed Conflict (United Nations Educational, Scientific and Cultural Organization [UNESCO]) 249 UNTS 240, UN Reg No I-3511, Ch.VI Scope of Application of the Convention, Art.19.
16 Second Protocol to The Hague Convention of 1954 for the Protection of Cultural Property in the Event of Armed Conflict (United Nations Educational, Scientific and Cultural Organization [UNESCO]) 2253 UNTS 172, UN Reg No A-3511.

International Humanitarian Law has mostly been described in this section with reference to treaty law, but of course, it also exists as customary international law. Customary International Humanitarian Law with respect to non-international armed conflict is somewhat controversial, particularly with respect to the role of role and status of combatants. Nonetheless, the jurisprudence of international criminal tribunals, the efforts of jurists such as Theodor Meron,[17] and notably the International Committee of the Red Cross's customary international humanitarian law study[18] have developed the basic argument with respect to the application of *jus in bello* rules in international armed conflicts to *jus in bello* in non-international armed conflicts:

> Indeed, elementary considerations of humanity and common sense make it preposterous that the use by States of weapons prohibited in armed conflicts between themselves be allowed when States try to put down rebellion by their own nationals on their own territory. What is inhumane, and consequently proscribed, in international wars cannot but be inhumane and inadmissible in civil strife.[19]

C   *Jus Ad Bellum* in IAC and NIAC

"*Jus ad bellum*" is a phrase normally used only with respect to international armed conflict. There is no prohibition of rebellion (nor of putting down rebellion) as such in international law. In contrast, Article 2(4) of the United Nations Charter famously commands:

> All Members shall refrain in their international relations from the threat or use of force against the territorial integrity or political independence of any state, or in any other manner inconsistent with the Purposes of the United Nations.[20]

---

17 Meron, Theodor. "The continuing role of custom in the formation of international humanitarian law." *American Journal of International Law* (1996): 238–249.

18 Henckaerts, Jean-Marie, Louise Doswald-Beck, and Carolin Alvermann, eds.*Customary International Humanitarian Law: Volume 1, Rules*. Vol. 1. Cambridge University Press, 2005.

19 ICTY, *The Prosecutor v. Duško Tadić aka "Dule,"* Decision on the Defence Motion for Interlocutory Appeal on Jurisdiction, Appeals Chamber, 2 October 1995, Case No. IT-94-1-AR72, § 119.

20 Charter of the United Nations (done at San Francisco, United States, on 26 June 1945) (United Nations [UN]) 1 UNTS XVI, 892 UNTS 119, 59 Stat 1031, TS 993, 3 Bevans 1153, 145 BSP 805, Ch.I Purposes and Principles, Art.2(4).

Thus, *jus ad bellum* is sometimes now declared to be *jus contra bellum*, restricting resort to force in international armed conflict to self-defence or United Nations-authorized use of force. That said, a broader view of *jus ad bellum* has implications for the treatment of non-international armed conflict.

International law is not simply mute on the issue of the (*jus ad bellum*) issue of the resort to the use of force amounting to an armed conflict when both parties are not states, particularly in the context of decolonization and self-determination. Indeed, the context of decolonization has helped to redraw the boundaries of international armed conflict and non-international armed conflict. The concept of self-determination can be found at least as far back as the late 18th century, with the United States of America proclaiming the principle in the Declaration of Independence[21] and was further promoted by the leaders of the (First) French Republic. The concept was further developed after the First World War, and found truly modern expression in the United Nations Charter and subsequent practice. Three chapters of the United Nations Charter are of particular interest: Chapter XI: Declaration regarding Non-Self-Governing Territories; Chapter XII: International Trusteeship System; and Chapter XIII: The Trusteeship Council.

Self-determination is a right enjoyed by, at a minimum, people under colonial rule. There is a legal obligation not to use force to frustrate that right. The keystone for this clarification of this area of law is the Declaration on Principles of International Law concerning Friendly Relations and Co-operation among States in Accordance with the Charter of the United Nations, annexed to United Nations General Assembly Resolution 2625, widely known as the "Friendly Relations Declaration" of 1970.[22] Similarly, the 1973 United Nations General Assembly Resolution 3103 on the Basic Principles of the Legal Status of the Combatants Struggling against Colonial and Alien Domination and Racist Regimes:

> [t]he armed conflicts involving the struggle of peoples against colonial and alien domination and racist regimes are to be regarded as international armed conflicts in the sense of the 1949 Geneva Conventions, and the legal status envisaged to apply to the combatants in the 1949 Geneva Conventions and other international instruments is to apply to the

---

21 Declaration of Independence of the United States of America (United States) 51 BSP 847.
22 Declaration on Principles of International Law Concerning Friendly Relations and Cooperation among States in Accordance with the Charter of the United Nations (United Nations [UN]) UN Doc A/RES/2625(XXV), Annex.

persons engaged in armed struggle against colonial and alien domination and racist regimes[23]

This was given additional weight by Additional Protocol I, as previously described.[24] It says in Article 1, paragraphs 3 and 4:

> 3. This Protocol, which supplements the Geneva Conventions of 12 August 1949 for the protection of war victims, shall apply in the situations referred to in Article 2 common to those Conventions.
>
> 4. The situations referred to in the preceding paragraph include armed conflicts in which peoples are fighting against colonial domination and alien occupation and against racist régimes in the exercise of their right of self-determination, as enshrined in the Charter of the United Nations and the Declaration on Principles of International Law concerning Friendly Relations and Co-operation among States in accordance with the Charter of the United Nations.[25]

While Additional Protocol I governs *jus in bello* concerns, its emphasis on the right of self-determination again complicates the *jus ad bellum* concerns regarding the right to enter into armed conflict, and the recharacterization of certain armed conflicts as international armed conflicts rather than non-international armed conflicts.

While this section focuses on the contemporary *jus ad bellum* in international armed conflict and non-international armed conflict, later sections will discuss the long history of *jus ad bellum*. There was nothing like the prohibition on the use of force in Article 2 of the United Nations Charter in the time of Hugo Grotius, but there were still clear *jus ad bellum* limits. Grotius wrote that it was not "right to take up arms in order to weaken a power which, if it becomes too great, may be a source of danger" for example.[26]

---

23   United Nations General Assembly Resolution 3103 (XXVIII) on the basic principles of the legal status of the combatants struggling against colonial and alien domination and racist regimes (United Nations General Assembly [UNGA]) UN Doc A/RES/3103(XXVIII), para. 3.
24   Protocol Additional to the Geneva Conventions of 12 August 1949, and relating to the Protection of Victims of International Armed Conflicts (Protocol I) (adopted 8 June 1977, entered into force 7 December 1978) 1125 UNTS 3.
25   Geneva Conventions Additional Protocol I (1977).
26   H Grotius De iure belli ac pacis, vol II, Ch l, sec XVII.

It is also worth looking at domestic law approaches to armed conflict. In the United States, in theory, native tribes were protected from attack, except when Congress authorized a just and lawful war against them.

> The utmost good faith shall always be observed towards the Indians; their land and property shall never be taken from them without their consent; and in their property, rights and liberty, they never shall be invaded or disturbed, unless in just and lawful wars authorized by Congress; but laws founded in justice and humanity shall from time to time be made, for preventing wrongs being done to them, and for preserving peace and friendship with them.[27]

Whether armed conflict with native groups would constitute an international armed conflict or non-international armed conflict is somewhat anachronistic, although the issue of an international legal personality and legitimacy for national liberation movement has 20th-century echoes.

This section was not intended to exhaust the issue of *jus ad bellum*, but rather to introduce *jus ad bellum* with respect to international armed conflict and non-international armed conflict and set the stage for a discussion of *jus post bellum* in the context of international armed conflict and non-international armed conflict.

D *Jus Post Bellum* in IAC and NIAC

What *jus post bellum* looks like in international armed conflict and non-international armed conflict depends on what one means by *jus post bellum*. As described above, there are two major ways to approach *jus post bellum* and its relationship to its sister terms, as well as a hybrid approach. With the temporal approach, *jus ad bellum*, governs the beginning of armed conflict, *jus in bello* governs the armed conflict from beginning to end, and *jus post bellum* governs directly after armed conflict is terminated, in effect restricted to early peace. With the functional approach, *jus post bellum* applies to the entire function of transition from armed conflict to peace, even if some of that function occurs during armed conflict. Taken together, there is also the possibility of a hybrid approach, which is defined both by time and function, rooted temporally

---

27   An Act to provide for the government of the territory northwest of the river Ohio. The Ordinance of July 13, 1787 (1 Stat. 52). Available at http://avalon.law.yale.edu/18th_century/nworder.asp last visited 24 March 2015.

in the period of transition from conflict and the achievement of a positive peace, and functionally restricted to the construction of positive peace.

1 Complications

Addressing *jus post bellum* with respect to international and non-international armed conflict is complicated by at least three factors, which will be described before looking at the subject matter placed within a general schematic representation of the subject matter of *jus post bellum*. Each complication will be addressed now in turn.

First, the status of an armed conflict as a non-international armed conflict or international armed conflict is not static. An international armed conflict can be transformed into a non-international armed conflict in practice. The reverse is also true. Afghanistan's recent history provides a good example of this. In Afghanistan, there was arguably a non-international armed conflict between the forces later characterized as the "Northern Alliance" and the Taliban government, although one could argue with the requirement of sufficient ongoing intensity. The best understanding is that this then became an "internationalized" international armed conflict between the United States/NATO conflict with Afghanistan until the Taliban were overthrown. Once a new government was established and widely recognized, the armed conflict between the government and the Taliban (as well as other organized armed groups), the armed conflict is best characterized as a non-international armed conflict. One could argue whether Pakistan's alleged support for organized armed groups "internationalizes" the conflict again. Similarly, the long civil war in Sudan was a non-international armed conflict until South Sudan seceded, any further armed conflict between Sudan and those who now constitute the government of South Sudan would then be characterized as an international armed conflict.

Second, non-international armed conflicts and international armed conflicts can co-exist at the same time and place (a "mixed conflict") or in ways that influence each other. Pakistan arguably provides an example of this. The United States asserts it is in a non-international armed conflict with organized armed groups based at least in part in Pakistan. Formally, the repeated use of force by the United States in the territory of Pakistan may satisfy the requirements for an international armed conflict, if the government of Pakistan has not consented to the use of force. While related, and in fact springing from the same use of force, as a legal matter the (potential) non-international armed conflict and international armed conflict must be analysed separately.

Third, non-international armed conflict may be increasingly less limited to one state territory per conflict, and non-international armed conflicts may be more difficult to separate than previously. Organized armed groups party to non-international armed conflicts may have no inherent need to remain in a single territory, and indeed crossing territories or being based across territories can provide advantages or be necessary for the survival of organized armed groups. The Taliban and the Haqqani Network are examples of organized armed groups straddling the Afghani-Pakistan border. The Islamic State is operating in both Iraqi and Syrian territory. The various armed groups in the Great Lakes region of Africa do not have great respect for national boundaries.

2 Prohibitions and Facilitations

As a general note, while *jus ad bellum* and *jus in bello* generally but not exclusively consist of prohibitions, *jus post bellum* has both prohibitions and facilitative functions. *Jus ad bellum, jus in bello*, and *jus post bellum* will now be briefly examined with respect to prohibitions, obligations, facilitative opportunities.

The general rule of contemporary *jus ad bellum* is prohibition, with limited exceptions for the use of force in international affairs for self-defence and United Nations Security Council authorized actions. Arguably the inclusion of the option for collective security mechanisms and Security Council resolutions are facilitative, but the general tendency is prohibition. Those agreements themselves can create specific obligations dependent on the particular situation.

Jus in bello is usually phrased in the form of prohibition regarding the particular uses of force, such as prohibiting attacks against civilians, indiscriminate attacks, disproportionate attacks, attacks that create unnecessary suffering, or prohibited means and methods. *Jus in bello*/international humanitarian law/law of armed conflict does, however, include affirmative obligations, such as care for those rendered *hors de combat* and for prisoners of war, and obligations on occupiers. Interestingly, while these affirmative obligations are normally squarely placed as part of *jus in bello*, they often involve obligations that extend beyond active combat—occupations have no inherent time limit, and obligations to prisoners of war can take years to discharge. While not obligatory, the possibility of *jus in bello* facilitative activity like exchanges of prisoners of war is certainly possible.

3 More Procedural Aspects
a) Treaty and Agreement Law

As discussed above, this author finds the hybrid functional approach the better reading of *jus post bellum*, allowing a full incorporation of *jus terminatio* and *lex pacificatoria* into the concept and keeping the focus on the function of the law and noting the important but sometimes arbitrary temporal delimitation between the end of an armed conflict and early peace. Using this approach, one formal distinction that can be made is the distinction between an armed conflict terminating through a peace treaty (or series of peace treaties) in the case of an international armed conflict, and a peace agreement (or series of peace agreements) in the case of a non-international armed conflict. The term "peace treaty" is generally reserved for agreements not signed by non-state organized armed groups, whereas the more general term "peace agreement" can include peace treaties but is used more frequently for agreements that are not technically treaties because they include non-state groups (other than intergovernmental organizations) in the agreement.

In an international armed conflict, during *lex pacificatoria* or *jus terminatio*, the application of the Vienna Convention on the Law of Treaties[28] and associated customary international law of treaties is a critical facilitative law that is a key part of *jus post bellum*. The customary international law of state recognition may come into play if there has been an attempted or successful secession or annexation, although secession may be more likely in (what started as) a non-international armed conflict. The customary international law of state recognition is also important if a government has been overthrown or if an occupying power attempts to install a puppet government. The recognition of states and governments applies to states, but can also come into play for intergovernmental organizations as well.

b)   Amnesty and *Aut Dedere Aut Judicare*

One tension that may come into play in the transition from armed conflict to peace, perhaps particularly in international armed conflict, is the obligation that exists to prosecute or extradite for prosecution the alleged perpetration of certain crimes. The fight against impunity that creates this tension, often at the heart of the "peace vs. justice" debate, may complicate the short-term transition to peace but is often helpful to make the transition to peace successful in the long run.[29] This is often described using the Latin term *aut dedere aut judicare*, although it is common now to tamp down the demand to prosecute to merely "submit for prosecution" because of varied responsibilities and procedures at the domestic level and the presumption of innocence in criminal law.

---

28   United Nations, *Vienna Convention on the Law of Treaties*, 23 May 1969, (Entry into force: 27 January 1980) United Nations Treaty Series, vol. 1155, p. 331.

29   *See e.g.* Darehshori, Sara. *Selling justice short: why accountability matters for peace*. Human Rights Watch, 2009.

Given actual state practice and demonstrated opinio juris, one cannot generally assert there is a yet a general customary duty to prosecute or extradite for all alleged international criminal law violations. This is explored in greater detail in Chapter 6.b.2.b *infra*.

c)   The Responsibility to Protect

The Responsibility to Protect doctrine[30] is one of general application as a matter of international law and policy. It does not require armed conflict of any sort for its application. Rather, as part of the "just cause," it requires either large-scale loss of life or "ethnic cleansing."[31]

The Responsibility to Protect doctrine includes the Responsibility to Prevent, Responsibility to Respond, and the Responsibility to Rebuild. The Responsibility to Prevent and the Responsibility to Rebuild are more tightly tied to *jus post bellum*. In comparison with the Responsibility to Respond, these aspects of the Responsibility to Protect (Prevent and Rebuild) apply more generally to international armed conflict and non-international armed conflict, but are probably still envisaged to apply more to non-international armed conflict. This subject is treated in more detail in Chapter 6.B.2.b *infra*.

4   *Mixed Procedural and Substantive Aspects*

Reviewing the schematic depiction of examples of law and norms regarding the transition to peace reproduced above, most of the material under the first column, titled "Procedural" has been addressed in this section (*Jus post bellum* in IAC and NIAC). The Vienna Convention on the Law of Treaties and the customary law of treaties has been briefly examined (a very general/global law), as opposed to intrastate/domestic peace negotiations (which can be very specific/local). Both are part of the *lex pacificatoria* or *jus terminatio*. Similarly, the general laws and norms regarding the recognition of states and government

---

30   See International Commission on Intervention and State Sovereignty, *The Responsibility to Protect: Report of the International Commission on Intervention and State Sovereignty* (International Development Research Centre 2001) 39–45; see also United Nations Secretary General's High-Level Panel on Threats, Challenges and Change, *A More Secure World: Our Shared Responsibility, Report of the High-level Panel on Threats, Challenges and Change* (2004) 65–7; United Nations General Assembly, *2005 World Summit Outcome*, UN Doc. A/60/L.1 (15 September 2005) paras 138–9; United Nations General Assembly, *Implementing the Responsibility to Protect: Report of the Secretary-General*, UN Doc. A/63/677 (12 January 2009) para. 48.

31   International Commission on Intervention and State Sovereignty, *The Responsibility to Protect: Report of the International Commission on Intervention and State Sovereignty* (International Development Research Centre 2001) p. XII.

apply as a general matter, and the specific case-by-case state recognition and government recognition on the local matter also makes law and norms that apply to the transition to peace. Also discussed above—the treaty and customary international law regarding the prosecution or extradition of individuals accused of certain international crimes, in tension with local amnesty laws. Finally, on the procedural end of law and norms regarding the transition to peace, the "Responsibility to Protect" doctrine was discussed.

Moving to law and norms that are a mixture of procedural and substance, several issues are worth particular consideration in distinguishing between international armed conflict and non-international armed conflict. These include United Nations Security Council Resolutions, customary international law on post-conflict administration, the existence of global judicial bodies with jurisprudence relating to *jus post bellum*, regional judicial bodies jurisprudence relating to *jus post bellum*, multilateral disarmament treaties, specific disarmament/demobilization reintegration efforts, and domestic judicial bodies jurisprudence relating to *jus post bellum*.

The authority of United Nations Security Council resolutions derives from the United Nations Charter, particularly Chapters VI and VII.[32] The Charter itself derives its legal status not only from the general force of treaty law as an almost universally ratified treaty, but from Article 103 of the Charter, which states "In the event of a conflict between the obligations of the Members of the United Nations under the present Charter and their obligations under any other international agreement, their obligations under the present Charter shall prevail."[33] Article 25 obliges Members of the United Nations to carry out the decisions of the Security Council.[34] While the United Nations Security Council was not intended to function as a legislative body, it has wide powers on matters touching upon peace and security, and the restraints on its acting in a tailored fashion and to avoid *ultra vires* action are more practical and political than through a formal institutional check.

The United Nations Security Council has issued a number of resolutions of relevance regarding the transition from armed conflict to peace, including resolutions that have applicability outside a particular territorial situation.

---

32   United Nations, Charter of the United Nations, 24 October 1945, 1 UNTS XVI. Chapters that pertain to the powers of the Security Council (V, VI, VII, VIII, and XII), with Chapters VI and VII of the most relevance for resolutions.
33   United Nations, Charter of the United Nations, 24 October 1945, 1 UNTS XVI.
34   United Nations, Charter of the United Nations, 24 October 1945, 1 UNTS XVI, Art. 25.

United Nations Security Council Resolutions 1325[35] and 1889[36] are of particular note. In general terms, United Nations Security Council Resolution 1325 enunciates both procedural norms for the resolution of armed conflict and norms for the substance of peace agreements. With respect to procedural norms, see for example paragraph 1: "1. Urges Member States to ensure increased representation of women at all decision-making levels in national, regional and international institutions and mechanisms for the prevention, management, and resolution of conflict[.]"[37] With respect to substantive norms, see for example paragraph 8:

8. Calls on all actors involved, when negotiating and implementing peace agreements, to adopt a gender perspective, including, inter alia: (a) The special needs of women and girls during repatriation and resettlement and for rehabilitation, reintegration and post-conflict reconstruction; (b) Measures that support local women's peace initiatives and indigenous processes for conflict resolution, and that involve women in all of the implementation mechanisms of the peace agreements; (c) Measures that ensure the protection of and respect for human rights of women and girls, particularly as they relate to the constitution, the electoral system, the police and the judiciary[.][38]

United Nations Security Council Resolution 1889 also enunciates procedural norms for the resolution of armed conflict as well as substantive requirements in the post-conflict phase. With respect to procedural aspects of United Nations Security Council 1889, see for example, from the preambular language:

> Reiterating the need for the full, equal and effective participation of women at all stages of peace processes given their vital role in the prevention and resolution of conflict and peacebuilding, reaffirming the key role women can play in re-establishing the fabric of recovering society and stressing the need for their involvement in the development and implementation of post-conflict strategies in order to take into account their perspectives and needs, Expressing deep concern about the

---

35 UN Security Council, Security Council resolution 1325 (2000) [on women and peace and security], 31 October 2000, S/RES/1325 (2000).

36 UN Security Council, Security Council resolution 1889 (2009) [on women and peace and security], 5 October 2009, S/RES/1889 (2009).

37 UN Security Council, Security Council resolution 1325 (2000) [on women and peace and security], 31 October 2000, S/RES/1325 (2000).

38 UN Security Council, Security Council resolution 1325 (2000) [on women and peace and security], 31 October 2000, S/RES/1325 (2000).

under-representation of women at all stages of peace processes, particularly the very low numbers of women in formal roles in mediation processes and stressing the need to ensure that women are appropriately appointed at decision-making levels, as high level mediators, and within the composition of the mediators' teams, Remaining deeply concerned about the persistent obstacles to women's full involvement in the prevention and resolution of conflicts and participation in postconflict public life, as a result of violence and intimidation, lack of security and lack of rule of law, cultural discrimination and stigmatization, including the rise of extremist or fanatical views on women, and socio-economic factors including the lack of access to education, and in this respect, recognizing that the marginalization of women can delay or undermine the achievement of durable peace, security and reconciliation[.][39]

Further, United Nations Security Council Resolution 1889 states:

1. Urges Member States, international and regional organisations to take further measures to improve women's participation during all stages of peace processes, particularly in conflict resolution, post-conflict planning and peacebuilding, including by enhancing their engagement in political and economic decision-making at early stages of recovery processes, through inter alia promoting women's leadership and capacity to engage in aid management and planning, supporting women's organizations, and countering negative societal attitudes about women's capacity to participate equally;

[...]

Urges Member States to ensure gender mainstreaming in all post-conflict peacebuilding and recovery processes and sectors[.][40]

With respect to substantive aspects of United Nations Security Council Resolution 1889, see the language in the preamble and paragraph 10:

Expresses its intention, when establishing and renewing the mandates of United Nations missions, to include provisions on the promotion of gender equality and the empowerment of women in post-conflict situations, and requests the Secretary-General to continue, as appropriate, to appoint gender advisors and/or women-protection advisors to United

---

39 UN Security Council, Security Council resolution 1889 (2009) [on women and peace and security], 5 October 2009, S/RES/1889 (2009).
40 Ibid.

Nations missions and asks them, in cooperation with United Nations Country Teams, to render technical assistance and improved coordination efforts to address recovery needs of women and girls in postconflict situations;

[...]

10. Encourages Member States in post-conflict situations, in consultation with civil society, including women's organizations, to specify in detail women and girls' needs and priorities and design concrete strategies, in accordance with their legal systems, to address those needs and priorities, which cover inter alia support for greater physical security and better socio-economic conditions, through education, income generating activities, access to basic services, in particular health services, including sexual and reproductive health and reproductive rights and mental health, gender-responsive law enforcement and access to justice, as well as enhancing capacity to engage in public decision-making at all levels[.][41]

In addition to the United Nations Security Council Resolutions 1325 and 1889, there are international standards for peace agreements emerging from the United Nations.[42] The Secretaries-General of the United Nations have taken particular interest in this subject in recent decades.

Of course, in addition to United Nations Security Council resolutions and United Nations guidelines of general application, United Nations Security Council resolutions also can regulate specific transitions to peace. Rather than simply putting an end to conflict, they often attempt to establish future good governance—part of the transition to a just and sustainable peace. United Nations Security Council Resolution 1244[43] drew upon the Rambouillet Accords[44] to regulate the transition to peace in Kosovo. One can see similar regulation

---

41   Ibid.
42   See, e.g., UN Press Release SG/SM/7257, Secretary-General Comments on Guidelines Given to Envoys (10 December 1999) (guidelines on human rights and peace negotiations); The Rule of Law and Transitional Justice in Conflict and Post-conflict Societies, Report of the Secretary General, UN Doc. S/2004/616 (including recommendations for negotiations, peace agreements, and Security Council mandates); Report of the Panel on United Nations Peace Operations [Brahimi Report], UN Doc. A/55/305-S/2000/809, 158 (mandating the UN's capacity to put conditions on peace agreements).
43   UN Security Council, *Security Council resolution 1244 (1999)* [*on the deployment of international civil and security presences in Kosovo*], 10 June 1999, S/RES/1244 (1999).
44   Rambouillet Accords: Interim Agreement for Peace and Self-Government in Kosovo, Feb. 23, 1999, UN Doc. S/1999/648, annex.

with the transition to peace in, for example, Cambodia,[45] elsewhere in the former Yugoslavia,[46] Liberia,[47] East Timor,[48] Afghanistan,[49] and Iraq.[50] Most of these examples cannot always be neatly categorized into international armed conflict or non-international armed conflict—Cambodia was largely a non-international armed conflict but had significant foreign involvement that may have internationalized it; the conflicts in the former Yugoslavia included organized armed groups, states, and organized armed conflict under some degree of control of states; Liberia's conflict was a non-international armed conflict with significant foreign involvement, East Timor may have amounted to a non-international armed conflict before independence, at which point any armed conflict would be an international armed conflict; and Afghanistan's history of conflict (as already detailed) is remarkably baroque.

The Security Council's role in the transition to peace in Liberia exemplifies the emphasis on future-oriented goals of good-governance; not simply focused on the cessation of armed conflict. The Security Council has passed a great number of resolutions on the UN Mission in Liberia (UNMIL) and the situation in Liberia between 2002 and 2016. These included Preliminary matters;[51]

---

45 E.g. UN Security Council, *Resolution 745 (1992) Adopted by the Security Council at its 3057th meeting, on 28 February 1992*, 28 February 1992, S/RES/745 (1992).

46 E.g. UN Security Council, *On Basic Agreement on the Region of Eastern Slavonia, Baranja and Western Sirmium between the Government of Croatia and the local Serb representatives Resolution 1023 (1995) Adopted by the Security Council at its 3596th meeting, on 22 November 1995*, 22 November 1995, S/RES/1023 (1995).

47 E.g. UN Security Council, *Resolution 788 (1992) Adopted by the Security Council at its 3138th meeting, on 19 November 1992*, 19 November 1992, S/RES/788 (1992).

48 E.g. UN Security Council, *Resolution 1277 (1999) Adopted by the Security Council at its 4074th meeting, on 30 November 1999*, 30 November 1999, S/RES/1277 (1999).

49 E.g. UN Security Council, *Security Council Resolution 1378 (2001) on the situation in Afghanistan*, 14 November 2001, S/RES/1378 (2001).

50 E.g. UN Security Council, *Security Council Resolution 1483 (2003) on the situation between Iraq and Kuwait*, 22 May 2003, S/RES/1483 (2003).

51 UN Security Council, *Security Council resolution 1408 (2002) [on the situation in Liberia]*, 6 May 2002, S/RES/1408 (2002); UN Security Council, *Security Council resolution 1458 (2003) [on the situation in Liberia]*, 28 January 2003, S/RES/1458 (2003); UN Security Council, *Security Council resolution 1343 (2001) [on the situation in Sierra Leone]*, 7 March 2001, S/RES/1343 (2001); UN Security Council, *Security Council resolution 1478 (2003) [on the situation in Liberia]*, 6 May 2003, S/RES/1478 (2003); UN Security Council, *Security Council resolution 1497 (2003) [on the situation in Liberia]*, 1 August 2003, S/RES/1497 (2003); UN Security Council, *Security Council resolution 1521 (2003) [on dissolution of the Security Council Committee established pursuant to Resolution 1343 (2001) concerning Liberia]*, 22 December 2003, S/RES/1521 (2003).

establishment of UNMIL;[52] continuing its mandate;[53] other matters, including targeted sanctions against Liberian President Charles Taylor and others.[54]

---

52   UN Security Council, *Security Council resolution 1509 (2003)* [*on establishment of the UN Mission in Liberia (UNMIL)*], 19 September 2003, S/RES/1509 (2003).

53   UN Security Council, *Security Council resolution 1836 (2008)* [*on extension of the mandate of the UN Mission in Liberia (UNMIL)*], 29 September 2008, S/RES/1836 (2008); UN Security Council, *Security Council resolution 1938 (2010)* [*on extension of the mandate of the UN Mission in Liberia (UNMIL)*], 15 September 2010, S/RES/1938 (2010); UN Security Council, *Security Council resolution 1885 (2009)* [*on extension of the mandate of the UN Mission in Liberia (UNMIL)*], 15 September 2009, S/RES/1885 (2009); UN Security Council, *Security Council resolution 2008 (2011)* [*on extension of the mandate of the UN Mission in Liberia (UNMIL) until 30 Sept. 2012*], 16 September 2011, S/RES/2008(2011); UN Security Council, *Security Council resolution 2066 (2012)* [*on extension of the mandate of the UN Mission in Liberia (UNMIL) until 30 Sept. 2013*], 17 September 2012, S/RES/2066 (2012); UN Security Council, *Security Council resolution 2176 (2014)* [*on extension of the mandate of the UN Mission in Liberia (UNMIL) until 31 Dec. 2014*], 15 September 2014, S/RES/2176 (2014); UN Security Council, *Security Council resolution 2190 (2014)* [*on extension of the mandate of the UN Mission in Liberia (UNMIL) until 30 Sept. 2015*], 15 December 2014, S/RES/2190 (2014); UN Security Council, *Security Council resolution 2215 (2015)* [*on the drawdown of the UN Mission in Liberia (UNMIL)*], 2 April 2015, S/RES/2215 (2015); UN Security Council, *Security Council resolution 2239 (2015)* [*on extension of the mandate of the UN Mission in Liberia (UNMIL) until 30 Sept. 2016*], 17 September 2015; UN Security Council, *Security Council resolution 2308 (2016)* [*on extension of the mandate of the UN Mission in Liberia (UNMIL) until 31 Dec. 2016*], 17 September 2015, S/RES/2308 (2016).

54   UN Security Council, *Security Council resolution 1532 (2004)* [*on preventing former Liberian President Charles Taylor, his immediate family members and senior officials of the former Taylor regime from using misappropriated funds and property*], 12 March 2004, S/RES/1532 (2004); UN Security Council, *Security Council resolution 1549 (2004)* [*on re-establishment of the Panel of Experts to monitor fulfilling the conditions for the lifting of sanctions*], 17 June 2004, S/RES/1549 (2004); UN Security Council, *Security Council resolution 1561 (2004)* [*on UNMIL*], 17 September 2004, S/RES/1561 (2004); UN Security Council, *Security Council resolution 1579 (2004)* [*on the Situation in Liberia and West Africa*], 21 December 2004, S/RES/1579 (2004); UN Security Council, *Security Council resolution 1607 (2005)* [*on the Situation in Liberia and West Africa*], 21 June 2005, S/RES/1607 (2005); UN Security Council, *Security Council resolution 1626 (2005)* [*The situation in Liberia*], 19 September 2005, S/RES/1626 (2005); UN Security Council, *Security Council resolution 1638 (2005)* [*The situation in Liberia*], 11 November 2005, S/RES/1638 (2005); UN Security Council, *Security Council resolution 1647 (2005)* [*Liberia renews the measures on arms and travel imposed by paragraphs 2 and 4 of resolution 1521 (2003) for a further period of 12 months*], 20 December 2005, S/RES/1647 (2005); UN Security Council, *Security Council resolution 1667 (2006)* [*The situation in Liberia*], 31 March 2006, S/RES/1667 (2006); UN Security Council, *Security Council resolution 1683 (2006)* [*The Situation in Liberia*], 13 June 2006, S/RES/1683 (2006); UN Security Council, *Security Council resolution 1688 (2006)* [*Sierra Leone*], 16 June 2006, S/RES/1688 (2006); UN Security Council, *Resolution 1689 (2006) The Situation in Liberia*, 20 June 2006, S/RES/1689 (2006); UN Security Council, *Resolution 1694 (2006) The Situation in Liberia*, 13 July 2006, S/RES/1694 (2006); UN Security Council, *Security Council resolution 1712 (2006)* [*Liberia*], 29 September 2006, S/RES/1712 (2006); UN Security Council, *Resolution 1731*

It is worth noting that a strictly temporal approach to *jus post bellum* would necessarily cut off early United Nations Security Council resolutions that occurred during armed conflict.[55] Similarly, a definition of *jus post bellum* that focused on backwards-looking criminal justice measures and not forward-looking establishment of a just and sustainable peace (particularly good governance) would overlook some of the most important regulation in the transition from armed conflict in Liberia.

As Aboagye and Rupiya note in their 2005 work on democratic governance and security sector reform in Liberia, in the previous 15 years more than half of the armed conflicts "ended" by peace agreements restarted.[56] They evaluate the early implementation of the 2003 Comprehensive Peace Agreement[57] by

---

(2006) *The Situation in Liberia*, 20 December 2006, S/RES/1731 (2006); UN Security Council, *Security Council resolution 1750 (2007)* [*Liberia*], 30 March 2007, S/RES/1750 (2007); UN Security Council, *Resolution 1753 (2007) The Situation in Liberia*, 27 April 2007, S/RES/1753(2007); UN Security Council, *Security Council resolution 1777 (2007)* [*Liberia*], 20 September 2007, S/RES/1777 (2007); UN Security Council, *Security Council resolution 1792 (2007)* [*on renewal of measures on arms and travel imposed by resolution 1521 (2003) and on extension of the mandate of the current Panel of Experts on Liberia*], 19 December 2007, S/RES/1792 (2007); UN Security Council, *Security Council resolution 1819 (2008)* [*on extension of the mandate of the Panel of Experts on Liberia*], 18 January 2008, S/RES/1819 (2008); UN Security Council, *Security Council resolution 1854 (2008)* [*on extension of the mandate of the Panel of Experts on Liberia*], 19 December 2008, S/RES/1854 (2008); UN Security Council, *Security Council resolution 2025 (2011)* [*Liberia*], 14 December 2011, S/RES/2025(2011); UN Security Council, *Security Council resolution 2079 (2012)* [*on the situation in Liberia*], 12 December 2012, S/RES/2079 (2012); UN Security Council, *Security Council resolution 2116 (2013)* [*on Liberia*], 18 September 2013, S/RES/2116 (2013); UN Security Council, *Security Council resolution 2128 (2013)* [*on the situation in Liberia and West Africa*], 10 December 2013, S/RES/2128 (2013); UN Security Council, *Security Council resolution 2188 (2014)* [*on the situation in Liberia*], 9 December 2014, S/RES/2188 (2014).

55 UN Security Council, *Security Council resolution 1408 (2002)* [*on the situation in Liberia*], 6 May 2002, S/RES/1408 (2002); UN Security Council, *Security Council resolution 1458 (2003)* [*on the situation in Liberia*], 28 January 2003, S/RES/1458 (2003); UN Security Council, *Security Council resolution 1343 (2001)* [*on the situation in Sierra Leone*], 7 March 2001, S/RES/1343 (2001); UN Security Council, *Security Council resolution 1478 (2003)* [*on the situation in Liberia*], 6 May 2003, S/RES/1478 (2003); UN Security Council, *Security Council resolution 1497 (2003)* [*on the situation in Liberia*], 1 August 2003, S/RES/1497 (2003).

56 Aboagye, Festus B., and Martin R. Rupiya. "Enhancing post-conflict democratic governance through effective security sector reform in Liberia." *A tortuous road to peace. The dynamics of regional, UN and international humanitarian interventions in Liberia*, Festus Aboagye and Alhaji M.S. Bah eds (Pretoria: Institute for Security Studies 2005): 249–280, 249.

57 *Peace Agreement between the Government of Liberia, the Liberians United for Reconciliation and Democracy (LURD), the Movement of Democracy in Liberia (MODEL) and the Political Parties*, 18 August 2003, Annexed to Letter dated 27 August 2003 from the Permanent

the national transitional government of Liberia with the support of UNMIL.⁵⁸ They note that United Nations Security Council Resolution 1509 (2003)⁵⁹ mandated UNMIL to focus not only on traditional peacekeeping but on supporting the institutionalization of human rights and the rule of law in Liberia, giving UNMIL wide-ranging responsibilities including humanitarian assistance, establishing security conditions, human rights monitoring, restructuring the security sector, legal reform, judicial reform, and correctional reform.⁶⁰ UNMIL established a Human Rights and Protection Unit with a role in child protection, rule of law, gender and trafficking advisors, as well as the institutionalisation and operationalisation of the Truth and Reconciliation Commission and an Independent National Commission on Human Rights pursuant to the Comprehensive Peace Agreement.⁶¹ While Aboagye and Rupiya's critiques of the state of democratic governance and security sector reform in 2005 are warranted, the United Nations Security Council and ECOWAS's efforts in combination with local efforts in the subsequent decade are not without merit, providing some indication of the benefits of a comprehensive, future-oriented approach. United Nations Security Council resolutions regulating the transition to peace are increasingly oriented towards building a positive peace, not merely putting an end to past conflict.

The customary and treaty law, as well as regulation coming from the United Nations regarding post-conflict/transitional administration, are also part of *jus post bellum*. As pointed out by Carsten Stahn, criminal justice under transitional administration does not neatly fall within domestic, international, or hybrid criminal justice.⁶² It is unique for two reasons. First, there is a particular emphasis on restoring public order and safety, not simply safeguarding the

---

Representative of Ghana to the United Nations addressed to the President of the Security Council, S/2003/850 (2003).

58 Aboagye, Festus B., and Martin R. Rupiya. "Enhancing post-conflict democratic governance through effective security sector reform in Liberia." *A tortuous road to peace. The dynamics of regional, UN and international humanitarian interventions in Liberia*, Festus Aboagye and Alhaji M.S. Bah eds (Pretoria: Institute for Security Studies 2005): 249–280, 251.

59 UN Security Council, *Security Council resolution 1509 (2003) [on establishment of the UN Mission in Liberia (UNMIL)]*, 19 September 2003, S/RES/1509 (2003).

60 Aboagye, Festus B., and Martin R. Rupiya. "Enhancing post-conflict democratic governance through effective security sector reform in Liberia." *A tortuous road to peace. The dynamics of regional, UN and international humanitarian interventions in Liberia*, Festus Aboagye and Alhaji M.S. Bah eds (Pretoria: Institute for Security Studies 2005): 249–280, 256–257.

61 Ibid 257.

62 Stahn, Carsten. "Justice under transitional administration: contours and critique of a paradigm." *Hous. J. Int'l L.* 27 (2004): 311.

interests of victims or the other typical goals of criminal law.[63] Second, there is often an emphasis on justifying any intervention (often post-hoc justified on the basis of human rights) that made the transitional administration possible.[64] It is unclear that the distinction between international armed conflict and non-international armed conflict makes a great deal of inherent, generalizable difference in terms of the practice of transitional administration. Transitional administrations, of course, have a much wider role in *jus post bellum*

It is also important to note that courts and tribunals at every level play an important role in developing and effectuating *jus post bellum*. At the global level, institutions such as the International Court of Justice, the Permanent Court of Arbitration (and other arbitral bodies), and the International Criminal Court are not specialized *jus post bellum* institutions, but they can play an important role in establishing the general rules for transitions to peace and can perform specific functions in particular transitions to peace. The International Court of Justice's decision on Kosovo,[65] for example, clarified that declaring independence was not itself a violation of international law—a helpful, if limited, general rule that also probably helped to move the situation in Kosovo towards a sustainable peace. Of the ten situations before the International Criminal Court as of this writing[66] (Democratic Republic of the Congo, Central African Republic, Uganda, Darfur (Sudan), Kenya, Libya, Cote d'Ivoire, Mali, Comoros (Situation on Registered Vessels of the Union of the Comoros, the Hellenic Republic and the Kingdom of Cambodia), and Georgia),[67] all except for perhaps the cases of post-election violence (Kenya and Cote d'Ivoire) involve an armed conflict, generally one that is dormant, although not necessarily truly finished. The International Criminal Court does not have inherent global jurisdiction. That said, with the potential of new accessions, ad hoc Article 12.3 referrals from non-member states, jurisdiction on the basis of nationality of the alleged perpetrator, and referrals by the United Nations Security Council, the International Criminal Court has no inherent territorial limit to its jurisdiction, and can be considered in a certain sense a global court. While its norms and development of law with an impact on the transition to peace are of wide and general application, the development of each investigation, case, and charge can have particular effects on local transitions to peace.

---

63   See ibid 315.
64   See ibid 315–316.
65   Accordance with International Law of the Unilateral Declaration of Independence in Respect of Kosovo, Advisory Opinion (Int'l Ct. Justice July 22, 2010).
66   3 May 2016.
67   See https://www.icc-cpi.int/en_menus/icc/situations%20and%20cases/Pages/situations%20and%20cases.aspx last visited 3 May 2016.

The situations before the International Criminal Court are generally non-international armed conflict (with the possible exception of the Comoros referral[68]) although many have international involvement. That said, the norms emerging from the International Criminal Court's jurisprudence are likely to have general application to international armed conflicts and non-international armed conflicts.

Regional judicial bodies also can play an important role in establishing regional norms and influencing local transitions to peace. The Inter-American and European systems of human rights courts are perhaps best known, but other regional courts are also potentially useful sources of jurisprudence and dispute resolution with respect to both transitions out of international armed conflict and non-international armed conflict. In Africa, such regional judicial bodies that are likely to have potential impacts on transitions to peace include the African Court on Human and Peoples' Rights, the Community Court of Justice of the Economic Community of West African States, and the East African Court of Justice. In the Americas, there is not only the Inter-American Court of Human Rights (with its feeder institution the Inter-American Commission on Human Rights) but also the Central American Court of Justice, the Caribbean Court of Justice, and the East Caribbean Supreme Court. In Europe, the leading institutions are the European Court of Justice and the European Court of Human Rights.

Multilateral disarmament and weapons control treaties are typically categorized under *jus in bello* if they are categorized under the *jus ad bellum/jus in bello/jus post bellum* trichotomy (or the *jus ad bellum/jus in bello* dichotomy) at all. For treaties that focus on the *use* of weapons, that seems the most appropriate choice. So, for example, the use of exploding projectiles weighing less than 400 grams;[69] bullets that flatten upon entering the human body;[70] poison and

---

[68] Decision on the admissibility of the Prosecutor's appeal against the "Decision on the request of the Union of the Comoros to review the Prosecutor's decision not to initiate an investigation," Situation on Registered Vessels of the Union of the Comoros, the Hellenic Republic and the Kingdom of Cambodia, ICC-01/13-51, 6 November 2015, Appeals Chamber.

[69] Short title: Declaration of Saint Petersburg (1868); Declaration Renouncing the Use, in Time of War, of Explosive Projectiles Under 400 Grammes Weight. Saint Petersburg, adopted 11 December 1868, D.Schindler and J.Toman, The Laws of Armed Conflicts, Martinus Nihjoff Publisher, 1988, p.102.

[70] Short title: Hague Declaration (1899); International Peace Conference 1899, Declaration (IV,3) concerning Expanding Bullets. The Hague, adopted 29 July 1899, (entry into force 4 September 1900).

poisoned weapons;[71] chemical weapons and bacteriological methods;[72] biological weapons;[73] certain conventional weapons[74] including incendiary weapons,[75] mines,[76] booby traps,[77] blinding laser weapons,[78] explosive remnants of war,[79] and munitions that create fragments not detectable by X-ray;[80]

---

71 Short title: Hague Regulations (1907); International Conferences (The Hague), Hague Convention (IV) Respecting the Laws and Customs of War on Land and Its Annex: Regulations Concerning the Laws and Customs of War on Land, 18 October 1907.

72 Short title: Geneva Protocol (1925); United Nations, Protocol for the Prohibition of the Use in War of Asphyxiating, Poisonous or other Gases, and of Bacteriological Methods of Warfare, 17 June 1925 (Entry into force: 8 February 1928); Short title: Convention on the prohibition of chemical weapons (1993); Convention on the Prohibition of the Development, Production, Stockpiling and Use of Chemical Weapons and on their Destruction, 3 September 1992 (Entry into force: 29 April 1997); *see also* UN General Assembly, Implementation of the Convention on the Prohibition of the Development, Production, Stockpiling and Use of Chemical Weapons and on Their Destruction: Resolution adopted by the General Assembly, 17 December 2003, A/RES/58/52.

73 Short title: 1972 Biological Weapons Convention; 1972 Convention on the Prohibition of the Development, Production and Stockpiling of Bacteriological (Biological) and Toxin Weapons and on their Destruction, 1015 UNTS 163 / [1977] ATS 23 / 11 ILM 309 (1972) , 10 April 1972 (Entry into force: 26 March 1975).

74 Short title: Convention on Certain Conventional Weapons; United Nations, Convention on Prohibitions or Restrictions on the Use of Certain Conventional Weapons Which May be Deemed to be Excessively Injurious or to Have Indiscriminate Effects (and Protocols) (As Amended on 21 December 2001), 10 October 1980, 1342 UNTS 137 (Entry into force: 2 December 1983; Registered No. 22495).

75 Short title: Protocol III (1980) to the Convention on Certain Conventional Weapons; Protocol on Prohibitions or Restrictions on the Use of Incendiary Weapons (Protocol III). Geneva, 10 October 1980 (Entry into force: 2 December 1983).

76 Short title: Protocol II, as amended (1996), to the Convention on Certain Conventional Weapons; Protocol (II) on Prohibitions or Restrictions on the Use of Mines, Booby-Traps and Other Devices. Geneva, 10 October 1980 (Entry into force: 2 December 1983).

77 Short title: Protocol II, as amended (1996), to the Convention on Certain Conventional Weapons; Protocol (II) on Prohibitions or Restrictions on the Use of Mines, Booby-Traps and Other Devices. Geneva, 10 October 1980 (Entry into force: 2 December 1983).

78 Short title: Protocol IV (1995) to the Convention on Certain Conventional Weapons; Protocol on Blinding Laser Weapons (Protocol IV to the 1980 Convention), 13 October 1995 (Entry into force: 30 July 1998).

79 Short title: Protocol V (2003) to the Convention on Certain Conventional Weapons; Protocol on Explosive Remnants of War (Protocol V to the 1980 CCW Convention), 28 November 2003 (Entry into force: 12 November.2006).

80 Short title: Protocol I (1980) to the Convention on Certain Conventional Weapons; Protocol on Non-Detectable Fragments (Protocol I). Geneva, 10 October 1980 (Entry into force: 2 December 1983).

anti-personnel mines;[81] and cluster munitions[82]—are all functionally part of *jus in bello*. Many of these treaties, particularly the more modern treaties, are also potentially important in the transition from armed conflict to peace. New regimes can be "joiners" and joining well-regarded treaties such as human rights treaties and weapons treaties can signal their status. Many weapons treaties do not only bar use of weapons, but also bar their stockpiling, production and transfer and require their destruction. Examples of such Treaties include the 1972 Biological Weapons Convention,[83] the 1993 Chemical Weapons Convention,[84] the 1980 Convention on Certain Conventional Weapons (CCW)[85] and its Protocols ,the 1997 Convention on the Prohibition of the Use, Stockpiling, Production and Transfer of Anti-Personnel Mines and on their Destruction[86] and the 2008 Convention on Cluster Munitions.[87] The 2013 Arms Trade Treaty[88] regulating the international trade in conventional weapons also may aid in the transition to peace not only by limiting stockpiles but by reinforcing the norm against arming entities engaged in international criminal law violations. Of particular importance is the emphasis on removing the explosive

---

81 Short title: Convention on the Prohibition of Anti-Personnel Mines (Ottawa Treaty) (1997); The 1997 Convention on the Prohibition of the Use, Stockpiling, Production and transfer of Anti-Personnel Mines and on their Destruction (Entry into force: 1 March 1999).

82 Convention on Cluster Munitions, Dublin Diplomatic Conference on Cluster Munitions, 30 May 2008 (Entry into force: 1 August 2010).

83 Short title: 1972 Biological Weapons Convention; 1972 Convention on the Prohibition of the Development, Production and Stockpiling of Bacteriological (Biological) and Toxin Weapons and on their Destruction, 1015 UNTS 163 / [1977] ATS 23 / 11 ILM 309 (1972), 10 April 1972 (Entry into force: 26 March 1975).

84 Short title: Convention on the prohibition of chemical weapons (1993); Convention on the Prohibition of the Development, Production, Stockpiling and Use of Chemical Weapons and on their Destruction, 3 September 1992 (Entry into force: 29 April 1997); *see also* UN General Assembly, Implementation of the Convention on the Prohibition of the Development, Production, Stockpiling and Use of Chemical Weapons and on Their Destruction: Resolution adopted by the General Assembly, 17 December 2003, A/RES/58/52.

85 Short title: Convention on Certain Conventional Weapons; United Nations, Convention on Prohibitions or Restrictions on the Use of Certain Conventional Weapons Which May be Deemed to be Excessively Injurious or to Have Indiscriminate Effects (and Protocols) (As Amended on 21 December 2001), 10 October 1980, 1342 UNTS 137 (Entry into force: 2 December 1983; Registered No. 22495).

86 Short title: Convention on the Prohibition of Anti-Personnel Mines (Ottawa Treaty) (1997); The 1997 Convention on the Prohibition of the Use, Stockpiling, Production and transfer of Anti-Personnel Mines and on their Destruction (Entry into force: 1 March 1999).

87 Convention on Cluster Munitions, Dublin Diplomatic Conference on Cluster Munitions, 30 May 2008 (Entry into force: 1 August 2010).

88 United Nations, Arms Trade Treaty, 2 April 2013 (Entry into force: 24 December 2014).

remnants of war in the 1997 Convention on the Prohibition of the Use, Stockpiling, Production and Transfer of Anti-Personnel Mines and on their Destruction[89] and the 2008 Convention on Cluster Munitions.[90] Generally, these treaties are more relevant in international armed conflict than non-international armed conflict, although that may be less true for the Landmine Treaty and the Arms Control Treaty. Destruction of landmines can be an enduring postconflict concern in non-international armed conflicts such as in Cambodia, Afghanistan, and Colombia, as well as in the technically ongoing international armed conflict between the Democratic Republic of Korea and the Republic of Korea. The Arms Control Treaty helps to address the inflows and outflows of small arms that can determine the outcome of transitions to peace.

Not all law restricting arms in the transition from armed conflict to peace takes the form of multilateral treaties. After international armed conflict, victors or the international community may demand disarmament from defeated states, as happened after the First and Second World War (imposed by victorious states) or during and after the first Gulf War.[91] These international efforts to impose disarmament may result in enduring domestic law mandating restrictions on armament and militarization, as with the Second World War, or less enduring, as with the First. More widespread is the common domestic law practice after non-international armed conflicts involving programs to mandate and facilitate the disarmament, demobilization and reintegration of members of organized armed groups—so-called "DDR" programs. These disarmament programs are usually framed as part of "transitional justice" and, alongside "security sector reform" are widely considered vital for a successful transition from non-international armed conflict to peace. Disarmament is inherently a process-driven process, not merely a simple prohibition, so it inevitably inhabits a middle ground between purely procedural and purely substantive law.

---

89 Short title: Convention on the Prohibition of Anti-Personnel Mines (Ottawa Treaty) (1997); The 1997 Convention on the Prohibition of the Use, Stockpiling, Production and transfer of Anti-Personnel Mines and on their Destruction (Entry into force: 1 March 1999).

90 Convention on Cluster Munitions, Dublin Diplomatic Conference on Cluster Munitions, 30 May 2008 (Entry into force: 1 August 2010).

91 See e.g. UN Security Council, *Security Council Resolution S/RES/689 (1991) Resolution 689 (1991) Adopted by the Security Council at its 2983rd meeting on 9 March 1991*, 9 April 1991, S/RES/689 (1991).

5 More Substantive Aspects

Again using the schematic depiction above as a guide, it is possible to examine a variety of more substantive *jus post bellum* law and norms with respect to international armed conflicts and non-international armed conflicts. The substantive elements of *jus post bellum* are more thoroughly examined in Chapter 4.B Contrasting the Content of Transitional Justice and *Jus Post Bellum*, but are briefly explored here with an emphasis on the difference between International Armed Conflict and Non-International Armed Conflict.

Such law and norms include resolving the *res*/just cause in traditional just war thinking, treaty and customary law on occupation and post-occupation, the customary international law of state responsibility (particularly with regards to new states and reparations), peacekeeping norms, down to particular implementations of the above. These are generally issues of international armed conflict, although they may be present by analogy with non-international armed conflict. For example, while successfully transitioning from armed conflict to peace in international armed conflict may require resolving the *res*, in non-international armed conflict the complaints that led to armed conflict may need to be substantively resolved on the domestic level for the successful transition from armed conflict to peace. For International Armed Conflicts, the prohibition of annexation as the *res*[92] of armed conflict is tied to the prohibition of acts of aggression, a *jus ad bellum* concern with *jus post bellum* implications. International armed conflict has implications with respect to occupation and post-occupation obligations and prohibitions.

Regardless of the international or non-international nature of the conflict, there are a variety of substantive prohibitions that take on particular importance in *jus post bellum*. Genocide, expulsion, persecution, slavery are prohibited and are non-derogable in times of armed conflict or national emergency, and are binding on those crafting peace agreements, those who enjoy transitional governmental authority, and new states or governments. United Nations Security Council Chapter VII resolutions frequently provide specific binding law that applies to particular transitions from armed conflict to peace.

---

92 The traditional criteria of *persona, res, causa, animus* and *auctoritas* dates from the *Apparatus glossarum Laurentii Hispanii in Compilationem tertiam* of Laurentius Hispanus (c. 1180–1248). See generally Frederick H. Russell, *The Just War in the Middle Ages*, p. 128. "*Res*" or "thing" was the territory, property, or other object over which the just war was fought, and was intimately connected to the idea of *causa* or *justa causa* which was the characterization of the *res*, that is, that it was just to pursue the *res* in war, for example to lawfully recover territory.

E   Conclusion

This section, *Jus Post Bellum* in the Context of International and Non-International Armed Conflict, has focused on the distinguishing the operation of *jus post bellum* in the two canonical types of armed conflict. It introduces the concept of international armed conflict and non-international armed conflict and how those terms operate with *jus in bello* and *jus ad bellum*, before providing exploring the subject matter of *jus post bellum*—locating where the type of armed conflict made a substantial difference, and where it did not.

Fundamentally, resolving non-international armed conflicts is primarily an issue of what sort of state (or in the case of secession, states) will be built in the aftermath of war, whereas international armed conflicts inevitably are not only an issue of the post-war nature of the states involved (particularly if there is a clear-cut losing state) but also the nature of interstate relations afterwards. The issues involved can, of course, be largely bilateral (for instance, a piece of territory such as Alsace-Lorraine can change hands) but there is also inevitably often a question as to the nature of international relations, governed by law more generally. This phenomenon is most powerfully exemplified in The Peace of Westphalia (the peace made after the Thirty Years' War in the Holy Roman Empire and the Eighty Years' War) and the United Nations Charter—both developments closing terrible armed conflicts and (in different ways) establishing a new foundational reference point for international peace.[93] This struggle

---

93   For a classic work on the importance of the Peace of Westphalia, see Gross, Leo. "The Peace of Westphalia 1648–1948." *American Journal of International Law* 42 (1948): 20. The author agrees with Gross that the peace agreements generally collectively referenced as the "Peace of Westphalia" are in some ways comparable to the United Nations Charter (p. 20) and that while in many ways simply followed previous practice and was part of a gradual process (p. 27), that by increasing the possibility of equality and lasting peace between states of "any particular religious background" ("p. 26") the Peace of Westphalia has rightly come to be seen as a cornerstone of a system of sovereign states. Of course, in reality, there are clear differences between the Peace of Westphalia and the (global, multilateral) United Nations Charter. The mythology has been somewhat problematized by e.g. Beaulac, Stéphane. "The Westphalian Legal Orthodoxy-Myth or Reality?." *Journal of the History of International Law* 2.2 (2000): 148–177 (focusing on the continuing multilayered authority in Europe); but in the author's view the problematization can be overstated and "miss the forest for the trees"—the fundamental drive for a sovereign state system that could be at peace not through a unified Christendom, as symbolized by the Peace of Westphalia, generally justifies the shorthand status "Westphalia" has earned. For additional critical approaches, see e.g. Osiander, Andreas. "Sovereignty, international relations, and the Westphalian myth." *International organization* 55.02 (2001): 251–287; Beaulac, Stéphane. "The Westphalian model in defining international law: challenging the myth." *Austl. J. Legal Hist.* 8 (2004): 181; Beaulac, Stéphane. *The power of language in the*

to establish the nature of the international order is an old one. A pessimistic approach goes back to for example Niccolo Machiavelli's *The Prince*,[94] Thomas Hobbes' *Leviathan*[95] and Baruch Spinoza's *Tractatus theologico-politicus*,[96] or even back to Thucydides *History of the Peloponnesian War*[97]—a tradition that sees the nature of international relations as fundamentally and irrevocably lawless. But there is also a long tradition, that a collective effort to construct a peaceful order, as proposed in the various treaties that constituted the Peace of Westphalia, can be successful. Many of these efforts were detailed in Chapter 1: "Past – The Deep Roots of Jus Post Bellum." Continuing the analysis of the substance of jus post bellum, the current tensions within the use of the term jus post bellum should be further examined, a problem to which this work now turns. The next chapter will include analysis of odious debt and jus post bellum in the context of international armed conflict and non-international armed conflict, building on the foundation of this chapter.

making of international law: the word sovereignty in Bodin and Vattel and the myth of Westphalia. Vol. 46. Martinus Nijhoff Publishers, 2004; De Carvalho, Benjamin, Halvard Leira, and John M. Hobson. "The big bangs of IR: The myths that your teachers still tell you about 1648 and 1919." *Millennium* 39.3 (2011): 735–758; Schmidt, Sebastian. "To Order the Minds of Scholars: The Discourse of the Peace of Westphalia in International Relations Literature " *International Studies Quarterly* 55.3 (2011): 601–623. These efforts to demythologize "Westphalia" are welcome if they do not cause the reader to understate the importance of the developments generally referenced in shorthand as the "Peace of Westphalia."

94 Machiavelli, Niccolò, 1515. *The Prince*, trans. Harvey C. Mansfield, Jr., Chicago: Chicago University Press, 1985.
95 Hobbes, Thomas, and Edwin Curley. *Leviathan: with selected variants from the Latin edition of 1668*. Vol. 2. Hackett Publishing, 1994.
96 See e.g. Israel, Jonathan, and Michael Silverthorne, eds. *Spinoza: Theological-Political Treatise*. Cambridge University Press, 2007, p. 195:

   By the right and order of nature I merely mean the rules determining the nature of each individual thing by which we conceive it is determined naturally to exist and to behave in a certain way. For example fish are determined by nature to swim and big fish to eat little ones, and therefore it is by sovereign natural right that fish have possession of the water and that big fish eat small fish.

97 Thucydides. *History of the Peloponnesian War*, trans. Rex Warner, Harmondsworth: Penguin Books, 1972.

CHAPTER 7

Contemporary Legal Content of *Jus Post Bellum*

A   Introduction

1   *Chapter Focus*

Jus post bellum has a particular function in international law, to organize the application of law and principles in order to successfully guide the transition from armed conflict to a just and sustainable (or "positive") peace.[1] This chapter demonstrates the application of the hybrid functional approach described *supra* in core areas of law Stahn asserts (and the author concurs) are central to achieving the goals of *jus post bellum*.

This work has addressed *jus post bellum* in a variety of ways: its origins, the contemporary debate around its meaning, contrasting it with related concepts and bodies of law (such as transitional justice, *jus ad bellum*, and *jus in bello*), and describing it in both International Armed Conflict and Non-International Armed Conflict. This chapter draws upon and extends what has been discussed earlier, to provide a specific thematic focus on the contemporary legal content of *jus post bellum*. It builds upon and extends the framework earlier laid out by Stahn[2] because, in the author's view and the view of the many scholars who have used Stahn's work as a starting point, the legal components identified by Stahn are some of the most crucial for the successful transition from armed conflict to peace (with slight modifications such as the inclusion of odious debt as a potentially regulated subject).

These components are usefully considered together as part of *jus post bellum* because they provide legal substance and applied principles to the hybrid functional approach already described and propounded in Part I of this work. Given the scope of this work, it cannot review the entire scholarship in each of these areas, but rather provide a more concrete guide to the legal foundations and principles of *jus post bellum*, building on the theoretical and definitional structure of Part I.

This chapter provides analysis as to how the hybrid functional approach would apply in eight substantive areas. The eight areas discussed are:

---

1   See Part 1 of this work.
2   Stahn, Carsten. "'Jus ad bellum,'jus in bello'...'jus post bellum'?–Rethinking the Conception of the Law of Armed Force." *European Journal of International Law* 17.5 (2006): 921–943, p. 937.

1) Procedural fairness and peace agreements; 2) The Responsibility to Protect; 3) Territorial dispute resolution; 4) Consequences of an act of aggression; 5) International territorial administration and the prohibition of 'trusteeship'; 6) The law applicable in a territory in transition; 7) The scope of individual criminal responsibility; and 8) The nexus of *jus post bellum* and odious debt. Alternative frameworks are also examined. These eight areas are not comprehensive, but they are at the core of *jus post bellum*. By drawing upon analysis used throughout this work to emphasize the contemporary legal content of *jus post bellum*, the more practical aspects of this work can be brought to the fore.

What follows then in this chapter is primarily a significant expansion of the efforts of one leading scholar, Stahn, to outline the core legal substance of *jus post bellum*, using the hybrid functional approach already described in this work. While Stahn's work is often referenced,[3] expanding his framework in this manner has never been done properly.

2   Responses to Critical Approaches to Jus Post Bellum

It is worth detailing further what this chapter does and what it will not attempt to do. There is a strain of criticism of *jus post bellum* that indicates the term should be avoided because it is a new term that does not represent a new body of laws. This chapter will not convince such critics that *jus post bellum* contains only laws that apply only within the framework of *jus post bellum* and in no other framework. It does not follow, however, that the concept of *jus post bellum* should not be used and developed. *Jus post bellum*, properly conceived, plays a vital function in international law, for the international community, and for survivors of armed conflict—to guide the transition from armed conflict to a just and sustainable peace. How these laws and principles can be applied in this transition remains worthy of study, regardless of the term applied.

Many critics of *jus post bellum* are very specific in the particular norms and addressees they address. Three notable scholars who have taken a sceptical approach to *jus post bellum* are Eric De Brabandere, Antonia Chayes, and Gelijn Molier. Even an unapologetically pro-*jus post bellum* advocate should recognize the value of their contributions and the salience of some their specific points. Critical to understanding their approaches is how they define *jus post bellum* and their overall approach to *lex lata*. Recognizing certain commonalities in critical approaches these scholars have demonstrated with respect to *jus*

---

3   As best as the author can tell, the referenced work (Stahn, Carsten. "Jus ad bellum,"jus in bello'...'jus post bellum'?–Rethinking the Conception of the Law of Armed Force." *European Journal of International Law* 17.5 (2006): 921–943) is the most frequently cited legal (as opposed to philosophical) article on the subject.

post bellum allows for an appreciation for the productive role such scholars can play in the ongoing discussion on *jus post bellum*, while respectfully disagreeing with certain broader conclusions.

De Brabandere has authored a number of works on the theme of *jus post bellum*.[4] In 2010, he argued that "recent cases have shown that there already exists an adequate, flexible, and neutral legal framework to address" the transition from armed conflict to peace, but rejects the label *jus post bellum* for that framework.[5] His later work on the subject, in an area bringing together two areas of his expertise (transitions to peace and foreign direct investment), admits the use of the term *jus post bellum* as the "legal regime governing post-conflict reconstruction, a use of the concept to which no normative implications should be attached."[6] Chayes squarely asks whether there is a freestanding, universally applicable post-conflict obligation to rebuild a vanquished society after war and answers in the negative.[7] Molier[8] addresses *jus post*

---

[4] De Brabandere, Eric. "The Responsibility for Post-Conflict Reforms: A Critical Assessment of Jus Post Bellum as a Legal Concept"(2010)." *Vanderbilt Journal of Transnational Law* 43: 119; De Brabandere, Eric. "International Territorial Administrations and Post-Conflict Reforms: Reflections on the Need of a Jus Post Bellum as a Legal Framework." *Belgisch Tijdschrift voor Internationaal Recht / Revue Belge de Droit International* 44(1–2): 69–90; Eric De Brabandere, 'The Concept of Jus Post Bellum in International Law: A Normative Critique, in Carsten Stahn, Jennifer S. Easterday, and Jens Iverson (eds.), Jus Post Bellum: Mapping the Normative Foundations (Oxford: Oxford University Press, 2014); De Brabandere, Eric. "Jus Post Bellum and Foreign Direct Investment: Mapping the Debate." *The Journal of World Investment & Trade* 16.4 (2015): 590–603. See more generally, Eric De Brabandere, Post-conflict Administrations in International Law: International Territorial Administration, Transitional Authority and Foreign Occupation in Theory and Practice, Leiden: Martinus Nijhoff, 2009, particularly pp. 289–93.

[5] De Brabandere, Eric. "The Responsibility for Post-Conflict Reforms: A Critical Assessment of Jus Post Bellum as a Legal Concept"(2010)." *Vanderbilt Journal of Transnational Law* 43: 119, 134.

[6] De Brabandere, Eric. "Jus Post Bellum and Foreign Direct Investment: Mapping the Debate." *The Journal of World Investment & Trade* 16.4 (2015): 590–603, 591.

[7] Chayes, Antonia. "Chapter VII½: Is Jus Post Bellum Possible?." *European Journal of International Law* 24.1 (2013): 291–305. For a response, see Verdirame, Guglielmo. "What to Make of Jus Post Bellum: A Response to Antonia Chayes." *European Journal of International Law* 24.1 (2013): 307–313.

[8] Molier, Gelijn. "Rebuilding after Armed Conflict: Towards a Legal Framework of "The Responsibility to Rebuild" or a "Ius post Bellum"?." *Peace, Security and Development in an Era of Globalization: The Integrated Security Approach Viewed from a Multidisciplinary Perspective* (2009): 317–53; in Dutch see also Molier G. (2007), Wederopbouw na gewapend conflict: naar juridificering van 'the responsibility to rebuild' of een 'ius post bellum?.' In: Bomert B., Hoogen T. van den (Eds.) *Jaarboek Vrede en Veiligheid 2007*. Nijmegen: Centrum voor Internationaal Conflict-Analyse & Management 2007. 1–34.

bellum, primarily through criticism of the contributions of Stahn,[9] Boon,[10] and Orend.[11]

This subsection will not attempt to defend, point by point, the scholarship criticised by De Brabandere, Chayes, and Molier. Many of their specific criticisms (e.g. Molier's objection to Orend's tearing down the wall between the application of *jus ad bellum* and *jus in bello*[12] or his critique of Orend's assertion that a *jus post bellum* violation is a just cause for the use of force[13]) have merit. De Brabandere's documentation of the varied usage of the term is accurate and worthy of systematic expansion.[14] Other criticism regarding the purported lack of utility of the principles identified by Boon and Stahn is less persuasive. While useful and worthy of further development elsewhere, there is a risk of "missing the forest for the trees" in extending the implications of such arguments too far.

The underlying question is whether a criticism of a specific assertion as to the law and principles of the transition to armed peace has the broader effect of overturning the entire field of *jus post bellum*. A useful, specific disagreement on a particular point or series of points of law does not negate the primary assertion that *jus post bellum* exists, nor does it (in this author's view) undermine the argument that *jus post bellum* functions to guide the transition from armed conflict to a just and sustainable peace. One might trace a particular argument from, for example, William Martel's assertion that victory "imposes political, economic, human and moral responsibilities — on the victorious state"[15] to Chayes assertion that such responsibilities cannot amount to a

---

9   Stahn, Carsten, and Jann K. Kleffner eds. *Jus post bellum: towards a law of transition from conflict to peace*. TMC Asser Press, 2008; Stahn, Carsten. "Jus ad bellum,'jus in bello'...'jus post bellum'?–Rethinking the Conception of the Law of Armed Force." *European Journal of International Law* 17.5 (2006): 921–943; Stahn, Carsten. "Jus Post Bellum: Mapping the Discipline (s)." *Am. U. Int'l L. Rev.* 23 (2007): 311.

10 Boon, Kristen. "Legislative reform in post-conflict zones: Jus post bellum and the contemporary occupant's law-making powers." *McGill LJ* 50 (2005): 285.

11 Orend, Brian. "Jus post bellum: The perspective of a just-war theorist." *Leiden Journal of International Law* 20.03 (2007): 571–591.

12 Molier, Gelijn. "Rebuilding after Armed Conflict: Towards a Legal Framework of "The Responsibility to Rebuild" or a "Ius post Bellum"?." *Peace, Security and Development in an Era of Globalization: The Integrated Security Approach Viewed from a Multidisciplinary Perspective* (2009): 317–53, 332.

13 Ibid. 333.

14 De Brabandere, Eric. "The Responsibility for Post-Conflict Reforms: A Critical Assessment of Jus Post Bellum as a Legal Concept"(2010)." *Vanderbilt Journal of Transnational Law* 43: 119. For such a systematic expansion, see Chapter 5 of this work.

15 Martel, William C. *Victory in War: Foundations of Modern Strategy*. Cambridge University Press, 2011, 5.

general legal requirement,[16] to a further response that victories are regulated by certain laws and principles (e.g. regarding the prohibition of annexation, the right of self-determination, the prohibition of aggression, the requirements of human rights law, the obligations of occupation law, etc.) that may impose legal requirements on the victor in certain particular situations. This ongoing discussion does not disprove *jus post bellum*, it elucidates and amplifies it.

As a review of the chapter below demonstrates, the laws and principles involved in a hybrid functional approach to *jus post bellum,* as well as their addressees, are diverse, ranging from the international community and the United Nations Security Council down to organized armed groups and individuals. A hybrid functional approach to *jus post bellum* allows for a spectrum of law and principles, from global to local, and from the more general to the more specific.

The general stance of many critics is not to deny the existence of law that applies to the transition from armed conflict to peace,[17] but to deny it exists independently of other areas of law, and to further suggest that it serves no purpose to use the term. De Brabandere is particularly articulate on these points in his early scholarship on the subject.[18] Such scepticism has been an important part of the further development of scholarship on the subject, underlining the need for a richer articulation of a *jus post bellum* with a clearer telos: one of establishing a just and sustainable peace. Dieter Fleck's scholarship has been particularly useful in establishing the utility of partially-independent legal frameworks in regulation and norm generation in the transition to peace.[19] James Gallen has pioneered the utility of *jus post bellum* as an interpretive framework.[20] De Brabandere consents in his later work to use the term *jus post bellum* to help elucidate the particularities of foreign direct investment

---

16   Chayes, Antonia. "Chapter VII ½: Is Jus Post Bellum Possible?." *European Journal of International Law* 24.1 (2013): 291–305.

17   Verdirame, Guglielmo. "What to Make of Jus Post Bellum: A Response to Antonia Chayes." *European Journal of International Law* 24.1 (2013): 307–313.

18   See particularly De Brabandere, Eric. "The Responsibility for Post-Conflict Reforms: A Critical Assessment of Jus Post Bellum as a Legal Concept"(2010)." *Vanderbilt Journal of Transnational Law* 43: 119, 134.

19   Fleck, Dieter. "The Responsibility to Rebuild and Its Potential for Law-Creation: Good Governance, Accountability and Judicial Control." *Journal of International Peacekeeping* 16.1–2 (2012): 84–98; Fleck, Dieter "*Jus post bellum* as a partly independent legal framework" in Stahn, Carsten, Jennifer S. Easterday, and Jens Iverson, eds. Jus Post Bellum. Oxford University Press, 2014, 43–57.

20   Gallen, James "*Jus post bellum*: an interpretive framework" in Stahn, Carsten, Jennifer S. Easterday, and Jens Iverson, eds. Jus Post Bellum. Oxford University Press, 2014, 43–57.

in post-conflict rebuilding.[21] While *jus post bellum* is not fully independent as a legal regime, that does not mean it lacks utility as a concept—particularly when conceptualized as having the function to the international community described in this work. Scholars of *jus post bellum* should take note of warranted and particularized criticism, proceed with caution, but nonetheless proceed.

Perhaps many with a skeptical but reasoned approach to aspects of *jus post bellum* scholarship can admit that there is a sense in which "the train has left the station" or "the genie has left the bottle" in terms of *jus post bellum* entering widespread use in scholarship and playing an increasing role in shaping and describing law and practice. One can imagine scholars with a similar critical approach realizing in the early 1900s that-while they may not find the law of occupation, weapons law, targeting law, and the law regarding prisoners of war *new* or (in their view) *worthy* of a specific new term that included those elements but excluded the legality of the use of force overall—it was nonetheless worth analyzing, unifying, and encouraging the expansion of these areas in order to successfully minimize the harm of armed conflict and occupation. The need for a coherent body of laws and principles that guide the transition to peace is enduring, as demonstrated in Chapter 1. If the term is disputed, this need will not disappear. Criticism of particular points is always welcome. That said, at this point in the development of the concept, wholesale critics of *jus post bellum* would be well-served to also propose alternative unifying frameworks that comprehensively address this need and describe the varied laws and principles that function to guide the transition from armed conflict to peace, or to more fully and persuasively explain why such an effort is not worthwhile.

Some critical insistence on the overweening importance of *lex lata*, as a general matter, is also laudable and a productive part of the overall development of scholars' understanding of the law as it is. That said, extreme scepticism on matters which go beyond clearly settled law can itself pose difficulties. This is particularly true in areas on the frontiers of international law. C. Wilfred Jenks' dictum regarding the need for thoughtfulness in being over-cautious with respect to uncertain *lex lata* is worth repeating here:

> Certainty and predictability in respect of matters governed by well-established precedent are an important element in the rule of law, but to treat as speculation *de lege ferenda*, rather than as speculation concerning

---

21 De Brabandere, Eric. "Jus Post Bellum and Foreign Direct Investment: Mapping the Debate." *The Journal of World Investment & Trade* 16.4 (2015): 590–603.

an uncertain *lex lata*, everything which goes beyond clearly settled law is to arrest processes of growth without which the law will be atrophied and the rule of law perish.[22]

Jus post bellum has ancient roots, but it is not static. The "processes of growth" praised by Jenks are ongoing. Applying the rule of law to this most difficult area of human conduct, building peace from the ruins of war, remains an enormous challenge. The more limited task of clarifying core areas of the contemporary legal content of *jus post bellum* is the work of the remainder of this chapter.

B   Procedural Fairness and Peace Agreements

1   *Article 52 of the Vienna Convention on the Law of Treaties*

As discussed regarding in sections *supra* (Chapter 4.B.4.d) regarding procedural *jus post bellum*, The Vienna Convention on the Law of Treaties[23] is widely ratified and is generally accepted as customary international law. Article 52 of the Vienna Convention on the Law of Treaties states in full: "A treaty is void if its conclusion has been procured by the threat or use of force in violation of the principles of international law embodied in the Charter of the United Nations."[24] A literal reading of this Article applied to any peace treaty indicates that the validity of the peace treaty, the foundation of a transition from international armed conflict to peace, depends on whether there has been an illegal threat or use of force to procure that treaty.

For international armed conflict, the legal validity of the foundation of the transition to peace may formally depend on what is typically considered a question of *jus ad bellum*, the legality of the use or threat of force. This connection between *jus ad bellum* and *jus post bellum* emerges not through an analysis of *substantive* rights and restrictions during the transition to peace, but through

---

22   Jenks, C. Wilfred. "The challenge of universality." Proceedings of the American Society of International Law at Its Annual Meeting (1921–1969). Vol. 53. American Society of International Law, 1959, 85–98, at 95.

23   United Nations, *Vienna Convention on the Law of Treaties*, 23 May 1969, United Nations, Treaty Series, vol. 1155, p. 331 (Entry into force: 27 January 1980). See generally, Villiger, M.E. (2009). *Commentary on the 1969 Vienna Convention on the Law of Treaties*. Leiden: Nijhoff; Dörr, O., & Schmalenbach, K. (2012). *Vienna Convention on the Law of Treaties: A Commentary*. (Vienna convention on the law of treaties.) Berlin, Heidelberg: Springer-Verlag Berlin Heidelberg; Sinclair, Ian M.T. *The Vienna Convention on the Law of Treaties*. Manchester: Manchester University Press, 1984.

24   *Vienna Convention on the Law of Treaties*, Art. 52.

an analysis of the legitimate procedure for creating a peace treaty. The difficulty arises, of course, in that each side may believe that the other used not merely the threat of force, but actual use of force in violation of the principles of international law in order to achieve whatever negotiating position they have achieved at the peace table. Further, the threat of ongoing or renewed force almost inevitably forms the backdrop of peace negotiations—otherwise peace negotiations would not be required.

The interpretation of Article 52 in the context of peace agreements thus requires special consideration so as not to invalidate peace treaties in general, while retaining a disincentive for states to use force or the threat of force to create grossly unfair treaties. This may be done in part through Article 43 ("Obligations imposed by international law independently of a treaty"), Article 44.5 (disallowing separation of the treaty in cases governed by Article 52), Article 53 ("Treaties conflicting with a peremptory norm of general international law"), Article 71 ("Consequences of the invalidity of a treaty which conflicts with a peremptory norm of general international law"), Article 73 ("Cases of State succession, State responsibility and outbreak of hostilities"), and Article 75 ("Case of an aggressor State").[25] Article 73 and Article 75 in particular limits the application of the Vienna Convention on the Law of Treaties regarding questions arising from the outbreak of hostilities between states or treaty obligations of an aggressor state.[26] These limitations of the Vienna Convention on the Law of Treaties, however, raise more questions as to the effect of the use or threat of force on the validity and effects of peace treaties. To fully understand the general rulemaking peace treaties valid despite the context of the use of force, it is very helpful to have recourse to the tradition of *jus post bellum avant la lettre*, particularly with respect to Gentili, Wolff, and Vattel.[27] There seems little doubt that state practice and opinio juris dating back to the 16th century indicate peace treaties are binding, despite the fact that most peace treaties are procured by, or at least concluded in the context of, the threat or use of force.

---

25 Article 75 states in whole: "The provisions of the present Convention are without prejudice to any obligation in relation to a treaty which may arise for an aggressor State in consequence of measures taken in conformity with the Charter of the United Nations with reference to that State's aggression."
26 For more on the interaction of Article 75 and 52, see e.g. Villiger, M.E. (2009). *Commentary on the 1969 Vienna Convention on the Law of Treaties*. Leiden: Nijhoff, p. 915; Dörr, O., & Schmalenbach, K. (2012). *Vienna Convention on the Law of Treaties: A Commentary*. (Vienna convention on the law of treaties.) Berlin, Heidelberg: Springer-Verlag Berlin Heidelberg, p. 1284; Sinclair, Ian M.T. *The Vienna Convention on the Law of Treaties*. Manchester: Manchester University Press, 1984, p. 178.
27 See Chapter 1 of this work.

Again, one formal distinction that can be made is the distinction between an armed conflict terminating through a peace treaty (or series of peace treaties) in the case of an international armed conflict, and a peace agreement (or series of peace agreements) in the case of a non-international armed conflict. The term "peace treaty" is generally reserved for agreements not signed by non-state organized armed groups, whereas the more general term "peace agreement" can include peace treaties but is used more frequently for agreements that are not technically treaties because they include non-state groups (other than inter-governmental organizations) in the agreement.

One could argue that peace agreements that are not peace treaties (binding non-state actors) are guided by similar considerations of procedural fairness, but only by analogy, as the VCLT and the customary law it represents does not apply directly. In terms of lex lata, this argument by analogy is not terribly persuasive. As a prudential matter, however, the warning for the party to the potential peace agreement not to rely entirely on the threat of future force and demand an entirely one-sided agreement is sensible, lest the peace created be unjust or unsustainable.

2   Other Considerations of Procedural Fairness

a)   Treaty and Agreement Law

Several other articles in the Vienna Convention on the Law of Treaties are specifically relevant for the formation of peace treaties with respect to procedural fairness. Article 47 reads as follows:

> If the authority of a representative to express the consent of a State to be bound by a particular treaty has been made subject to a specific restriction, his omission to observe that restriction may not be invoked as invalidating the consent expressed by him unless the restriction was notified to the other negotiating States prior to his expressing such consent.[28]

This is straightforward as it goes, although there is a long tradition stating that there are limits to what a state representative may alienate (see above), ultimately culminating in the prohibition on annexation (see below).

Article 48 reads as follows:

1.   A State may invoke an error in a treaty as invalidating its consent to be bound by the treaty if the error relates to a fact or situation which was

---

28   Ibid, Art. 47.

assumed by that State to exist at the time when the treaty was concluded and formed an essential basis of its consent to be bound by the treaty.
2. Paragraph 1 shall not apply if the State in question contributed by its own conduct to the error or if the circumstances were such as to put that State on notice of a possible error.
3. An error relating only to the wording of the text of a treaty does not affect its validity; article 79 then applies.[29]

This presumably is not meant to invalidate peace treaties due to the notoriously difficult to ascertain battlefield facts or strategic position. Use of this Article with respect to peace treaties, or by analogy to peace agreements, should be depreciated. Article 49 covers fraud. Article 50 addresses the corruption of a representative of a state. These are likewise unlikely to affect the validity of a peace treaty or agreement. Of more potential impact is Article 51, which deals with coercion of a representative of a state:

> The expression of a State's consent to be bound by a treaty which has been procured by the coercion of its representative through acts or threats directed against him shall be without any legal effect.

This mirrors Article 52, but instead of the threat of the use of force against a state, it concerns coercion of a state's representative. While normal diplomatic immunity and IHL protections for those seeking to negotiate a ceasefire or peace treaty (inviolability of parlementaires)[30] should shield representatives from harm, but should those not be respected, and should representatives be coerced into signing a peace treaty, that treaty would be void.

b) Amnesty and *Aut Dedere Aut Judicare*

This section amplifies what this work has previously described with respect to amnesty and *aut dedere aut judicare* (Latin for "extradite or prosecute.") This is a modern implementation of the legal principle coined by Grotius, "*aut dedere aut punire*" (either extradite or punish).[31] The section below on individual criminal responsibility also touches on this point. The procedural law

---

29 Ibid, Art. 48.
30 *See e.g.* Article 32 1899 Hague Regulations, Article 32 International Conferences (The Hague), *Hague Convention (IV) Respecting the Laws and Customs of War on Land and Its Annex: Regulations Concerning the Laws and Customs of War on Land*, 18 October 1907, Article 43 of the 1874 Brussels Declaration, International Committee of the Red Cross (ICRC), *Customary International Humanitarian Law*, 2005, Volume I: Rules, Rules 66 and 67.
31 Grotius, De Jure Belli ac Pacis, Book II, Chap. XXI, paras. 3–4.

applicable to substantive criminal law is part of the transition to peace. This is not only with respect to the high profile, highly contested issues such as amnesties for the perpetration of alleged crimes related to the armed conflict. It includes questions of jurisdiction, immunities, statutes of limitation, and other questions of admissibility. How these laws are interpreted can influence the formation of peace agreements, and conversely, peace agreements may mandate procedural law changes to criminal and civil law. This section will focus on amnesty and *aut dedere aut judicare*.

The obligation to prosecute or extradite for prosecution the alleged perpetration of certain crimes is well-established, but can create tensions. The fight against impunity that creates this tension, often at the heart of the "peace vs. justice" debate, may complicate the short-term transition to peace but is often helpful to make the transition to peace successful in the long run.[32] This is often described using the Latin term *aut dedere aut judicare*, although it is common now to tamp down the demand to prosecute to merely "submit for prosecution" because of varied responsibilities and procedures at the domestic level and the presumption of innocence in criminal law. The Convention on the Prevention and Punishment of the Crime of Genocide,[33] for example, requires the state on whose territory a genocide allegedly occurred to prosecute the genocide. The Geneva Conventions of 1949[34] likewise require prosecution (or extradition for prosecution) of alleged grave breaches. The Convention Against

---

32 See e.g. Darehshori, Sara. *Selling justice short: why accountability matters for peace*. Human Rights Watch, 2009.

33 UN General Assembly, Convention on the Prevention and Punishment of the Crime of Genocide, 9 December 1948, (Entry into force: 12 January 1951) United Nations Treaty Series, vol. 78, p. 277. Article 6 states:
    Persons charged with genocide or any of the other acts enumerated in article III shall be tried by a competent tribunal of the State in the territory of which the act was committed, or by such international penal tribunal as may have jurisdiction with respect to those Contracting Parties which shall have accepted its jurisdiction.

34 International Committee of the Red Cross (ICRC), Geneva Convention for the Amelioration of the Condition of the Wounded and Sick in Armed Forces in the Field (First Geneva Convention), 12 August 1949, 75 UNTS 31 ("GCI"); International Committee of the Red Cross (ICRC), Geneva Convention for the Amelioration of the Condition of Wounded, Sick and Shipwrecked Members of Armed Forces at Sea (Second Geneva Convention), 12 August 1949, 75 UNTS 85 ("GCII"); International Committee of the Red Cross (ICRC), Geneva Convention Relative to the Treatment of Prisoners of War (Third Geneva Convention), 12 August 1949, 75 UNTS 135 ("GCIII"); International Committee of the Red Cross (ICRC), Geneva Convention Relative to the Protection of Civilian Persons in Time of War (Fourth Geneva Convention), 12 August 1949, 75 UNTS 287 ("GCIV").

Torture and Other Cruel, Inhuman or Degrading Treatment or Punishment[35] likewise requires prosecution or extradition, as does the Hague Convention for the Protection of Cultural Property in the Event of Armed Conflict.[36] This set of obligations also extends to issues less central although potentially relevant to *jus post bellum*, such as terrorism,[37] apartheid,[38] crimes against internationally protected persons,[39] and corruption.[40] Aside from direct treaty obligations to extradite or prosecute, indirect treaty obligations, such as human rights law obligations, also often create the duty to prosecute or extradite. Particularly in the Inter-American system[41] the duty to respect and ensure rights, as explained in the *Barrios Altos* case.[42] In certain cases, such as with genocide, there also exists a customary international law norm with respect to the duty to prosecute or extradite.[43] All of that said, given actual state practice and demonstrated opinio juris, one cannot generally assert there is a yet a general customary duty to prosecute or extradite for all alleged international criminal law violations.

---

35   UN General Assembly, *Convention Against Torture and Other Cruel, Inhuman or Degrading Treatment or Punishment*, 10 December 1984, (Entry into force 26 June 1987) United Nations Treaty Series, vol. 1465, p. 85.

36   UN Educational, Scientific and Cultural Organisation (UNESCO), *Convention for the Protection of Cultural Property in the Event of Armed Conflict*, 14 May 1954 (Entry into force: 7 August 1956).

37   United Nations, *Convention for the Suppression of Unlawful Seizure of Aircraft*, 16 December 1970, (Entry into force: 14 October 1971) UN Treaty Series 1973; UN General Assembly, *International Convention against the Taking of Hostages*, 17 November 1979, (Entry into force: 3 June 1983) No. 21931; UN General Assembly, *International Convention for the Suppression of Terrorist Bombings*, 15 December 1997, (Entry into force: 23 May 2001) No. 37517; UN General Assembly, *International Convention for the Suppression of the Financing of Terrorism*, 9 December 1999, (Entry into force: 10 April 2002) No. 38349.

38   UN General Assembly, *International Convention on the Suppression and Punishment of the Crime of Apartheid*, 30 November 1973, (Entry into force: 18 July 1976) A/RES/3068(XXVIII).

39   UN General Assembly, Convention on the Prevention and Punishment of Crimes against Internationally Protected Persons, including Diplomatic Agents, 14 December 1973, (Entry into force: 20 February 1977) No. 15410.

40   UN General Assembly, *United Nations Convention Against Corruption*, 31 October 2003, (Entry into force: 14 December 2005) A/58/422.

41   See generally Organization of American States (OAS), *American Convention on Human Rights, "Pact of San Jose," Costa Rica*, 22 November 1969, Entry into force: 18 July 1978.

42   Barrios Altos Case, Judgment of November 30, 2001, Inter-Am Ct. H.R. (Ser. C) No. 87 (2001). See particularly para. 19, citing Article 63(1) of the American Convention:
      If the Court finds that there has been a violation of a right or freedom protected by this Convention, the Court shall rule that the injured party be ensured the enjoyment of his right or freedom that was violated.

43   See Application of the Convention on the Prevention and Punishment of the Crime of Genocide (Bosnia and Herzegovina v. Serbia and Montenegro), 2007 I.C.J. 191.

C   The Responsibility to Protect

The Responsibility to Protect, including (and perhaps in particular) the Responsibility to Prevent and the Responsibility to Rebuild[44] are at best emerging legal norms rather than hard *lex lata*.[45] That said the norms described by this doctrine are worth noting in the context of *jus post bellum*. Fleck in particular makes a compelling case that the Responsibility to Rebuild, while not *lex lata*, is likely to be a productive norm in terms of additional rule generation in the future.[46]

The Responsibility to Protect doctrine[47] does not require armed conflict of any sort for its application. Rather, as part of the "just cause" it requires either large-scale loss of life or "ethnic cleansing":

A.   large scale loss of life, actual or apprehended, with genocidal intent or not, which is the product either of deliberate state action, or state neglect or inability to act, or a failed state situation; or

B.   large scale 'ethnic cleansing,' actual or apprehended, whether carried out by killing, forced expulsion, acts of terror or rape.[48]

---

44   For a particular focus on the Responsibility to Rebuild and *jus post bellum*, arguing that the Responsibility to Rebuild in particular is phrased in terms of policy rather than legal principle, see Molier, Gelijn. "Rebuilding after Armed Conflict: Towards a Legal Framework of "The Responsibility to Rebuild" or a "Ius post Bellum"?." *Peace, Security and Development in an Era of Globalization: The Integrated Security Approach Viewed from a Multidisciplinary Perspective* (Martinus Nijhoff 2009): 317–353. For a highly critical approach, see Robinson, Paul. "Is There an Obligation to Rebuild?." *Justice, Responsibility and Reconciliation in the Wake of Conflict*. Springer Netherlands, 2013. 105–116.

45   See Stahn, Carsten. "Responsibility to protect: political rhetoric or emerging legal norm." *Am. J. Int'l L.* 101 (2007): 99; Jovanović, Miodrag A. "Responsibility to Protect and the International Rule of Law." *Chinese Journal of International Law* 14.4 (2015): 757–776.

46   Fleck, Dieter. "The Responsibility to Rebuild and Its Potential for Law-Creation: Good Governance, Accountability and Judicial Control." *Journal of International Peacekeeping* 16.1–2 (2012): 84–98.

47   See International Commission on Intervention and State Sovereignty, *The Responsibility to Protect: Report of the International Commission on Intervention and State Sovereignty* (International Development Research Centre 2001) 39–45; see also United Nations Secretary General's High-Level Panel on Threats, Challenges and Change, *A More Secure World: Our Shared Responsibility, Report of the High-level Panel on Threats, Challenges and Change* (2004) 65–7; UN General Assembly, *2005 World Summit Outcome : resolution / adopted by the General Assembly*, 24 October 2005, A/RES/60/1, paras 138–9; United Nations General Assembly, *Implementing the Responsibility to Protect: Report of the Secretary-General*, UN Doc. A/63/677 (12 January 2009) para. 48.

48   International Commission on Intervention and State Sovereignty, *The Responsibility to Protect: Report of the International Commission on Intervention and State Sovereignty* (International Development Research Centre 2001) p. XII.

The Responsibility to Protect doctrine includes the Responsibility to Prevent, Responsibility to React, and the Responsibility to Rebuild. Of these three components, the Responsibility to React (particularly the section dealing with military intervention) has the most bearing on questions related to *jus ad bellum* and *jus in bello*, as it seeks to replace the rhetoric and framework of humanitarian intervention with guidelines of responses short of the use of armed force and constraints on the resort to armed force and how it is used. While the Responsibility to React could apply both to international armed conflict and non-international armed conflict, it is more likely to come into play in a non-international armed conflict that becomes internationalized (and thus becomes an international armed conflict), or a situation that did not amount to an armed conflict (either international or non-international) that becomes an international armed conflict once foreign military intervention occurs. Even a cursory reading of this doctrine with someone with a passing familiarity of just war doctrine will recognize the debt the International Commission on Intervention and State Sovereignty owes to the authors referenced in Chapter 1 of this work, requiring just cause, right intention, last resort, proportional means, and reasonable prospects as criteria for military intervention.[49]

The Responsibility to Prevent and the Responsibility to Rebuild are more tightly tied to *jus post bellum*. In comparison with the Responsibility to Respond, these aspects of the Responsibility to Protect (Prevent and Rebuild) apply more generally to international armed conflict and non-international armed conflict, but are probably still envisaged to apply more to non-international armed conflict.

The norms contained in The Responsibility to Prevent come into play with respect to *jus post bellum* given the goal of *jus post bellum* to create a sustainable peace, thus one that prevents future armed conflict. As described in *The Responsibility to Protect: Report of the International Commission on Intervention and State Sovereignty*,[50] the emphasis of the Responsibility to Prevent is the "[p]revention of deadly conflict and other forms of man-made catastrophe"[51] which is the responsibility of sovereign states[52] but is also within the portfolio of international mechanisms such as the Organization of African Unity's Mechanism for Conflict Prevention, Management, and Settlement and the Organization for Security Cooperation in Europe.[53] Early warning efforts by

---

49   Ibid 32–37.
50   Ibid 19.
51   Ibid.
52   Ibid.
53   Ibid 20.

non-governmental organizations such as the International Crisis Group, Amnesty International, Human Rights Watch, and the Fédération international des ligues des droits de l'homme, as well as the United Nations Secretary-General play an important role.[54] Root cause prevention efforts should be undertaken not only by states but by the United Nations, given that "the creation of conditions of stability and well-being [...] are necessary for peaceful and friendly relations among nations."[55] Direct prevention measures from fact-finding missions, mediation, arbitration, adjudication, legal sanction, the creation of international criminal law institutions, and even preventative measures of a military nature such as the UN Preventative Deployment Force in Macedonia are all referenced.[56]

With respect to the Responsibility to Rebuild, the International Commission on Intervention and State Sovereignty emphasized first and foremost post-intervention obligations—that is, if military intervention is pursued (under the rubric of Responsibility to React) that necessarily implies the "genuine commitment to helping to build a durable peace."[57] Much of the "Peace Building" subcomponent of post-intervention obligations are squarely in line with *jus post bellum* approaches found elsewhere.[58] This section relies heavily on previous efforts such as the Report of the United Nations Secretary-General to the Security Council, *The Causes of Conflict and the Promotion of Durable Peace and Sustainable Development in Africa*.[59] The Secretary-General's report describes post-conflict peacebuilding as follows:

> By post-conflict peace-building, I mean actions undertaken at the end of a conflict to consolidate peace and prevent a recurrence of armed

---

54 Ibid 21–22.
55 United Nations Charter, Article 55. Those conditions are listed in Article 55 as "a. higher standards of living, full employment, and conditions of economic and social progress and development;
  b. solutions of international economic, social, health, and related problems; and international cultural and educational cooperation; and
  c. universal respect for, and observance of, human rights and fundamental freedoms for all without distinction as to race, sex, language, or religion."
56 International Commission on Intervention and State Sovereignty, *The Responsibility to Protect: Report of the International Commission on Intervention and State Sovereignty* (International Development Research Centre 2001) pp. 23–25.
57 Ibid 39.
58 Ibid.
59 Report of the United Nations Secretary-General to the Security Council, The Causes of Conflict and the Promotion of Durable Peace and Sustainable Development in Africa, A/52/871 – S/1998/318 (New York: United Nations, 13 April 1998).

confrontation. Experience has shown that the consolidation of peace in the aftermath of conflict requires more than purely diplomatic and military action, and that an integrated peace building effort is needed to address the various factors which have caused or are threatening a conflict. Peace building may involve the creation or strengthening of national institutions, monitoring elections, promoting human rights, providing for reintegration and rehabilitation programmes, as well as creating conditions for resumed development.[60]

The Secretary-General's report continues:

A smooth and early transition to post-conflict peace-building is critical, and I urge the Security Council to look favourably on the establishment of post-conflict peace-building support structures similar to the one in Liberia. *Even prior to the end of the conflict*, there must be a clear assessment of key post-conflict peace-building needs and of ways to meet them.[61]

As to the priorities of post-conflict peacebuilding, the Secretary-General's report emphasizes the interconnectedness of a diverse set of priorities:

Societies which have emerged from conflict have special needs. To avoid a return to conflict while laying a solid foundation for development, emphasis must be placed on critical priorities such as encouraging reconciliation and demonstrating respect for human rights; fostering political inclusiveness and promoting national unity; ensuring the safe, smooth and early repatriation and resettlement of refugees and displaced persons; reintegrating ex-combatants and others into productive society; curtailing the availability of small arms; and mobilizing the domestic and international resources for reconstruction and economic recovery. Each priority is linked to every other, and success will require a concerted and coordinated effort on all fronts.[62]

One aspect emphasized by the International Commission on Intervention and State Sovereignty as part of post-conflict peacebuilding after an intervention is the provision of basic security, both in the form of avoiding revenge killings

---

60   Ibid, p. 13, para. 63.
61   Ibid, p. 14, para 65 (emphasis supplied). For more on Liberia, see Chapter 5.D *supra*.
62   Ibid, p. 14, para 66.

and in disbarment, demobilization and reintegration of former members of armed groups.⁶³ Criminal justice and administrative reform to ensure non-discrimination, particularly for returning refugees and internally displaced persons is emphasized.⁶⁴ The International Commission on Intervention and State Sovereignty concludes by accentuating the limits to occupation and the need for local ownership, both legally (given the underlying norm of sovereignty) and practically (given the treats of dependency and economic distortion).⁶⁵

Ultimately the main impact of the Responsibility to Protect doctrine has been to shift the rhetoric around "humanitarian intervention" to a different vocabulary, but has not fully changed the shared understanding of the norm of sovereignty in the way many hoped,⁶⁶ despite being referenced in the 2005 World Summit Outcome Document.⁶⁷ In the heat of the discussion over military intervention, some broader pragmatic points regarding the need to prevent and to rebuild have been underemphasized. By including these points as part of a hybrid functional concept of *jus post bellum*, the effort to establish a system of laws and norms that function together to help establish a just and sustainable peace should be strengthened.

D   Territorial Dispute Resolution

1   *Prohibition of Annexation*

The prohibition on the annexation of territory is central not only in determining the legality of particular post-conflict settlement, but also in underpinning the entire order of stable and pacific interstate relations. The prohibition on transformative occupation takes its ultimate form in the prohibition of annexation—the customary international law norm against any right of annexation by an occupier is reflected in Article 2(4) of the UN Charter and in the Declaration on Principles of International Law Concerning Friendly Relations and Co-operation Among States in Accordance with the Charter of the

---

63 International Commission on Intervention and State Sovereignty, *The Responsibility to Protect: Report of the International Commission on Intervention and State Sovereignty* (International Development Research Centre 2001) pp. 40–41.
64 Ibid. 41–42.
65 Ibid. 44–45.
66 Jovanović, Miodrag A. "Responsibility to Protect and the International Rule of Law." *Chinese Journal of International Law* 14.4 (2015): 757–776.
67 UN General Assembly, *2005 World Summit Outcome : resolution / adopted by the General Assembly*, 24 October 2005, A/RES/60/1, particularly paras. 138–139.

United Nations, GA Res. 2625 (XXV), annex (Oct. 24, 1970) and the prohibition against aggression.

The prohibition of annexation as the result of armed conflict is tied to the prohibition of acts of aggression, a clear *jus ad bellum* concern. For International Armed Conflicts, the prohibition of annexation as the *res*[68] of armed conflict is tied to the prohibition of acts of aggression, a *jus ad bellum* concern with *jus post bellum* implications. While annexation could be agreed upon in the text of a peace treaty, such an agreement would be void on that point. Were that not the case, little would remain of the prohibition of annexation. Further, the Vienna Convention on the Law of Treaties, reflecting customary international law on this point, clearly states in Article 53:

> A treaty is void if, at the time of its conclusion, it conflicts with a peremptory norm of general international law. For the purposes of the present Convention, a peremptory norm of general international law is a norm accepted and recognized by the international community of States as a whole as a norm from which no derogation is permitted and which can be modified only by a subsequent norm of general international law having the same character.[69]

A good list of peremptory norms (*jus cogens* norms) can be found in the commentary to the Draft Articles on Responsibility of States for Internationally Wrongful Acts: "Those peremptory norms that are clearly accepted and recognized include the prohibitions of aggression, genocide, slavery, racial discrimination, crimes against humanity and torture, and the right to self-determination."[70]

Annexation may often be the result of prohibited acts of aggression, and more to the point, will almost always violate the right to self-determination, being the imposition of a new territorial arrangement from the outside.

---

68   The traditional criteria of *persona, res, causa, animus* and *auctoritas* dates from the *Apparatus glossarum Laurentii Hispanii in Compilationem tertiam* of Laurentius Hispanus (c. 1180–1248). See generally Frederick H. Russell, *The Just War in the Middle Ages*, p. 128. "*Res*" or "thing" was the territory, property, or other object over which the just war was fought, and was intimately connected to the idea of *causa* or *justa causa* which was the characterization of the *res*, that is, that it was just to pursue the *res* in war, for example to lawfully recover territory.

69   United Nations, Vienna Convention on the Law of Treaties, 23 May 1969, United Nations, Treaty Series, vol. 1155, p. 331, art. 53.

70   International Law Commission. "Draft articles on Responsibility of States for Internationally Wrongful Acts, with commentaries." Report of the International Law Commission on the Work of its 53rd session (2001), Commentary on Article 26, paragraph 5, p. 85.

Following the *principle ex injuria jus non oritur* ("law does not arise from injustice"), Meron has put forward the view that unilateral State action can have no legal effect when it is in contravention of *jus cogens*.[71] This echoes Lauterpacht, who is worth quoting at length:

> Thus it follows from the principle *ex injuria jus non oritur* that a peace treaty imposed by the victorious aggressor has no legal validity. This is so notwithstanding the rule of orthodox international law which disregards the vitiating effect of duress in the conclusion of treaties. For that rule can reasonable be held to apply only to a war which the victor is entitled to wage. So long as international law permitted resort to war as an instrument of national policy and as an undisputed prerogative of national sovereignty it was inevitable that it should countenance the validity of treaties imposed by the victor. That consideration does not apply, in relation to an aggressor, in a system of international law in which war no longer occupies that position—although it is a consideration which continues to be valid in relation to the State which has been the victim of aggression.[72]

While the typical remedy for annexation subsequent to aggression is non-recognition,[73] it is unclear how the international community will handle cases of annexation in the truly long term.[74] Forbidding this result as a general matter, however, should provide a disincentive to begin armed conflicts in the first place.

2 *Self-determination*

Additional Protocol II explains that what is normally described as "International Armed Conflict" "include[s] armed conflicts in which peoples are fighting against colonial domination and alien occupation and against racist régimes in the exercise of their right of self-determination[.]"[75] International law

---

71 T. Meron, 'On a Hierarchy of International Human Rights,' 80 *AJIL* 1, 19–21 (1986).

72 Lauterpacht, Hersch. "The Limits of the Operation of the Law of War." *Brit. YB Int'l L.* 30 (1953): 206, pp. 233–234.

73 UN General Assembly, Definition of Aggression, 14 December 1974, A/RES/3314, at 123.

74 Dinstein, Yoram. *War, Aggression and Self-Defence*. Cambridge University Press, 2011, pp. 182–183.

75 International Committee of the Red Cross (ICRC), Protocol Additional to the Geneva Conventions of 12 August 1949, and relating to the Protection of Victims of Non-International Armed Conflicts (Protocol II), 8 June 1977, 1125 UNTS 609, Article 1.

is not simply mute on the issue of resort to the use of force amounting to an armed conflict when both parties are not states, particularly in the context of decolonization and self-determination. Indeed, the context of decolonization has helped to redraw the boundaries of international armed conflict and non-international armed conflict. The concept of self-determination can be found at least as far back as the late 18th century, with the United States of America proclaiming the principle in the Declaration of Independence[76] and was further promoted by the leaders of the (First) French Republic. The concept was further developed after the First World War, and found truly modern expression in the United Nations Charter and subsequent practice. Three chapters of the United Nations Charter are of particular interest: Chapter XI: Declaration regarding Non-Self-Governing Territories; Chapter XII: International Trusteeship System; and Chapter XIII: The Trusteeship Council.

Self-determination is a right enjoyed by, at a minimum, people under colonial rule. There is a legal obligation not to use force to frustrate that right. The keystone for this clarification of this area of law is the Declaration on Principles of International Law concerning Friendly Relations and Co-operation among States in Accordance with the Charter of the United Nations, annexed to United Nations General Assembly Resolution 2625, widely known as the "Friendly Relations Declaration" of 1970.[77] Similarly, the 1973 United Nations General Assembly Resolution 3103 on the Basic Principles of the Legal Status of the Combatants Struggling against Colonial and Alien Domination and Racist Regimes:

> [t]he armed conflicts involving the struggle of peoples against colonial and alien domination and racist regimes are to be regarded as international armed conflicts in the sense of the 1949 Geneva Conventions, and the legal status envisaged to apply to the combatants in the 1949 Geneva Conventions and other international instruments is to apply to the persons engaged in armed struggle against colonial and alien domination and racist regimes[78]

---

76 Declaration of Independence of the United States of America (United States) 51 BSP 847.
77 Declaration on Principles of International Law Concerning Friendly Relations and Cooperation among States in Accordance with the Charter of the United Nations (United Nations [UN]) UN Doc A/RES/2625(XXV), Annex.
78 United Nations General Assembly Resolution 3103 (XXVIII) on the basic principles of the legal status of the combatants struggling against colonial and alien domination and racist regimes (United Nations General Assembly [UNGA]) UN Doc A/RES/3103(XXVIII), para. 3.

This was given additional weight by Additional Protocol I, as previously described.[79] It says in Article 1, paragraphs 3 and 4:

> 3. This Protocol, which supplements the Geneva Conventions of 12 August 1949 for the protection of war victims, shall apply in the situations referred to in Article 2 common to those Conventions.
>
> 4. The situations referred to in the preceding paragraph include armed conflicts in which peoples are fighting against colonial domination and alien occupation and against racist régimes in the exercise of their right of self-determination, as enshrined in the Charter of the United Nations and the Declaration on Principles of International Law concerning Friendly Relations and Co-operation among States in accordance with the Charter of the United Nations.[80]

As expressed by many authors, protection of minorities is the necessary corollary of self-determination, two sides of the same coin.[81] While international protection of minorities was an intense focus after the First World War (but even then of limited application), after the second interest in the subject dropped markedly, replaced to some degree by a focus on human rights.[82]

E Consequences of an Act of Aggression

The prohibition of annexation as the result of armed conflict is tied to the prohibition of acts of aggression, a clear *jus ad bellum* concern. Acts of aggression also raise the question of response in the transition to peace, including the question of reparations—an issue that implicates the law of state responsibility. United Nations Security Council resolutions under Chapter VII authority

---

79 Protocol Additional to the Geneva Conventions of 12 August 1949, and relating to the Protection of Victims of International Armed Conflicts (Protocol I) (adopted 8 June 1977, entered into force 7 December 1978) 1125 UNTS 3.
80 Geneva Conventions Additional Protocol I (1977).
81 Kunz, Josef L. "The future of the international law for the protection of national minorities." *American Journal of International Law* (1945): 89–95; Thornberry, Patrick. "Self-determination, minorities, human rights: a review of international instruments." *International and Comparative Law Quarterly* 38.04 (1989): 867–889.
82 Kunz, Josef L. "The present status of the international law for the protection of minorities." *American Journal of International Law* (1954): 282–287, pp. 282–283.

frequently provide specific binding law that applies to particular transitions from armed conflict to peace.[83]

The prohibition on transformative occupation takes its ultimate form in the prohibition of annexation—the customary international law norm against any right of annexation by an occupier is reflected in Article 2(4) of the UN Charter and in the Declaration on Principles of International Law Concerning Friendly Relations and Co-operation Among States in Accordance with the Charter of the United Nations, GA Res. 2625 (XXV), annex (Oct. 24, 1970) and the prohibition against aggression. Section III of the Fourth Geneva Convention of 1949[84] imposes substantial restrictions on the conduct of occupations, and Article 47 in particular notes: The prohibition of annexation as the result of armed conflict is tied to the prohibition of acts of aggression, a clear *jus ad bellum* concern.

This section focuses on the consequences of an *act* of aggression, a state act, as opposed to the *crime* of aggression. The general matter of individual criminal responsibility is addressed in Chapter 6.G ("The scope of individual criminal responsibility") and elsewhere in the work.[85]

F   International Territorial Administration and Trusteeship

It is important to distinguish at the outset between the *principle* of trusteeship (as opposed to a formal trusteeship through the UN trusteeship system). This section will first discuss the formal prohibition of trusteeship for UN Members, then turn to the principle of trusteeship as it applies to international

---

83 The United Nations Charter does not limit its application to *jus post bellum* to providing for the authority of the Security Council to act under Chapter VI or Chapter VII to restore peace. Article 78 of the United Nations Charter states in full: "The trusteeship system shall not apply to territories which have become Members of the United Nations, relationship among which shall be based on respect for the principle of sovereign equality." The trusteeship system, like the mandate system before it, was in part an effort to realize the principle of self-determination and to move away from colonialism and empire as a post-war norm. While the United Nations Trusteeship Council is moribund and widely considered obsolete, the history of colonization and decolonization must inform an analysis of the normative and historical foundations of *jus post bellum*.
84 Geneva Convention Relative to the Protection of Civilian Persons in Time of War (Fourth Geneva Convention), 12 August 1949, 75 UNTS 287.
85 For more on this definitional issue, see e.g. O'Connell, Mary Ellen, and Mirakmal Niyazmatov. "What is Aggression? Comparing the Jus ad Bellum and the ICC Statute." *Journal of International Criminal Justice* 10.1 (2012): 189–207.

territorial administration. Finally, it will turn to the principles of accountability and proportionality as they apply to *jus post bellum* as described by Boon.[86]

Article 78 of the UN Charter reads as follows: "The trusteeship system shall not apply to territories which have become Members of the United Nations, relationship among which shall be based on respect for the principle of sovereign equality."[87] The prohibition of 'trusteeship' (over UN members) under Article 78 of the Charter limits the options in the transition from armed conflict to peace. It has implications for occupation law under the Fourth Geneva Convention, as well as the powers of the Security Council under the Charter. Given near universal membership in the United Nations, trusteeship in its original sense is essentially prohibited. The reincarnation of the United Nations Trusteeship Council to address such issues as failing states does not seem realistic, given the legal and political difficulties surrounding the issue.[88]

The principles of trusteeship may nonetheless be helpful for instances of international territorial administration.[89] As described by Article 76 of the UN Charter:

> The basic objectives of the trusteeship system, in accordance with the Purposes of the United Nations laid down in Article 1 of the present Charter, shall be:
>
> a. to further international peace and security;
>
> b. to promote the political, economic, social, and educational advancement of the inhabitants of the trust territories, and their progressive development towards self-government or independence as may be appropriate to the particular circumstances of each territory and its peoples and the freely expressed wishes of the peoples concerned, and as may be provided by the terms of each trusteeship agreement;
>
> c. to encourage respect for human rights and for fundamental freedoms for all without distinction as to race, sex, language, or religion, and to encourage recognition of the interdependence of the peoples of the world; and

---

86 *See* particularly Boon, Kristen. "Legislative reform in post-conflict zones: Jus post bellum and the contemporary occupant's law-making powers." *McGill LJ* 50 (2005): 285.
87 United Nations, *Charter of the United Nations*, 24 October 1945, 1 UNTS XVI.
88 Stahn, Carsten. The Law and Practice of International Territorial Administration: Versailles to Iraq and Beyond. Cambridge: Cambridge University Press, (2008), p. 440.
89 Ibid. 422.

d. to ensure equal treatment in social, economic, and commercial matters for all Members of the United Nations and their nationals, and also equal treatment for the latter in the administration of justice, without prejudice to the attainment of the foregoing objectives and subject to the provisions of Article 80.[90]

A series of International Court of Justice cases have a direct bearing on the obligations and principles governing an administering authority. These obligations and principles governing administering authority demand that the authority act in the interest of the inhabitants of the administered territory,[91] including self-governance.[92] The authority should bear responsibility for unlawful acts it commits.[93]

International territorial administration is no longer done through the trusteeship system but through the United Nations Security Council. There are essentially two types, those with the consent of the sovereign or former sovereign pursuant to Chapter VI (operations such as those in El Salvador ("UNOSAL") and Cambodia ("UNTAC")) and those without such consent pursuant to Chapter VII (operations such as the United Nations Mission in Kosovo ("UNMIK") and the United Nations Administration in East Timor ("UNTAET")). One principle emerging from the United Nations Security Council itself it that the authority should provide regular reports to the international community.[94]

Boon emphasizes that trusteeship is implicit in what she calls multilateral interim administrations or functional occupants.[95] While international humanitarian law binds belligerent occupants to an usufructuary or trusteeship role (see *infra*), one must look elsewhere for this principle to be applied to multilateral interim administrations. Boon also finds trusteeship obligations for international financial institutions involved in post-conflict economic reform, although the contours of those obligations beyond avoiding self-dealing are could be further developed.[96]

---

90   United Nations, *Charter of the United Nations*, 24 October 1945, 1 UNTS XVI.
91   See *International Status of South-West Africa (Advisory Opinion)* [1950] ICJ Rep 128, 132.
92   See *Legal Consequences for States of the Continued Presence of South Africa in Namibia (South West Africa) notwithstanding Security Council Resolution 276* (1970) (Advisory Opinion) ([1971] ICJ Rep 16, 31.
93   See Northern Cameroons Case [Preliminary Objections] (1963) ICJ Rep 15, 26, 35.
94   See UN Security Council, *Security Council resolution 1511 (2003) on authorizing a multinational force under unified command to take all necessary measures to contribute to the maintenance of security and stability in Iraq*, 16 October 2003, S/RES/1511 (2003).
95   Boon, Kristen. "Legislative reform in post-conflict zones: Jus post bellum and the contemporary occupant's law-making powers." *McGill LJ* 50 (2005): 285, 311.
96   Boon, Kristen E. "Open for Business: International Financial Institutions, Post-Conflict Economic Reform, and the Rule of Law." *NYUJ Int'l L. & Pol.* 39 (2006): 513, 572 et seq.

Where then to find the regulations of such administrations? Boon identifies at least three sources. First, there are the limits imposed by the United Nations Charter.[97] , there exist the baseline *jus cogens* restrictions.[98] Again, a good list of peremptory norms (*jus cogens* norms) can be found in the commentary to the Draft Articles on Responsibility of States for Internationally Wrongful Acts: "Those peremptory norms that are clearly accepted and recognized include the prohibitions of aggression, genocide, slavery, racial discrimination, crimes against humanity and torture, and the right to self-determination."[99] Aside from hopefully rare, rogue instances of racial discrimination, attacks on a civilian population, or torture, the main norm at play in such administrations is likely to be self-determination—an area that raises the question of trusteeship. (For more on self-determination, see Chapter 6.D.2 *supra*.) Rather than trusteeship for a displaced sovereign, trusteeship in an instance of these administrations is likely to be for the population within the administered territory, particularly a population engaged in a struggle for self-determination. Third, United Nations missions established by Security Council resolutions are of course regulated by the resolutions themselves.[100]

The *jus post bellum* principles identified by Boon extend beyond trusteeship to also include accountability (to the population of the administered territory) and proportionality.[101] With respect to accountability, both UNMIK and UNTAET included consultative mechanisms with local representatives.[102] This limited practice is not a strong evidentiary basis for this principle, although local-ownership as a prudential mantra has become widespread for any sort of external intervention in post-conflict justice. A stronger theoretical and legal basis for the principle of accountability is likely found in the peremptory norm of self-determination and the aforementioned evidence of a duty towards trusteeship as applied to accountability to the people in the administered territory. If self-determination applies, it limits the degree to which an administration can be unaccountable to the local population. The words of Article 73

---

97 United Nations, Charter of the United Nations, 24 October 1945, 1 UNTS XVI, particularly the chapters pertaining to the powers of the Security Council (V, VI, VII, VIII, and XII).
98 Boon, Kristen. "Legislative reform in post-conflict zones: Jus post bellum and the contemporary occupant's law-making powers." *McGill LJ* 50 (2005): 285, 312.
99 International Law Commission. "Draft articles on Responsibility of States for Internationally Wrongful Acts, with commentaries." Report of the International Law Commission on the Work of its 53rd session (2001), Commentary on Article 26, paragraph 5, p. 85.
100 Boon, Kristen. "Legislative reform in post-conflict zones: Jus post bellum and the contemporary occupant's law-making powers." *McGill LJ* 50 (2005): 285, 318.
101 Ibid. 294–295.
102 Ibid. 320–321.

of the United Nations Charter, while not directly applicable to such administration, are worthy of note. They read in pertinent part:

> Members of the United Nations which have or assume responsibilities for the administration of territories whose peoples have not yet attained a full measure of self-government recognize the principle that the interests of the inhabitants of these territories are paramount, and accept as a sacred trust the obligation to promote to the utmost, within the system of international peace and security established by the present Charter, the well-being of the inhabitants of these territories, and, to this end:
>
> a. to ensure, with due respect for the culture of the peoples concerned, their political, economic, social, and educational advancement, their just treatment, and their protection against abuses;
>
> b. to develop self-government, to take due account of the political aspirations of the peoples, and to assist them in the progressive development of their free political institutions, according to the particular circumstances of each territory and its peoples and their varying stages of advancement;
>
> c. to further international peace and security;[103]

As a matter of guiding principle, it would be odd if these obligations bound member states individually but not collectively. The language in Article 73 requires not only the trusteeship values (promoting the interests of the inhabitants, respecting their culture, advancing them, treating them justly, and protecting them from abuses), but also to develop self-government. Again, while not a strong argument for a *lex lata* obligation of accountability to the local population for international territorial administrations (let alone a clear determination of the operationalizations of such an obligation), the overall thrust of the obligations inherent in the peremptory norm of self-determination and the trusteeship obligations described in Article 73 are orthogonal with existing practice requiring some accountability mechanisms between the international territorial administration and the populations of the administered territory. As argued by Gordon, there is a strong case to be made that the right of self-determination applies to non-self governing people in general.[104] The shorter the period of administration and the greater the accountability, the less tension there is with the principle of self-determination.

---

103   United Nations, Charter of the United Nations, 24 October 1945, 1 UNTS XVI, Article 73.
104   Gordon, Ruth E. "Some Legal Problems with Trusteeship." *Cornell Int'l LJ* 28 (1995): 301.

Boon suggests a tension between the obligations of trusteeship (what inhabitants "should" want) and the obligations of accountability (what inhabitants do or do not want in fact) that can be resolved with the principle of proportionality.[105] While helpful, this general term could be further operationalized. In general, there is a potential for paternalism in any exercise of trusteeship—in assuming that the administrators are better placed to determine the obligations of trusteeship (what inhabitants "should" want) better than the inhabitants themselves. Ideally, there should be no tension between the two, and the administrator should, unless there is a compelling not to do so, be led by the expressed will of the inhabitants of the territory.[106] One notable exception to this general rule would be when the will of the majority of inhabitants is at odds with the rights or interests of a minority. Ethnic Serbs in Kosovo or Ethnic Indonesians in East Timor are pertinent examples. Then, presumably, one way to operationalize the norm of proportionality between trusteeship and accountability as introduced by Boon is to tie it to the overall *telos* of *jus post bellum*: taking the rights and interest of minorities into account not only for their own sake but to serve the overall goals of societal reconciliation and a just, sustainable, positive peace.

G   The Law Applicable in a Territory in Transition

1   *The Law of State Succession*

State succession is the replacement of one State by another in the responsibility for the international relations of territory.[107] It occurs in situations when

---

105   Boon, Kristen. "Legislative reform in post-conflict zones: Jus post bellum and the contemporary occupant's law-making powers." *McGill LJ* 50 (2005): 285, 323–325.

106   For more on subjective and objective public reasoning on collective goods, the foremost scholar on the subject may be Amartya Sen. *See* e.g. Sen, Amartya Kumar. *Collective choice and social welfare*. Vol. 11. Elsevier, 2014; Sen, Amartya. *The Idea of Justice*. Harvard University Press, 2011 (particularly Part IV); Sen, Amartya. *Development as freedom*. Oxford Paperbacks, 2001. The concept of a "right to development" has faded from scholarly and United Nations discourse, but if given credence would also have bearing on the obligations of an administrator, particularly a long-term administrator or one that radically changed regulations in terms of investment, property, and resource exploitation.

107   *See* Vienna Convention on Succession of States in Respect of Treaties (United Nations [UN]) 1946 UNTS 3, UN Reg No I-33356, Part I General Provisions, Art.2, (1), (b); Vienna Convention on Succession of States in respect of State Property, Archives and Debts (United Nations [UN]) UN Doc A/CONF.117/14, Part I General Provisions, Art.2, (1), (a); Arbitral Award of 31 July 1989, Guinea-Bissau v Senegal, Judgment, [1991] ICJ Rep 53, ICGJ 90 (ICJ 1991), (1992) 31 ILM 32, 12th November 1991, International Court of Justice [ICJ].

territorial change occurs, such as decolonization, cession of territory, secession, dismemberment of a state, incorporation of one state into another, or merger of multiple states into a new state. These can all be the result of an armed conflict. It has to be distinguished from situations where no territorial changes occur, such as military occupation, a change in government, or a failed state.

With respect to the law of state succession with respect to treaties, two dichotomous approaches collectively dominate.[108] The first approach uses the principle of universal succession, upholding past treaty obligations. The second *tabula rasa* approach emphasizes sovereignty at the expense of prior obligations. The dominance of these approaches varies with the type of succession.

In decolonization, the newly independent state is not bound to maintain in force a treaty of the predecessor state, but may establish its status as a party to such a treaty through unilateral declaration.[109] Decolonization frequently happened as a result of armed conflict, so this practice is particularly relevant for *jus post bellum* historically, although likely lacks contemporary relevance.

With cession of territory from one sovereign to another (e.g. Hong Kong) the general rule is the moving treaty frontiers principle:

> When part of the territory of a State, or when any territory for the international relations of which a State is responsible, not being part of the territory to that State, becomes part of the territory of another State: (a) treaties of the predecessor State cease to be in force in respect of the territory to which the succession of States relates from the date of the succession of States and (b) treaties of the successor State are in force in respect of the territory to which the succession of States relates from the date of the succession of States, unless It appears from the treaty or Is otherwise established that the application of the treaty to that territory would be incompatible with the object and purpose of the treaty or would radically change the conditions for its operation.[110]

This scenario, however, should be inoperative in an ordinary contemporary post-conflict scenario, as annexation of territory through conquest is prohibited

---

108 See Craven, Matthew CR. "The problem of state succession and the identity of states under international law." *European Journal of International Law* 9.1 (1998): 142–162.
109 UN General Assembly, *Vienna Convention on Succession of States in respect of Treaties*, 6 November 1996, (Entry into force 6 November 1996, United Nations, Treaty Series, vol. 1946, p. 3), Article 16.
110 Ibid, Article 15.

under international law (see e.g. Chapter 6.E "Prohibition of an act of annexation" *supra*.) That said, contested borders may be resolved during peace treaties, so this law may theoretically be operative.

If one state is voluntarily incorporated into another (e.g. German Democratic Republic into the Federal Republic of Germany), the obligations of the absorbed state would not normally be taken on by the incorporating state unless the parties decide otherwise, while the obligations of the incorporating state would be extended to the territory of the absorbed state, excepting localized treaties. Again, this scenario is problematic in a post-conflict context, as one would question the voluntary nature of the incorporation.

To the degree that the *Vienna Convention on Succession of States in respect of Treaties* is applied, if two or more states merge to form a new state (e.g. Yemen), all treaties continue to be enforced on the previous with their previous territorial scope unless further action is taken: "Any treaty continuing in force [...] shall apply only in respect of the part of the territory of the successor State in respect of which the treaty was in force at the date of the succession of States[.]"[111]

In the case of a complete dissolution of a state into multiple states (Yugoslavia), the treaties of the predecessor state continue in force for each successor state.[112] In contrast, when one of the entities on the territory continues the legal personality of the predecessor state (USSR, Russian Federation) the continuing state continues all treaty relations (excepting localized treaties).[113] These scenarios can come into play in the post-conflict environment, and can thus be important components of *jus post bellum*.

Of course, not all issues in the law of state succession regard treaty law. Some issues include property, archives and debts, for example. The *Vienna Convention on Succession of States in respect of State Property, Archives and Debts*[114] has not yet entered into force, and currently[115] has only seven state parties. Customary law seems governed mostly by equitable, negotiated settlements (e.g. USSR, Yugoslavia, Czechoslovakia). Again, these examples are not post bellum, so the law in that context is likely unsettled. This area is further explored in the section on odious debt, *infra*.

---

111 Ibid, Art. 31.
112 Ibid, Art. 34.
113 Ibid, Art. 35.
114 Vienna Convention on Succession of States in respect of State Property, Archives and Debts (United Nations [UN]) UN Doc A/CONF.117/14, 8 April 1983.
115 9 April 2017.

2 Human Rights Law and the Rights and Interests of Minorities

Human rights law generally applies in times of war and peace, and so would apply during the transition from armed conflict to peace. The full spectrum of applicable human rights law is beyond the scope of this work. Three aspects of human rights law merit particular attention with respect to the application of human rights law in the context of the transition from armed conflict to peace: states of emergency; the simultaneous application of international humanitarian law and human rights law; and the rights and interests of minorities in the transition to peace.

Human rights conventions limit the general doctrine of necessity by proclaiming non-derogable human rights guarantees[116] and allowing measures derogating from their obligations only (e.g.):

> to the extent strictly required by the exigencies of the situation, provided that such measures are not inconsistent with their other obligations under international law and do not involve discrimination solely on the ground of race, colour, sex, language, religion or social origin.[117]

While the International Covenant on Civil and Political Rights, European Convention on Human Rights, and American Convention on Human Rights have differing non-derogable rights, they all protect the right to life; the right not to be free from torture or other forms of cruel, inhuman or degrading treatment or punishment, the right to be free from slavery and servitude, and the right to be free from retroactive punishment.

Derogation in states of emergency is only potentially applicable in situations of "public emergency which threatens the life of the nation."[118] The Human Rights Committee's General Comment No 29 (Derogations from Provisions of the Covenant during a State of Emergency)'[119] makes clear that such states are exceptional. The American Convention on Human Rights phrases the suspension of guarantees:

---

116 E.g. "No derogation from articles 6, 7, 8 (paragraphs 1 and 2), 11, 15, 16 and 18 may be made under this provision." UN General Assembly, *International Covenant on Civil and Political Rights*, 16 December 1966, United Nations, Treaty Series, vol. 999, p. 171, Article 4.2.

117 E.g. "No derogation from articles 6, 7, 8 (paragraphs 1 and 2), 11, 15, 16 and 18 may be made under this provision." Ibid, Article 4.1.

118 Ibid.

119 Human Rights Committee, General Comment 29, States of Emergency (article 4), U.N. Doc. CCPR/C/21/Rev.1/Add.11 (2001). *See also* Lawless v Ireland, Admissibility, App No 332/57, B/1, (1958–59) 2 YB Eur Conv HR 324, 30th August 1959, European Commission on Human Rights.

> In time of war, public danger, or other emergency that threatens the independence or security of a State Party, it may take measures derogating from its obligations under the present Convention to the extent and for the period of time strictly required by the exigencies of the situation, provided that such measures are not inconsistent with its other obligations under international law and do not involve discrimination on the ground of race, color, sex, language, religion, or social origin.[120]

The possibility of a state of emergency may change over the course of the transition from armed conflict to peace, depending on whether conditions exist that meet the required standard. The European Commission of Human Rights described the criteria justifying a declaration of a state of emergency as follows:

a) the emergency must already exist or be imminent;
b) it must affect the whole of the nation;
c) the organized life of the community must be threatened;
d) the situation must be such that normal measures permitted under the Convention will not be adequate to address that situation.[121]

With respect to the application of human rights alongside international humanitarian law, a critical case is the recent *Hassan v. United Kingdom*.[122] The particular concern was the application of the right to liberty, enshrined in Article 5 of the ECHR, was violated by the United Kingdom's detention of an individual in accordance with the Third and Fourth Geneva Conventions in an international armed conflict. The European Court of Human Rights rejected the argument that international humanitarian law was *lex specialis* that precluded jurisdiction.[123] Instead, the Court rejected complaints under Articles 2 and 3 of the ECHR (failure to investigate detention, ill-treatment and death) for lack of evidence, and found that deprivation of liberty pursuant to powers under international law could be lawful and not arbitrary. The Court relied on the principle that the ECHR can be modified by a consistent practice by High Contracting Parties.[124] Of particular importance is the application of human rights

---

[120] American Convention on Human Rights (Organization of American States [OAS]) OASTS No 36, 1144 UNTS 123, B-32, OEA/Ser.L.V/II.82 doc.6 rev.1, 25, Part I State Obligations and Rights Protected, Chapter IV Suspension of Guarantees, Interpretation and Application, Art.27.

[121] Greek Case, Denmark v Greece, Report of the Commission, App No 3321/67, (1969) 12 YB Eur Conv Hum Rts 1, (1972) 12 YB Eur Conv Hum Rts 186, 5th November 1969, European Commission on Human Rights.

[122] Hassan v. United Kingdom, 2014 Eur. Ct. H.R., available at http://hudoc.echr.coe.int/sites/eng/pages/search.aspx?i001-146501 (9 December 2015).

[123] Ibid., para. 77).

[124] Ibid., para. 101. *See* United Nations, *Vienna Convention on the Law of Treaties*, 23 May 1969, United Nations, Treaty Series, vol. 1155, p. 331, Article 31(3)(c).

law extraterritorially, even if read in light of international humanitarian law. This also has implications for the laws of occupation, which this work addresses *infra*.

There is a robust ongoing discussion as to how, for example, international humanitarian law and human rights law operate during periods of armed conflict.[125] William Schabas contrasts the approach taken by the International Court of Justice (in which international humanitarian law is the *lex specialis* through which the human rights concept of "arbitrary deprivation of life" is to be understood during armed conflict) with the approach taken by the Human Rights Committee in which the individual benefits from both bodies of law.[126] For Schabas, the tension between these two approaches to international human rights law and international humanitarian law cannot be understood without understanding the relationship with a third body of law, *jus ad bellum*. International humanitarian law is built on neutrality with respect to the legality of the war itself and human rights law tends to view war itself as a violation of the human right to peace. This analysis regarding the choice of approach may be useful with respect to *jus post bellum* as well. If one attempts to find a neat and seamless relationship between potentially conflicting areas of law, one is likely to compromise essential aspects of at least one body of law.

It is worth noting that a number of international treaties and instruments since 1989 include both human rights and international humanitarian law provisions. These include the Convention on the Rights of the Child,[127] the Rome Statute of the International Criminal Court,[128] the Optional Protocol to the Convention on the Rights of the Child on the Involvement of Children in Armed Conflict,[129] the Basic Principles and Guidelines on the Right to a Remedy and

---

125   See e.g., Schabas, William A. "Lex Specialis-Belt and Suspenders-the Parallel Operation of Human Rights Law and the Law of Armed Conflict, and the Conundrum of Jus Ad Bellum." Isr. L. Rev. 40 (2007): 592; Droege, Cordula. "Interplay between International Humanitarian Law and International Human Rights Law in Situations of Armed Conflict, The." Isr. L. Rev. 40 (2007): 310; Orakhelashvili, Alexander. "The interaction between human rights and humanitarian law: fragmentation, conflict, parallelism, or convergence?." European Journal of International Law 19.1 (2008): 161–182; Cassimatis, Anthony E. "International humanitarian law, international human rights law, and fragmentation of international law." International and Comparative Law Quarterly 56.03 (2007): 623–639.

126   Schabas, William A. "Lex Specialis-Belt and Suspenders-the Parallel Operation of Human Rights Law and the Law of Armed Conflict, and the Conundrum of Jus Ad Bellum." Isr. L. Rev. 40 (2007): 592.

127   Convention on the Rights of the Child of 1989, art. 38, Nov. 20, 1989, 1577 U.N.T.S. 3.

128   Rome Statute of the International Criminal Court, July 1, 2002, 2187 U.N.T.S. 3.

129   UN General Assembly, *Optional Protocol to the Convention on the Rights of the Child on the Involvement of Children in Armed Conflict*, 25 May 2000 (Entered into force 12 February

Reparation for Victims of Gross Violations of International Human Rights Law and Serious Violations of International Humanitarian Law[130] and the Convention on the Rights of Persons with Disabilities.[131]

International law and international organizations have long been concerned with the venerable problem of "national minorities." As far back as the Peace of Westphalia, religious minorities were a central concern. The fate of minorities was at issue in the 1814 Congress of Vienna, the 1856 Congress of Paris, and the 1878 Congress of Berlin. The Paris Minority Treaties that emerged after World War I were the result of distrust of municipal law's treatment of minorities.[132] The Paris Minority Treaties were an innovative regulation of a state's treatment of its own citizens based on international law pertaining to minority groups.[133] As expressed by many authors, protection of minorities is the necessary corollary of self-determination, two sides of the same coin.[134] While international protection of minorities was an intense focus after the First World War (but even then of limited application), after the second interest in the subject dropped markedly, replaced to some degree by a focus on human rights.[135] Increasingly, protection of minorities was not seen as a separate

---

2002, Adopted and opened for signature, ratification and accession by General Assembly resolution A/RES/54/263 of 25 May 2000).

130   G.A. Res. 60/147, UN Doc. A/RES/60/147 (Dec. 16, 2005).
131   UN General Assembly, Convention on the Rights of Persons with Disabilities : resolution / adopted by the General Assembly, 24 January 2007, A/RES/61/106, *see especially* Article 11: States Parties shall take, in accordance with their obligations under international law, including international humanitarian law and international human rights law, all necessary measures to ensure the protection and safety of persons with disabilities in situations of risk, including situations of armed conflict, humanitarian emergencies and the occurrence of natural disasters. See 40 Isr. L. Rev. 317 (2007) Interplay between International Humanitarian Law and International Human Rights Law in Situations of Armed Conflict, The; Droege, Cordula.
132   Kunz, Josef L. "The future of the international law for the protection of national minorities." *American Journal of International Law* (1945): 89–95, p. 91.
133   Kunz, Josef L. "The future of the international law for the protection of national minorities." *American Journal of International Law* (1945): 89–95, p. 91; Kunz, Josef L. "The present status of the international law for the protection of minorities." *American Journal of International Law* (1954): 282–287, pp. 282–283.
134   Kunz, Josef L. "The future of the international law for the protection of national minorities." *American Journal of International Law* (1945): 89–95; Thornberry, Patrick. "Self-determination, minorities, human rights: a review of international instruments." *International and Comparative Law Quarterly* 38.04 (1989): 867–889.
135   Kunz, Josef L. "The present status of the international law for the protection of minorities." *American Journal of International Law* (1954): 282–287, pp. 282–283.

area, but a mere subset of human rights.[136] Human rights, with its focus on the individual as its natural unit, can be limited with respect to providing special protection from the majority; limited to general statements such as Article 27 of the ICCPR:

> In those States in which ethnic, religious or linguistic minorities exist, persons belonging to such minorities shall not be denied the right, in community with the other members of their group, to enjoy their own culture, to profess and practise their own religion, or to use their own language.[137]

Again, in the *Declaration on the Rights of Persons Belonging to National or Ethnic, Religious and Linguistic Minorities*,[138] what is protected is the "rights" of "persons" not protecting the broader interests of groups (beyond mere existence). At the United Nations, the body with the primary responsibility for protecting minorities is the Human Rights Council.[139] Similarly, the Lisbon Treaty refers to the rights of persons belonging to minorities[140] including the right to be free from discrimination.[141] The strongest protection of national minority groups *qua* groups remains in Europe (specifically the Council of Europe), with instruments such as the European Charter for Regional or Minority Languages[142] and the Framework Convention for the Protection of National

---

136   See e.g. Brownlie, Ian. "Rights of Peoples in Modern International Law, The." *Bull. Austl. Soc. Leg. Phil.* 9 (1985): 104.
137   UN General Assembly, *International Covenant on Civil and Political Rights*, 16 December 1966, United Nations, Treaty Series, vol. 999, p. 171. See also e.g. e.g. the International Convention on the Elimination of all Forms of Racial Discrimination, U.K.T.S. 77 (1969), Cmnd.41088; The UNESCO Convention against Discrimination in Education (1960) 156 U.N.T.S. 93.
138   UN General Assembly, *Declaration on the Rights of Persons Belonging to National or Ethnic, Religious and Linguistic Minorities*, 3 February 1992, A/RES/47/135.
139   See e.g. UN Human Rights Council, *Rights of persons belonging to national or ethnic, religious and linguistic minorities : report of the United Nations High Commissioner for Human Rights* , 17 December 2012, A/HRC/22/27. The Sub-Commission on Prevention of Discrimination and Protection of Minorities under the United Nations Commission on Human Rights was renamed the Sub-Commission on the Promotion and Protection of Human Rights in 1999 and then ended in 2006.
140   European Union, *Treaty of Lisbon Amending the Treaty on European Union and the Treaty Establishing the European Community*, 13 December 2007, 2007/C 306/01, Art. 2.
141   Ibid, Art. 21.
142   Council of Europe: Parliamentary Assembly, *The European Charter for Regional or Minority Languages*, 21 October 2010, Doc. 12422.

Minorities.[143] While laudable, these efforts within the Council of Europe lack universality and specific application in the *jus post bellum* context.

One of the most interesting offices with respect to minorities and *jus post bellum* is likely the Organization for Security and Co-operation in Europe's High Commissioner on National Minorities, which gets involved in a situation if, in her judgement, there are tensions involving national minorities which could develop into a conflict. The portfolio of this office is more conflict prevention than peacemaking, peacekeeping, or peacebuilding, however. Human rights can sometimes trump and override arrangements meant to keep a sustainable peace between various national groups—see for example *Sejdić and Finci v. Bosnia and Herzegovina* in which the human rights of the applicants overrode the power-sharing arrangements between national groups in Bosnia and Herzegovina.[144]

When groups are recognized in laws applied during transitions to peace, they are typically rather limited, such as organized armed groups in international humanitarian law as applied to non-international armed conflicts, or a "people" fighting for self-determination. The right of certain groups not to be destroyed under the concept of Genocide is an extremely limited protection, not applicable to all groups and not protective of all of the interests of listed groups. The collective political interests of, for example, women, children, the poor, or indigenous populations are poorly served by the traditional bases of international law (particularly) during the transition to peace, when the urgent demands of ending organized violence may tend to trump all other concerns.

Jus post bellum, as part of a venerable legal and normative tradition, is well placed to fill the gap between states and individuals with respect to the interests of groups during the transition to peace. It could be a useful tool to create or recreate a sense of a social contract necessary for successful counterinsurgency and democracy-building, even in the midst of occupation or in post-occupation. After all, armed conflicts are often fought due to the political interests of groups being underserved by the pre-war political structure. A case study in how *jus post bellum* principles can be used to structure the transition

---

143 Council of Europe, *Framework Convention for the Protection of National Minorities*, 1 February 1995, ETS 157.

144 ECtHR 22 Dec. 2009, Case No. 27996/06 and 34836/06, *Sejdić and Finci v. Bosnia and Herzegovina*. For more on this case, see Milanovic, Marko. "Sejdic and Finci v. Bosnia and Herzegovina." *American Journal of International Law* 104 (2010); Bardutzky, Samo. "The Strasbourg Court on the Dayton Constitution: Judgment in the case of Sejdić and Finci v. Bosnia and Herzegovina, 22 December 2009." *European Constitutional Law Review* 6.02 (2010): 309–333.

to peace relates to the question of whether there should be any bias towards a more democratic, equitable distribution of political power in the aftermath of war.

3   The Laws of Occupation

The modern understanding of occupation is rooted in Article 42 of the 1907 Hague Regulations[145] and the identical text in the 1874 Brussels Declaration.[146] That text simply reads: "Territory is considered occupied when it is actually placed under the authority of the hostile army. The occupation extends only to the territory where such authority has been established and can be exercised."[147]

The test as to whether or not territory is occupied or not is thus factual, with two conditions: the sovereign power has cannot exercise authority and the occupying power can. With respect to the second condition, the International Court of Justice has clarified that the hostile army has actual, not potential control.[148] Belligerent occupation does not require active resistance, and may lead to a sustained peace without shots being fired.[149] Common Article 2 of the Geneva Conventions of 1949 explains their applicability with the following language:

> [a]ll cases of declared war or of any other armed conflict which may arise between two or more of the High Contracting Parties, even if the state of war is not recognized by one of them. The Convention shall also apply to all cases of partial or total occupation of the territory of a High Contracting Party, even if the said occupation meets with no armed resistance.[150]

---

[145]   Hague Convention (Date signed: 18th October 1907), IV (Convention Relating to the Laws and Customs of War on Land), Annex (Regulations respecting the Laws and Customs of War on Land), Section III (Military Authority over the Territory of the Hostile State), Art. 42.

[146]   Project of an International Declaration concerning the Laws and Customs of War ((signed 27 August 1874) (1873–74) 65 BFSP 1005 (1907) 1 AJIL 96).

[147]   Hague Convention (Date signed: 18th October 1907), IV (Convention Relating to the Laws and Customs of War on Land), Annex (Regulations respecting the Laws and Customs of War on Land), Section III (Military Authority over the Territory of the Hostile State), Art. 42. The authentic (French) text reads: "Un territoire est considéré comme occupé lorsqu'il se trouve placé de fait sous l'autorité de l'armée ennemie.

   L'occupation ne s'étend qu'aux territoires où cette autorité est établie et en mesure de s'exercer."

[148]   Armed Activities on the Territory of the Congo, Congo, Democratic Republic of the v Uganda, Merits, ICJ GL No 116, [2005] ICJ Rep 168, ICGJ 31 (ICJ 2005), (2006) 45 ILM 271, 19th December 2005, International Court of Justice [ICJ].

[149]   See generally, Benvenisti, The International Law of Occupation (2nd ed 2012 OUP); Yoram Dinstein, The International Law of Belligerent Occupation (CUP 2009).

[150]   Common Article 2 of each of the Geneva Conventions of 1949.

This was extended to Additional Protocol I.[151] As described in Article 1, paragraph 3:

3. This Protocol, which supplements the Geneva Conventions of 12 August 1949 for the protection of war victims, shall apply in the situations referred to in Article 2 common to those Conventions.

The Hague Regulations, Geneva Convention IV and Additional Protocol I are the main sources for determining the law of armed conflict in a belligerent occupation. Also of note is the Convention for the Protection of Cultural Property in the Event of Armed Conflict.

Traditionally, occupation was treated as a difficult exception under public international law.[152] Occupation was seen as an extraordinary situation, where the identity between the sovereign state and its territory was ruptured, and the occupying force in effect held the territory in trust or at most as a usufructuary, until control would be restored to the sovereign. Radical transformation of the occupied territory and its laws was thus traditionally prohibited. This was eventually reflected in Article 43 of the Hague Convention of 1907.

Human rights law can also apply in occupied territories. This is the case for at least three reasons: the finding that human rights protections continue during international armed conflict,[153] the obligations of governments for areas under their effective control,[154] and the obligation for the occupying power to respect the laws in force in the country under Article 43 of the Hague Regulations.[155]

The literature on *jus post bellum* and occupation demonstrates the need for understanding the laws applicable to occupation with an eye towards a

---

151   Protocol Additional to the Geneva Conventions of 12 August 1949, and relating to the Protection of Victims of International Armed Conflicts (Protocol I) (adopted 8 June 1977, entered into force 7 December 1978) 1125 UNTS 3.

152   See generally Eyal Benvenisti, *The International Law of Occupation* (2nd ed 2012 OUP).

153   *See Advisory Opinion Concerning Legal Consequences of the Construction of a Wall in the Occupied Palestinian Territory*, International Court of Justice (ICJ), 9 July 2004*Legality of the Threat or Use of Nuclear Weapons, Advisory Opinion*, I.C.J. Reports 1996, p. 226, International Court of Justice (ICJ), 8 July 1996.

154   *See Advisory Opinion Concerning Legal Consequences of the Construction of a Wall in the Occupied Palestinian Territory, International Court of Justice (ICJ)*, 9 July 2004, para. 112.

155   Convention concerning the Laws and Customs of War on Land between the Argentine Republic, Austria-Hungary, Belgium, Bolivia, Brazil, Bulgaria, Chile, Colombia, Cuba, Denmark, Dominican Republic, Ecuador, France, Germany, Great Britain, Greece, Guatemala, Haiti, Italy, Japan, Luxemburg, Mexico, Montenegro, the Netherlands, Norway, Panama, Paraguay, Persia, Peru, Portugal, Roumania, Russia, El Salvador, Servia, Siam, Sweden, Switzerland, Turkey, the United States, Uruguay and Venezuela, signed at The Hague, 18 October 1907, Annex Regulations respecting the Laws and Customs of War on Land, Section III Military Authority over the Territory of the Hostile State, Art.43.

successful transition to a just and sustainable peace. Stahn[156] points out the demands for a substantive *jus post bellum* to manage the difficulties of occupation and post-occupation, citing the legal dilemmas posed by interventions in Kuwait and Iraq[157] (and indeed Japan and Germany[158]), specifically referencing the practice of the United Nations Security Council in Resolution 1483, which combined continued application of the law of occupation alongside the principles of state-building.[159] Boon states "Yet with the exception of the law of belligerent occupation, neither jus ad bellum nor jus in bello provide much guidance on temporary interventions after war and before peace."[160]

For the sake of concision, the analysis on trusteeship, accountability, and proportionality contained in the section on international territorial administration and trusteeship *supra* is not repeated here, although much of it applies with equal or greater force to belligerent occupation. Boon's work on *jus post bellum*, occupation and trusteeship referenced earlier[161] should be read alongside Walzer,[162] Cohen,[163] Benvenisti,[164] and Roberts[165] as well as classics such as von Glahn.[166]

---

156 Stahn, Carsten. "'Jus ad bellum,''jus in bello'...'jus post bellum'?–Rethinking the Conception of the Law of Armed Force." *European Journal of International Law* 17.5 (2006): 921–943.
157 Ibid 926–929.
158 Ibid 928–929.
159 Ibid 929.
160 Boon, Kristen E., Obligations of the New Occupier: The Contours of a Jus Post Bellum (June, 29 2009). Loyola of Los Angeles International and Comparative Law Review, Vol. 31, No. 2, 2008, p. 102.
161 Boon, Kristen E., Obligations of the New Occupier: The Contours of a Jus Post Bellum (June, 29 2009). Loyola of Los Angeles International and Comparative Law Review, Vol. 31, No. 2, 2008, p. 102; Boon, Kristen E. "The Future of the Law of Occupation." *The Canadian Yearbook of International Law* 46 (2008): 107–142; Boon, Kristen. "Legislative reform in post-conflict zones: Jus post bellum and the contemporary occupant's law-making powers." *McGill LJ* 50 (2005): 285.
162 Walzer, Michael. "The Aftermath of War." in *Ethics beyond war's end. Patterson, Eric. Ed. Georgetown University Press, 2012*.: 35–46 (obligation to create social justice); Walzer, Michael. *Arguing about war*. Yale University Press, 2008.
163 Cohen, Jean L. "The Role of International Law in Post-Conflict Constitution-Making toward a Jus Post Bellum for Interim Occupations." *NYL Sch. L. Rev.* 51 (2006): 497.
164 Benvenisti, Eyal. "Security Council and the Law on Occupation: Resolution 1483 on Iraq in Historical Perspective, The." IDF LR 1 (2003): 19; Benvenisti, Eyal. *The International Law of Occupation*. 2d ed. Oxford: Oxford University Press 2012.
165 Roberts, Adam. "What is a military occupation?." *British Yearbook of International Law* 55.1 (1985): 249–305; Roberts, Adam. "Transformative military occupation: applying the laws of war and human rights."*American Journal of International Law* (2006): 580–622.
166 Von Glahn, Gerhard. *The Occupation of Enemy Territory: A commentary on the law and practice of belligerent occupation*. University of Minnesota Press, 1957, 6.

Why is transformative occupation a problem under occupation law?[167] To briefly review Articles 43 and 46 of the Hague Convention of 1907,[168] Article 43 states:

> The authority of the legitimate power having in fact passed into the hands of the occupant, the latter shall take all the measures in his power to restore, and ensure, as far as possible, public order and safety, while respecting, unless absolutely prevented, the laws in force in the country.

Article 46 states: "Family honour and rights, the lives of persons, and private property, as well as religious convictions and practice, must be respected. Private property cannot be confiscated."

The prohibition on transformative occupation takes its ultimate form in the prohibition of annexation—the customary international law norm against any right of annexation by an occupier is reflected in Article 2(4) of the UN Charter and in the Declaration on Principles of International Law Concerning Friendly Relations and Co-operation Among States in Accordance with the Charter of the United Nations, GA Res. 2625 (XXV), annex (Oct. 24, 1970) and the prohibition against aggression. Section III of the Fourth Geneva Convention of 1949[169] imposes substantial restrictions on the conduct of occupations, and Article 47 in particular notes:

> Art. 47. Protected persons who are in occupied territory shall not be deprived, in any case or in any manner whatsoever, of the benefits of the

---

[167] For more on the heated discussion regarding transformative occupation, see e.g. Österdahl, Inger, and Esther Van Zadel. "What will jus post bellum mean? Of new wine and old bottles." *Journal of Conflict and Security Law* 14.2 (2009): 175–207; Boon, Kristen. "Obligations of the New Occupier: The Contours of a Jus Post Bellum." *Loyola of Los Angeles International and Comparative Law Review* 31.2 (2008); Zahawi, Hamada. "Redefining the Laws of Occupation in the Wake of Operation Iraqi Freedom": *California Law Review* (2007): 2295–2352; Roberts, Adam. "Transformative military occupation: applying the laws of war and human rights." *American Journal of International Law* (2006): 580–622; Cohen, Jean L. "Role of International Law in Post-Conflict Constitution-Making toward a Jus Post Bellum for Interim Occupations, The." *NYL Sch. L. Rev.* 51 (2006): 497; 580–622; Bhuta, Nehal. "The antinomies of transformative occupation." *European Journal of International Law* 16.4 (2005): 721–740; Yoo, John. "Iraqi Reconstruction and the Law of Occupation." *UC Davis J. Int'l L. & Pol'y* 11 (2004): 7.

[168] International Conferences (The Hague), *Hague Convention (IV) Respecting the Laws and Customs of War on Land and Its Annex: Regulations Concerning the Laws and Customs of War on Land*, 18 October 1907.

[169] Geneva Convention Relative to the Protection of Civilian Persons in Time of War (Fourth Geneva Convention), 12 August 1949, 75 UNTS 287.

present Convention by any change introduced, as the result of the occupation of a territory, into the institutions or government of the said territory, nor by any agreement concluded between the authorities of the occupied territories and the Occupying Power, nor by any annexation by the latter of the whole or part of the occupied territory.

Pictet's commentary notes that the traditional concept of occupation puts the occupying Authority to be considered merely as a de facto administrator.[170] The Public Trust Doctrine provided the occupier by analogy with usufructuary obligations during occupation.

The Fourth Geneva Convention[171] continues in Article 64:

> The penal laws of the occupied territory shall remain in force, with the exception that they may be repealed or suspended by the Occupying Power in cases where they constitute a threat to its security or an obstacle to the application of the present Convention. Subject to the latter consideration and to the necessity for ensuring the effective administration of justice, the tribunals of the occupied territory shall continue to function in respect of all offences covered by the said laws.
>
> The Occupying Power may, however, subject the population of the occupied territory to provisions which are essential to enable the Occupying Power to fulfil its obligations under the present Convention, to maintain the orderly government of the territory, and to ensure the security of the Occupying Power, of the members and property of the occupying forces or administration, and likewise of the establishments and lines of communication used by them.

In short, under this article, the Occupying Party may only do what is necessary for order and security, not radical transformation of the penal code—even if, presumably, the penal code is inequitable. With that as the traditional basis for the restriction of transformative occupation, it must be noted that transformative occupation nonetheless has a long history, and has been particularly challenged since World War II, first with the axis powers, with Czechoslovakia after 1968, northern Cyprus after 1974, Cambodia after 1978, Grenada in 1983, and

---

170   International Committee Of The Red Cross, Commentary On The Geneva Convention (IV) Relative To The Protection Of Civilian Persons In Time Of War 273 (Jean Pictet gen. ed., 1958), Article 47.
171   Geneva Convention Relative to the Protection of Civilian Persons in Time of War (Fourth Geneva Convention), 12 August 1949, 75 UNTS 287.

with United States policy in Iraq after 2003.[172] The occupation of Iraq, including the import of United Nations Security Council Resolution 1483[173] is primarily responsible for the current heated debate on the subject.

H   The Scope of Individual Criminal Responsibility

The section regarding amnesty and *aut dedere aut judicare* (Chapter 6.B.2.b *supra*) has already touched upon the scope of individual criminal responsibility. This section also amplifies the material covered in Chapter 3 ("Present – An Exploration of Contemporary Usage") Of the ten situations before the International Criminal Court as of this writing[174] (Democratic Republic of the Congo, Central African Republic, Uganda, Darfur (Sudan), Kenya, Libya, Cote d'Ivoire, Mali, and Georgia),[175] all except for perhaps the cases of post-election violence (Kenya and Cote d'Ivoire) involve an armed conflict, generally one that is dormant, although not necessarily truly finished.

While its norms and development of law with an impact on the transition to peace are of wide and general application, the development of each investigation, case, and charge can have particular effects on local transitions to peace. The situations before the International Criminal Court are generally non-international armed conflict (with the possible exception of the Comoros referral) although many have international involvement. That said, the norms emerging from the International Criminal Court's jurisprudence are likely to have general application to international armed conflicts and non-international armed conflicts.

In its current usage, International Criminal Law involves the application of international law to determine the individual criminal responsibility of

---

172   For more on this subject see e.g. Roberts, Adam. "Transformative military occupation: applying the laws of war and human rights."*American Journal of International Law* (2006): 580–622; Bhuta, Nehal. "The antinomies of transformative occupation." *European Journal of International Law*16.4 (2005): 721–740; Fox, Gregory H. "Transformative occupation and the unilateralist impulse." *International Review of the Red Cross* 94.885 (2012): 237–266.

173   UN Security Council, *Security Council Resolution 1483 (2003) on the situation between Iraq and Kuwait*, 22 May 2003, S/RES/1483 (2003). For more on this subject, see Benvenisti, Eyal. "Security Council and the Law on Occupation: Resolution 1483 on Iraq in Historical Perspective, The." *IDF LR* 1 (2003): 19; Orakhelashvili, Alexander. "Post-War Settlement in Iraq: The UN Security Council Resolution 1483 (2003) and General International Law, The." *J. Conflict & Sec. L.* 8 (2003): 307.

174   24 March 2017.

175   See https://www.icc-cpi.int/en_menus/icc/situations%20and%20cases/Pages/situations%20and%20cases.aspx last visited 3 May 2016.

defendants under that law while protecting the rights of the accused against the power of the state, regardless of how that power is institutionalized. The critical aspect of International Criminal Law is not the forum, whether that forum is international, domestic, or hybrid. The central hypothesis of International Criminal Law is the existence of international law that creates individual criminal responsibility for prohibited conduct.

The modern touchstone for the substantive content of International Criminal Law may be the four categories of crimes identified in the Rome Statute of the International Criminal Court: Genocide, Crimes against Humanity, War Crimes, and Aggression. A historical approach might tease out the criminalization of separate crimes (such as slavery, torture, or forced marriage) now lumped together under general headings such as Crimes against Humanity and War Crimes. The substantive portfolio of International Criminal Law is likely to continue to expand. For example, should the controversial Draft Protocol on Amendments to the Protocol on the Statute of the African Court of Justice and Human Rights be adopted, pursuant to Article 28A "International Criminal Jurisdiction of the Court," the International Criminal Law Section of the Court would have the power to try persons for fourteen crimes, not four.[176] Influences on international criminal law may have influences from unlikely places. The 2013 Arms Trade Treaty[177] regulating the international trade in conventional weapons also may aid in the transition to peace not only by limiting stockpiles but by reinforcing the norm against arming entities engaged in international criminal law violations.

The substance of International Criminal Law continues to change over time. Some developments, like the attempted criminalization as a matter of international law of "The Crime of Unconstitutional Change of Government" may tend to reinforce the status quo, putting it potentially at odds with other dynamics such as the original conception of Transitional Justice that might tend to oppose any status quo not sufficiently protective of human rights.

I   Odious Debt

The section *supra* regarding the law applicable to state succession with respect to a territory in transition naturally leads to the question as to whether there

---

176 First Meeting of the Specialized Technical Committee on Justice and Legal Affairs, 15–16 May 2014, STC/Legal/Min/7(I) Rev. 1, Draft Protocol on Amendments to the Protocol on the Statute of the African Court of Justice and Human Rights, Article 28A.
177 United Nations, Arms Trade Treaty, 2 April 2013 (Entry into force: 24 December 2014).

are laws of state and governmental succession in matters other than territory that relate to *jus post bellum*. In particular, the idea of "odious debt" as a species of "odious finance" may raise important legal and normative questions in the transition from armed conflict to peace. The key work in this area is James Gallen's article *Odious Debt and Jus Post Bellum*,[178] which addresses the issue directly.

The idea of "odious debt" dates primarily from the work of Alexander Sack from the 1920s onwards[179] and has reemerged since the invasion of Iraq in 2003.[180] Sack defines the principle of "odious debt" as follows:

> The new Government would have to prove and an international tribunal would have to ascertain the following:
>
> a. That the needs which the former Government claimed in order to contract the debt in question, were odious and clearly in contradiction to the interests of the people of the entirety of the former State or a part thereof
>
> b. That the creditors at the moment of paying out the loan were aware of its odious purpose.
>
> 2. Upon establishment of these two points, the creditors must then prove that the funds for this loan were not utilized for odious purposes – harming the people of the entire State or part of it – but for general or specific purposes of the State, which do not have the character of being odious.[181]

---

178 Gallen, James. "Odious Debt and Jus Post Bellum." *The Journal of World Investment & Trade* 16.4 (2015): 666–694.

179 Alexander N Sack, *Les effets de transformations des États sur leur dettes publiques et autres obligations financières* (Recueil Sirey 1927); Alexander N Sack, 'The Judicial Nature of the Public Debt of States' (1932) 10 NYU L Q 341; Alexander N Sack, 'Diplomatic Claims Against the Soviets (1918–1938)' (1938) 15 NYU Review of Law 507–35.

180 Patricia Adams, 'Iraq's Odious Debts' Policy Analysis No 526 (28 September 2004); Justin Alexander and Colin Rowat, 'A Clean Slate in Iraq: From Debt to Development' (2003) 33 Middle East Report No 228, 32–36; Jürgen Kaiser and Antje Queck, 'Odious Debts – Odious Creditors? – International Claims in Iraq' *Friedrich Ebert Stiftung: Occasional Paper No 2* (March 2004) <http://library.fes.de/pdf-files/iez/global/02018.pdf> accessed 2 May 2016; Nehru, Vikram. "The concept of odious debt: some considerations." *World Bank Policy Research Working Paper Series, Vol* (2008).

181 Alexander N Sack, *Les effets de transformations des États sur leur dettes publiques et autres obligations financières* (Recueil Sirey 1927), p. 163.

The concept of "odious debt" is consistently associated with Sack's definition.¹⁸² An alternative definition of "odious debt" can be found in the reports of Mohammed Bedjaoui, UN Special Rapporteur on the succession of States for the International Law Commission.¹⁸³ He proposed the definition:

(a) All debts contracted by the predecessor State with a view to attaining objectives contrary to the major interests of the successor State or the transferred territory:

(b) All debts contracted by the predecessor State with an aim and for a purpose not in conformity with international law and, in particular, the principles of international law embodied in the Charter of the United Nations.¹⁸⁴

Anupam Chander has usefully and compellingly clarified that the concept of odious debt should not be restricted to traditional forms of indebtedness, but also other "long-term obligations invented by modem finance."¹⁸⁵ For the purposes of this section, "odious debt" should be read to include such long-term obligations more generally, without devolving unnecessarily into a discussion of "odious finance."¹⁸⁶

Of particular note for the purposes of *jus post bellum*, "war debts" (debts raised for the purpose of war but possibly passed to the successor/victor state) were not passed in a number of cases,¹⁸⁷ while they were in others.¹⁸⁸ Similarly, Bedjaoui in his role as Special Rapporteur identified a number of cases of the non-passing to a successor state of "subjugation debts."¹⁸⁹ Despite these reports, the text of the treaty that might have dealt with odious debt, *Vienna Convention on Succession of States in Respect of State Property, Archives and Debts*,¹⁹⁰ does not mention odious debt. The idea of odious debt as a blanket

---

182 Gallen, James. "Odious Debt and Jus Post Bellum." *The Journal of World Investment & Trade* 16.4 (2015): 666–694, 670.
183 Mohammed Bedjaoui, Special Rapporteur, 'Ninth Report on Succession of States in Respect of Matters other than Treaties' (1977) UN Doc A/CN.4/301 and Add.1, 67.
184 Mohammed Bedjaoui, Special Rapporteur, 'Ninth Report on Succession of States in Respect of Matters other than Treaties' (1977) UN Doc A/CN.4/301, 66.
185 Anupam Chander, 'Odious Securitization' (2004) 53 Emory L J 923, 924.
186 Gallen, James. "Odious Debt and Jus Post Bellum." *The Journal of World Investment & Trade* 16.4 (2015): 666–694, 677.
187 Mohammed Bedjaoui, Special Rapporteur, 'Ninth Report on Succession of States in Respect of Matters other than Treaties' (1977) UN Doc A/CN.4/301, fn 276.
188 Mohammed Bedjaoui, Special Rapporteur, 'Ninth Report on Succession of States in Respect of Matters other than Treaties' (1977) UN Doc A/CN.4/301.
189 Ibid, fn 278.
190 UN General Assembly, *Vienna Convention on Succession of States in Respect of State Property, Archives and Debts*, 8 April 1983, available at: http://www.refworld.org/docid/3ae6b3961c.html [accessed 2 May 2016].

exception to the obligation to repay probably does not yet reflect customary international law.[191]

What is more intriguing is the possibility that through the application of principles of *jus post bellum*, the specific contours of odious debt may be made more specific and compelling as law and equitable principles that may form the basis of renegotiation during the transition from armed conflict to peace. Mohammed Bedjaoui, in his role as Special Rapporteur of the International Law Commission, viewed "odious debt" as an umbrella concept covering a range of specific debt categories,[192] including the two classical and most common types of odious debt: "hostile debt" and "war debt."[193] "Hostile debts" are debts incurred to suppress secessionist movements,[194] wars of liberation,[195] (implicating primarily non-international armed conflict) or wars to conquer peoples[196] (implicating in contemporary terms primarily international armed conflicts). Examples include the repudiation of Tsarist debts by the Union of Soviet Socialist Republics, and the refusal of the United States to repay formerly Spanish debt associated with Cuba, the Philippines, Puerto Rico, and other territories.[197] "War debts" are debts contracted by the State for the purpose of funding a war which the State eventually loses and whereby the victor is not obliged to repay the debt.[198] The majority of examples of war debt as odious debt seem to be antiquated from a contemporary perspective where the victor in a war might assume debt from the loser due to annexation of territory in an international armed conflict, but the term may also be applied to a non-international armed conflict that results in a regime overthrow. An example of this is the refusal of the new government in Costa Rica to pay back loans made by the Royal Bank of Canada after the overthrow of a dictator.[199]

---

191 Gallen, James. "Odious Debt and Jus Post Bellum." *The Journal of World Investment & Trade* 16.4 (2015): 666–694.

192 *Ninth Report on the Succession of States in Respect of Matters other than Treaties*, 1977 Yearbook of the International Law Commission, Vol. 2 (Part 1): 68 and 70.

193 Robert Howse, 'The Concept of Odious Debt in Public International Law' UNCTAD Discussion Paper No 185 (2007) UNCTAD/OSG/DP/2007/4, p. 3.

194 Ibid.

195 Gallen, James. "Odious Debt and Jus Post Bellum." *The Journal of World Investment & Trade* 16.4 (2015): 666–694, p. 671.

196 Robert Howse, 'The Concept of Odious Debt in Public International Law' UNCTAD Discussion Paper No 185 (2007) UNCTAD/OSG/DP/2007/4, p. 3.

197 Gallen, James. "Odious Debt and Jus Post Bellum." *The Journal of World Investment & Trade* 16.4 (2015): 666–694, p. 672.

198 Robert Howse, 'The Concept of Odious Debt in Public International Law' UNCTAD Discussion Paper No 185 (2007) UNCTAD/OSG/DP/2007/4, p. 3.

199 *Great Britain v Costa Rica* (1923) 2 Annual Digest 34, 176; See Odette Lienau, 'Who Is the "Sovereign" in Sovereign Debt?: Reinterpreting a Rule-of-Law Framework from the Early

The application of Additional Protocol I, Article 1.4 (defining "armed conflicts in which people are fighting against colonial domination and alien occupation and against racist regimes in the exercise of their right of self-determination" as international armed conflict)[200] may complicate the division between non-international armed conflict and international armed conflict—should AP 1 apply, the debt would be associated with international armed conflict.

Beyond war debt and hostile debt, Jeff King categorizes illegal occupation debts and fraudulent, illegal and corruption debts as species of odious debt.[201] As Gallen notes, these varieties of odious debt cover most of the scenarios in which a debt may be repudiated after a conflict.[202] Regardless of the type of odious debt, the application of the principles informing *jus post bellum* should assist in the resolution of the issue of repayment of obligations in the transition to peace.

Gallen focuses on equity as a general principle of law that informs the resolution of odious debt in the transition from armed conflict to peace. Other scholars such as Jure Zrilič and Merryl Lawry-White focus on equity in the application of investment claims in the transition to peace.[203] While equity is a system rooted in a variety of legal traditions[204] its generality is both a strength and a weakness—flexible but potentially over-flexible. Focusing the principle of equity (or related principles such as *meionexia*[205] and proportionality[206])

Twentieth Century' (2008) 33(1) Yale J Intl L 63–111; Gallen, James. "Odious Debt and Jus Post Bellum." *The Journal of World Investment & Trade* 16.4 (2015): 666–694, pp. 672–673.

200 International Committee of the Red Cross (ICRC), Protocol Additional to the Geneva Conventions of 12 August 1949, and relating to the Protection of Victims of International Armed Conflicts (Protocol I), 8 June 1977, 1125 UNTS 3.

201 Jeff King, 'Odious Debt: The Terms of the Debate' (2007) 32 NC J Intl L & Comm Reg 605–67.

202 Gallen, James. "Odious Debt and Jus Post Bellum." *The Journal of World Investment & Trade* 16.4 (2015): 666–694, pp. 673.

203 Jure Zrilič, 'International Investment Law in the Context of *Jus Post Bellum:* Are Investment Treaties Likely to Facilitate or Hinder the Transition to Peace?' (2015) 16 *The Journal of World Investment & Trade* 604; Merryl Lawry-White, 'A Context Specific and Holistic Approach to Post-Conflict International Investment Claims' (2015) 16 *The Journal of World Investment & Trade* 633.

204 Akehurst, Michael. "Equity and general principles of law." *International and Comparative Law Quarterly* 25.04 (1976): 801–825; Justice Margaret White, 'Equity – A General Principle of Law Recognised by Civilised Nations?' (2004) 4(1) Queensland University of Technology Law Journal 103, 106–07.

205 See Larry May, *After War Ends: A Philosophical Perspective* (CUP 2012), 6–10; Larry May, 'Jus Post Bellum, Grotius and Meionexia' in Carsten Stahn, Jennifer S Easterday and Jens Iverson (eds), *Jus Post Bellum: Mapping the Normative Foundations* (OUP 2014) 15–25, 21.

206 See Jure Zrilič, 'International Investment Law in the Context of *Jus Post Bellum:* Are Investment Treaties Likely to Facilitate or Hinder the Transition to Peace?' (2015) 16 *The*

on the particular goal of achieving a just and sustainable peace may help guide the application of these principles to make sure that the repudiation is not done to the level that actually degrades the post-conflict government's access to credit, nor cripples them with unsustainable or unjust debt. This may also allow a varied application depending on whether the creditors are private, sovereign, or international financial institutions.[207]

J   Alternative Structuring of *Jus Post Bellum*

It is also helpful to look at other leading authors and their approach to the substance of *jus post bellum*. In Carsten Stahn's classic *Jus ad bellum,' 'jus in bello'...'jus post bellum'?–Rethinking the Conception of the Law of Armed Force*[208] points out the demands for a substantive *jus post bellum*, citing the legal dilemmas posed by interventions in Kuwait and Iraq[209] (and indeed Japan and Germany[210]), specifically referencing the practice of the United Nations Security Council in Resolution 1483, which combined continued application of the law of occupation alongside the principles of state-building.[211] He points to the Responsibility to Rebuild pillar of *The Responsibility to Protect*, as reflected not only in the work of the International Commission on Intervention and State Sovereignty[212] but also the High-Level Panel Report on Threats, Challenges and Change,[213] the Report of the Secretary-General entitled 'In Larger Freedom: Towards Development, Security and Human Rights for All'[214] and in the

---

Journal of World Investment & Trade 604; Larry May and Michael Newton, *Proportionality in International Law* (OUP 2014); Emiliou, Nicholas. *The principle of proportionality in European law: a comparative study*. Vol. 10. Kluwer Law Intl, 1996.

207 Gallen, James. "Odious Debt and Jus Post Bellum." *The Journal of World Investment & Trade* 16.4 (2015): 666–694, pp. 686.

208 Stahn, Carsten. "Jus ad bellum,'jus in bello'...'jus post bellum'?–Rethinking the Conception of the Law of Armed Force." *European Journal of International Law* 17.5 (2006): 921–943.

209 Ibid 926–29.

210 Ibid 928–929.

211 Ibid 929.

212 Report of the International Commission on Intervention and State Sovereignty, The Responsibility to Protect (Dec. 2001), para. 5.1.

213 UN General Assembly, *Note [transmitting report of the High-level Panel on Threats, Challenges and Change, entitled "A more secure world : our shared responsibility"]*, 2 December 2004, A/59/565.

214 The Report of the UN High-level Panel on Threats, Challenges, and Change, A More Secure World: Our Shared Responsibility (2004), at paras 201–203.

Outcome Document of the 2005 World Summit.[215] One can also look to the work of the Peacebuilding Commission.[216] He points specifically to requirements that may exist for liberal interventions in order to restore human rights and standards of good governance during the transition to peace.[217] For concrete examples, Stahn notes that the formation of peace agreements is governed by

> Article 52 of the Vienna Convention on the Law of Treaties and considerations of procedural fairness; the limits of territorial dispute resolution are defined by the prohibition of annexation and the law of self-determination; the consequences of an act of aggression are inter alia determined by parameters of the law of state responsibility, Charter-based considerations of proportionality and human rights-based limitations on reparations; the exercise of foreign governance over territory is limited by the principle of territorial sovereignty, the prohibition of 'trusteeship' (over UN members) under Article 78 of the Charter limits occupation law under the Fourth Geneva Convention, as well as the powers of the Security Council under the Charter; the law applicable in a territory in transition is determined by the law of state succession as well as certain provisions of human rights law (for instance, non-derogable human rights guarantees) and the laws of occupation; finally, the scope of individual criminal responsibility is defined by treaty-based and customary law-based prohibitions of international criminal law.[218]

To help organize this substance, Stahn lists six principles of *jus post bellum*, namely Fairness and Inclusiveness of Peace Settlements,[219] The Demise of the Concept of (Territorial) Punishment for Aggression,[220] The Humanization of Reparations and Sanctions,[221] The Move from Collective Responsibility to Individual Responsibility,[222] A Combined Justice and Reconciliation Model,[223] and People-Centred Governance.[224]

---

215 GA Res. 60/1 (2005 World Summit Outcome) of 24 Oct. 2005.
216 Ibid, paras 97–105.
217 Stahn, Carsten. "'Jus ad bellum,' 'jus in bello'... 'jus post bellum'?–Rethinking the Conception of the Law of Armed Force." *European Journal of International Law* 17.5 (2006): 921–943, p. 932.
218 Ibid 937 (internal citations omitted).
219 Ibid 938.
220 Ibid 939 ("Territorial" added).
221 Ibid.
222 Ibid 940.
223 Ibid ("Towards" omitted).
224 Ibid 941.

Similarly, in the concluding chapter of *Jus Post Bellum – Towards a Law of Transition from Conflict to Peace* Stahn lists seven substantive areas of *jus post bellum*, namely 1) Treaty obligations, 2) Institutional frameworks for the management of transition from conflict to peace, 3) Definition of the law applicable in transitions from conflict to peace, 4) Management of individual responsibility, 5) Management of collective responsibility, 6) Structural principles for institution-building, and 7) Parameters of economic reconstruction.[225]

Guglielmo Verdirame points out that it is obvious that post-conflict situations are not exempt from the application of international law.[226] There are important law of armed conflict rules which extend to *post bellum*, including the rules applicable to 'protected persons' who remain in the hands of the detaining state,[227] a duty to repatriate prisoners of war after the cessation of active hostilities,[228] duties under the law of occupation that continue after the cessation of hostilities,[229] and in non-international armed conflicts a duty to "endeavour to grant the broadest possible amnesty to persons who have participated in the armed conflict, or those deprived of their liberty for reasons related to the armed conflict, whether they are interned or detained."[230] An expanding body of human rights case law in post-conflict situations is also available.[231] He also points to a growing body of state and international institutional practice on post-war situations, at least since the 1992 Agenda for Peace.[232] Since that 1992 Agenda for Peace, the four main elements of

---

225   Carsten Stahn, 'The Future of Jus Post Bellum' in Carsten Stahn and Jann K Kleffner (eds), Jus Post Bellum – Towards a Law of Transition from Conflict to Peace (T·M·C·Asser Press 2008) 231–237, p. 236–237.

226   Verdirame, Guglielmo. "What to Make of Jus Post Bellum: A Response to Antonia Chayes." *European Journal of International Law* 24.1 (2013): 307–313.

227   I.e. Art. 5 of Geneva Convention (III) relative to the Treatment of Prisoners of War (signed 12 Aug. 1949, entered into force 21 Oct. 1950), 75 UNTS 135, and Art. 6 of Geneva Convention (IV) relative to the Protection of Civilian Persons in Time of War (signed 12 Aug. 1949, entered into force 21 Oct. 1950) 75 UNTS 287, Art. 3 of Protocol Additional to the Geneva Conventions of 12 Aug. 1949, and relating to the Protection of Victims of International Armed Conflicts, 8 June 1977, 1125 UNTS 3.

228   Art. 118 of Geneva Convention III.

229   Art. 6 of Geneva Convention IV.

230   Art. 6(5) of Protocol Additional to the Geneva Conventions of 12 Aug. 1949, and relating to the Protection of Victims of Non-International Armed Conflicts (Protocol II) (signed 12 Dec. 1977, entered into force 7 Dec. 1978) 1125 UNTS 609.

231   App. No. 27021/08, Al-Jedda v. United Kingdom, ECHR, Judgment (2011); App. Nos. 71412/01 & 78166/01, Behrami and Behrami v. France, Saramati v. France, Germany and Norway, ECHR, Decision on Admissibility (2007).

232   UN SG Report, 'An Agenda for Peace Preventive Diplomacy, Peacemaking and Peace-Keeping,' UN Doc A/47/277-S/24111 (June 1992). See also UN SG Report, 'Supplement to An Agenda for Peace: Position Paper of the Secretary-General on the Occasion of the Fiftieth Anniversary of the United Nations,' UN Doc A/50/60 -S/1995/1 (Jan. 1995).

post-conflict peacebuilding from the perspective of the United Nations are 1) Disarmament, Demobilization, and Reintegration (DDR); Security Sector Reform (SSR), reestablishment of the rule of law, and democratization. Verdirame points out that

> Key aspects of the legal relationship between the victors and the defeated are already governed by rules of international law. On the front of prohibitions, in particular, it is noteworthy that outcomes of war previously treated as lawful are unlawful under modern international law. For example, war can no longer result in the dissolution or annexation of the vanquished state through debellatio or conquest.[233]

Veridame concludes with a delightful modification of the so-called "Pottery Barn rule" that reflects the combination of onus on the intervenor and the need for local ownership: "if you break it, you have a duty to help fix it but you still do not own it."[234]

Similarly, as Vincent Chetail has argued, post-conflict peacebuilding alone includes

> [I]nternational humanitarian law; international human rights law; international criminal law; international refugee law; international development law; international economic law; the law of international organizations; the law of international responsibility; the law relating to the peaceful settlement of disputes; treaty law which governs in particular ceasefire agreements; and the law relating to the succession of states in the case of territorial dismemberment due to conflict.[235]

Similarly, Larry May's discussion of *jus post bellum* focuses only on "the moral principles after a transition from war to peace has been achieved,"[236] following David Rodin's definitional lead.[237] Even within that limited definition, May isolates six normative principles of *jus post bellum*: rebuilding, retribution,

---

233   Verdirame, Guglielmo. "What to Make of Jus Post Bellum: A Response to Antonia Chayes." *European Journal of International Law* 24.1 (2013): 307–313, p. 309.
234   Ibid. 312.
235   Vincent Chetail, "Introduction: Post-conflict Peacebuilding – Ambiguity and Identity" in Vincent Chetail (ed), *Post-Conflict Peacebuilding: A Lexicon* (OUP 2009) 1–33, 18.
236   See e.g. May, Larry. "Jus Post Bellum Proportionality and the Fog of War." *European Journal of International Law* 24.1 (2013): 315–333, p. 317.
237   Rodin, David. "Two emerging issues of jus post bellum: War termination and the liability of soldiers for crimes of aggression." Jus Post Bellum: Towards a Law of Transition from Conflict to Peace (2008): 123–136.

reconciliation, restitution, reparation, and proportionality.[238] He insists that the addressee of these principles are not only political leaders but average citizens.[239] The ultimate goal of May's *jus post bellum* is the same as the hybrid functional approach outlined in this work, a just and lasting peace.[240] (In the end, May essentially rejects the main thrust of Just War thinking, opting instead for contingent pacifism.)[241]

Dieter Fleck likewise outlines three areas of *jus post bellum* that deviate from *jus in bello* on the one hand and peacetime international law on the other: 1) assistance in performing regime change, 2) robust law enforcement post-conflict, and 3) international territorial administration.[242] Fleck's watchword is cooperation, with *jus post bellum* operating primarily as an enabling framework more than a restrictive series of regulations. Similarly, James Gallen's conception of *jus post bellum* as an interpretive framework more than a series of restrictions is useful, although a hybrid functional conception of *jus post bellum* clearly extends beyond this limited role.[243]

The substance of *jus post bellum* also includes specialist areas of international law, such as investment law. A special 2015 edition of *The Journal of World Investment and Trade* focuses on *jus post bellum* provides a series of ground-breaking treatments of this issue. Gallen provides an analysis of "odious debt"[244]—an idea with significant potential for clarifying the legitimate expectations of foreign investors in the aftermath of conflict, while at the same time potentially freeing a post-conflict society from an unsustainable post-conflict debt burden. Merryl Lawry-White[245] and Jure Zrilič[246] provide an exploration of bilateral investment treaties and investment arbitration in the

---

238 See e.g. May, Larry. "Jus Post Bellum Proportionality and the Fog of War." European Journal of International Law 24.1 (2013): 315–333, p. 316.
239 Ibid 318–319.
240 Ibid 320.
241 Ibid 328–331.
242 Fleck, Dieter "*Jus post bellum* as a partly independent legal framework" in Stahn, Carsten, Jennifer S. Easterday, and Jens Iverson, eds. Jus Post Bellum. Oxford University Press, 2014, 43–57.
243 Gallen, James "*Jus post bellum*: an interpretive framework" in Stahn, Carsten, Jennifer S. Easterday, and Jens Iverson, eds. Jus Post Bellum. Oxford University Press, 2014, 43–57.
244 Gallen, James. 2015. Odious Debt and Jus Post Bellum. *The Journal Of World Investment And Trade*.
245 Lawry-White Merryl. 2015. International Arbitration in a *Jus Post Bellum* Framework. *The Journal Of World Investment And Trade*.
246 Zrilič Jure. 2015. International Investment Law in the Context of *Jus Post Bellum*: Are Investment Treaties Likely to Facilitate or Hinder the Transition to Peace? *The Journal Of World Investment And Trade*.

context of the transition from armed conflict. These are potentially critical issues not only in terms of resolving claims from foreign investors but for attracting investment critical to a sustainable *post bellum* future. Eric de Brabandere highlights the tension between the potential backlash from protecting foreign investors and the need to attract them.[247]

K   Conclusion

Building on the Stahn's 2006 framework for the substantive content of *jus post bellum*,[248] this chapter drew upon and extends what has been discussed earlier, to provide a specific focus on the contemporary legal content of *jus post bellum*. Seven basic areas were discussed: 1) Procedural fairness and peace agreements; 2) The Responsibility to Protect; 3) Territorial dispute resolution; 4) Consequences of an act of aggression; 5) International territorial administration and trusteeship; 6) The law applicable in a territory in transition; 7) The scope of individual criminal responsibility; and 8) The nexus of *jus post bellum* and odious debt. These areas are not comprehensive, and other frameworks could be used, as described in the alternative structuring section of this work *supra* —but it does highlight some of the major categories of legal content of *jus post bellum*.

---

247   De Brabandere, Eric. "Jus Post Bellum and Foreign Direct Investment: Mapping the Debate." *The Journal of World Investment & Trade* 16.4 (2015): 590–603.
248   Stahn, Carsten. "'Jus ad bellum,'jus in bello'...'jus post bellum'?–Rethinking the Conception of the Law of Armed Force." *European Journal of International Law* 17.5 (2006): 921–943, p. 937.

CHAPTER 8

Future? Rethinking Transformative Occupation and Democratization

A   Introduction

Previous sections of this work have detailed differing conceptions of *jus post bellum*, expanded on a hybrid functional theory of *jus post bellum*, contrasted the idea with other related ideas, and explored the roots of *jus post bellum* as an integrated part of the just war tradition. This section is also rooted in the past and present, but admittedly includes a greater portion of *lex ferenda*[1] than in previous sections. Ideally, the future of *jus post bellum* described here is *jus nascendi*, a body of law and principles in the process of being born.

This chapter makes the case for increased attention to the interests of groups and for a preference towards democratization in the transition to peace. A preference for democratization is in potential tension with the prohibition on transformative occupation and a neutral stance towards political systems, but is nonetheless justified, due to the value of democratization in *jus post bellum*. The value of democratization as part of *jus post bellum* is in part due to the democratic peace hypothesis, and in part due to the inherent value of providing protections for and empowerment of otherwise-disadvantaged groups such as minorities and women (as described below).

B   The Interests of Groups in the Transition to Peace

The interests of groups are a difficult subject for international law to address, but they are of critical concern for the transition to a just and sustainable peace, particularly in the context of post-occupation, democracy-building, and counterinsurgency. As the emphasis on successful transitions from armed conflict to peace grows, the management of the interests of groups merits further attention. The interests of groups may be seen to be an issue of political science more than law or normative principles. The interests of groups tend to

---

1 *Lex ferenda* is a Latin expression that translates as "future law," meaning what the law should be (see also *de lege ferenda*, with a view towards the future law). It contrasts with *lex lata* or *de lege lata* meaning "the law as it exists."

"fall between two chairs" that contemporary international law addresses most comfortably: the rights of states and the rights of individuals. For example, the simple version of nineteenth-century positivist public international law treats sovereign states as the subjects and objects of international law, with other entities existing as tacked on as an asterisk or exception. International human rights law typically focuses on the rights of the individual person, as does asylum and refugee law. International Criminal Law focuses on individual criminal responsibility (the designation of criminal organizations and joint criminal enterprises notwithstanding). The main focus of these bodies of law is not groups, and certainly not the distribution of political power of groups, despite the importance of that subject during the transition from armed conflict.

This is not to say international law is not aware of other entities aside from states and individuals. To take the most pertinent example, international law and international organizations have long been concerned with the venerable problem of "national minorities." As far back as the Peace of Westphalia, religious minorities were a central concern. The fate of minorities was at issue in the 1814 Congress of Vienna, the 1856 Congress of Paris, and the 1878 Congress of Berlin. The Paris Minority Treaties that emerged after World War I were the result of distrust of municipal law's treatment of minorities.[2] The Paris Minority Treaties were an innovative regulation of a state's treatment of its own citizens based on international law pertaining to minority groups.[3] As expressed by many authors, protection of minorities is the necessary corollary of self-determination, two sides of the same coin.[4] While international protection of minorities was an intense focus after the First World War (but even then of limited application), after the second interest in the subject dropped markedly, replaced to some degree by a focus on human rights.[5] Increasingly, protection of minorities was not seen as a separate area, but a mere subset of human

---

2 Kunz, Josef L. "The future of the international law for the protection of national minorities." *American Journal of International Law* (1945): 89–95, p. 91.
3 Kunz, Josef L. "The future of the international law for the protection of national minorities." *American Journal of International Law* (1945): 89–95, p. 91; Kunz, Josef L. "The present status of the international law for the protection of minorities." *American Journal of International Law* (1954): 282–287, pp. 282–283.
4 Kunz, Josef L. "The future of the international law for the protection of national minorities." *American Journal of International Law* (1945): 89–95; Thornberry, Patrick. "Self-determination, minorities, human rights: a review of international instruments." *International and Comparative Law Quarterly* 38.04 (1989): 867–889.
5 Kunz, Josef L. "The present status of the international law for the protection of minorities." *American Journal of International Law* (1954): 282–287, pp. 282–283.

rights.⁶ Human rights, with its focus on the individual as its natural unit, can be limited with respect to providing special protection from the majority; limited to general statements such as Article 27 of the ICCPR:

> In those States in which ethnic, religious or linguistic minorities exist, persons belonging to such minorities shall not be denied the right, in community with the other members of their group, to enjoy their own culture, to profess and practise their own religion, or to use their own language.⁷

Again, in the *Declaration on the Rights of Persons Belonging to National or Ethnic, Religious and Linguistic Minorities*,⁸ what is protected is the "rights" of "persons" not protecting the broader interests of groups (beyond mere existence). At the United Nations, the body with the primary responsibility for protecting minorities is the Human Rights Council.⁹ Similarly, the Lisbon Treaty refers to the rights of persons belonging to minorities¹⁰ including the right to be free from discrimination.¹¹ The strongest protection of national minority groups *qua* groups remains in Europe (specifically the Council of Europe), with instruments such as the European Charter for Regional or Minority Languages¹² and the Framework Convention for the Protection of National Minorities.¹³ While

---

6   See e.g. Brownlie, Ian. "Rights of Peoples in Modern International Law, The." *Bull. Austl. Soc. Leg. Phil.* 9 (1985): 104.
7   UN General Assembly, *International Covenant on Civil and Political Rights*, 16 December 1966, United Nations, Treaty Series, vol. 999, p. 171. See also e.g. e.g. the International Convention on the Elimination of all Forms of Racial Discrimination, U.K.T.S. 77 (1969), Cmnd.41088; The UNESCO Convention against Discrimination in Education (1960) 156 U.N.T.S. 93.
8   UN General Assembly, *Declaration on the Rights of Persons Belonging to National or Ethnic, Religious and Linguistic Minorities*, 3 February 1992, A/RES/47/135.
9   See e.g. UN Human Rights Council, *Rights of persons belonging to national or ethnic, religious and linguistic minorities : report of the United Nations High Commissioner for Human Rights*, 17 December 2012, A/HRC/22/27. The Sub-Commission on Prevention of Discrimination and Protection of Minorities under the United Nations Commission on Human Rights was renamed the Sub-Commission on the Promotion and Protection of Human Rights in 1999 and then ended in 2006.
10 European Union, *Treaty of Lisbon Amending the Treaty on European Union and the Treaty Establishing the European Community*, 13 December 2007, 2007/C 306/01, Art. 2.
11 European Union, *Treaty of Lisbon Amending the Treaty on European Union and the Treaty Establishing the European Community*, 13 December 2007, 2007/C 306/01, Art. 21.
12 Council of Europe: Parliamentary Assembly, *The European Charter for Regional or Minority Languages*, 21 October 2010, Doc. 12422.
13 Council of Europe, *Framework Convention for the Protection of National Minorities*, 1 February 1995, ETS 157.

laudable, these efforts within the Council of Europe lack universality and specific application in the *jus post bellum* context.

One of the most interesting offices with respect to minorities and *jus post bellum* is likely the Organization for Security and Co-operation in Europe's High Commissioner on National Minorities, which gets involved in a situation if, in her judgement, there are tensions involving national minorities which could develop into a conflict. The portfolio of this office is more conflict prevention than peacemaking, peacekeeping, or peacebuilding, however. Human rights can sometimes trump and override arrangements meant to keep a sustainable peace between various national groups—see for example *Sejdić and Finci v. Bosnia and Herzegovina* in which the human rights of the applicants overrode the power-sharing arrangements between national groups in Bosnia and Herzegovina.[14]

When groups are recognized in laws applied during transitions to peace, they are typically rather limited, such as organized armed groups in international humanitarian law as applied to non-international armed conflicts, or a "people" fighting for self-determination. The right of certain groups not to be destroyed under the concept of Genocide is an extremely limited protection, not applicable to all groups and not protective of all of the interests of listed groups. The collective political interests of, for example, women, children, the poor, or indigenous populations are poorly served by the traditional bases of international law (particularly) during the transition to peace, when the urgent demands of ending organized violence may tend to trump all other concerns.

Jus post bellum, as part of a venerable legal and normative tradition, is well placed to fill the gap between states and individuals with respect to the interests of groups during the transition to peace. It could be a useful tool to create or recreate a sense of a social contract necessary for successful counterinsurgency and democracy-building, even in the midst of occupation or in post-occupation. After all, armed conflicts are often fought due to the political interests of groups being underserved by the pre-war political structure. A case

---

14   ECtHR 22 Dec. 2009, Case No. 27996/06 and 34836/06, *Sejdić and Finci v. Herzegovina*. For more on this case, see Milanovic, Marko. "Sejdic and Finci v. Bosnia and Herzegovina." *American Journal of International Law*104 (2010); Bardutzky, Samo. "The Strasbourg Court on the Dayton Constitution: Judgment in the case of Sejdić and Finci v. Bosnia and Herzegovina, 22 December 2009." *European Constitutional Law Review* 6.02 (2010): 309–333.

study in how *jus post bellum* principles can be used to structure the transition to peace relates to the question of whether there should be any bias towards a more democratic, equitable distribution of political power in the aftermath of war.

C   *Jus Post Bellum* and Democratization

What role, if any, does *jus post bellum* have in democratization of post-conflict societies? There are many ways to rephrase this question. If *Jus Post Bellum* plays the particular function of structuring the production and application of laws in favour of a just and sustainable peace during the transition from armed conflict, is *jus post bellum* neutral with respect to the allocation of post-conflict political power? Or does *jus post bellum* militate against a democratic allocation of power in some instances? Or, in turn, does it favour a democratic allocation of power, with structural protections for groups potentially underrepresented at the table that sets the terms of the peace? This section will argue for the third interpretation: against neutrality and against anti-democratic bias, with a preference towards structural protections for and empowerment of certain otherwise-disadvantaged groups.

The hybrid functional conception of *jus post bellum* provides a framework for the allocation of post-conflict political power in the context of the transition to peace. Normally, international law is relatively neutral as to municipal arrangements of political power. Human rights law may protect individuals on an ongoing basis, international humanitarian law may serve a limited role to protect certain individuals from selected horrors of war, but as a general matter the approach taken since the Peace of Westphalia is to treat the sovereignty of all states as equal, regardless of their internal allocation of power, and thus limit the capacity of international law or foreign actors to interfere with domestic political arrangements. Even during occupation, a moment when a foreign sovereign has displaced local state authority, the general rule is against transformation and for a conservative preservation of the *status quo ante bellum*.[15] How then could *jus post bellum* provide a framework for a *post bellum* state with a preference for democratic political aspects?

---

15   See Fox, Gregory H. "Occupation of Iraq, The." *Geo. J. Int'l L.* 36 (2004): 195, p. 199.

The answer lies not only in human rights,[16] in the idea of a democratic peace, an idea with both a long pedigree and contemporary application. In the simplest form, the idea of "a democratic peace" is the idea that democracies do not go to war against each other. Stated with more nuance, this hypothesis asserts that given the unit of analysis of a "dyad-year," where any two states constitute a "dyad" and their relations over a year constitute a "dyad-year," as the democratic nature of the two states increases, the probability for substantial armed conflict during the dyad-year decreases.

More specifically, the explanation of *jus post bellum*'s potential democratic preference is best exemplified in the idea of a democratic peace providing an exception to the normal prohibition on transformative occupation and the normal prohibition for interference with a state's domestic political independence. While normally an occupier is restricted from transforming an occupied country, there is a traditional exception to this restriction, dating back to Immanuel Kant, that allows for the transformation of the conquered in order to achieve lasting peace. During the period when the new form of post bellum politics is being resolved, *jus post bellum* has a role to play.

D The Problem of Undemocratic Transitions to Peace

1 *The Natural Tendencies of Unguided Transitions to Peace to Favor the Powerful*

The natural tendency in the transition from armed conflict to peace is for political power to reflect the degree of military supremacy or influence of the armed groups involved in the conflicts. Democracy-building is a goal easily jettisoned under the pressure of security needs, and counterinsurgency can easily devolve into the reinforcement of the most powerful rather than building a positive peace. While this may make short-term sense in terms of pausing the organized violence of armed conflict, it is often not conducive to creating a just and sustainable peace. Often, those with military supremacy achieve this supremacy at the expense of democratic norms or social harmony. This raises the possibility that the need for a democratic arrangement of political power that includes protections for such groups as minorities and women should inform *jus post bellum* as a framework for the allocation of post-conflict political power.

---

16   See Eyal Benvenisti, The International Law of Occupation, 2d ed. Oxford: Oxford University Press 2012, 349–350.

Of course, if other areas of law or approaches to law, such as international humanitarian law, human rights law, or transitional justice, are able to address the natural tendencies of unguided transitions to peace to reinforce the political power of those victorious on the battlefield, there is less need for *jus post bellum* to apply. Accordingly, the limitations of traditional international humanitarian law, human rights law, and transitional justice will be detailed below.

2   The Limitations of Public International Law and Traditional International Humanitarian Law

A good place to begin is the Hague Convention of 1907 (Hague Convention IV, Respecting the Laws and Customs of War on Land).[17] Article 43 states:

> The authority of the legitimate power having in fact passed into the hands of the occupant, the latter shall take all the measures in his power to restore, and ensure, as far as possible, public order and safety, while respecting, unless absolutely prevented, the laws in force in the country.

Article 46 states: "Family honour and rights, the lives of persons, and private property, as well as religious convictions and practice, must be respected. Private property cannot be confiscated."

These Articles, and the thrust of occupation law generally as traditionally interpreted, is conservative in nature, even if the laws in force, family rights, private property arrangements, and/or religious convictions and practice reinforce gross inequities and power imbalances. Traditionally interpreted international humanitarian law (that traditionally includes occupation law) is thus unlikely to solve the problem of rectifying distributional injustices.

Traditionally, occupation was treated as a difficult exception under public international law.[18] Occupation was seen as an extraordinary situation, where the identity between the sovereign state and its territory was ruptured, and the occupying force in effect held the territory in trust or at most as a usufructuary, until control would be restored to the sovereign. Radical transformation of the occupied territory and its laws was thus traditionally prohibited. This was eventually reflected in Article 43 of the Hague Convention of 1907.

---

[17]   International Conferences (The Hague), *Hague Convention (IV) Respecting the Laws and Customs of War on Land and Its Annex: Regulations Concerning the Laws and Customs of War on Land*, 18 October 1907.

[18]   See generally Eyal Benvenisti, *The International Law of Occupation* (2nd ed 2012 OUP).

International Humanitarian Law has numerous protections for civilians generally and in certain cases for vulnerable groups in particular, but many of those interests are short-term, often simply avoiding death or damage. Occupation law may have progressed from being primarily concerned with the rights of the displaced sovereign to the rights of the people under occupation,[19] but it is not geared to address domestic political inequities.

More generally, Public International Law has no (or very little) preference for equitable and democratic structuring of group political interests within municipal government. As reflected in Article 2.4 of the United Nations Charter,[20] and the Declaration on Principles of International Law concerning Friendly Relations and Co-operation among States in Accordance with the Charter of the United Nations ("Friendly Relations Declaration"),[21] the political independence of each sovereign state is theoretically sacrosanct. As stated in the preamble of the Friendly Relations Declaration:

> Recalling the duty of States to refrain in their international relations from military, political, economic or any other form of coercion aimed against the political independence or territorial integrity of any State[.][22]

Thus, from a generic public international law perspective or a specific occupation law perspective, one would be hard-pressed to make out a preference for equitable and democratic political arrangements of municipal power—indeed, a plain reading of occupation law may at times be specifically anti-democratic in nature, preserving the status quo ante bellum. If *jus post bellum* can be argued to counteract this potentially anti-democratic nature of occupation law, then *a fortiori, jus post bellum* may have a role in promoting democratic regimes when such barriers to democratic change are not in place.

---

19   See generally Eyal Benvenisti, *The International Law of Occupation* (2nd ed 2012 OUP).
20   Charter of the United Nations (done at San Francisco, United States, on 26 June 1945) (United Nations [UN]) 1 UNTS XVI, 892 UNTS 119, 59 Stat 1031, TS 993, 3 Bevans 1153, 145 BSP 805, Ch.I Purposes and Principles, Art.2(4).
21   Declaration on Principles of International Law Concerning Friendly Relations and Cooperation among States in Accordance with the Charter of the United Nations (United Nations [UN]) UN Doc A/RES/2625(XXV), Annex.
22   Declaration on Principles of International Law Concerning Friendly Relations and Cooperation among States in Accordance with the Charter of the United Nations (United Nations [UN]) UN Doc A/RES/2625(XXV), Annex.

3 The Limitations of Human Rights Law, Transitional Justice, and International Criminal Law

Human rights concerns may be at their weakest when the terms of the new peace are being resolved. For those interested in these protecting and promoting these rights and interests as part of a just and sustainable peace, the limits of human rights at this moment can be a problem. Human rights are seen as binding, first and foremost, on the sovereign state with respect to those in its territory. Human rights law can, of course, have extra-territorial effect, but the initial and primary concern of human rights law has been the restraint of the state with respect to those in its territory. The context of armed conflict, occupation, and post-occupation can limit the territorial state's control over the conditions in its territory.

While there are certainly human rights relating to democratic political participation, non-discrimination, and other issues that relate to the issue of the arrangement of political power, there is no clear hierarchy of norms in the vast panoply of potentially applicable human rights that would guide the application of human rights to adequately ensure structuring the post-conflict peace in an equitable manner. It is not so much that human rights themselves are inadequate in the abstract for the needs of constructing a just and sustainable peace, but that they need an organizing mechanism during the delicate transition from armed conflict to maximize the chances of long-term success.

As described in Chapter 3, Section B *supra*, Transitional Justice ought to be focused on legal responses to confront the wrongdoings of repressive predecessor regimes. As stated in *Transitional Justice Genealogy*,[23] "Transitional justice can be defined as the conception of justice associated with periods of political change, characterized by legal responses to confront the wrongdoings of repressive predecessor regimes."[24] That said, Transitional Justice does not typically come into full effect until after the regime change has occurred, and has played a limited role in negotiating the terms of the peace, particularly in international armed conflict. It suffers from the same structural weaknesses as the application of international human rights law generally with respect to the transition to a just and sustainable peace.

Transitional Justice has its roots in a focus on past atrocities, ideally as a means to cementing a new human-rights respecting regime, but does not necessarily place issues of equitable structuring political power of various groups as a high-priority. There has been excellent work to ensure that distributional

---

23 Teitel, "Transitional Justice Genealogy" 3.
24 Teitel, "Transitional Justice Genealogy" 69.

justice is taken seriously in transitional justice,[25] but in daily practice, most transitional justice remains tightly tied to international criminal law or truth-seeking mechanism that are decidedly backwards-looking and focused on rectificatory and retributive justice, not distributional justice. It would be highly inappropriate for International Criminal Law institutions, with International Criminal Law's focus on individual criminal responsibility, to involve themselves in matters of the political interests of groups.

E   Transformative Occupation and Democratic Peace

1   *The Problem of Transformative Occupation*
Why is transformative occupation a problem under occupation law?[26] To briefly review Articles 43 and 46 of the Hague Convention of 1907,[27] Article 43 states:

> The authority of the legitimate power having in fact passed into the hands of the occupant, the latter shall take all the measures in his power to restore, and ensure, as far as possible, public order and safety, while respecting, unless absolutely prevented, the laws in force in the country.

Article 46 states: "Family honour and rights, the lives of persons, and private property, as well as religious convictions and practice, must be respected. Private property cannot be confiscated."

---

25   See e.g. Mani, Rama. *Beyond Retribution: Seeking Justice in the Shadows of War.* Polity, 2002.
26   For more on the heated discussion regarding transformative occupation, see e.g. Österdahl, Inger, and Esther Van Zadel. "What will jus post bellum mean? Of new wine and old bottles." *Journal of Conflict and Security Law* 14.2 (2009): 175–207; Boon, Kristen. "Obligations of the New Occupier: The Contours of a Jus Post Bellum." *Loyola of Los Angeles International and Comparative Law Review* 31.2 (2008); Zahawi, Hamada. "Redefining the Laws of Occupation in the Wake of Operation Iraqi Freedom": *California Law Review* (2007): 2295–2352; Roberts, Adam. "Transformative military occupation: applying the laws of war and human rights." *American Journal of International Law* (2006): 580–622; Cohen, Jean L. "Role of International Law in Post-Conflict Constitution-Making toward a Jus Post Bellum for Interim Occupations, The." *NYL Sch. L. Rev.* 51 (2006): 497; 580–622; Bhuta, Nehal. "The antinomies of transformative occupation." *European Journal of International Law* 16.4 (2005): 721–740; Yoo, John. "Iraqi Reconstruction and the Law of Occupation." *UC Davis J. Int'l L. & Pol'y* 11 (2004): 7.
27   International Conferences (The Hague), *Hague Convention (IV) Respecting the Laws and Customs of War on Land and Its Annex: Regulations Concerning the Laws and Customs of War on Land*, 18 October 1907.

The prohibition on transformative occupation takes its ultimate form in the prohibition of annexation—the customary international law norm against any right of annexation by an occupier is reflected in Article 2(4) of the UN Charter and in the Declaration on Principles of International Law Concerning Friendly Relations and Co-operation Among States in Accordance with the Charter of the United Nations, GA Res. 2625 (XXV), annex (Oct. 24, 1970) and the prohibition against aggression. Section III of the Fourth Geneva Convention of 1949[28] imposes substantial restrictions on the conduct of occupations, and Article 47 in particular notes:

> Art. 47. Protected persons who are in occupied territory shall not be deprived, in any case or in any manner whatsoever, of the benefits of the present Convention by any change introduced, as the result of the occupation of a territory, into the institutions or government of the said territory, nor by any agreement concluded between the authorities of the occupied territories and the Occupying Power, nor by any annexation by the latter of the whole or part of the occupied territory.

Pictet's commentary notes that the traditional concept of occupation puts the occupying Authority to be considered merely as a de facto administrator.[29] The Public Trust Doctrine provided the occupier by analogy with usufructuary obligations during occupation.

The Fourth Geneva Convention[30] continues in Article 64:

> The penal laws of the occupied territory shall remain in force, with the exception that they may be repealed or suspended by the Occupying Power in cases where they constitute a threat to its security or an obstacle to the application of the present Convention. Subject to the latter consideration and to the necessity for ensuring the effective administration of justice, the tribunals of the occupied territory shall continue to function in respect of all offences covered by the said laws.

---

28 Geneva Convention Relative to the Protection of Civilian Persons in Time of War (Fourth Geneva Convention), 12 August 1949, 75 UNTS 287.

29 International Committee Of The Red Cross, Commentary On The Geneva Convention (IV) Relative To The Protection Of Civilian Persons In Time Of War 273 (Jean Pictet gen. ed., 1958), Article 47.

30 Geneva Convention Relative to the Protection of Civilian Persons in Time of War (Fourth Geneva Convention), 12 August 1949, 75 UNTS 287.

The Occupying Power may, however, subject the population of the occupied territory to provisions which are essential to enable the Occupying Power to fulfil its obligations under the present Convention, to maintain the orderly government of the territory, and to ensure the security of the Occupying Power, of the members and property of the occupying forces or administration, and likewise of the establishments and lines of communication used by them.

In short, under this article, the Occupying Party may only do what is necessary for order and security, not radical transformation of the penal code—even if, presumably, the penal code is inequitable. With that as the traditional basis for the restriction of transformative occupation, it must be noted that transformative occupation nonetheless has a long history, and has been particularly challenged since World War II, first with the axis powers, with Czechoslovakia after 1968, northern Cyprus after 1974, Cambodia after 1978, Grenada in 1983, and with United States policy in Iraq after 2003.[31] The occupation of Iraq, including the import of United Nations Security Council Resolution 1483[32] is primarily responsible for the current heated debate on the subject.

2   Kant's Concept of a Warlike Constitution

In Perpetual Peace, Kant emphasizes this conservative principle. Article 5 of the *Preliminary Articles for Perpetual Peace Among States* reads simply "No state shall by force interfere with either the constitution or government of another state." Shortly thereafter, however, Kant includes a caveat, recognizing the tension that endures to this day. He suggests that a defeated aggressor "can be made to accept a new constitution of a nature that is unlikely to encourage their warlike inclinations."[33]

---

31   For more on this subject see e.g. Roberts, Adam. "Transformative military occupation: applying the laws of war and human rights."*American Journal of International Law* (2006): 580–622; Bhuta, Nehal. "The antinomies of transformative occupation." *European Journal of International Law*16.4 (2005): 721–740; Fox, Gregory H. "Transformative occupation and the unilateralist impulse." *International Review of the Red Cross* 94.885 (2012): 237–266.

32   UN Security Council, *Security Council Resolution 1483 (2003) on the situation between Iraq and Kuwait*, 22 May 2003, S/RES/1483 (2003). For more on this subject, see Benvenisti, Eyal. "Security Council and the Law on Occupation: Resolution 1483 on Iraq in Historical Perspective, The." *IDF LR* 1 (2003): 19; Orakhelashvili, Alexander. "Post-War Settlement in Iraq: The UN Security Council Resolution 1483 (2003) and General International Law, The." *J. Conflict & Sec. L.* 8 (2003): 307.

33   I. Kant, The Doctrine of Right, in his Political Writings, trans. H.B. Nisbet (1995), pp. 169–171 (P 348–49).

Kant's vision of the possibility of perpetual peace was based partially on states sharing "republican" constitutions. By "republican," Kant was referring to certain basic elements core to what is thought of as "democratic today: liberty, equal treatment under the law, representative government, and separation of powers.[34] Kant's vision was thus very much a precursor of our modern conception of a democratic peace.

3   *Democratic Peace*

Kant's ultimate hope was not merely that single states be made free or peaceful, but that there could be a systematic effect on the international plane, what he called a "federation of free states."[35] As said before, in the simplest form, the idea of "a democratic peace" is the idea that democracies do not go to war against each other. Stated with more nuance, this hypothesis asserts that given the unit of analysis of a "dyad-year," where any two states constitute a "dyad" and their relations over a year constitute a "dyad-year," as the democratic nature of the two states increases, the probability for substantial armed conflict during the dyad-year decreases. This is one of the most significant theses in statistical studies of world politics.[36] Bruce Russett, Zeev Maoz, and others have convincingly shown this to be the case, given the datasets available to him for post-World War II, and for the ancient world.[37] The result that democracies rather fight each other is even more impressive given that democracies are not less conflict-prone than non-democracies.[38] There are, however, limitations to the data used. The Polity dataset is often used to determine the degree to which a state is democratic, but it is less clear whether particular arguably democratic attributes, such as women's rights, are properly reflected in the dataset either directly or by proxy.

---

34   See Immanuel Kant, Toward Perpetual Peace, 1932, U.S. Library Association, Westwood Hills Press, Los Angeles, California, U.S.A; Russett, Bruce. Grasping the democratic peace: Principles for a post-Cold War world. Princeton University Press, 1994, p. 4.

35   Immanuel Kant, Toward Perpetual Peace, 1932, U.S. Library Association, Westwood Hills Press, Los Angeles, California, U.S.A.

36   Maoz, Zeev, and Bruce Russett. "Normative and Structural Causes of Democratic Peace, 1946–1986." American Political Science Review 87.03 (1993): 624–638.

37   Maoz, Zeev, and Bruce Russett. "Normative and Structural Causes of Democratic Peace, 1946–1986." American Political Science Review 87.03 (1993): 624–638; Russett, Bruce. Grasping the democratic peace: Principles for a post-Cold War world. Princeton university press, 1994; Russett, Bruce, et al. "The democratic peace."*International Security* (1995): 164–184.

38   Maoz, Zeev, and Bruce Russett. "Normative and Structural Causes of Democratic Peace, 1946–1986." American Political Science Review 87.03 (1993): 624–638.

4 The Role of Protecting the Rights and Interests of Women in a Democracy

There has been increasing recognition that a state suffers from a democratic deficit without adequate representation of women and women's interests.[39] This has been recognized by the Beijing Declaration and Platform of Action, which states "No government can claim to be democratic until women are guaranteed the right to equal representation."[40] Relatively recently, datasets such as the Cingranelli-Richards (CIRI) Human Rights Data Project[41] contains quantitative indicators of 15 human rights for 195 countries including Women's Economic Rights, Women's Political Rights, and Women's Social Rights. There are also datasets such as WomenStats that focus specifically on cross-national data and information on women[42] and indices to show relative empowerment and development such as the GEM (Gender Empowerment Measure) and GDI (Gender Development Index). Datasets such as these allow for statistical analysis of women's rights and political power, and how these relate to world political theories such as the democratic peace hypothesis.

F Argument for Democratization in the Transition to Peace

During the transition from armed conflict to peace, local structural factors (such as who controls military, political, economic, and social power) can hinder the establishment or re-establishment of a democratic post bellum regime. International law prohibitions on transformative occupation can also hinder, in theory at least, the establishment of a democratic post bellum regime. If in fact, democratic states are less likely to enter into armed conflict with other democratic states, these barriers to democratization are a potential

---

39 See, e.g. Moghadam, Valentine M. "The gender of democracy: The link between women's rights and democratization in the Middle East." Arab reform bulletin 2.7 (2004): 2–3; Phillips, Anne. 1991. Engendering Democracy. University Park, PA: University of Pennsylvania Press; Phillips, Anne. 1995. The Politics of Presence: The Political Representation of Gender, Ethnicity and Race. Oxford, UK: Clarendon Press.

40 United Nations, Beijing Declaration and Platform of Action, adopted at the Fourth World Conference on Women, 27 October 1995.

41 Cingranelli, David L., David L. Richards, and K. Chad Clay. 2014. "The CIRI Human Rights Dataset." http://www.humanrightsdata.com. Version 2014.04.14; Cingranelli, David L., and David L. Richards. "The Cingranelli and Richards (CIRI) human rights data project." Human Rights Quarterly 32.2 (2010): 401–424; Cingranelli, David L. "The Cingranelli-Richards (CIRI) Human Rights Data Project." Human Rights Quarterly 32 (2008): 395–418.

42 Caprioli, Mary, et al. "The WomanStats project database: advancing an empirical research agenda." Journal of Peace Research (2009). http://www.womanstats.org.

international *jus post bellum* problem in that they lessen the sustainability of the peace between the new regime and other states that are democracies. Regardless of this democratic peace factor, avoidable post bellum deficits pose a domestic *jus post bellum* problem in that they tend to reduce the justness and possibly the sustainability of the peace within the new polity.

While these are *jus post bellum* problems (in terms of maximizing the chances for a transition to a just and sustainable peace), *jus post bellum* as a concept also holds promise as a solution—it can provide an organizing framework for the response. As far back as Kant, ethical philosophers have posited an exception to the prohibition of transformative occupation based on the possibility of a democratic peace. Efforts are underway on a variety of levels to ensure a just and equitable process and outcome for the termination of armed conflict and construction of early peace, including the full participation of women and inclusion of women's issues, but these efforts risk being treated more as an add-on or an afterthought.[43] The typical prescription for increasing the representation of women and other groups in peace negotiations and the construction of the post bellum society is for additional political will, but being backed by a legal and normative framework to prioritize these factors as important for building a just and sustainable peace would do more than an empty request for additional will. The idea of *jus post bellum* is ideally suited as a framework for addressing group issues structurally placed between the rights of states and individuals by placing those group issues within a more universal set of goals—a just and sustainable peace.

G Transformative Occupation that Considers Group Interests and Participation Aiding the Transition to Peace

The United Nations Security Council has passed several resolutions on women, peace, and security, including the specific issues of women's representation during the construction of peace and ensuring that women's issues are addressed.[44] On reflection, from a traditional public international law perspective, this may seem like odd work for the Security Council to take on. While this may be laudable policy, how does it relate to international peace and security, the supposed portfolio of the Security Council? Why is this not left to the

---

43 Women, U.N. "Women's participation in peace negotiations: Connections between presence and influence." *New York* (2010).

44 See UNSC Res. 1325 (2000), UNSC Res. 1820 (2008), UNSC Res. 1888 (2009), UNSC Res. 1889 (2009), UNSC Res. 1960 (2010), and UNSC Res. 2242(2015).

Human Rights Council, or some other United Nations organ or institution? Is it a human right that is being protected here, or something broader—protecting the political interests of a group (women) that is systematically and structurally underserved by existing peacemaking practices?

This practice of the United Nations Security Council, focusing on the protection of the long-term rights and interests of women during armed conflict and its aftermath, is a good example of the (underdeveloped) promise of *jus post bellum* to address group issues structurally placed between the rights of the individual and the rights of states. More specifically, it is a good example of aiding in democratization of the process of peacemaking, and in democratization of the post-conflict society. After all, women constitute about half of the adult population in any particular society, and by contemporary standards must be included in a democratic society.

The United Nations Security Council resolutions on women, peace, and security provide evidence of the seriousness of the problem. They highlight the rights and interests of women in the context of the transition from armed conflict. They are, however, unsuccessful in fully addressing the problem.

Protecting and promoting the rights and interests of women during the transition to peace may be a legitimate interest of *jus post bellum*, not as part of a human rights regime, but more as part of the traditional concerns of public international law—international order— and in some cases part of a central obligation to an occupying power to make the resort to the use of force just, by helping to create a just and sustainable peace.

What would this look like in modern terms? The canonical modern occupations of Japan and Germany after World War II certainly were transformative. One aspect of this transformation was explicitly pacific in nature—the neutering of their militaries for any action except individual self-defence. This was far from the only transformative aspect of the occupation, as the domestic legal systems were refashioned as comparatively human rights-respecting regimes.[45] To understand not only the occupation but the post-occupation, a different approach is warranted. Had Article 43 of the Hague Convention of 1907 been over-enthusiastically observed and the laws in force in the occupied country been preserved to the point where Germany remained fascist and Japan remained non-democratic, not only would this have seemed absurd, but the justness of the war effort would have arguably been lessened. This is not simply because we value the rights of the Germans and Japanese. Rather, a democratic, human rights respecting regime has proven important for

---

45   This was, of course, uneven, particularly in the case of the German Democratic Republic, commonly known as East Germany.

constructing what Kant might have called a "federation of free states."[46] The democratic, human-rights respecting nature of Germany and Japan may prove a more durable change to their constitutions than the overtly anti-militarist restrictions, and more important for international peace.[47]

The general modern form of the hypothesis that democratic reform is important for peace is the "democratic peace hypothesis." In the simplest form, this hypothesis asserts democracies do not go to war against each other. More powerfully, this hypothesis asserts that given the unit of analysis of a "dyad-year," where any two states constitute a "dyad" and their relations over a year constitute a "dyad-year," as the democratic nature of the two states increases, the probability for substantial armed conflict during the dyad-year decreases. This will be discussed in more detail below, in particular, Bruce Russet's use of the Polity datasets and the Correlates of War datasets. This author suggests that a properly constructed modern democratic index should evaluate the rights and interests of women. Should this modern democratic peace hypothesis remain persuasive, then protecting and promoting the rights of women is important throughout the transition to peace, not only for their own sake but for the success of the project of a sustainable peace.

Thus, properly considered, protecting the rights and interests of women and girls is not a side-issue or epiphenomenon that can be considered once the "primary" issues of national security and inter-state relations are resolved—rather such protection falls within the legitimate transformative role of an occupying power and responds to the traditional justifications for going to war (resolving the *res* and satisfying the *justa causa* of the war).

To understand the argument made in this chapter, one must understand the problem of transformative occupation under the law of occupation, Kant's concept of a warlike constitution, the idea of peace emerging from dyads of democratic states (or as Kant puts it, a federation of free states), and the role of protecting the rights and interests of women and girls has in a democracy. Each of these issues was elucidated briefly above.

There are, of course, strong reasons to protect the rights of women and girls based purely on a human rights analysis, and powerful points to be made in favour of protecting women and girls' individual interests purely on normative and humanitarian grounds. The argument of this chapter is not intended to in any way undermine such arguments, but rather to supplement them. It does

---

46   Immanuel Kant, Toward Perpetual Peace, 1932, U.S. Library Association, Westwood Hills Press, Los Angeles, California, U.S.A.

47   There are currently efforts underway in both countries to be more militarily assertive abroad.

not take as its primary framework the rights of the individual girl or woman, nor their collective structural position within society as a matter of gender justice, although these issues will be referenced. Rather, it is essentially rooted in a traditional framework for public international law–the legal relationship between sovereign states.

The insight that protecting the rights and interests of women during the transition to peace is critical for establishing a just and sustainable peace is not new. It is the driving force behind the host of UN Security Council resolutions mentioned at the outset, and drives a host of international and domestic initiatives. But as long as these rights and interests are perceived as peripheral, rather than at the core of just war practice and the practice of building peace, they will likely be marginalized at crucial moments. In Afghanistan, there is a mixed record of partial success and potential disaster on women's rights. This points both to the promise of taking women's rights and interests seriously and the failure to put this promise at the core of the international effort to secure a just and sustainable peace. There is nothing wrong with pursuing human rights and humanitarian concerns for their own sake—unless that effort fails unnecessarily. Providing an additional public international law foundation for these rights and interests is worth the effort.

CHAPTER 9

Conclusions

War does not terminate, and peace is not built, in a moral or legal vacuum.[1] This thesis has attempted to clarify and refine some of the foundational parameters of the moral and legal framework that applies during the transition from armed conflict to peace, termed by some *"jus post bellum."* A necessary follow up question remains, however: What challenges lie ahead for this emerging concept?

Most authors on the subject recognize a need for *jus post bellum*. Given the complexity of the issues and the relatively recent nature of the contemporary discourse on the subject, it is also unsurprising that there remains substantial disagreement about it. While some of this disagreement may turn out to be short-term productive friction, there is a distinct risk that no enduring consensus will emerge that will frame and direct scholarship and practice in this area. There also remains a significant potential for original thinking about how *jus post bellum* relates to some of the most difficult problems of contemporary international legal scholarship and practice. *Jus post bellum* could strengthen and improve diverse areas of law and contemporary challenges that arise after war.

There are many other risks and benefits that arise with the concept of *jus post bellum*, some addressed by authors in this volume and others that remain un-examined. These concluding reflections address the strengths, weaknesses, opportunities, and threats of and for the concept of *jus post bellum*. This approach, modelled after what is sometimes known as SWOT analysis, is usually used for strategic planning for businesses.[2] This may seem like an unorthodox choice for the concluding remarks to a scholarly volume. This approach is not meant to deny the complexity of *jus post bellum,* nor should it be viewed as an attempt to understand the concept as an entrepreneurial construct.[3] It has the virtue of being simple to understand and given the risk that *jus post bellum* will

---

1 This section draws upon an early draft, written by this author, of the Epilogue from *Jus Post Bellum: Mapping the Normative Foundations* (OUP 2014).
2 See, for example, David W. Pickton and Sheila Wright, "What's SWOT in Strategic Analysis?" (1998) 7 Strategic Change 101. This type of analysis is not without its critics. See, for example, Terry Hill and Roy Westbrook, "SWOT Analysis: It's Time for a Product Recall" (1997) 30 Long Range Planning 46.
3 For an analogy of "business" and "war," see David Parrott, *The Business of War: Military Enterprise and Military Revolution in Early Modern Europe* (CUP 2012).

CONCLUSIONS

not cohere into a consensus definition and realize its potential, something akin to strategic analysis may be useful. Applying SWOT analysis to a subject matter it was never designed for may not produce the predictable results it is known for producing in the business sphere, but occasionally bringing approaches from one area and applying them to another can prove productive.

It is useful to analyze aspects of the subject across two dimensions: the internal/external dimension and the positive/negative dimension. Strengths are the internal, positive aspects of the subject. Weaknesses are the internal, negative aspects of the subject. Opportunities are the external, positive aspects of the subject. Threats are the external, negative aspects of the subject. This can be visualized in the following simple table.

In ordinary strategic planning, the internal/external divide is relatively clear-cut, with external aspects often involving entities such as business competitors or relationships with other entities. In this case, applying SWOT to *jus post bellum*, the "external" aspects are harder to define. *Jus post bellum* will be addressed in its current form with respect to internal factors (strengths and weaknesses), with opportunities and threats (external factors) focusing on the future of the concept.[4]

Rather than a comprehensive review of all of the strengths, weaknesses, opportunities, and threats, the following summary will focus on key factors that are of particular importance or which might otherwise be overlooked. The strengths, weaknesses, opportunities, and threats discussed below include:
- Key Strengths:
    - Broad and increasing interest
    - Solid foundation
- Key Weaknesses
    - Lack of consensus
    - Difficulties of integrating a range of sources

TABLE 7

	Internal	**External**
Positive	Strengths	Opportunities
Negative	Weaknesses	Threats

---

4 "Opportunities" and "threats" are more future-oriented terms than "strengths" and "weaknesses," so this modification makes some natural sense, particularly in a chapter ultimately focused on the future of the concept.

- Key Opportunities
    - The opportunity to clarify a range of areas of law
    - The opportunity to contribute to the establishment of just and enduring peace
- Key Threats
    - The threat of politicization
    - The threat of discouraging peace

There are certainly others that currently exist or that will emerge as the concept matures.

A Key Strengths

1 *Broad and Increasing Interest*

There has been an increasing number of references in published works overall. This can be illustrated in Figure 20 showing usage of the phrase "*jus post bellum*" in an extremely large corpus of printed work scanned by Google.

The increasing number of references indicates that scholars' interest in *jus post bellum* is more than superficial and is unlikely to disappear anytime soon. There is a risk, however, that with increased usage there will be an increased lack of clarity and consistency as to the meaning of the term.

In addition to increased usage of the term in general, there has recently been an increase in the study of the concept in various disciplines. As reflected by the authors in this volume, philosophers, lawyers, political scientists, and those studying international relations have taken an interest in *jus post bellum*. This shows that the concept has broad reach and applicability. However, there is a risk that the multi-disciplinary study of *jus post bellum* will lack

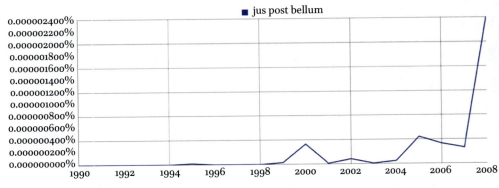

FIGURE 20   Frequency of the use of the term *jus post bellum* in published works.

inter-disciplinary dialogue—with each field taking siloed approaches—which could confuse or fragment the concept.

2 Foundation

While "*jus post bellum*" as a term is of relatively recent vintage, the just war tradition and history of thought and practice with respect to the transition from armed conflict to peace is ancient. To take just a few examples, St. Augustine, often referenced as the founder of the just war tradition, connected the goal of establishing peace to the justice of fighting a war.[5] Hugo Grotius, a foundational figure in international law, extensively discussed justice in the context of transition to peace.[6] Immanuel Kant stated "The Right of Nations in relation to the State of War may be divided into: 1. The Right of *going to* War; 2. Right *during* War; and 3. Right *after* War, the object of which is to constrain the nations mutually *to pass from this state of war, and to found a common Constitution establishing Perpetual Peace*."[7] This idea is not new, even if the surge of scholarship on the subject is vibrant.

Jus post bellum is founded not only on an ancient ethical tradition, but also builds upon a modern legal tradition that lies at the heart of the international system. The development of the concepts of *jus ad bellum* and *jus in bello* and their translation into law during the twentieth and twenty-first centuries has transformed the international order. The richness, depth, and power of these "sister concepts" of *jus post bellum* mean that *jus post bellum* is not operating in a vacuum or starting from scratch, but is working within a specific context and foundation regarding the regulation of armed force.

Jus post bellum not only builds upon a wealth of ethical thought and modern law, but also an extensive field of contemporary practice. *Jus post bellum* is emerging as a subject of renewed interest in the context of peacekeeping, peacebuilding, occupation, and international involvement and administration of territories such as East Timor, Bosnia and Herzegovina, and Kosovo. A nucleus of norms may be found in different areas, such as the law of peace operations, State responsibility, responsibility of international organizations, human rights instruments, international criminal law, or the law of peace

---

[5] St. Augustine, Concerning the City of God Against the Pagans, (originally published 426, tr Henry Bettenson, Penguin 1984), bk 19, ch 12, 866.

[6] Hugo Grotius, *De Jure Praedae* (On the Law of Prize and Booty, originally published 1605, tr by Gwladys L. Williams, Clarendon Press 1950); Hugo Grotius, *De Jure Belli Ac Pacis* (On the Law of War and Peace, originally published 1625, tr by Francis W. Kelsey, Clarendon Press, 1925).

[7] Immanuel Kant, *Metaphysische Anfangsgründe der Rechtslehre* (The Philosophy of Law: An Exposition of the Fundamental Principles of Jurisprudence as the Science of Right, originally published 1887, tr W. Hastie, The Lawbook Exchange 2002) (Emphasis added) 214.

treaties. Codifications in these areas provide an initial starting point. But in many cases further guidance must be sought in practice in order to solve specific conflicts of interests or tensions inherent in transitions from conflict to peace. This has ramifications for methodology. Some rules and principles may be derived from primary sources.[8] But many concepts will need to be specified inductively, that is, through a systematic look at practice.

Jus post bellum has institutional implications. It touches on challenges facing international and regional organizations such as the United Nations (UN) (and its various sub-organizations, including the UN Security Council, the Peacebuilding Commission, and others) the World Bank, the Organization for Security and Co-operation in Europe (OSCE) and the Economic Community of West African States (ECOWAS), to name a few. Practitioners across a wide range of professions are beginning to recognize *jus post bellum* norms as important for decisions related to various aspects of peacebuilding practice, including political and legal strategies; cooperating with domestic civil society; taking an inclusive and context-specific approach to their activities; sequencing and prioritization; and creating and interpreting mandates. It is likely that this practical foundation will continue to develop.

B   Key Weaknesses

1   *Lack of Consensus*
The challenges of transition from armed conflict to peace are inherently difficult, contentious, and pressing. The challenges raised in any one area—legal, moral, or practical—are complex on their own. Together, they present a thicket of interlocking problems. But as long as armed conflict exists, the challenge of ending it will have to be faced. Ideally, it will be faced not with blindness towards criticism, but with open eyes towards the pitfalls and problems of *jus post bellum*. However, there is a lack of consensus about important aspects of the concept—between critics and supporters as well as *among* supporters of the concept.

As reflected by authors in this volume, given the complexities and difficulties highlighted, one response would be to avoid the concept or proceed with extreme caution.[9] Analysis and development of *jus post bellum* might be too

---

[8] For a preliminary survey, see "*'Jus in Bello,' 'Jus ad Ad Bellum'* – *'Jus post Post Bellum'*?: Rethinking the Conception of the Law of Armed Force" (2006) 17 European Journal of International Law 921 937–41.

[9] See Robert Cryer, "Law and the *Jus Post Bellum*: Counseling Caution" in Larry May and Andrew Forcehimes, *Morality, Jus Post Bellum, and International Law* (CUP 2012) 223.

difficult or perilous a task. It might make the post-conflict environment worse, not better. It might detract from existing frameworks, such as transitional justice, or perpetuate existing injustices, such as unequal treatment of women. One might suggest that there is no need for any effort to integrate different legal areas, varied moral considerations, and practical difficulties under a common study—that the current conceptions are sufficient, but perhaps need more enforcement. Others might argue that the current conceptions are insufficient and should be further clarified and refined before serving as a basis for a new framework.

Even among those who agree that the concept should be embraced—albeit with full awareness of its potential risks—there is a lack of consensus about *jus post bellum*. In at least one key aspect, the definition of *jus post bellum* is unsettled. That respect has to do with the relative importance of fixing the definition by using a timeline with sharp divisions marking the end of armed conflict, which this chapter refers to as the "temporal aspect" or "temporal dimension" of *jus post bellum*. To be sure, the temporal aspect of *jus post bellum* is not a mere technical concern, but lies at the very heart of the concept.

However, although the temporal aspect is widely recognized as a critical one, its treatment can also be divisive amongst scholars. Some consider the temporal aspect to be determinative of all else related to the concept, and take a narrow view as to when *jus post bellum* can be said to "begin" and "end." Others see the temporal as one of many determinative aspects of the concept, which can vary in importance depending on the context. These scholars tend to focus more on the function of *jus post bellum*, which can apply before, during, and after the conflict. This division is a risk. If there is no agreement about what is meant by "post," the concept could quickly begin to lose value and import.

An example may help clarify the difference between the two approaches to *jus post bellum*. Imagine a targeting decision during an armed conflict. Specifically, imagine that a military target has been placed within an important cultural site in a manner such that attacking the target would destroy the cultural site. There is existing *jus in bello* law to help decide the legality of such an attack, but it is unclear whether *jus post bellum* would have anything to say about the question because of the definitional dichotomy between a temporal approach and a functional approach. A temporal approach would clearly rule out *jus post bellum* playing a role. Under a temporal approach, the armed conflict is ongoing, so *jus post bellum* has not begun. A primarily functional approach may allow *jus post bellum* to speak. While the normal application of *jus in bello* principles of proportionality and distinction might permit the destruction of a cultural site in some instances, the simultaneous application of *jus post bellum* principles, either as a second-order method of interpretation or as a first-order application of discrete rules, might forbid the destruction of the site.

The unclear definition of *jus post bellum* might be described as its original sin. Take the following quote from Brian Orend's foundational essay, *Jus Post Bellum*.

> It seems, then, that just war theorists must consider the justice not only of the resort to war in the first place, and not only of the conduct within war, once it has begun, but also of the termination phase of the war, in terms of the cessation of hostilities and the move back from war to peace. It seems, in short, that we also need to detail a set of just war norms or rules for what we might call *jus post bellum*: justice after war.[10]

On one hand, Orend refers to the termination phase of the war and the move back from war to peace. On the other hand, he speaks of "justice after war," which, taken literally, would not obviously include the termination phase of the war and the move back from war to peace. This ambiguity has been there from the beginning.

To explore this dichotomy, it is useful to point to a database of articles referencing *jus post bellum*, allowing for trends in *jus post bellum* scholarship to be analyzed systematically.[11] Some of this data is summarized in a graphical format below. Many of the works analyzed for this database are only ambiguously categorizable as using a temporal or functional definition of *jus post bellum*. Some are not categorizable one way or another. No work represents a Weberian "ideal type" of self-consciously using a temporal or functional definition of *jus post bellum*. However, the data shows interesting trends.

The overall findings could be summarized as follows: There has been an expansion of references to *jus post bellum* in a variety of journals. With the expansion of references, there has been an increase of ambiguity, not a consolidation around a consensus definition. The trend is generally an increase in trivial references to *jus post bellum*, in addition to a trend towards a simpler, literal temporal definition. Whether a consensus focus will be achieved, and what that consensus might be, is as yet unclear.

The following visualization excludes trivial references in the dataset:

---

10   Brian Orend, "*Jus Post Bellum*" (2000) 31 Journal of Social Philosophy 117, 118.
11   For more information on the methods of his research, see Jens Iverson's SSRN page, <http://ssrn.com/author=1861204> accessed 25 July 2013.

CONCLUSIONS

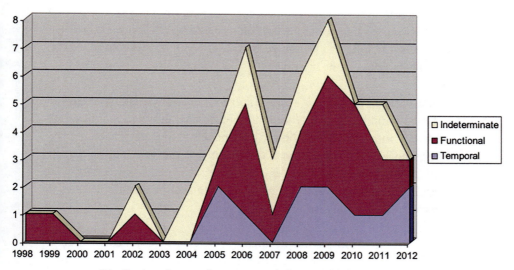

FIGURE 21 Distribution of approaches to *jus post bellum* in published works over time.

The graph shows the early use of functional definitions, a period of indeterminate definition, and an increasing use of temporal references compared to functional approaches in 2012, with fewer indeterminate usages.

The question "what is '*jus post bellum*'" ultimately brings us to the question: "Why use the term '*jus post bellum*?'" What are those interested in the subject of *jus post bellum* are trying to accomplish? It may be that in using the term, we are merely attempting to describe what law applies during early peace. An alternative effort would be to describe and advance the law that has the function of establishing a sustainable peace. Indeed, sustainable peace is often referenced as a goal of *jus post bellum*, which inherently implies the need for a functional approach—a body of law cannot be said to be aspirational unless it is assumed to have functional components. Indeed, it could be argued that the functional is inherent in the very concept of law. The ancient maxim *hominum causa omne jus constitutem est* (all law is created for the benefit of human beings) could certainly guide the development of any new law or means of legal interpretation in this area. One can hardly think of a greater benefit than the aim of *jus post bellum*: a just and sustainable peace. It is possible, however, that focusing on the functional or aspirational aspects of *jus post bellum* will cause clarity (or at least simplicity) to suffer.

2   *Difficulties of Integrating a Range of Sources*

Whichever definition of *jus post bellum* is used, *jus post bellum* will be informed by, operate upon, and may borrow from a diverse range of sources. While this diversity is a potential strength in many respects, the difficulty of integrating this range of sources in a coherent fashion is a serious challenge. As pointed out by Vincent Chetail (and reiterated by Dieter Fleck in this volume), post-conflict peacebuilding alone includes

> [I]nternational humanitarian law; international human rights law; international criminal law; international refugee law; international development law; international economic law; the law of international organizations; the law of international responsibility; the law relating to the peaceful settlement of disputes; treaty law which governs in particular ceasefire agreements; and the law relating to the succession of states in the case of territorial dismemberment due to conflict.[12]

Even beyond these diverse areas of law, *jus post bellum* can be considered as broader than the legal ambit of post-conflict peacebuilding, as it incorporates moral philosophy and is rooted in the long just war tradition. There is a danger that the discourse communities and interpretive communities that have been built around these various areas of law and philosophy will use terms in ways that will cause confusion when they are used in a cross-cutting manner.[13] From a practical perspective, the same risk applies: if practitioners working simultaneously in post-conflict situations adopt principles of *jus post bellum* but apply them inconsistently, it could create additional confusion and inconsistency in peacebuilding practice.

If people use multiple definitions of the same term, particularly without realizing it, the clarity of their communications lessens. This is true in an interpretive community or a discourse community. It may be particularly important

---

12   Vincent Chetail, "Introduction: Post-conflict Peacebuilding – Ambiguity and Identity" in Vincent Chetail (ed), *Post-Conflict Peacebuilding: A Lexicon* (OUP 2009) 1–33, 18.

13   Erik Borg contrasted the terms "discourse community" and "interpretive community" as follows:
> We do not generally use language to communicate with the world at large, but with individuals or groups of individuals. As in life, for discussion and analysis in applied linguistics these groups are gathered into communities. One such grouping that is widely used to analyse written communication is *discourse community*. John Swales, an influential analyst of written communication, described discourse communities as groups that have goals or purposes, and use communication to achieve these goals. [...] 'Interpretive community' (Fish 1980), on the other hand, refers not to a gathering of individuals, but to an open network of people who share ways of reading texts [...] [U]nlike an interpretive community, members of a discourse community actively share goals and communicate with other members to pursue those goals.

Erik Borg, "Key Concepts in ELT: Discourse Community" (2003) 57 English Language Teaching Journal 398.

with respect to *jus post bellum* if it is defined functionally, as a discourse community with actively shared goals.

C   Key Opportunities

1   *The Opportunity to Clarify a Range of Areas of Law and Practice*

This opportunity is, in a sense, the other aspect of the previous weakness. Should the difficulties inherent in integrating various areas of law and philosophy be overcome, these various areas of law themselves will be enriched and clarified with respect to their application to the specific *jus post bellum* context.

Including a philosophical dimension that is not encompassed by purely legal sources may present a singular opportunity to clarify the application of a variety of legal fields to the transition from armed conflict to peace. Larry May's work may be particularly important in this respect. James Gallen's suggestion that *jus post bellum* can function as an interpretive framework, providing second-order rules that act upon first-order rules in other areas of law is also extremely helpful on this point.[14]

Jus post bellum's potential to clarify a range of areas of law does not end with areas of law that might be partially included in *jus post bellum*—it also includes the potential to clarify issues in areas discreet from *jus post bellum*. Transitional Justice, properly understood, can be clearly defined as a separate concept from *jus post bellum*. The Responsibility to Protect and *lex pacificatoria* are likewise conceptually discreet from *jus post bellum*, albeit with some overlap. Clarity comes not only from what such concepts are, but also what they are not.

Jus post bellum also provides the opportunity to clarify the practice of peacebuilding. *Jus post bellum* can help clarify the obligations of interveners, whether they are individual states, international organizations, or multilateral groups. It could help set policy objectives and determine mandates. For example, *jus post bellum* is relevant to exit strategies, influencing political decisions, local ownership, and the practicalities of concluding peacebuilding missions.

The post-conflict environment can become crowded with various international organizations, regional organizations, donors, NGOs, civil society groups, and others working on a myriad of peacebuilding tasks. They might include,

---

14   Regarding first-order and second-order laws, see, for example, H.L.A. Hart, *The Concept of Law* (OUP 1961).

amongst others, lawyers, political advisors, economic advisors, public health specialists, doctors, journalists, development specialists, artists, or athletes. Each practitioner will come with her or his professional and personal worldview and priorities on how to tackle the challenges of peacebuilding. By setting out legal and moral rules, principles, and guidelines, *jus post bellum* can help streamline the practice of peacebuilding. If all of these various actors can speak a common *"jus post bellum"* language and understand its underlying values, it might help clarify mandates, reduce redundancies, or stimulate partnerships and collaboration amongst practitioners.

2 The Opportunity to Contribute to the Establishment of Just and Enduring Peace

Placing this opportunity so far down in this concluding chapter is an artefact of the SWOT format, not a measure of its importance. This opportunity is, in fact, the *raison d'être* of the concept and is mentioned extensively in this volume. However, it is probably the most difficult opportunity to evaluate or analyze. It is hard to define what a "peace" means, and even harder to define a "just peace." Beyond the well-known distinction between positive and negative peace,[15] Astri Suhrke argues persuasively in this volume that there are different "types" of peace, and examines how the differences in post-conflict situations can affect peacebuilding and state-building efforts. This opportunity also begs the question of what a "just" peace might look like. Does it involve addressing and solving the root causes of a conflict? This might be an impossible task, as root causes might be disputed by the parties to the conflict or might be so deeply entrenched into the social and economic fabric of the society (eg, conflicts arising out of ethnic divides or long-standing poverty) that *jus post bellum* would require or encourage extremely long-term interventions. Moreover, even if it were possible to claim that a just and enduring peace had been achieved, it would be difficult to attribute that to any single concept, even one as potentially broad as *jus post bellum*.

However, the opportunity exists. Some argue for the creation of a new Geneva Convention for *jus post bellum* and suggest that its contribution to legal certainty and the creation of obligation will contribute to peace. Others have suggested that *jus post bellum* can improve policy and practice, and have suggested that a *"Jus Post Bellum* for Dummies" might be useful for practitioners.[16]

---

15 Johan Galtung, "Violence, Peace, and Peace Research" (1969) 6 Journal of Peace Research 167.

16 Michael Semple, *"Jus Post Bellum* in the Age of Terrorism: Remarks by Michael Semple" (2012) 106 Proceedings of the Annual Meeting (American Society of International Law) 337.

However, perhaps the added value of *jus post bellum* to achieving peace will be subtle and nuanced, such as by the development of "soft law" and policy instruments, changing rules of engagement, newly emerging legal norms,[17] the encouragement of looking forward after conflict, instead of backwards,[18] or through promoting moral norms. Whatever the source of influence, it will be necessary for scholars and norm entrepreneurs who support the concept to take a humble and self-reflexive approach to their work.

D   Key Threats

1   *The Threat of Politicization*

The risk of manipulation and instrumentalization of the legal framework by international actors, as well as the embedding and legitimation of neo-colonial projects through law, are critical threats that advocates of *jus post bellum* would be wise to guard against. Indeed, a recognized shortcoming is the lack of diversity amongst the scholars who have formed the intellectual basis of the concept.

However, one interesting question that critical theorists and international relation theorists do not seem to have analyzed fully is why a tripartite, comprehensive just war theory that covers the initiation of armed conflict, prosecution of armed conflict, and transition out of armed conflict was *not* fully developed during the twentieth century (when the terms *jus ad bellum*, *jus in bello*, and *jus post bellum* were coined)[19] or previously. One possible answer might be that *jus post bellum* has in fact been *inconvenient* for great military and colonial powers, and that, *contra* Vatanparast, the emergence of *jus post bellum* may be a rejection of twentieth-century realpolitik and colonialism more than the fruit of neo-colonial projects. *Jus post bellum* might also provide

---

17   On the emergence and reception of norms, see Martha Finnemore and Kathryn Sikkink, "International Norm Dynamics and Political Chance" (1998) 52 International Organization at Fifty: Exploration and Contestation in the Study of World Politics 887, 895 (discussing a "norm lifecycle" in three stages: first a "norm emergence," then a "norm cascade," and finally "norm internalization.").

18   See, for example Ruti Teitel, "Rethinking *Jus Post Bellum* in an Age of Global Transitional Justice: Engaging with Michael Walzer and Larry May" (2013) 24 European Journal of International Law 335 (arguing that *jus post bellum* will be most useful if it is forward-looking.).

19   See Robert Kolb, "Origin of the Twin Terms *Jus Ad Bellum/Jus In Bello*" (1997) 37 International Review of the Red Cross 553; Carsten Stahn, "*Jus Post Bellum*: Mapping the Discipline(s)" (2008) 23 American University International Law Review 311, 312.

an opportunity to acknowledge the importance of local/national ownership over peacebuilding projects and the need to apply context-specific policy decisions in interventions, and help reduce the risk of neo-colonialism.

2   The Threat of Discouraging Peace

This threat is directly tied to the key opportunity listed previously, the opportunity to contribute to the establishment of just and enduring peace.

It is worth noting that, for Larry May, *jus post bellum* leads *away* from a more permissive structure for the use of force and towards a broad but not universal pacifism. In *After War Ends: A Philosophical Approach*,[20] May argues for contingent pacifism based on the unlikely nature of armed force passing the stringent standards of a modern tripartite just war theory.[21] Between a more warlike world and pacifism, there is certainly a broad range of predictions as to the effect of a more widespread adoption of *jus post bellum*.

E   Final Conclusion

Transitions to peace frequently fail. The pause in violence following the cessation of armed conflict often collapses into renewed armed conflict, or continues as a mere "negative" peace,[22] without a just resolution of the causes of the war or accountability for conduct within the conflict. While the international community's approach to restricting the use of force and regulating conduct within armed conflict has matured and consolidated considerably since the Second World War, efforts to systematize and regulate transitions out of armed conflict remain very much a work-in-progress. Restoring *jus post bellum* to the twentieth-century framework dominated by *jus in bello* and *jus ad bellum* is difficult and complex. Nonetheless, accomplishments in this field should be recognized, and further efforts are merited. This conclusion will provide a few final remarks on the relative importance of various areas of debate, appraise

---

20   See Larry May, *After War Ends: A Philosophical Approach* (CUP 2012).
21   Ibid 232.
22   The concepts of "negative" and "positive" peace were developed by Johan Galtung in his seminal 1964 article: Galtung, J. (1965). An Editorial. *Journal of Peace Research*, 1(1), 1–4. For more on Galtung's work on structural analysis of peace, *see also* Galtung, J. (1969). Violence, Peace and Peace Research. *Journal of Peace Research*, 6 (3), 167–191. Galtung, J. (1981). Social Cosmology and the Concept of Peace. *Journal of Peace Research*, 17 (2), 183–199. Galtung, J. (1985). Twenty-Five Years of Peace Research: Ten Challenges and Some Responses. *Journal of Peace Research*, 22 (2), 141–158. Galtung, J. (1990). Cultural Violence. *Journal of Peace Research*, 27 (3), 291–305.

the research aims of this work, revisit the propositions put forth in the introduction, and offer last thoughts on the subject of the transition to peace.

Before analyzing the research aims and propositions of this work, a comment on the relative importance of certain issues is merited. Many scholars, familiar with the term "*jus post bellum*" or less familiar, may reasonably reject the author's contention that *jus post bellum* is best understood through a hybrid functional approach. The definitional debate is ongoing, and this volume will not be the last word for all readers. Certain scholars may wish for the term to be abandoned and replaced with another term, perhaps based out of the inherent artificiality of Latin neoterisms in a post-Latin era, or out of a desire to protect the perceived clarity of a bipartite approach; defending *jus post bellum*'s sister terms *jus ad bellum* and *jus in bello* from any confusion introduced by adding another member to the family. Others may wish to keep the term *jus post bellum* but limit it to, for example, post-conflict criminal justice efforts, referring to each of the areas discussed in Chapter 6 by separate terms with no (or an alternate) unifying framework.

What is important to the author, in the final accounting, is not what term is used, but whether laws and principles that *can* be used to guide the successful transition from armed conflict to peace *are* used. Ultimately, the highest priority should be the quality and nature of the lives of those who live through the transition from armed conflict and may spend their days in the peace constructed thereafter. Unless there is an increasingly shared understanding of how laws and principles can be synthesized and synchronized to facilitate the successful and permanent cessation of armed conflict and the construction of a robust, positive peace, opportunities will be lost.

There is a need for what has been described as "*jus post bellum*" in this work. The need for a shared commitment by local actors to the most powerful sovereign forces in the international community to work for a just and sustainable peace, and an understanding that one cannot wait until the armed conflict is finished to apply the laws and principles needed to prevent its return—this commitment and understanding is far more significant than whether one chooses to describe this commitment and understanding as "*jus post bellum*" or any other plausible alternative that facilitates the organization, development, and application of laws and principles to the same end, be it "peacebuilding that begins in war" or "transitional justice as it applies to armed conflict" or "an expanded notion of *lex pacificatoria*."

The debate over the correct terminology can occasionally give the reader a sense that they have stepped through the looking glass, and lost sight of what is actually significant in the real world. This famous passage may spring to mind:

> 'When *I* use a word,' Humpty Dumpty said, in rather a scornful tone, 'it means just what I choose it to mean — neither more nor less.'
>
> 'The question is,' said Alice, 'whether you *can* make words mean so many different things.'
>
> 'The question is,' said Humpty Dumpty, 'which is to be master — that's all.'[23]

With respect to all of the philosophers of language and reference that have more or less taken Humpty Dumpty's side of the argument, "the question" in the sense of the normative question for those who value a just and sustainable peace, is how and whether such a peace can best be achieved in any particular instance. The author believes that the phenomenal growth in scholarship in *jus post bellum* itself provides evidence that the concept of *jus post bellum* may be a good vehicle to organize laws and principles towards a shared and laudable aim, but that the varied use of the term may lead to lost opportunities. The flip side of this emphasis on substance over rhetorical games was perhaps best emphasized by Abraham Lincoln. Abraham Lincoln liked to ask, "If you call a dog's tail a leg, how many legs does a dog have?" — and when given the answer "Five," he would respond," the correct answer is four. Calling a tail a leg does not make it a leg."[24]

This volume had three broad aims. First, it evaluated the history of *jus post bellum avant la lettre*, tracing important writings on the transition to peace from Augustine, Aquinas, and Kant to more modern jurists and scholars. Second, it explored definitional aspects of *jus post bellum*, including current its relationship to sister terms and related fields. Third, it explored the current state and possibilities for the future development of the law and normative principles that apply to the transition to peace.

In addition to these positive research aims, this work argued against certain ideas. Throughout the volume, the erroneous suggestion that *jus post bellum* does not exist was rebuffed, as is the idea that it has no content. It situated *jus post bellum* with its sister terms, *jus in bello* and *jus ad bellum* and explored the content and contours of *jus post bellum*. It specifically rejected the idea that transitional justice, post-conflict international criminal law and *jus post bellum* are interchangeable ideas. The claim that the just war tradition is devoid of discussion of the subject matter of *jus post bellum* or that discussing the just

---

23   C.L. Dodgson (Lewis Carroll), *Through the Looking-Glass*, in *The Complete Works of Lewis Carroll* (New York, 1936), pp. 213–214.

24   Gardner, James B. "The Redefinition of Historical Scholarship: Calling a Tail a Leg?." *The Public Historian* (1998): 43–57.

war tradition is meritless was specifically rejected. The thrust of this work is not to argue for the use of the term *jus post bellum*, although there are reasons to do so, but rather to examine the law and principles of the transition to peace regardless of the terminology used.

Often, the term "*jus post bellum*" is used by different authors without a common definition or theoretical approach. Throughout this volume, this definitional problem has been addressed. This work argues for a hybrid functional (rather than purely temporal) approach to *jus post bellum*, that is, to define an approach to this area of law that focuses on the goal of achieving a just and sustainable peace rather than a mere discussion of the law that applies during early peace.

The problems underlying armed conflict cannot be resolved, nor can a positive peace be constructed, without a sustainable foundation of justice and law. This research has clarified the moral and legal framework that applies during the transition from armed conflict to peace, termed by contemporary scholars and practitioners "*jus post bellum*." The need for *jus post bellum* is widely recognized, but given the complexity of the issues, it is unsurprising that there remains a certain lack of consensus about how to approach the principles and law regarding ending armed conflict in a just and sustainable manner. There is a distinct risk that until an enduring consensus emerges that frames and directs scholarship and practice in this area, communities will needlessly suffer the horrors of preventable war.

In order to light the way forward, it is worth considering the works of past jurists who have dedicated themselves to understanding the normative and practical difficulties of war and peace. A review of the works of Augustine and his peers, the Institutes of Justinian, the Decretals of Gregory IX, Thomas Aquinas, Baldus de Ubaldis, Francisco de Vitoria, Francisco Suarez, Alberico Gentili, Petrus Gudelinus, Hugo Grotius, Emer de Vattel, Christian Wolff and Immanuel Kant provides a rich heritage to guide, but not necessarily constrain, contemporary and future jurists. Perhaps the strongest practical lesson that can be learned is the importance of keeping the goal of a just and sustainable peace at the centre of policy-makers' concerns not only after the guns fall silent but whenever war is threatened and throughout the armed conflict itself.

Contemporary *jus post bellum* is rooted in a well-rooted normative and scholarly tradition, and also upon the concepts of *jus ad bellum* and *jus in bello* that remain the core underpinnings of international order. *Jus post bellum* operates within a specific context and foundation regarding the regulation of armed force, and benefits from the power of the general prohibition on recourse to the use of force and the richness and depth of contemporary international humanitarian law. *Jus post bellum* builds upon an extensive body of contemporary law and practice, including procedural fairness, territorial dispute resolution, regulating the consequences of an act of aggression, international territorial administration, territorial transition, state responsibility, the responsibility of international organizations, human rights instruments, international criminal law, and odious debt.

The ambition of *jus post bellum* is worth celebrating, but also worth noting with some caution. While *jus ad bellum* primarily seeks to preserve a negative peace between states, and *jus in bello* hopes to preserve a modicum of humanity during hostilities, *jus post bellum* dares to set a difficult additional goal. It demands prioritization of a robust and desirable solution to the problems that create armed conflict—even when humanitarian concerns are most pressing and the power imbalance between victor and vanquished are at their most extreme. This prioritization can take a variety of legal forms described throughout this work, from the prohibition of annexation, to respect for human rights, to limits on domestic amnesties. The dangers here should be obvious—by pushing too hard for an ideal long-term solution, an unwise or unlucky application of *jus post bellum* principles may risk overlooking the importance of short-term incremental gains, or may risk politicizing approaches that are better left neutral. The answer to these concerns should not be to reject the project of developing *jus post bellum*, but to further ground it in the practical wisdom of those involved in peacemaking, peacebuilding, and peace operations generally.

Shortly before his death, Tony Judt, the great historian and essayist, shared a few thoughts on learning from the history of war in an essay simply titled, "What have we learned, if anything?"

> War was not just a catastrophe in its own right; it brought other horrors in its wake. World War I led to an unprecedented militarization of society, the worship of violence, and a cult of death that long outlasted the war itself and prepared the ground for the political disasters that followed. States and societies seized during and after World War II by Hitler or Stalin (or by both, in sequence) experienced not just occupation and exploitation but degradation and corrosion of the laws and norms of civil society. The very structures of civilized life—regulations, laws, teachers, policemen, judges—disappeared or else took on sinister significance: far from guaranteeing security, the state itself became the leading source of insecurity. Reciprocity and trust, whether in neighbors, colleagues, community, or leaders, collapsed. Behavior that would be aberrant in conventional circumstances—theft, dishonesty, dissemblance, indifference to the misfortune of others, and the opportunistic exploitation of their suffering—became not just normal but sometimes the only way to save your family and yourself. Dissent or opposition was stifled by universal fear.

War, in short, prompted behavior that would have been unthinkable as well as dysfunctional in peacetime. It is war, not racism or ethnic antagonism or religious fervor, that leads to atrocity. War—total war—has been the crucial antecedent condition for mass criminality in the modern era. The first primitive concentration camps were set up by the British during the Boer War of 1899–1902. Without World War I there would have been no Armenian genocide and it is highly unlikely that either communism or fascism would have seized hold of modern states. Without World War II there would have been no Holocaust. Absent the forcible involvement of Cambodia in the Vietnam War, we would never have heard of Pol Pot. As for the brutalizing effect of war on ordinary soldiers themselves, this of course has been copiously documented.[25]

The challenge of building peace goes well beyond the cessation of violence. Judt's reminder of the horrific effects of war on individuals and society is helpful, particularly for those temporarily lost in legal abstraction. At the same time, Judt moves the focus beyond the immediate kinetic effect of war to the social devastation it causes. Beyond death and destruction, armed conflict fundamentally replaces trust with fear. This fear in time fuels atrocity beyond war itself, and can cause armed conflict to reoccur. Rebuilding communities and institutions at a core level means restoring trust in a better future and ameliorating fears of a failed peace. This is not done merely through the legal prohibition of war, nor through post-conflict justice alone, but rather with Galtung's conception of a positive peace squarely in mind—even before the conflict ends.[26]

Jus post bellum should be further developed to help all participants manage the complex process of ending armed conflict and developing early peace. No peace will be perfect. Some relapse into armed conflict is perhaps close to inevitable. But addressing the problem of transitions to peace as systematically and thoughtfully as possible remains one of the most pressing challenges in contemporary international law and practice. It demands our attention. It compels our effort. While the horrors of past failures should be kept in mind, so should the triumphs. The peace that is enjoyed simply, invisibly, and often thoughtlessly, is in fact the quiet victory of a vision that has inspired society for millennia—that wars must end, and that a just peace must be built to endure.

---

25   Judt, Tony. "What have we learned, if anything?." *New York Review of Books* 55.7 (2008): 16.
26   Galtung, Johan. "An Editorial." *Journal of Peace Research* 1(1) (1965):1–4.

Bibliography

A.   *Literature*

Aboagye, Festus B., and Martin R. Rupiya. "Enhancing post-conflict democratic governance through effective security sector reform in Liberia." *A tortuous road to peace. The dynamics of regional, UN and international humanitarian interventions in Liberia,* Festus Aboagye and Alhaji M.S. Bah eds (Pretoria: Institute for Security Studies 2005): 249–280.

Adams, Patricia. *Iraq's Odious Debts*. Cato Institute, 2004.

Akehurst, Michael. "Equity and general principles of law." *International and Comparative Law Quarterly* 25.04 (1976): 801–825.

Alexander, Justin, and Colin Rowat. "A clean slate in Iraq: From debt to development." *Middle East Report* 228 (2003): 32–36.

Alford, Roger Paul, On War as Hell. Chicago Journal of International Law, Vol. 3, No. 1, Spring 2002.

Amnesty International, "United Kingdom: Summary of Concerns Raised with the Human Rights Committee" (1 November 2001).

Aquinas, Thomas. "Summa Theologica. 3 vols." Trans. By the Fathers of the English Dominican Province. New York: Benziger Brothers 48 (1947).

Augustine, Saint, and Saint John Chrysostom. *Nicene and Post-Nicene Fathers: Homilies on the Acts of the apostles and the Epistle to the Romans*. Ed. Philip Schaff. Vol. 11. Hendrickson Pub, 1995.

Augustine, Saint. "On free choice of the will." *Trans. by Thomas Williams (Indianapolis: Hackett, 1993)* (1993).

Augustine, Saint. "Reply to Faustus the Manichaean." *Nicene and Post-Nicene Fathers* (1994): 1886–94.

Augustine, Saint. "The city of god, trans." *Markus Dods. New York, NY: Modern Library* (1950).

Augustine, Saint. *Commentary on the Lord's Sermon on the Mount with Seventeen Related Sermons*. Vol. 11. CUA Press, 2010.

Bainton, Roland H., Christian attitudes toward war and peace: a historical survey and critical re-evaluation. Wipf and Stock Publishers, 2008.

Baldus de Ubaldis, Petrus, The Oxford International Encyclopedia of Legal History, (Stanley N. Katz ed.), Oxford University Press, 2009.

Barbara F. Walter, *Conflict Relapse and the Sustainability of Post-Conflict Peace*, World Development Report Background Paper, 2010, World Bank.

Bardutzky, Samo. "The Strasbourg Court on the Dayton Constitution: Judgment in the case of Sejdić and Finci v. Bosnia and Herzegovina, 22 December 2009." *European Constitutional Law Review* 6.02 (2010): 309–333.

Barker, Kenneth L., Donald Burdick, and Donald W. Burdick. *The NIV study bible, new international version*. Zondervan Bible Publishers, 1995.

Beaulac, Stéphane. "The Westphalian Legal Orthodoxy-Myth or Reality?." *Journal of the History of International Law* 2.2 (2000): 148–177.

Beaulac, Stéphane. "The Westphalian model in defining international law: challenging the myth." *Austl. J. Legal Hist.* 8 (2004): 181.

Beaulac, Stéphane. *The power of language in the making of international law: the word sovereignty in Bodin and Vattel and the myth of Westphalia*. Vol. 46. Martinus Nijhoff Publishers, 2004.

Bell, Christine. "Peace agreements: Their nature and legal status." *American Journal of International Law* (2006): 373–412.

Bell, Christine. Peace Settlements and International Law: From Lex Pacificatoria to Jus Post Bellum (May 17, 2012). Edinburgh School of Law Research Paper No. 2012/16.

Bell, Christine. *On the law of peace: peace agreements and the Lex Pacificatoria*. Oxford University Press, 2008.

Bell, Christine. *Peace Agreements and Human Rights*. Oxford University Press, 2000.

Benson, Christina C. "Jus Post Bellum in Iraq: The Development of Emerging Norms for Economic Reform in Post Conflict Countries." *Rich. J. Global L. & Bus.* 11 (2011): 315.

Benvenisti, Eyal. "Security Council and the Law on Occupation: Resolution 1483 on Iraq in Historical Perspective, The." IDF LR 1 (2003): 19.

Benvenisti, Eyal. *The International Law of Occupation*. 2d ed. Oxford: Oxford University Press 2012.

Betsy, Baker. "The 'Civilized Nation' in the work of Johann Caspar Blutschli." Kremer, Markus, and Hans-Richard Reuter, eds. Macht und Moral: politisches Denken im 17. und 18. Jahrhundert. Vol. 31. W. Kohlhammer Verlag. (2007): 342.

Bhuta, Nehal. "New Modes and orders: the difficulties of a jus post bellum of constitutional transformation." *University of Toronto Law Journal* 60.3 (2010): 799–854.

Bhuta, Nehal. "The antinomies of transformative occupation." *European Journal of International Law* 16.4 (2005): 721–740.

Binder, Christina. "Uniting for Peace Resolution (1950)." *Max Planck Encyclopedia of Public International Law, Oxford* (2013).

Birks, Peter and Grant McLeod Trans. *Justinian's Institutes*. Cornell University Press (1987).

Blutschli, Johann Kaspar. *Das modern kriegsrecht der zivilisierten Staaten als Rechtsbuch dargestellt* (1866).

Boon, Kristen E. "Future of the Law of Occupation, The." *Can. YB Int'l L.* 46 (2008): 107.

Boon, Kristen. "Legislative reform in post-conflict zones: Jus post bellum and the contemporary occupant's law-making powers." *McGill LJ* 50 (2005): 285.

Boon, Kristen E. "Obligations of the New Occupier: The Contours of Jus Post Bellum." *Loy. L.A. Int'l & Comp. L. Rev.* 31 (2009): 57.

Boon, Kristen E. "Open for Business: International Financial Institutions, Post-Conflict Economic Reform, and the Rule of Law." *NYUJ Int'l L. & Pol.* 39 (2006): 513.

Borg, Erik. "Discourse community." *ELT journal* 57.4 (2003): 398–400.

Brett, Annabel. "Francisco De Vitoria (1483–1546) and Francisco Suárez (1548–1617)." *The Oxford Handbook of the History of International Law*. Eds. Bardo Fassbender and Anne Peters. Oxford University Press, 2012.

Brownlie, Ian. "Rights of Peoples in Modern International Law, The." Bull. Austl. Soc. Leg. Phil. 9 (1985): 104.

Bugnion, François. "Jus ad bellum, jus in bello and non-international armed conflicts." *Yearbook of International Humanitarian Law*, T.M.C. Asser Press, vol. VI, 2003.

Bull, Hedley. "The importance of Grotius in the study of international relations." Bull, Hedley, Benedict Kingsbury, and Adam Roberts, eds. Hugo Grotius and international relations. Oxford University Press, 1992. 65–93.

Burke, Edmund. *Reflections on the Revolution in France: and on the proceedings in certain societies in London relative to that event. In a letter intended to have been sent to a gentleman in Paris*. No. 1–2. J. Dodsley, 1790.

Cahn, Hans J. "The responsibility of the successor State for war debts." *The American Journal of International Law* 44.3 (1950): 477–487.

Canning, Joseph. The Political Thought of Baldus de Ubaldis . Cambridge, U.K.: Cambridge University Press, 1987.

Caprioli, Mary, et al. "The WomanStats project database: advancing an empirical research agenda." *Journal of Peace Research* (2009).

Carswell, Andrew J. "Unblocking the UN Security Council: The Uniting for Peace Resolution." *Journal of Conflict and Security Law* (2013).

Cassimatis, Anthony E. "International humanitarian law, international human rights law, and fragmentation of international law." *International and Comparative Law Quarterly* 56.03 (2007): 623–639.

Caverzasio, Sylvie Giossi. "Strengthening protection in war: A search for professional standards." Geneva: ICRC. (2001).

Chander, Anupam. "Odious Securitization." *Emory LJ* 53 (2004): 923.

Chayes, Antonia. "Chapter VII½: Is Jus Post Bellum Possible?." *European Journal of International Law* 24.1 (2013): 291–305.

Chetail, Vincent, ed. *Post-conflict peacebuilding: A lexicon*. OUP Oxford, 2009.

Chetail, Vincent, Post-Conflict Peacebuilding. Lexique de la consolidation de la paix. Ed. Vincent Chetail. Bruylant, 2009. 29–70.

Chetail, Vincent. "Introduction: Post-conflict Peacebuilding – Ambiguity and Identity" in Vincent Chetail (ed), *Post-Conflict Peacebuilding: A Lexicon* (OUP 2009) 1–33.

Chetail, Vincent. "Post-Conflict Peacebuilding – Ambiguity and Identity." Ed. Vincent Chetail. *Post-Conflict Peacebuilding: A Lexicon*. OUP Oxford, 2009. 1–33.

Cingranelli, David L. "The Cingranelli-Richards (CIRI) Human Rights Data Project." Human Rights Quarterly 32 (2004): 395–418.

Cingranelli, David L., and David L. Richards. "The Cingranelli and Richards (CIRI) human rights data project." Human Rights Quarterly 32.2 (2010): 401–424.

Cingranelli, David L., David L. Richards, and K. Chad Clay. "The CIRI human rights dataset." *CIRI Human Rights Data Project* 6 (2014).

Cohen, Jean L. "Role of International Law in Post-Conflict Constitution-Making toward a Jus Post Bellum for Interim Occupations, The." *NYL Sch. L. Rev.* 51 (2006): 497.

Cole, Elizabeth A. and Judy Barsalou. "Unite or Divide? The Challenges of Teaching History in Societies emerging from Violent Conflict" (United States Institute for Peace 2006).

Craven, Matthew CR. "The problem of state succession and the identity of states under international law." European Journal of International Law 9.1 (1998): 142–162.

Cryer, Robert. "Law and the Jus Post Bellum," Morality, Jus Post Bellum, and International Law. Ed. Larry May and Andrew Forcehimes. 1st ed. Cambridge: Cambridge University Press, 2012. 223–249.

Curran, Vivian. "The Politics of Memory/Errinerungspolitik and the Use and Propriety of Law in the Process of Memory Construction." *Law and Critique*, 19 October 2003, Springer, 316.

Da Legnano, Giovanni, Thomas Erskine Holland, and James Leslie Brierly. *Tractatus de bello, de represaliis et de duello*. Printed for the Carnegie Institution of Washington at the Oxford University Press, 1917.

Darehshori, Sara. *Selling Justice Short: Why Accountability Matters for Peace*. Human Rights Watch, 2009.

De Brabandere, Eric, Post-conflict Administrations in International Law: International Territorial Administration, Transitional Authority and Foreign Occupation in Theory and Practice, Leiden: Martinus Nijhoff, 2009.

De Brabandere, Eric. "International Territorial Administrations and Post-Conflict Reforms: Reflections on the Need of a Jus Post Bellum as a Legal Framework." *Belgisch Tijdschrift voor Internationaal Recht / Revue Belge de Droit International* 44(1–2): 69–90.

De Brabandere, Eric, 'The Concept of Jus Post Bellum in International Law: A Normative Critique, in Carsten Stahn, Jennifer S. Easterday, and Jens Iverson (eds.), Jus Post Bellum: Mapping the Normative Foundations (Oxford: Oxford University Press, 2014).

De Brabandere, Eric. "Jus Post Bellum and Foreign Direct Investment: Mapping the Debate." *The Journal of World Investment & Trade* 16.4 (2015): 590–603.

De Brabandere, Eric. "Responsibility for Post-Conflict Reforms: A Critical Assessment of Jus Post Bellum as a Legal Concept, The." *Vand. J. Transnat'l L.* 43 (2010): 119.

De Carvalho, Benjamin, Halvard Leira, and John M. Hobson. "The big bangs of IR: The myths that your teachers still tell you about 1648 and 1919." *Millennium* 39.3 (2011): 735–758.

De Greiff, Pablo, and Alexander Mayer-Rieckh. "Justice as prevention: vetting public employees in transitional societies." SSRC, 2007.

Dinstein, Yoram. "Comments on War." Harv. JL & Pub. Pol'y 27 (2003): 877.

Dinstein, Yoram. *The International Law of Belligerent Occupation* (CUP 2009).

Dinstein, Yoram. *War, aggression and self-defence.* Cambridge University Press, 2011.

Donovan, Dolores A. *Rebuilding Cambodia: human resources, human rights, and law: three essays.* Johns Hopkins Foreign Policy, 1993.

Dörr, O., & Schmalenbach, K. (2012). *Vienna Convention on the Law of Treaties: A Commentary.* (Vienna convention on the law of treaties.) Berlin, Heidelberg: Springer-Verlag Berlin Heidelberg.

Droege, Cordula. "The Interplay between International Humanitarian Law and International Human Rights Law in Situations of Armed Conflict." *Israel Law Review* 40.02 (2007): 310–355.

Dudziak, Mary L. *War time: an idea, its history, its consequences.* Oxford University Press, 2012.

Dudziak, Mary L., Law, War, and the History of Time, 98 Cal. L. Rev. 1669 (2010).

Elder, David A. "Historical Background of Common Article 3 of the Geneva Convention of 1949, The." *Case W. Res. J. Int'l L.* 11 (1979): 37.

Emerson, Rupert. "Self-determination." *Am. J. Int'l L.* 65 (1971): 459.

Emiliou, Nicholas. *The principle of proportionality in European law: a comparative study.* Vol. 10. Kluwer Law Intl, 1996.

Enriques, Giuliano. "Considerazioni sulla teoria della Guerra nel diritto Internazionale" (Considerations on the Theory of War in International Law) (1928) 7 Rivista Di Diritto Internazionale (Journal of International Law) 172.

Eppstein, John. *The Catholic Tradition of the Law of Nations.* The Lawbook Exchange, Ltd., 2012. Originally published: Washington, D.C.: Published for the Carnegie Endowment for International Peace by the Catholic Association for International Peace, 1935.

Feilchenfeld, Ernst Hermann. *Public debts and state succession.* Macmillan, 1931.

Fellmeth, Aaron Xavier, and Maurice Horwitz. *Guide to Latin in international law.* Oxford University Press, 2009.

Fellmeth, Aaron Xavier, and Maurice Horwitz. *Guide to Latin in international law.* Oxford University Press, 2009.

Finucane, Brian, Enforced Disappearance as a Crime Under International Law: A Neglected Origin in the Laws of War Yale Journal of International Law, Vol. 35, 171, 2010.

Fleck, Dieter. "The Responsibility to Rebuild and Its Potential for Law-Creation: Good Governance, Accountability and Judicial Control." *Journal of International Peacekeeping* 16.1–2 (2012): 84–98.

Fleck, Dieter "Jus post bellum as a partly independent legal framework" in Stahn, Carsten, Jennifer S. Easterday, and Jens Iverson, eds. *Jus Post Bellum.* Oxford University Press, 2014. 43–57.

Fox, Gregory H. "Occupation of Iraq, The." *Geo. J. Int'l L.* 36 (2004): 195.

Fox, Gregory H. "Transformative occupation and the unilateralist impulse." *International Review of the Red Cross* 94.885 (2012): 237–266.

Frängsmyr, Tore. "Christian Wolff's mathematical method and its impact on the eighteenth century." *Journal of the History of Ideas* 36.4 (1975): 653–668.

Gallen, James "Jus post bellum: an interpretive framework." Stahn, Carsten, Jennifer S. Easterday, and Jens Iverson, eds. *Jus Post Bellum*. Oxford University Press, 2014, 43–57.

Gallen, James. "Odious Debt and Jus Post Bellum." *The Journal of World Investment & Trade* 16.4 (2015): 666–694.

Galtung, Johan. "An Editorial." *Journal of Peace Research* 1(1) (1965):1–4.

Galtung, Johan. "Cultural Violence." *Journal of Peace Research*, 27 (3) (1990):291–305.

Galtung, Johan. "Social Cosmology and the Concept of Peace." *Journal of Peace Research*, 17 (2) (1981):183–199.

Galtung, Johan. "Twenty-Five Years of Peace Research: Ten Challenges and Some Responses." *Journal of Peace Research*, 22 (2) (1985):141–158.

Galtung, Johan. "Violence, Peace and Peace Research." *Journal of Peace Research*, 6 (3) (1969): 167–191.

Galtung, Johan. "Violence, Peace, and Peace Research" *Journal of Peace Research* 6 (3) (1969): 167.

Gardner, James B. "The Redefinition of Historical Scholarship: Calling a Tail a Leg?." *The Public Historian* (1998): 43–57.

Garner, Bryan A. "Black's Law Dictionary." (1991).

Gentili, Alberico. *De iure belli libri tres*. No. 16. 3 vols. Clarendon Press, John C. Rolfe trans., 1933.

Gordon, William M., and Olivia F. Robinson. *The Institutes of Gaius*. Duckworth, 1988.

Gross, Leo. "The Peace of Westphalia 1648–1948." *American Journal of International Law* 42 (1948): 20.

Grotius, Hugo, *Libri tres de jure belli ac pacis, in quibus ius naturae et gentium, item iuris publici praecipua explicantur*, 1st ed. (Paris, 1625). English translation: Francis W. Kelsey, et al. (Oxford, U.K.: Clarendon Press, 1925). Recent standard edition: Hugo Grotius, *Libri tres de jure belli ac pacis, in quibus ius naturae et gentium, item iuris publici praecipua explicantur*, edited by B.J.A. de Kanter-van Hettinga Tromp, annotationes novas addiderunt R. Feenstra et C.E. Persenaire, adjuvante E. Arps-de Wilde (Aalen, Germany: Scientia Verlag, 1993).

Grotius, Hugo. *Inleidinge tot de Hollandsche rechts-geleerdheid*. 1st ed. 1631. Latin version: J. van der Linden, *Institutiones juris hollandici et belgici*, 1835, edited by H.F.W.D. Fischer. Haarlem, Netherlands: H.D. Tjeenk Willink, 1962. English translation: R.W. Lee, An *Introduction to Roman-Dutch Law* (Oxford, U.K.: Clarendon Press, 1915 [5th ed. 1953]). Standard edition: Eduard M. Meijers, Folke Dovring, and H.F.W.D. Fischer (Leiden, Netherlands: Universitaire Pers Leiden, 1952 [2d ed. 1965]).

Grotius, Hugo, *Commentary on the Law of Prize and Booty*, Martine Julia van Ittersum (ed.), Liberty Fund (2006).

Grotius, Hugo. *Commentary on the Law of Prize and Booty (De Jure Praedae Commentarius)*, eds. Gwladys L. Williams and W.H. Zeydel (Oxford: Clarendon Press, 1950), vol. 1: A Translation of the Original Manuscript of 1604 by Gwladys L. Williams, with the collaboration of Walter H. Zeydel.

Grotius, Hugo. *Parallelon Rerum Publicarum de Moribus Ingenioque Populorum Atheniensium,Romanorum, Batavorum* (1601–1603).

Grotius, Hugo. *The Rights of War and Peace*, edited and with an Introduction by Richard Tuck, from the Edition by Jean Barbeyrac. 3 Vol. (Indianapolis: Liberty Fund, 2005).

Gudelinus, Petrus. "De jure pacis commentaries." *Opera Omnia* (Collected works). Antwerp, 1685.

Gudelinus, Petrus. *De jure pacis commentaries ad constitutionem Frederici de pace Constantiense*, Louvain, 1628.

Gudelinus, Petrus. *De jure pacis commentarius, in quo praecipuae de hoc jure quaestionis distinctis capitibus eleganter pertractantur*, Louvain, 1620.

Guilermo O'Donnell, Philippe C. Schmitter, and Laurence Whitehead, *Transitions from Authoritarian Rule: Tentative Conclusions about Uncertain Democracies* Vol. 4. Johns Hopkins University Press, 1986.

Haggenmacher, 'Grotius and Gentili: A Reassessment of Thomas E. Holland's Inaugural Lecture,' in H. Bull, B. Kingsbury, and A. Roberts (eds), *Hugo Grotius and International Relations* (1990): 13.

Haggenmacher, Peter. *Grotius et la doctrine de la guerre juste*. Paris: Presses universitaires de France, 1983.

Hart, Herbert Lionel Adolphus. *The concept of law*. OUP Oxford, 1961.

Henckaerts, Jean-Marie, Louise Doswald-Beck, and Carolin Alvermann. *Customary international humanitarian law*. Vol. 1: Rules. Cambridge University Press, 2005.

Henckaerts, Jean-Marie, Louise Doswald-Beck, and Carolin Alvermann. *Customary international humanitarian law*. Vol. 2: Practice. Cambridge University Press, 2005.

Henckaerts, Jean-Marie. *Mass expulsion in modern international law and practice*. Vol. 41. Martinus Nijhoff Publishers, 1995.

Hobbes, Thomas, and Edwin Curley. *Leviathan: with selected variants from the Latin edition of 1668*. Vol. 2. Hackett Publishing, 1994.

Holland, Thomas Erskine. *An Inaugural Lecture on Albericus Gentilis, Delivered at All Souls College, November 7, 1874*. Vol. 47. MacMilland and Company, 1874.

Howse, Robert. 'The Concept of Odious Debt in Public International Law' UNCTAD Discussion Paper No 185 (2007) UNCTAD/OSG/DP/2007/4.

International Commission on Intervention, State Sovereignty, and International Development Research Centre (Canada). *The Responsibility to Protect: Research, Bibliography, Background: Supplementary Volume to the Report of the International*

Commission on Intervention and State Sovereignty. International Development Research Centre, 2001.

International Commission on Intervention, State Sovereignty, and International Development Research Centre (Canada). *Report of the International Commission on Intervention and State Sovereignty, The Responsibility to Protect*. International Development Research Centre, 2001.

International Committee Of The Red Cross, *Commentary On The Geneva Convention (IV) Relative To The Protection Of Civilian Persons In Time Of War* (Jean Pictet gen. ed., 1958).

Israel, Jonathan, and Michael Silverthorne, eds. *Spinoza: Theological-Political Treatise*. Cambridge University Press, 2007.

Ittersum, Martine Julia van. "Dating the manuscript of De Jure Praedae (1604–1608): What watermarks, foliation and quire divisions can tell us about Hugo Grotius' development as a natural rights and natural law theorist."*History of European Ideas* 35.2 (2009): 125–193.

Iverson, Jens. "Contrasting the Normative and Historical Foundations of Transitional Justice and Jus Post Bellum: Outlining the Matrix of Definitions in Comparative Perspective": 80–101." Jus Post Bellum: Mapping the Normative Foundations. New York: OUP (2014).

Iverson, Jens. "Transitional Justice, Jus Post Bellum and International Criminal Law: Differentiating the Usages, History and Dynamics."*International Journal of Transitional Justice* 7.3 (2013): 413–433.

Jenks, C. Wilfred. "The challenge of universality." Proceedings of the American Society of International Law at Its Annual Meeting (1921–1969). Vol. 53. American Society of International Law, 1959, 85–98.

Johnson, James Turner, *Just War Tradition and the Restraint of War: A Moral and Historical Inquiry*, (Princeton University Press 1981).

Johnson, James Turner. *Ideology, reason, and the limitation of war: religious and secular concepts, 1200–1740*. Princeton University Press, 1975.

Johnson, Larry D. ""Uniting for Peace": Does it Still Serve Any Useful Purpose?" *American Journal of International Law* 108 (2014): 106–115.

Jouannet, Emmanuelle. *Emer de Vattel et l' émergence doctrinale du droit international classique*. Paris: A Pedone, 1998.

Jovanović, Miodrag A. "Responsibility to Protect and the International Rule of Law." *Chinese Journal of International Law* 14.4 (2015): 757–776.

Judt, Tony. "What have we learned, if anything?." *New York Review of Books* 55.7 (2008): 16.

Kaiser, Jürgen, and Antje Queck. *Odious Debts-Odious Creditors?: International Claims on Iraq*. Friedrich-Ebert-Stiftung, 2004.

Kant, Immanuel, "Toward Perpetual Peace: A Philosophical Sketch." (originally published 1795) *Toward perpetual peace and other writings on politics, peace, and history*. Yale University Press, 2006, 67–109.

Kant, Immanuel, *Eternal Peace (Continued)*, The Advocate of Peace (1894–1920), Vol. 59, No. 8 (American Peace Society, August and September 1897). 196–199.

Kant, Immanuel, *Eternal Peace*, The Advocate of Peace (1894–1920), Vol. 59, No. 5 (American Peace Society, May 1897). 111–116.

Kant, Immanuel. *Metaphysische Anfangsgründe der Rechtslehre* (The Philosophy of Law: An Exposition of the Fundamental Principles of Jurisprudence as the Science of Right, originally published 1887, tr W. Hastie, The Lawbook Exchange 2002).

Kant, Immanuel. *The Doctrine of Right, in his Political Writings*, trans. H.B. Nisbet (1995).

Kant, Immanuel. *Toward Perpetual Peace*, 1932, U.S. Library Association, Westwood Hills Press, Los Angeles, California, U.S.A.

Kantorowicz, Ernst H. *The King's Two Bodies: A Study in Medieval Political Theory*. Princeton University Press, 1957.

Kapossy, Béla and Richard Whitmore. "Introduction." *Emer de Vattel, The Law of Nations, Or, Principles of the Law of Nature, Applied to the Conduct and Affairs of nations and Sovereigns, with Three Early Essays on the Origin and Nature of Natural Law and on Luxury*. Ed. Béla Kapossy and Richard Whitmore (Indianapolis: Liberty Fund, 2008).

Kelsen, Hans. *Pure theory of law*. Univ of California Press, 1967.

King, Jeff. 'Odious Debt: The Terms of the Debate' (2007) 32 *NC J Intl L & Comm Reg* 605–67.

Kolb, Robert. "Origin of the twin terms jus ad bellum/jus in bello."*International Review of the Red Cross* 37.320 (1997): 553–562.

Koskenniemi, Martti. "The function of law in the international community: 75 years after." *The British Year Book of International Law* 79.1 (2009): 353.

Koskenniemi, Martti. "Lauterpacht: The Victorian Tradition in International Law" (1997) 8 *European Journal of International Law* 215.

Kritz, Neil J., *Transitional Justice: How Emerging Democracies Reckon With Former Regimes*. US Institute of Peace Press (1995).

Kunz, Josef L. "The future of the international law for the protection of national minorities." *American Journal of International Law* (1945): 89–95.

Kunz, Josef L. "The present status of the international law for the protection of minorities."*American Journal of International Law* (1954): 282–287.

Kunz, Josef L. "Vienna School and International Law, The." *NYULQ Rev.* 11 (1933): 370.

Kuttner, Stephan. "Raymond of Peñafort as Editor: The Decretales and Constitutiones of Gregory IX." *Bull. Medieval Canon L.* 12 (1982).

La Fontaine, Fannie, *No Amnesty or Statute of Limitation for Enforced Disappearances: the Sandoval Case before the Supreme Court of Chile*, 3 J. Int'l Crim. Just. 469 (2005).

LaForce, Glen W. "Trial of Major Henry Wirz-A National Disgrace, The."*Army Law.* (1988): 3.

Langan, John. "The elements of St. Augustine's just war theory." *The Journal of Religious Ethics* (1984): 19–38.

Lauterpacht, Hersch. "Limits of the Operation of the Law of War, The." *Brit. YB Int'l L.* 30 (1953): 206.

Lauterpacht, Hersch. "Non Liquet and the Function of Law in the International Community'(1959)." *BYIL* 35: 124.

Lauterpacht, Hersch. "Recognition of States in International Law." *The Yale Law Journal* 53.3 (1944): 385–458.

Lauterpacht, Hersch. "The Doctrine of Non-Justiciable Disputes in International Law." *Economica* 24 (1928): 277–317.

Lauterpacht, Hersch. "Rules of War in an Unlawful War," *Law and Politics in the World Community* 89 (Lipsky, ed., 1953).

Lauterpacht, Hersch. "The Grotian Tradition in International Law" (1946) 23 *British Year Book of International Law* 1.

Lauterpacht, Hersch. "The Problem of the Revision of the Law of War." *British Year Book of International Law* 29 (1952) 360.

Lauterpacht, Hersch. *Private Law Sources and Analogies of International Law.* London: Longmans, 1927. Reprints, Hamden, Conn.: Archon Books, 1970, and Union, N.J.: Lawbook Exchange, 2002.

Lauterpacht, Hersch. *The Function of Law in the International Community* (Oxford University Press 1933).

Lawry-White, Merryl. "International Investment Arbitration in a Jus Post Bellum Framework." *The Journal of World Investment & Trade* 16.4 (2015): 633–665.

Lerner, Nātān. *Group rights and discrimination in international law.* Vol. 77. Martinus Nijhoff Publishers, 2003.

Lesaffer, Randall. "Alberico Gentili's just post bellum and Early Modern Peace Treaties." in Kingsbury, Benedict, and Benjamin Straumann. The Roman foundations of the law of nations: Alberico Gentili and the justice of empire. Oxford University Press, 2010.

Lesaffer, Randall. "An early treatise on peace treaties: Petrus Gudelinus between Roman law and modern practice." *Journal of Legal History* 23.3 (2002): 223–252.

Lesaffer, Randall. "The medieval canon law of contract and early modern treaty law." *Journal of the History of International Law* 2.2 (2000): 178–198.

Lesaffer, Randall. "Peace treaties and the formation of international law." *The Oxford Handbook of the History of International Law* (2012): 71–94.

Lesaffer, Randall, ed. *Peace treaties and international law in European history: from the late Middle Ages to World War One.* Cambridge University Press, 2004.

Lesaffer, Randall. "A Schoolmaster Abolishing Homework? Vattel on Peacemaking and Peace Treaties." *Vattel's International Law from a XXI st Century Perspective/Le Droit International de Vattel vu du XXI e Siècle.* Brill, 2011. 353–384.

Lesaffer, Randall. "The Westphalia peace treaties and the development of the tradition of great European peace settlements prior to 1648." *Grotiana* 18 (1997).

Lewkowicz, Grégory. "Jus Post Bellum: vieille antienne ou nouvelle branche du droit? Sur le mythe de l'origine vénérable du Jus Post Bellum." *Revue belge de droit international* 1 (2011).

Lienau, Odette.'Who Is the "Sovereign" in Sovereign Debt?: Reinterpreting a Rule-of-Law Framework from the Early Twentieth Century' (2008) 33(1) *Yale J Intl L* 63–111.

Lin, Yuri, Jean-Baptiste Michel, Erez Lieberman Aiden, Jon Orwant, William Brockman, Slav Petrov. Syntactic Annotations for the Google Books Ngram Corpus. Proceedings of the 50th Annual Meeting of the Association for Computational Linguistics Volume 2: Demo Papers (ACL '12) (2012).

Linz, Juan J., and Alfred Stepan. *Problems of democratic transition and consolidation: Southern Europe, South America, and post-communist Europe*. Johns Hopkins University Press, 1996.

Lutz, Ellen, and Kathryn Sikkink. "Justice Cascade: The Evolution and Impact of Foreign Human Rights Trials in Latin America, The." *Chi. J. Int'l L.* 2 (2001): 1.

Machiavelli, Niccolò, 1515. *The Prince*, trans. Harvey C. Mansfield, Jr., Chicago: Chicago University Press, 1985.

Magnus Ryan, *Bartolus of Sassoferrato and Free Cities*. The Alexander Prize Lecture, Transactions of the Royal Historical Society, Vol. 10 (2000). 65–89. Published by: Cambridge University Press on behalf of the Royal Historical Society.

Mani, Rama. Beyond Retribution: Seeking Justice in the Shadows of War. Polity, 2002.

Maoz, Zeev, and Bruce Russett. "Normative and Structural Causes of Democratic Peace, 1946–1986." *American Political Science Review* 87.03 (1993): 624–638.

Martel, William C. *Victory in War: Foundations of Modern Strategy*. Cambridge University Press, 2011.

May, Larry. "Grotius and Contingent Pacifism." *Studies in the History of Ethics* (2006): 1–24.

May, Larry. "Jus Post Bellum Proportionality and the Fog of War." *European Journal of International Law* 24.1 (2013): 315–333.

May, Larry. "Jus Post Bellum, Grotius and Meionexia." Eds. Carsten Stahn, Jennifer S Easterday and Jens Iverson. *Jus Post Bellum: Mapping the Normative Foundations* (OUP 2014) 15–25.

May, Larry. *After war ends: a philosophical perspective*. Cambridge University Press, 2012.

Megret, Frederic. On the Legitimacy of 'Insurgency': Rise and Fall of the Idea of Resistance to Occupation (Grandeur Et Declin De L'Idee De Resistance a L'Occupation: Reflexions a Propos de la Legitimite des 'Insurges') (November 5, 2008). *Revue Belge de Droit International*, 2009. 18.

Meron, Theodor. "On a hierarchy of international human rights." *Am. J. Int'l L.* 80 (1986): 1.

Meron, Theodor. "The continuing role of custom in the formation of international humanitarian law." *American Journal of International Law* (1996): 238–249.

Meron, Theodor. "The Martens Clause, principles of humanity, and dictates of public conscience." *American Journal of International Law* (2000): 78–89.

Michel, Jean-Baptiste*, Yuan Kui Shen, Aviva Presser Aiden, Adrian Veres, Matthew K. Gray, William Brockman, The Google Books Team, Joseph P. Pickett, Dale Hoiberg, Dan Clancy, Peter Norvig, Jon Orwant, Steven Pinker, Martin A. Nowak, and Erez Lieberman Aiden*. Quantitative Analysis of Culture Using Millions of Digitized Books. Science (Published online ahead of print: 12/16/2010).

Michel, Jean-Baptiste, et al. "Quantitative analysis of culture using millions of digitized books." *Science* 331.6014 (2011): 176–182.

Milanovic, Marko, The Lost Origins of Lex Specialis: Rethinking the Relationship between Human Rights and International Humanitarian Law (July 9, 2014). *Theoretical Boundaries of Armed Conflict and Human Rights*, Jens David Ohlin ed., Cambridge University Press, Forthcoming, at 15. Available at SSRN: http://ssrn.com/abstract=2463957.

Milanovic, Marko. "Sejdic and Finci v. Bosnia and Herzegovina." *American Journal of International Law* 104 (2010).

Milanovic, Marko. *Extraterritorial application of human rights treaties: law, principles, and policy*. Oxford University Press, 2011.

Moghadam, Valentine M. "The gender of democracy: The link between women's rights and democratization in the Middle East." Arab reform bulletin 2.7 (2004): 2–3.

Molier, Gelijn. "Rebuilding after Armed Conflict: Towards a Legal Framework of "The Responsibility to Rebuild" or a "Ius post Bellum"?." *Peace, Security and Development in an Era of Globalization: The Integrated Security Approach Viewed from a Multidisciplinary Perspective* (Martinus Nijhoff 2009): 317–53.

Molier, Gelijn. (2007), Wederopbouw na gewapend conflict: naar juridificering van 'the responsibility to rebuild' of een 'ius post bellum?.' In: Bomert B., Hoogen T. van den (Eds.) *Jaarboek Vrede en Veiligheid 2007*. Nijmegen: Centrum voor Internationaal Conflict-Analyse & Management 2007. 1–34.

Mommsen, Theodor, and Paul Krueger, eds. *Corpus iuris civilis*. Vol. 1. Cambridge University Press, 2014.

Moore, John Norton. "Jus Ad Bellum Before the International Court of Justice."*Va. J. Int'l L.* 52 (2011): 903.

Moyle, John Baron, ed. *The Institutes of Justinian*. Clarendon Press, 1906.

Muldoon, James. "The contribution of the medieval canon lawyers to the formation of international law." *Traditio* 28 (1972): 483–497.

Neff, Stephen C. "Conflict Termination and Peace-Making in the Law of Nations: A Historical Perspective." *Jus Post Bellum: Towards a Law of Transition from Conflict to Peace*, ed. Carsten Stahn and Jann K. Kleffner (The Hague: T.M.C. Asser Press, 2008): 77–91.

Neff, Stephen C. *War and the law of nations: A general history.* Cambridge University Press, 2005.

Nehru, Vikram. "The concept of odious debt: some considerations." World Bank Policy Research Working Paper Series No. 4676 (2008).

Newton, Michael, and Larry May. *Proportionality in International Law.* Oxford University Press, 2014.

Niebuhr, Reinhold. *Moral Man and Immoral Society.* (New York: Charles Scribner's Sons, 1932).

Nystuen, Gro, Stuart Casey-Maslen, and Annie Golden Bersagel, eds. *Nuclear Weapons Under International Law.* Cambridge University Press, 2014.

Ocran, T. Modibo. "The Doctrine of Humanitarian Intervention in Light of Robust Peacekeeping." *BC Int'l Comp. L. Rev.* 25 (2002): 1.

O'Connell, Mary Ellen, and Mirakmal Niyazmatov. "What is Aggression? Comparing the Jus ad Bellum and the ICC Statute." *Journal of International Criminal Justice* 10.1 (2012): 189–207.

Orakhelashvili, Alexander. "Post-War Settlement in Iraq: The UN Security Council Resolution 1483 (2003) and General International Law, The." J. Conflict & Sec. L. 8 (2003): 307.

Orakhelashvili, Alexander. "The interaction between human rights and humanitarian law: fragmentation, conflict, parallelism, or convergence?." *European Journal of International Law* 19.1 (2008): 161–182.

Orend, Brian. "Jus post bellum." *Journal of Social Philosophy* 31.1 (2000): 117–137.

Orend, Brian. "Jus Post Bellum: A Just War Theory Perspective" in *Jus Post Bellum: Towards a Law of Transition from Conflict to Peace*, ed. Carsten Stahn and Jann K. Kleffner (The Hague: T.M.C. Asser Press, 2008), 39–40.

Orend, Brian. "Jus Post Bellum: The Perspective of a Just-War Theorist." *Leiden Journal of International Law*, 20 (2007), 579–580.

Orend, Brian. *The Morality of War.* Broadview Press, 2013.

Orend, Brian. *War and International Justice: A Kantian Perspective.* Wilfrid Laurier Univ. Press, 2000.

Osiander, Andreas. "Sovereignty, international relations, and the Westphalian myth." *International organization* 55.02 (2001): 251–287.

Österdahl, Inger, and Esther Van Zadel. "What will jus post bellum mean? Of new wine and old bottles." *Journal of Conflict and Security Law* 14.2 (2009): 175–207.

Pegis, Anton C. "Introduction." *Basic Writings of St. Thomas Aquinas*, Vol. 1. Ed. Anton C. Pegis, Hackett Publishing 1997.

Penn, William, and Andrew R. Murphy. *The political writings of William Penn.* Indianapolis: Liberty Fund, 2002.

Pennington, Kenneth. "Baldus de Ubaldis." *Rivista Internazionale di Diritto Comune* 8 (1997): 35.

Perkins, Merle L. *The moral and political philosophy of the Abbé de Saint-Pierre.* Vol. 24. Librairie Droz, 1959.

Persico, Joseph E. *Eleventh Month, Eleventh Day, Eleventh Hour.* Random House, 2005.

Phillips, Anne. 1995. *The Politics of Presence: The Political Representation of Gender, Ethnicity and Race.* Oxford, UK: Clarendon Press.

Phillips, Anne. *Engendering democracy.* Penn State Press, 1991.

Pictets, Jean. "The Geneva Conventions of 12 August 1949, Commentary, Vol. I (Geneve, 1952), Vol. II (Geneve, 1960), Vol. III (Geneve, 1960), Vol. IV (Geneve, 1958), [Kommentarutgave, Den internasjonale Røde Kors-komiteen]." (1949).

Pilloud, Claude, et al., eds. *Commentary on the additional protocols: of 8 June 1977 to the Geneva Conventions of 12 August 1949.* Martinus Nijhoff Publishers, 1987.

Quinn, Joanna R. "Chicken and Egg? Sequencing in Transitional Justice: The Case of Uganda" (Autumn/Winter 2009) 14(2) *International Journal of Peace Studies* 35–53.

Ratner, Steven R. "The Cambodia settlement agreements." *The American Journal of International Law* 87.1 (1993): 1–41.

Robinson, Paul. "Is There an Obligation to Rebuild?." *Justice, Responsibility and Reconciliation in the Wake of Conflict.* Springer Netherlands, 2013. 105–116.

Roberts, Adam. "What is a military occupation?." *British Yearbook of International Law* 55.1 (1985): 249–305.

Roberts, Adam. "Transformative military occupation: applying the laws of war and human rights."*American Journal of International Law* (2006): 580–622.

Rodin, David. "Ending war." *Ethics & International Affairs* 25.03 (2011): 359–367.

Rodin, David. "Two Emerging Issues of Jus Post Bellum: War Termination and the Liability of Soldiers for Crimes of Aggression." *Jus Post Bellum: Towards a Law of Transition from Conflict to Peace.* Ed. Carsten Stahn and Jann K. Kleffner (The Hague: T.M.C. Asser Press, 2008), 53–62.

Rodin, David. "The War Trap: Dilemmas of jus terminatio." *Ethics* 125.3 (2015): 674–695.

Roht-Arriaza, Naomi, and Javier Mariezcurrena, eds. *Transitional justice in the twenty-first century: beyond truth versus justice.* Cambridge: Cambridge University Press, 2006.

Roht-Arriaza, Naomi. "Transitional Justice and Peace Agreements." Working Paper, International Council on Human Rights Policy (2005).

Roht-Arriaza, Naomi. *The Pinochet Effect: Transnational Justice in the Age of Human Rights.* University of Pennsylvania Press, 2005.

Russell, Frederick H. *The Just War in the Middle Ages.* Cambridge University Press, 1977.

Russett, Bruce, et al. "The Democratic Peace."*International Security* (1995): 164–184.

Russett, Bruce. *Grasping the Democratic Peace: Principles for a Post-Cold War World.* Princeton University Press, 1994.

Sack, Alexander N. "Diplomatic Claims Against the Soviets (1918–1938)." *New York University Law Quarterly Rev.* 15 (1937): 507.

Sack, Alexander N. 'The Judicial Nature of the Public Debt of States' *New York University Law Quarterly* 10 (1932): 341.

Sack, Alexander Nahum. *Les effets des transformations des états sur leurs dettes publiques et autres obligations financièrs. Traité juridique et financier*. Vol. 7. Recueil Sirey, 1927.

Scattola, Merio Fassbender, "Alberico Gentili (1552–1608)" in Bardo, et al. *The Oxford handbook of the history of international law*. Oxford University Press, 2012.

Schabas, William A. "Lex Specialis-Belt and Suspenders-the Parallel Operation of Human Rights Law and the Law of Armed Conflict, and the Conundrum of Jus Ad Bellum." *Isr. L. Rev.* 40 (2007): 592.

Schaff, Philip, ed. *A Select Library of the Nicene and Post-Nicene Fathers of the Christian Church*. Series I, Vol. I. Parker, 1890. (Letters of St Augustin, Ch. 142).

Schaff, Philip, ed. *A Select Library of the Nicene and Post-Nicene Fathers of the Christian Church*. Series I, Vol. IV. Parker, 1890. (Against Faustus).

Schaff, Philip, ed. *A Select Library of the Nicene and Post-Nicene Fathers of the Christian Church*. Series II, Vol. I. Parker, 1890. (Church History of Eusebius, Book IV, Ch. 6).

Schaff, Philip, ed. *A Select Library of the Nicene and Post-Nicene Fathers of the Christian Church*. Series II, Vol. III. Parker, 1890. (Theodoret, Ecclesiastical History, Book V, Ch 38).

Schaff, Philip, ed. *A Select Library of the Nicene and Post-Nicene Fathers of the Christian Church*. Series II, Vol. VI. Parker, 1890. (The Letters of St. Jerome, Letter 125).

Schaff, Philip, ed. *A Select Library of the Nicene and Post-Nicene Fathers of the Christian Church*. Series II, Vol. XIII. Parker, 1890. (Ephraim the Syrian and Aphrahat, Introductory Dissertation, Ephrahat the Persian Sage; Ephraim the Syrian and Aphrahat, Select Demonstrations of Aphrahat, Demonstration V "Of Wars").

Schauer, Frederick F., *Playing by the rules: a philosophical examination of rule-based decision-making in law and in life* (1991) Oxford University Press.

Schmidt, Sebastian. "To Order the Minds of Scholars: The Discourse of the Peace of Westphalia in International Relations Literature1." *International Studies Quarterly* 55.3 (2011): 601–623.

Schwarzenberger, Georg, Jus pacis ac belli? Prolegomena to a sociology of International Law, 37 Am. J. Int'l L. 460 (1943).

Schwarzenberger, Georg. "Jus Pacis Ac Belli? Prolegomena to a Sociology of International Law" (1943) 37 *American Journal of International Law* 460.

Scott, James Brown. *The Spanish Origin of International law: Francisco de Vitoria and his Law of Nations*. Oxford University Press, 1934.

Scott, James Brown. *The Catholic Conception of International Law. Francisco de Vitoria, founder of the modern law of nations; Francisco Suarez, founder of the modern philosophy of law in general and in particular of the law of nations; A critical examination and a justified appreciation*. Georgetown University, 1934.

Scott, James Brown. *The Spanish Origin of International Law: Lectures on Francisco de Vitoria (1480–1546) and Francisco Suarez (1548–1617)*, Washington, 1928.

Sen, Amartya Kumar. *Collective choice and social welfare*. Vol. 11. Elsevier, 2014.

Sen, Amartya. *The Idea of Justice*. Harvard University Press, 2011.

Sen, Amartya. *Development as freedom*. Oxford Paperbacks, 2001.

Seneca, Lucius Annaeus, and Robin Campbell. *Epistulae morales ad Lucilium*. Vol. 210. Penguin UK, 1969.

Sharma, Serena K. "The Legacy of Jus Contra Bellum: Echoes of Pacifism in Contemporary Just War Thought." Journal of Military Ethics 8.3 (2009): 217–230.

Sinclair, Ian M.T. *The Vienna Convention on the Law of Treaties*. Manchester: Manchester University Press, 1984.

Sikkink, Kathryn. *The Justice Cascade: How Human Rights Prosecutions Are Changing World Politics (The Norton Series in World Politics)*. WW Norton & Company, 2011.

Slim, Hugo, and Andrew Bonwick. *Protection: An ALNAP guide for humanitarian agencies*. Oxfam, 2006.

Solis, Gary D. *The law of armed conflict: international humanitarian law in war*. Cambridge University Press, 2010.

Stahn, Carsten "Jus Ad Bellum," "Jus In Bello," "Jus Post Bellum?" Rethinking the Conception of the Law of Armed Force, ASIL Proceedings, 2006, 159.

Stahn, Carsten, and Jann K. Kleffner eds. *Jus post bellum: towards a law of transition from conflict to peace*. TMC Asser Press, 2008.

Stahn, Carsten. "'Jus ad bellum,' 'jus in bello'...'jus post bellum'?–Rethinking the Conception of the Law of Armed Force." *European Journal of International Law* 17.5 (2006): 921–943.

Stahn, Carsten. "Jus Post Bellum: Mapping the Discipline (s)." *Am. U. Int'l L. Rev.* 23 (2007): 311.

Stahn, Carsten. "Justice under transitional administration: contours and critique of a paradigm." *Hous. J. Int'l L.* 27 (2004): 311.

Stahn, Carsten. "Jus Post Bellum, Mapping the Discipline(s)." *Jus Post Bellum: Towards a Law of Transition from Conflict to Peace*. Ed. Carsten Stahn and Jann K. Kleffner (The Hague: T.M.C. Asser Press, 2008), 105.

Stahn, Carsten. "The Future of Jus Post Bellum." Eds. Carsten Stahn and Jann K Kleffner. *Jus Post Bellum – Towards a Law of Transition from Conflict to Peace* (T·M·C·Asser Press 2008) 231–237.

Stahn, Carsten. *The law and practice of international territorial administration: Versailles to Iraq and beyond*. Vol. 57. Cambridge University Press, 2008.

Stevenson, Drury. "To Whom Is the Law Addressed?." Yale Law & Policy Review 21.1 (2003): 105–167.

Stevenson, Drury D. "Kelsen's View of the Addressee of the Law: Primary and Secondary Norms." *Hans Kelsen in America-Selective Affinities and the Mysteries of Academic Influence*. Springer International Publishing, 2016. 297–317.

Stevenson, Drury D., Kelsen's View of the Addressee of the Law: Primary and Secondary Norms (June 21, 2014). Kelsen in America Interdisciplinary Conference hosted by Valparaiso University School of Law at the Lutheran School of Theology at Chicago, June 27 – 28, 2014. Available at SSRN: https://ssrn.com/abstract=2457480 or http://dx.doi.org/10.2139/ssrn.2457480.

Svensson, Patrik. The Landscape of Digital Humanities, *Digital Humanities Quarterly*, 2010 Volume 4 Number 1.

Tardy, Thierry. "A critique of robust peacekeeping in contemporary peace operations." *International Peacekeeping* 18.2 (2011): 152–167.

Teitel, Ruti G. "The Law and Politics of Comtemporary Transitional Justice."*Cornell International Law Journal* 38 (2005): 837.

Teitel, Ruti G. "Transitional justice genealogy." *Harv. Hum. Rts. J.* 16 (2003): 69.

Teitel, Ruti G. *Humanity's law*. OUP USA, 2011.

Teitel, Ruti G. *Transitional justice*. Oxford University Press, 2000.

Tencati, Antonio and Francesco Perrini, Business Ethics and Corporate Sustainability, 2011, Edward Elgar Publishing Limited.

Terrie, Jim. "The use of force in UN peacekeeping: The experience of MONUC." *African Security Studies* 18.1 (2009): 21–34.

The Holy Bible, King James Version. Cambridge Edition: 1769.

Thornberry, Patrick. "Self-determination, minorities, human rights: a review of international instruments." *International and Comparative Law Quarterly* 38.04 (1989): 867–889.

Thucydides. History of the Peloponnesian War, trans. Rex Warner, Harmondsworth: Penguin Books, 1972.

Tondini, Matteo, Putting an End to Human Rights Violations by Proxy: Accountability of International Organizations and Member States in the Framework of Jus Post Bellum (2008). C. Stahn, Carsten and J. Kleffner (eds.), Jus Post Bellum: Towards a Law of Transition From Conflict to Peace, The Hague: TMC Asser Press, 2008, pp. 187–212.

Torrel, Jean-Pierre. "Thomas Aquinas (1224/1225–1274), Thomism." *Encyclopedia of the Middle Ages*, (Vauchez André ed., James Clarke & Co. 2002).

Turgis, Noémie. "What is Transitional Justice?" (2010) 1 *International Journal of Law, Transitional Justice and Human Rights* 9.

Van Der Molen, Gezina Hermina Johanna. *Alberico Gentili and the development of international law: his life, work and times*. Diss. 1937.

Vanderpol, Alfred, and Emile Chénon. *La doctrine scolastique du droit de guerre*. A. Pedone, 1919.

Vattel, Emerich. De *Le Droit des Gens, ou Principes de la Loi Naturelle, appliqués à la Conduite et aux Affaires des Nations et des Souverains* (1758), The Law of Nations, Or, Principles of the Law of Nature, Applied to the Conduct and Affairs of Nations and Sovereigns, with Three Early Essays on the Origin and Nature of Natural Law and on

Luxury, edited and with an Introduction by Béla Kapossy and Richard Whitmore (Indianapolis: Liberty Fund, 2008).

Verdirame, Guglielmo. "What to Make of Jus Post Bellum: A Response to Antonia Chayes." European Journal of International Law 24.1 (2013): 307–313.

Villiger, M.E. (2009). *Commentary on the 1969 Vienna Convention on the Law of Treaties*. Leiden: Nijhoff.

Vitoria, Francisco. De *Francisci de Victoria De Indis et De ivre belli relectiones*. No. 7. The Carnegie Institution of Washington, 1917.

Von Glahn, Gerhard. *The Occupation of Enemy Territory: A commentary on the law and practice of belligerent occupation*. University of Minnesota Press, 1957.

Wahl, J.A. "Baldus de Ubaldis and the Foundations of the Nation-State." *Manuscripta* 21.2 (1977):80.

Walter, Barbara F. *Conflict Relapse and the Sustainability of Post-Conflict Peace*, World Development Report Background Paper, 2010, World Bank.

Waltz, Kenneth Neal. *Man, the State, and War: a theoretical analysis*. Columbia University Press, 2001.

Walzer, Michael. "The Aftermath of War." in *Ethics beyond war's end*. Patterson, Eric. Ed. Georgetown University Press, 2012.: 35–46.

Walzer, Michael. *Arguing about war*. Yale University Press, 2008.

White, Margaret. "Equity-A General Principle of Law Recognised by Civilised Nations." *Queensland U. Tech. L. & Just. J.* 4 (2004): 103.

White, Nigel D. "The relationship between the UN Security Council and General Assembly in matters of international peace and security." *The Oxford Handbook of the Use of Force in International Law*. 2015.

Wilde, Ralph. *International Territorial Administration: How Trusteeship and the Civilizing Mission Never Went Away* (Oxford University Press 2010).

Williams, Gwladys L., Ammi Brown, and John Waldron Eds. "Selections from Three Works of Francisco Suárez." Oxford: Clarendon Press, 1944.

Williams, Robert E., and Dan Caldwell. "Jus Post Bellum: Just war theory and the principles of just peace." *International Studies Oerspectives* 7.4 (2006): 309–320.

Winkel, Laurens. "Grotius, Hugo" *The Oxford International Encyclopedia of Legal History* (Stanley N Katz ed. Oxford University Press 2009).

Wolff, Christian. "Dissertatio algebraica de algorithmo infinitesimali differentiali quam gratioso indultu amplissimi philosophorum ordinis." (1704).

Wolff, Christian. *Institutiones juris naturae et gentium: In quibus ex ipsa hominis natura continuo nexu omnes obligationes et jura omnia deducuntur* (Halle and Magdeburg, Germany, 1750).

Wolff, Christian, *Jus gentium methodo scientifica pertractatum*, Clarendon press (1934) Volume Two, p. 426. Translation by Francis J. Hemelt.

Wolff, Christian. *Jus naturae methodo scientifico pertractatum.* 8 vols. Leipzig, Germany: Prostat in Officina Libraria Rengeriana, 1741–1748.
Yoo, John. "Iraqi Reconstruction and the Law of Occupation." *UC Davis J. Int'l L. & Pol'y* 11 (2004): 7.
Zahawi, Hamada. "Redefining the Laws of Occupation in the Wake of Operation Iraqi Freedom." *California Law Review* (2007): 2295–2352.
Zrilič, Jure. "International Investment Law in the Context of Jus Post Bellum: Are Investment Treaties Likely to Facilitate or Hinder the Transition to Peace?." *The Journal of World Investment & Trade* 16.4 (2015): 604–632.

a. Table of Cases

Accordance with International Law of the Unilateral Declaration of Independence in Respect of Kosovo (Request for Advisory Opinion), General List No. 141, 2010 I.C.J. 1, International Court of Justice (ICJ), 22 July 2010.

Advisory Opinion Concerning Legal Consequences of the Construction of a Wall in the Occupied Palestinian Territory, 43 ILM 1009; International Court of Justice (ICJ), 9 July 2004.

Al-Jedda v. United Kingdom, 2011 E.C.H.R. 1092 (2011).

Application of the Convention on the Prevention and Punishment of the Crime of Genocide (Bosnia and Herzegovina v. Serbia and Montenegro), 2007 I.C.J. 191.

Arbitral Award of 31 July 1989, Guinea-Bissau v Senegal, Judgment, [1991] ICJ Rep 53, ICGJ 90 (ICJ 1991), (1992) 31 ILM 32, 12th November 1991, International Court of Justice.

Armed Activities on the Territory of the Congo, Congo, Democratic Republic of the v Uganda, Merits, ICJ GL No 116, [2005] ICJ Rep 168, ICGJ 31 (ICJ 2005), (2006) 45 ILM 271, 19th December 2005, International Court of Justice.

Barrios Altos Case, Judgment of November 30, 2001, Inter-Am Ct. H.R. (Ser. C) No. 87 (2001).

Behrami and Behrami v. France, Saramati v. France, Germany and Norway, ECHR, Decision on Admissibility (2007) 45 Eur. Ct. H.R. 10 (2007) App. Nos. 71412/01 & 78166/01.

Case Concerning Military and Paramilitary Activities in and against Nicaragua (Nicaragua v. United States of America), Merits [1986] I.C.J. Rep. 14.

Case concerning the Northern Cameroons (Cameroon v. UK), Preliminary Objections, 1963 ICJ Rep. 15 (Judgment of 2 December 1963).

ICC, Decision on the admissibility of the Prosecutor's appeal against the "Decision on the request of the Union of the Comoros to review the Prosecutor's decision not to initiate an investigation," Situation on Registered Vessels of the Union of the Comoros, the Hellenic Republic and the Kingdom of Cambodia, ICC-01/13-51, 6 November 2015, Appeals Chamber.

Great Britain v Costa Rica (1923) 2 Annual Digest 34, 1 RIAA 369.

Greek Case, Denmark v Greece, Report of the Commission, App No 3321/67, (1969) 12 YB Eur Conv Hum Rts 1, (1972) 12 YB Eur Conv Hum Rts 186, 5th November 1969, European Commission on Human Rights.

Hassan v. United Kingdom, 2014 Eur. Ct. H.R., (9 December 2015).

ICTY, The Prosecutor v. Duško Tadić aka "Dule," Decision on the Defence Motion for Interlocutory Appeal on Jurisdiction, Appeals Chamber, 2 October 1995, Case No. IT-94-1-AR72.

Lawless v Ireland, Admissibility, App No 332/57, B/1, (1958–59) 2 YB Eur Conv HR 324, 30th August 1959, European Commission on Human Rights.

Legal Consequences for States of the Continued Presence of South Africa in Namibia (South West Africa) notwithstanding Security Council Resolution 276 (1970) (Advisory Opinion) [1971] ICJ Rep 16.

Legality of the Threat or Use of Nuclear Weapons, Advisory Opinion, I.C.J. Reports 1996, p. 226, International Court of Justice (ICJ), 8 July 1996.

Prosecutor v. Dragoljub Kunarac, Radomir Kovac and Zoran Vukovic (Trial Judgment), IT-96-23-T & IT-96-23/1-T, International Criminal Tribunal for the former Yugoslavia (ICTY), 22 February 2001.

Sejdić and Finci v. Bosnia and Herzegovina, ECtHR 22 Dec. 2009, Case No. 27996/06 and 34836/06.

South-West Africa Cases; Advisory Opinion Concerning the International Status, International Court of Justice (ICJ), 11 July 1950 (Advisory Opinion) [1950] ICJ Rep 128.

b. Table of Treaties

1972 Convention on the Prohibition of the Development, Production and Stockpiling of Bacteriological (Biological) and Toxin Weapons and on their Destruction, 1015 UNTS 163 / [1977] ATS 23 / 11 ILM 309 (1972), 10 April 1972 (Entry into force: 26 March 1975).

1995 Protocol on Blinding Laser Weapons (Protocol IV; adopted 13 October 1995, entered into force 30 July 1998; 2024 UNTS 163).

Allied and Associated Powers (1914–1920). Treaty of Peace Between the Allied And Associated Powers And Germany, And Other Treaty Engagements Signed At Versailles, June 28th, 1919: Together With the Reply of the Allied And Associated Powers to the Observations of the German Delegation On the Conditions of Peace. [Versailles Treaty] London: H.M. Stationery off., 1920.

American Convention on Human Rights (Organization of American States) OASTS No 36, 1144 UNTS 123, B-32, OEA/Ser.L.V/II.82 doc.6 rev.1.

Charter of the United Nations (done at San Francisco, United States, on 26 June 1945) (United Nations) 1 UNTS XVI, 892 UNTS 119, 59 Stat 1031, TS 993, 3 Bevans 1153, 145 BSP 805 (entered into force 24 October 1945).

Convention (IV) respecting the Laws and Customs of War on Land and its annex: Regulations concerning the Laws and Customs of War on Land (adopted 18 October 1907, entered into force 26 January 1910), 36 Stat. 2277, 1 Bevans 631, 205 Consol TS 277.

Convention Against Torture and Other Cruel, Inhuman or Degrading Treatment or Punishment, 10 December 1984, (Entry into force 26 June 1987) United Nations Treaty Series, vol. 1465, p. 85.

Convention for the Protection of Cultural Property in the Event of Armed Conflict (United Nations Educational, Scientific and Cultural Organization) 249 UNTS 240, UN Reg No I-3511.

Convention on Certain Conventional Weapons; United Nations, Convention on Prohibitions or Restrictions on the Use of Certain Conventional Weapons Which May be Deemed to be Excessively Injurious or to Have Indiscriminate Effects (and Protocols) (As Amended on 21 December 2001), 10 October 1980, 1342 UNTS 137 (Entry into force: 2 December 1983; Registered No. 22495).

Convention on Cluster Munitions, Dublin Diplomatic Conference on Cluster Munitions, 30 May 2008 (Entry into force: 1 August 2010).

Convention on the Physical Protection of Nuclear Material, 1456 UNTS 101, 26 October 1979, No. 24631, (Entry into force: 8 February 1987).

Convention on the Prevention and Punishment of Crimes against Internationally Protected Persons, including Diplomatic Agents, 14 December 1973, 1035 UNTS 167; 28 UST 1975; 13 ILM 41 (1974); 68 AJIL 383 (Entry into force: 20 February 1977) No. 15410.

Convention on the Prevention and Punishment of the Crime of Genocide, 9 December 1948, (Entry into force: 12 January 1951) United Nations Treaty Series, vol. 78, p. 277.

Convention on the Prohibition of the Development, Production, Stockpiling and Use of Chemical Weapons and on their Destruction, 3 September 1992, 1974 UNTS 45 (Entry into force: 29 April 1997).

Convention on the Rights of Persons with Disabilities : resolution / adopted by the General Assembly, 24 January 2007, A/RES/61/106.

Convention on the Rights of the Child of 1989, 20 November 1989, 1577 UNTS 3 (Entry into force: 2 September 1990).

Council of Europe, Framework Convention for the Protection of National Minorities, 1 February 1995, ETS 157.

Council of Europe, *European Convention for the Protection of Human Rights and Fundamental Freedoms, as amended by Protocols Nos. 11 and 14*, 4 November 1950, ETS 5, 213 UNTS 222.

Council of Europe: Parliamentary Assembly, The European Charter for Regional or Minority Languages, 21 October 2010, Doc. 12422.

Declaration Renouncing the Use, in Time of War, of Explosive Projectiles Under 400 Grammes Weight. Saint Petersburg, adopted 11 December 1868, D. Schindler and J. Toman, The Laws of Armed Conflicts, Martinus Nihjoff Publisher, 1988, p.102.

European Union, Treaty of Lisbon Amending the Treaty on European Union and the Treaty Establishing the European Community, 13 December 2007, 2007/C 306/01.

Hague Convention II with Respect to the Laws and Customs of War on Land and its annex: Regulation concerning the Laws and Customs of War on Land: 29 July 1899, 32 Stat. 1803, 1 Bevans 247, 26 Martens Nouveau Recueil (ser. 2) 949, 187 Consol. T.S. 429 (Entered into force 4 September 1900).

Hague Convention No. II of 1899 with Respect to the Laws and Customs of War on Land, with annex of regulations, July 29, 1899, 32 Stat. 1803, 1 Bevans 247.

Hague Declaration (1899); International Peace Conference 1899, Declaration (IV,3) concerning Expanding Bullets. The Hague, adopted 29 July 1899, (entry into force 4 September 1900).

International Committee of the Red Cross (ICRC), *Protocol Additional to the Geneva Conventions of 12 August 1949, and relating to the Protection of Victims of International Armed Conflicts (Protocol I)*, 8 June 1977, 1125 UNTS 3 (Entry into force: 7 December 1978).

International Committee of the Red Cross (ICRC), *Protocol Additional to the Geneva Conventions of 12 August 1949, and relating to the Adoption of an Additional Distinctive Emblem (Protocol III)*, 8 December 2005 (Not yet entered into force).

International Committee of the Red Cross (ICRC), *Geneva Convention for the Amelioration of the Condition of the Wounded and Sick in Armed Forces in the Field (First Geneva Convention)*, 12 August 1949, 75 UNTS 31 (entered into force 21 Oct. 1950).

International Committee of the Red Cross (ICRC), *Geneva Convention for the Amelioration of the Condition of Wounded, Sick and Shipwrecked Members of Armed Forces at Sea (Second Geneva Convention)*, 12 August 1949, 75 UNTS 85 (entered into force 21 Oct. 1950).

International Committee of the Red Cross (ICRC), *Geneva Convention Relative to the Treatment of Prisoners of War (Third Geneva Convention)*, 12 August 1949, 75 UNTS 135 (entered into force 21 Oct. 1950).

International Committee of the Red Cross (ICRC), *Geneva Convention Relative to the Protection of Civilian Persons in Time of War (Fourth Geneva Convention)*, 12 August 1949, 75 UNTS 287 (Entry into force: 21 October 1950).

International Committee of the Red Cross (ICRC), *Protocol Additional to the Geneva Conventions of 12 August 1949, and relating to the Protection of Victims of Non-International Armed Conflicts (Protocol II)*, 8 June 1977, 1125 UNTS 609 (Entry into force: 7 December 1978).

International Conferences (The Hague), *Hague Convention (IV) Respecting the Laws and Customs of War on Land and Its Annex: Regulations Concerning the Laws and Customs of War on Land*, 18 October 1907.

International Convention against the Taking of Hostages, 17 November 1979, (Entry into force: 3 June 1983) No. 21931.

International Convention for the Suppression of Terrorist Bombings, 15 December 1997, (Entry into force: 23 May 2001) No. 37517.

International Convention for the Suppression of the Financing of Terrorism, 9 December 1999, (Entry into force: 10 April 2002) No. 38349.

International Convention on the Suppression and Punishment of the Crime of Apartheid, 30 November 1973, (Entry into force: 18 July 1976) A/RES/3068(XXVIII).

International Covenant on Civil and Political Rights, 16 December 1966, United Nations Treaty Series, vol. 999, p. 171 (Entry into force: 23 March 1976).

International Peace Conference 1899, Declaration (IV,3) concerning Expanding Bullets. The Hague, adopted 29 July 1899, (entry into force 4 September 1900).

North Atlantic Treaty (signed 4 April 1949, entered into force 24 August 1949) 34 UNTS 243.

Optional Protocol to the Convention on the Rights of the Child on the Involvement of Children in Armed Conflict, 25 May 2000 (Entered into force 12 February 2002, Adopted and opened for signature, ratification and accession by General Assembly resolution A/RES/54/263 of 25 May 2000).

Organization of American States (OAS), American Convention on Human Rights, "Pact of San Jose," Costa Rica, 22 November 1969, Entry into force: 18 July 1978.

Organization of American States (OAS), *Inter-American Convention on Forced Disappearance of Persons*, 9 June 1994, OAS Treaty Series 68.

Protocol (II) on Prohibitions or Restrictions on the Use of Mines, Booby-Traps and Other Devices. Geneva, 10 October 1980 (Entry into force: 2 December 1983).

Protocol for the Prohibition of the Use in War of Asphyxiating, Poisonous or other Gases, and of Bacteriological Methods of Warfare, 17 June 1925 (Entry into force: 8 February 1928), D. Schindler and J. Toman, The Laws of Armed Conflicts, Martinus Nihjoff Publisher, 1988, p.116.

Protocol IV (1995) to the Convention on Certain Conventional Weapons; Protocol on Blinding Laser Weapons (Protocol IV to the 1980 Convention), 13 October 1995 (Entry into force: 30 July 1998).

Protocol on Explosive Remnants of War (Protocol V to the 1980 CCW Convention), 28 November 2003.

Protocol on Non-Detectable Fragments (Protocol I). Geneva, 10 October 1980 (Entry into force: 2 December 1983).

Protocol on Prohibitions or Restrictions on the Use of Incendiary Weapons (Protocol III). Geneva, 10 October 1980 (Entry into force: 2 December 1983).

Protocol V (2003) to the Convention on Certain Conventional Weapons; Protocol on Explosive Remnants of War (Protocol V to the 1980 CCW Convention), 28 November 2003 (Entry into force: 12 November.2006).

Rambouillet Accords: Interim Agreement for Peace and Self-Government in Kosovo, Feb. 23, 1999, UN Doc. S/1999/648, annex.

Rome Statute of the International Criminal Court, July 1, 2002, 2187 U.N.T.S. 90. (Entered into force on 1 July 2002).

Second Protocol to The Hague Convention of 1954 for the Protection of Cultural Property in the Event of Armed Conflict (United Nations Educational, Scientific and Cultural Organization) 2253 UNTS 172, UN Reg No A-3511 (Entry into force: 9 March 2004).

Second Review Conference of the States Parties to the Convention on Prohibitions or Restrictions on the Use of Certain Conventional Weapons which may be Deemed to be Excessively Injurious or to have Indiscriminate Effects – Final Document, Part II Final Declaration (Doc.CCW/CONF.II/2 (2001)).

The 1997 Convention on the Prohibition of the Use, Stockpiling, Production and transfer of Anti-Personnel Mines and on their Destruction, 2056 UNTS 211 (Entry into force: 1 March 1999).

The Treaty of Lausanne, League of Nations Treaty Series, vol. XXVIII, p. 41.

The Treaty of Neuilly-sur-Seine (British and Foreign State Papers, 1919, vol. CXII (London, H.M. Stationery Office, 1922), p: 821.

The Treaty of Saint-Germain-en-Laye (British and Foreign State Papers, 1919, vol. CXII (London, H.M. Stationery Office, 1922), pp. 405–407.

The Treaty of Trianon (British and Foreign State Papers, 1919, vol. CXII (London, H.M. Stationery Office, 1922), vol. CXIII, pp. 556–568.

UN Educational, Scientific and Cultural Organisation (UNESCO), Convention for the Protection of Cultural Property in the Event of Armed Conflict, 249 U.N.T.S. 240 14 May 1954 (Entry into force: 7 August 1956).

UN Educational, Scientific and Cultural Organisation (UNESCO), *Convention Against Discrimination in Education*, 14 December 1960, 156 U.N.T.S. 93. (Entry into force: 22 May 1962).

UN General Assembly, *International Convention on the Elimination of All Forms of Racial Discrimination*, 21 December 1965, United Nations, Treaty Series, vol. 660, p. 195 (Entry into force: 4 January 1969).

UN General Assembly, *Optional Protocol to the Convention on the Rights of the Child on the Involvement of Children in Armed Conflict*, 25 May 2000 (Entry into force: 12 February 2002).

United Nations Convention Against Corruption, 31 October 2003, (Entry into force: 14 December 2005) A/58/422.

United Nations, Arms Trade Treaty, 2 April 2013 (Entry into force: 24 December 2014).

United Nations, Convention for the Suppression of Unlawful Seizure of Aircraft, 16 December 1970, (Entry into force: 14 October 1971) UN Treaty Series 1973.

United Nations, Vienna Convention on the Law of Treaties, 23 May 1969, (Entry into force: 27 January 1980) United Nations Treaty Series, vol. 1155, p. 331.

United Nations, *Convention on Prohibitions or Restrictions on the Use of Certain Conventional Weapons Which May be Deemed to be Excessively Injurious or to Have Indiscriminate Effects (and Protocols) (As Amended on 21 December 2001)*, 10 October 1980, 1342 UNTS 137 (Entry into force: 2 December 1983; Registered No. 22495).

United Nations, *Protocol on Explosive Remnants of War (Protocol V)*, 23 November 2003, (Entry into force: 12 November 2006) (protocol to Convention on Prohibitions or Restrictions on the Use of Certain Conventional Weapons Which May be Deemed to be Excessively Injurious or to Have Indiscriminate Effects (and Protocols) (As Amended on 21 December 2001)).

United Nations, *Protocol on Prohibitions or Restrictions on the Use of Mines, Booby-Traps and Other Devices (Protocol II) (As Amended on 3 May 1996)*, 10 October 1980 (Entry into force: 3 December 1998).

Vienna Convention on Succession of States in respect of State Property, Archives and Debts (United Nations) UN Doc A/CONF.117/14, 8 April 1983.

Vienna Convention on Succession of States in respect of Treaties, 6 November 1996, (Entry into force 6 November 1996, United Nations, Treaty Series , vol. 1946, p. 3).

Vienna Convention on the Law of Treaties, May 23, 1969, 1155 U.N.T.S. 331.

c.   UN Documents

Bedjaoui, Mohammed. Special Rapporteur, 'Ninth Report on Succession of States in Respect of Matters other than Treaties' (1977) UN Doc A/CN.4/301: Vol. 1.

Bedjaoui, Mohammed. Special Rapporteur, 'Ninth Report on Succession of States in Respect of Matters other than Treaties' (1977) UN Doc A/CN.4/301: Vol. 2.

Bedjaoui, Mohammed. Special Rapporteur, 'Ninth Report on Succession of States in Respect of Matters other than Treaties' (1977) UN Doc A/CN.4/30: Add.1.

Human Rights Committee, General Comment 29, States of Emergency UN Doc. CCPR/C/21/Rev. 1, Add. 11, 31 August 2001 (adopted 24 July 2001, 9 IHRR 303 (2002)).

International Conference on Human Rights, Proclamation of Teheran, Final Act of the International Conference on Human Rights, Teheran, 22 April to 13 May 1968, U.N. Doc. A/CONF. 32/41 at 3 (1968).

International Law Commission, Draft Articles on Responsibility of States for Internationally Wrongful Acts, November 2001, Supplement No. 10 (A/56/10), Chp.IV.E.1, Adopted by the General Assembly in resolution 56/83 of 12 December 2001, corrected by a/56/49(Vol. I)/Corr. 4.

International Law Commission, Draft Articles on the Effects of Armed Conflict on Treaties, UN Doc. A/66/10.

UN General Assembly, *2005 World Summit Outcome : resolution / adopted by the General Assembly*, 24 October 2005, A/RES/60/1.

UN General Assembly, 2005 World Summit Outcome, UN Doc. A/60/L.1 (15 September 2005).

UN General Assembly, Declaration on Principles of International Law Concerning Friendly Relations and Cooperation among States in Accordance with the Charter of the United Nations (United Nations) UN Doc A/RES/2625(XXV), Annex.

UN General Assembly, Declaration on the Rights of Persons Belonging to National or Ethnic, Religious and Linguistic Minorities, 3 February 1992, A/RES/47/135.

UN General Assembly, Definition of Aggression, 14 December 1974, A/RES/3314.

UN General Assembly, GA Res. 377 (V) 'Uniting for Peace' (3 November 1950) UN Doc A/1775.

UN General Assembly, GA Res. 60/1 (2005 World Summit Outcome) of 24 Oct. 2005.

UN General Assembly, GA Res. 60/147, UN Doc. A/RES/60/147 (Dec. 16, 2005).

UN General Assembly, Implementation of the Convention on the Prohibition of the Development, Production, Stockpiling and Use of Chemical Weapons and on Their Destruction: Resolution adopted by the General Assembly, 17 December 2003, A/RES/58/52.

UN General Assembly, United Nations General Assembly Resolution 3103 (XXVIII) on the basic principles of the legal status of the combatants struggling against colonial and alien domination and racist regimes (United Nations General Assembly) UN Doc A/RES/3103(XXVIII).

UN General Assembly, *Identical letters dated 21 August 2000 from the Secretary-General to the President of the General Assembly and the President of the Security Council : report of the Panel on United Nations Peace Operations* [Brahimi Report], 21 August 2000, A/55/305–S/2000/809.

UN General Assembly, *Note* [*transmitting report of the High-level Panel on Threats, Challenges and Change, entitled "A more secure world : our shared responsibility"*], 2 December 2004, A/59/565.

UN General Assembly, *Note* [*transmitting report of the High-level Panel on Threats, Challenges and Change, entitled "A more secure world : our shared responsibility"*], 2 December 2004, A/59/565.

UN General Assembly, Implementing the Responsibility to Protect: Report of the Secretary-General, UN Doc. A/63/677 (12 January 2009).

UN Human Rights Council, Rights of persons belonging to national or ethnic, religious and linguistic minorities : report of the United Nations High Commissioner for Human Rights, 17 December 2012, A/HRC/22/27.

UN Press Release SG/SM/7257, Secretary-General Comments on Guidelines Given to Envoys (10 December 1999) (guidelines on human rights and peace negotiations).

UN Security Council, "The Rule of Law and Transitional Justice in Conflict and Post-conflict Societies: Report of the Secretary-General" (23 August 2004) UN Doc. S/2004/616, 4.

UN Security Council, On Basic Agreement on the Region of Eastern Slavonia, Baranja and Western Sirmium between the Government of Croatia and the local Serb representatives Resolution 1023 (1995) Adopted by the Security Council at its 3596th meeting, on 22 November 1995, 22 November 1995, S/RES/1023 (1995).

UN Security Council, *Resolution 592 (1986) Adopted by the Security Council at its 2727th meeting, on 8 December 1986*, 8 December 1986, S/RES/592 (1986).

UN Security Council, *Resolution 688 (1991) Adopted by the Security Council at its 2982nd meeting on 5 April 1991*, 5 April 1991, S/RES/688 (1991).

UN Security Council, *Resolution 689 (1991)* Adopted by the Security Council at its 2983rd meeting on 9 March 1991, 9 April 1991, S/RES/689 (1991).

UN Security Council, *Resolution 745 (1992)* Adopted by the Security Council at its 3057th meeting, on 28 February 1992, 28 February 1992, S/RES/745 (1992).

UN Security Council, *Resolution 788 (1992)* Adopted by the Security Council at its 3138th meeting, on 19 November 1992, 19 November 1992, S/RES/788 (1992).

UN Security Council, *Resolution 1244 (1999)* [*on the deployment of international civil and security presences in Kosovo*], 10 June 1999, S/RES/1244 (1999).

UN Security Council, *Resolution 1277 (1999)* Adopted by the Security Council at its 4074th meeting, on 30 November 1999, 30 November 1999, S/RES/1277 (1999).

UN Security Council, *Resolution 1325 (2000)* [*on women and peace and security*], 31 October 2000, S/RES/1325 (2000).

UN Security Council, *Resolution 1378 (2001) on the situation in Afghanistan*, 14 November 2001, S/RES/1378 (2001).

UN Security Council, *Resolution 1483 (2003) on the situation between Iraq and Kuwait*, 22 May 2003, S/RES/1483 (2003).

UN Security Council, *Resolution 1511 (2003) on authorizing a multinational force under unified command to take all necessary measures to contribute to the maintenance of security and stability in Iraq*, 16 October 2003, S/RES/1511 (2003).

UN Security Council, *Resolution 1559 (2004)* [*on the political independence and withdrawal of foreign forces from Lebanon*], 2 September 2004, S/RES/1559 (2004).

UN Security Council, *Resolution 1701 (2006)* [*on full cessation of hostilities in Lebanon and on extending and strengthening the mandate of the UN Interim Force in Lebanon (UNIFIL) to monitor the ceasefire*], 11 August 2006, S/RES/1701 (2006).

UN Security Council, *Resolution 1803 (2008)* [*on further measures against Iran in connection with its development of sensitive technologies in support of its nuclear and missile programmes*], 3 March 2008, S/RES/1803(2008).

UN Security Council, *Resolution 1820 (2008)* [*on acts of sexual violence against civilians in armed conflicts*], 19 June 2008, S/RES/1820 (2008).

UN Security Council, *Resolution 1835 (2008)* [*on Iran's obligations to comply with Security Council's resolutions and meeting the requirements of the IAEA Board of Governors*], 27 September 2008, S/RES/1835 (2008).

UN Security Council, *Resolution 1888 (2009)* [*on acts of sexual violence against civilians in armed conflicts*], 30 September 2009, S/RES/1888 (2009).

UN Security Council, *Resolution 1889 (2009)* [*on women and peace and security*], 5 October 2009, S/RES/1889 (2009).

UN Security Council, *Resolution 1929 (2010)* [*on measures against Iran in connection with its enrichment-related and reprocessing activities, including research and development*], 9 June 2010, S/RES/1929 (2010).

UN Security Council, *Resolution 1960 (2010)* [*on women and peace and security*], 16 December 2010, S/RES/1960(2010).

UN Security Council, *Resolution 2242 (2015)* [*on women and peace and security*], 13 October 2015, S/RES/2242 (2015).

UN Security Council, *Resolution 1689 (2006) The Situation in Liberia*, 20 June 2006, S/RES/1689 (2006).

UN Security Council, *Resolution 1694 (2006) The Situation in Liberia*, 13 July 2006, S/RES/1694 (2006).

UN Security Council, *Resolution 1696 (2006) Non-proliferation*, 31 July 2006, S/RES/1696 (2006).

UN Security Council, *Resolution 1731 (2006) The Situation in Liberia*, 20 December 2006, S/RES/1731 (2006).

UN Security Council, *Resolution 1737 (2006) Non-proliferation*, 27 December 2006, S/RES/1737 (2006).

UN Security Council, *Resolution 1747 (2007) Non-proliferation*, 24 March 2007, S/RES/1747 (2007).

UN Security Council, *Resolution 1753 (2007) The Situation in Liberia*, 27 April 2007, S/RES/1753(2007).

UN Security Council, *Security Council resolution 1343 (2001)* [*on the situation in Sierra Leone*], 7 March 2001, S/RES/1343 (2001).

UN Security Council, *Security Council resolution 1408 (2002)* [*on the situation in Liberia*], 6 May 2002, S/RES/1408 (2002).

UN Security Council, *Security Council resolution 1458 (2003)* [*on the situation in Liberia*], 28 January 2003, S/RES/1458 (2003).

UN Security Council, *Security Council resolution 1478 (2003)* [*on the situation in Liberia*], 6 May 2003, S/RES/1478 (2003).

UN Security Council, *Security Council resolution 1497 (2003)* [*on the situation in Liberia*], 1 August 2003, S/RES/1497 (2003).

UN Security Council, *Security Council resolution 1509 (2003)* [*on establishment of the UN Mission in Liberia (UNMIL)*], 19 September 2003, S/RES/1509 (2003).

UN Security Council, *Security Council resolution 1521 (2003)* [*on dissolution of the Security Council Committee established pursuant to Resolution 1343 (2001) concerning Liberia*], 22 December 2003, S/RES/1521 (2003).

UN Security Council, *Security Council resolution 1532 (2004)* [*on preventing former Liberian President Charles Taylor, his immediate family members and senior officials of the former Taylor regime from using misappropriated funds and property*], 12 March 2004, S/RES/1532 (2004).

UN Security Council, *Security Council resolution 1549 (2004)* [*on re-establishment of the Panel of Experts to monitor fulfilling the conditions for the lifting of sanctions*], 17 June 2004, S/RES/1549 (2004).

UN Security Council, *Security Council resolution 1561 (2004)* [*on UNMIL*], 17 September 2004, S/RES/1561 (2004).

UN Security Council, *Security Council resolution 1579 (2004)* [*on the Situation in Liberia and West Africa*], 21 December 2004, S/RES/1579 (2004).

UN Security Council, *Security Council resolution 1607 (2005)* [*on the Situation in Liberia and West Africa*], 21 June 2005, S/RES/1607 (2005).

UN Security Council, *Security Council resolution 1626 (2005)* [*The situation in Liberia*], 19 September 2005, S/RES/1626 (2005).

UN Security Council, *Security Council resolution 1638 (2005)* [*The situation in Liberia*], 11 November 2005, S/RES/1638 (2005).

UN Security Council, *Security Council resolution 1647 (2005)* [*Liberia renews the measures on arms and travel imposed by paragraphs 2 and 4 of resolution 1521 (2003) for a further period of 12 months*], 20 December 2005, S/RES/1647 (2005).

UN Security Council, *Security Council resolution 1667 (2006)* [*The situation in Liberia*], 31 March 2006, S/RES/1667 (2006).

UN Security Council, *Security Council resolution 1683 (2006)* [*The Situation in Liberia*], 13 June 2006, S/RES/1683 (2006).

UN Security Council, *Security Council resolution 1688 (2006)* [*Sierra Leone*], 16 June 2006, S/RES/1688 (2006).

UN Security Council, *Security Council resolution 169 (1961)* [*The Congo Question*], 24 November 1961, S/RES/169 (1961).

UN Security Council, *Security Council resolution 1712 (2006)* [*Liberia*], 29 September 2006, S/RES/1712 (2006).

UN Security Council, *Security Council resolution 1750 (2007)* [*Liberia*], 30 March 2007, S/RES/1750 (2007).

UN Security Council, *Security Council resolution 1777 (2007) [Liberia]*, 20 September 2007, S/RES/1777 (2007).

UN Security Council, *Security Council resolution 1792 (2007) [on renewal of measures on arms and travel imposed by resolution 1521 (2003) and on extension of the mandate of the current Panel of Experts on Liberia]*, 19 December 2007, S/RES/1792 (2007).

UN Security Council, *Security Council resolution 1819 (2008) [on extension of the mandate of the Panel of Experts on Liberia]*, 18 January 2008, S/RES/1819 (2008).

UN Security Council, *Security Council resolution 1836 (2008) [on extension of the mandate of the UN Mission in Liberia (UNMIL)]*, 29 September 2008, S/RES/1836 (2008).

UN Security Council, *Security Council resolution 1854 (2008) [on extension of the mandate of the Panel of Experts on Liberia]*, 19 December 2008, S/RES/1854 (2008).

UN Security Council, *Security Council resolution 1885 (2009) [on extension of the mandate of the UN Mission in Liberia (UNMIL)]*, 15 September 2009, S/RES/1885 (2009).

UN Security Council, *Security Council resolution 1938 (2010) [on extension of the mandate of the UN Mission in Liberia (UNMIL)]*, 15 September 2010, S/RES/1938 (2010).

UN Security Council, *Security Council resolution 2008 (2011) [on extension of the mandate of the UN Mission in Liberia (UNMIL) until 30 Sept. 2012]*, 16 September 2011, S/RES/2008(2011).

UN Security Council, *Security Council resolution 2025 (2011) [Liberia]*, 14 December 2011, S/RES/2025(2011).

UN Security Council, *Security Council resolution 2066 (2012) [on extension of the mandate of the UN Mission in Liberia (UNMIL) until 30 Sept. 2013]*, 17 September 2012, S/RES/2066 (2012).

UN Security Council, *Security Council resolution 2079 (2012) [on the situation in Liberia]*, 12 December 2012, S/RES/2079 (2012).

UN Security Council, *Security Council resolution 2116 (2013) [on Liberia]*, 18 September 2013, S/RES/2116 (2013).

UN Security Council, *Security Council resolution 2128 (2013) [on the situation in Liberia and West Africa]*, 10 December 2013, S/RES/2128 (2013).

UN Security Council, *Security Council resolution 2176 (2014) [on extension of the mandate of the UN Mission in Liberia (UNMIL) until 31 Dec. 2014]*, 15 September 2014, S/RES/2176 (2014).

UN Security Council, *Security Council resolution 2188 (2014) [on the situation in Liberia]*, 9 December 2014, S/RES/2188 (2014).

UN Security Council, *Security Council resolution 2190 (2014) [on extension of the mandate of the UN Mission in Liberia (UNMIL) until 30 Sept. 2015]*, 15 December 2014, S/RES/2190 (2014).

UN Security Council, *Security Council resolution 2215 (2015)* [*on the drawdown of the UN Mission in Liberia (UNMIL)*], 2 April 2015, S/RES/2215 (2015).

UN Security Council, *Security Council resolution 2239 (2015)* [*on extension of the mandate of the UN Mission in Liberia (UNMIL) until 30 Sept. 2016*], 17 September 2015.

UN Security Council, *Security Council resolution 2308 (2016)* [*on extension of the mandate of the UN Mission in Liberia (UNMIL) until 31 Dec. 2016*], 17 September 2015, S/RES/2308 (2016).

UN Security Council, *The rule of law and transitional justice in conflict and post-conflict societies : report of the Secretary-General*, 23 August 2004, S/2004/616.

UN SG Report, 'An Agenda for Peace Preventive Diplomacy, Peacemaking and Peace-Keeping,' UN Doc A/47/277-S/24111 (June 1992).

UN SG Report, 'Supplement to An Agenda for Peace: Position Paper of the Secretary-General on the Occasion of the Fiftieth Anniversary of the United Nations,' UN Doc A/50/60 -S/1995/1 (Jan. 1995).

UN SG Report, Report on the Secretary General on Respect for Human Rights in Armed Conflict, UN Doc. A/8052, 18 September 1970.

UN SG Report, Report on the Secretary General on Respect for Human Rights in Armed Conflicts, UN Doc. A/7 720, 20 November 1969.

UN SG Report, Report of the United Nations Secretary-General to the Security Council, The Causes of Conflict and the Promotion of Durable Peace and Sustainable Development in Africa, A/52/871 – S/1998/318 (New York: United Nations, 13 April 1998).

UN Women, "Women's participation in peace negotiations: Connections between presence and influence." New York (2010).

United Nations, Beijing Declaration and Platform of Action, adopted at the Fourth World Conference on Women, 27 October 1995.

d.   Miscellaneous Sources

An Act to provide for the government of the territory northwest of the river Ohio. The Ordinance of July 13, 1787 (1 Stat. 52). Available at http://avalon.law.yale.edu/18th_century/nworder.asp last visited 24 March 2015.

Declaration of Independence of the United States of America (United States) 51 BSP 847.

Dep't of the Army, The Law Of Land Warfare, Para. 6 (Field Manual No. 27-10, 1956).

First Meeting of the Specialized Technical Committee on Justice and Legal Affairs, 15–16 May 2014, STC/Legal/Min/7(I) Rev. 1, Draft Protocol on Amendments to the Protocol on the Statute of the African Court of Justice and Human Rights, Article 28A.

German Federal Ministry of Defense, Humanitarian Law In Armed Conflict-Manual, (Zav 15/2, 1992).

Peace Agreement between the Government of Liberia, the Liberians United for Reconciliation and Democracy (LURD), *the Movement of Democracy in Liberia* (MODEL) *and the Political Parties*, 18 August 2003, Annexed to Letter dated 27 August 2003 from the Permanent Representative of Ghana to the United Nations addressed to the President of the Security Council, S/2003/850 (2003).

Project of an International Declaration concerning the Laws and Customs of War ("1874 Brussels Declaration") ((signed 27 August 1874) (1873–74) 65 BFSP 1005 (1907) 1 AJIL 96).

Shorter Oxford English Dictionary, Vol. 1, (Oxford University Press 1973).

U.S. Dept of the Air Force, International Law—The Conduct of Armed Conflict and Air Operations 1–7(B) (Afp No. 110–31, 1976).

UCDP/PRIO Armed Conflict Dataset.

United Kingdom War Office, The Law of War On Land, Being Part III of The Manual of Military Law, (1958).

e.   Online Sources

http://chronicle.nytlabs.com.

http://plato.stanford.edu/entries/war.

http://thomsonreuters.com/products_services/science/science_products/a-z/journal_citation_reports/.

http://www.humanrightsdata.com.

http://www.icrc.org/eng/war-and-law/weapons/overview-weapons.htm.

https://books.google.com/ngrams.

https://vre.leidenuniv.nl/vre/jpb/definitions/default.aspx.

https://www.icc-cpi.int/en_menus/icc/situations%20and%20cases/Pages/situations%20and%20cases.aspx.

IHL and other legal regimes – jus ad bellum and jus in bello, available at http://www.icrc.org/eng/war-and-law/ihl-other-legal-regmies/jus-in-bello-jus-ad-bellum/overview-jus-ad-bellum-jus-in-bello.htm (accessed 17 October 2012).

Impact Factor of the Washington and Lee University School of Law Most-Cited Legal Periodicals, available at http://law.wlu.edu/library/mostcited/method.asp.

International Center for Transitional Justice (ICTJ), "What is Transitional Justice" available at http://ictj.org/about/transitional-justice (accessed 27 May 2016).

Journal Citation Reports, available at http://thomsonreuters.com/products_services/science/science_products/a-z/journal_citation_reports/.

See Social Science Research Network Frequently Asked Questions, available at http://www.ssrn.com/update/general/ssrn_faq.html#what_is.

Who will assist the victims of nuclear weapons? Statement by Peter Maurer, President of the ICRC, International conference on the humanitarian impact of nuclear weapons, Oslo, 4–5 March 2013, available at http://www.icrc.org/eng/resources/documents/statement/2013/13-03-04-nuclear-weapons.htm.

Zsolnai, Laszlo, Corporate Legitimacy (March 18, 2011). Available at SSRN: http://ssrn.com/abstract=1789884 or http://dx.doi.org/10.2139/ssrn.1789884.

Index

Accountability   113, 121, 146–147, 150–151, 173, 188–189, 254, 256–258, 269, 314
Administration, transition   223–224
Afghanistan   170, 212–213, 220, 228, 301
Africa   39, 170, 213, 221–222, 225, 246, 273
Aggression   11–12, 15, 44–45, 59–60, 89, 137, 153, 164, 167, 249–253, 270, 273, 279, 281, 283
  crime of   15–16, 113, 169, 253
  prohibitions of   236, 249, 256
America   14, 51, 205, 209, 225, 251
American Convention on Human Rights   243, 261
Amnesties   17–18, 19, 72, 75, 83, 85–86, 91, 113, 156, 157–158, 159–160, 241–242
Annexation   229, 236, 240, 248–250, 252–253, 260, 270–271, 276, 279, 281, 294
  prohibition of   17, 229, 236, 249, 253, 270, 279, 294, 318
Apartheid   243
Armed conflict   8–14, 16–24, 94–95, 102–103, 104–109, 115–133, 136–138, 145–148, 151–153, 154–157, 176–179, 203–216, 227–230, 231–237, 242–245, 249–254, 261–264, 296–302, 305–307, 313–319
  international   16–18, 83–84, 103–104, 111, 203–209, 210–214, 220, 225, 228–231, 238, 245, 249–251, 268, 272, 276–277
  internationalized   15, 212
  law of   88, 95, 98–99, 100–102, 106–108, 112–113, 137, 141, 146–147, 153, 158, 263, 268
  non-international   8, 13, 16, 18, 20, 83–84, 104, 105, 203–209, 210–216, 220, 228–230, 245, 276–277, 280
Armed forces   4, 13, 95, 104, 106–108, 143, 145, 154–155, 165, 176–177, 203, 206, 232–233, 242, 278–279
Armed groups   18, 173, 205–206, 213–214, 220, 248, 289
Arms Trade Treaty   97, 227, 273
Attack   29, 30, 37, 52, 120–121, 130, 211, 213, 256
Augustine of Hippo   19, 26, 28–37, 42, 44–48, 51–52, 55, 62–65, 68, 90, 305

Aquinas, Thomas   24, 26, 28–29, 41, 42–48, 51, 90

Bell, Christine   17, 113, 122, 137, 151, 152, 165–166, 189, 191
Belligerents   43, 45, 52, 69, 82, 87, 104, 176–177
  occupation   95, 129, 132–133, 153, 167, 187, 255, 267–269
Biological Weapons   227
Biological Weapons Convention   95, 226–227
Boon, Kristen   133, 185, 186, 187, 235, 254–255, 256, 258, 269, 293
Bosnia and Herzegovina   244, 267, 288, 306

Cambodia   154–155, 162–163, 220, 224–225, 228, 255, 271, 295, 319
  Extraordinary Chambers in the Courts of Cambodia   162–163
  Khmer Rouge   162
Central African Republic   224, 272
Chemical Weapons   95, 226
Chetail, Vincent   189, 190, 281
Chile   159–160, 268
Christian thought   25, 28–29, 46, 52, 79–80, 81–83, 86, 143
Civil society   219, 306, 311, 318
Civilians   4, 13, 15, 94, 104, 213, 242, 253, 270–271, 280, 291, 294
Civilised Nations   104, 110, 205, 277
Civilizing Mission   153
Cold War   146, 173
Colombia   170, 228, 268
Colonialism   18, 174, 204, 209–210, 250–252, 253, 277, 313
Combatants   94–95, 137, 164, 208, 209–210, 251
Comoros   224–225, 272
Congo   224, 267, 272
Convention Against Discrimination in Education   265, 286
Convention Against Torture and Other Cruel, Inhuman or Degrading Treatment or Punishment   18, 243

INDEX 355

Convention for the Protection of Cultural Property   18, 208, 244, 269
Convention on Cluster Munitions   97, 120–121, 228–229
Convention on the Prevention and Punishment of the Crime of Genocide   151, 242, 243
Convention on the Prohibition of the Development, Production, Stockpiling and Use of Chemical Weapons and on their Destruction   96, 226
Convention on the Rights of the Child   263
Council of Europe   265–266, 286–287
Counter-insurgency   3, 20, 129, 132, 137, 266, 284, 287, 289
Croatia   220
Cultural Property   18, 130, 207, 243, 268, 307
Customary international law   205, 214, 216, 229, 238, 276

Darfur   224, 272
Debts   19, 80, 83, 245, 258, 260, 274–278, 282
  hostile   276–277
  odious   11, 231–233, 260, 274–277, 282–283
De Brabandere, Eric   142, 189, 190, 191, 233, 234, 235, 236, 237, 283
de Ubaldis, Baldus (*See* Ubaldis, Baldus de)
de Vitoria, Francisco (*See* Vitoria, Francisco de)
Declaration on Principles of International Law concerning Friendly Relations   209–210, 248, 251–253, 270, 291, 294
Decolonization   209, 251, 253, 259
Democracy   139, 163, 173, 175, 222, 289, 296, 297–298, 300
  democracy-building   266, 284, 287, 289
  democratic peace   34–35, 55, 88–91, 284, 289, 293, 296–298, 300
Dinstein, Yoram   95, 108, 167, 250, 267
Disarmament   68, 97, 125–126, 171, 228, 281
Draft articles on Responsibility of States for Internationally Wrongful Acts   18, 154, 159, 249, 256

East Timor   220, 255, 258, 305
Enslavement   11, 40, 142
Equity and general principles of law   54, 66, 277
Ethics   5, 30, 33, 59, 110, 122, 137, 269

Ethnic cleansing   215, 244
Ethnicity   258, 297
Europe   9, 24, 87–88, 225, 230, 245, 265–266, 286–287, 306
European Commission on Human Rights   261–262
European Court of Human Rights   225, 262
European Union   265, 286
Extradition   17, 19, 214–215, 216, 241–243
  aut dedere aut judicare   17, 214, 241–242, 272

Fleck, Dieter.   236, 244, 282, 310
Framework Convention for the Protection of National Minorities   265, 286

Galtung, Johan   5, 12, 116, 117, 148, 314, 319
General international law   239, 249, 272, 295
Geneva Conventions   4, 13, 18, 94–95, 102, 104–108, 167, 203–206, 209–210, 242, 250–252, 267–268, 277, 280
  Geneva Convention for the Amelioration of the Condition of the Wounded and Sick in Armed Forces in the Field (First Geneva Convention)   4, 14, 203, 242
  Geneva Convention for the Amelioration of the Condition of Wounded, Sick and Shipwrecked Members of Armed Forces at Sea (Second Geneva Convention)   4, 13, 242
  Geneva Convention Relative to the Treatment of Prisoners of War (Third Geneva Convention)   4, 13, 242
  Geneva Convention Relative to the Protection of Civilian Persons in Time of War (Fourth Geneva Convention)   4, 13, 94, 104, 242, 253–254, 262, 270–271, 279–280, 294
  Protocol Additional to the Geneva Conventions of 12 August 1949, and relating to the Protection of Victims of Non-International Armed Conflicts (Protocol II)   13, 18, 204, 205, 206, 207, 280
  Protocol Additional to the Geneva Conventions of 12 August 1949, and relating to the Protection of Victims of International Armed Conflicts (Protocol I)   108, 167, 210, 252, 268

INDEX

Gender (see also Women)   126, 149, 156, 217, 218, 219, 223, 297, 301
Genocide   18, 151, 229, 242–243, 249, 256, 266, 273, 287
Gentili, Alberico   60–71, 82, 91, 239
Grotian Tradition in International Law   9, 25, 59–61, 76–79, 90–91, 139–142, 143–144, 148, 177–179, 204, 210, 305, 317
Grotius, Hugo (see also Grotian Tradition in International Law)   25, 45, 59, 61, 71, 72, 75, 76–79, 81–83, 90–92, 140–144, 148, 176, 204, 210, 241, 277, 305
Gudelinus, Petrus   50, 71–75, 91

Human rights   102–104, 119–121, 146–148, 150–153, 156–158, 168, 170–171, 172–173, 178, 223–224, 225, 246–247, 252, 261–263, 264–266, 269–270, 272–273, 278–279, 285–287, 292–293
    law   102–103, 119–121, 261, 263–264, 268, 279, 281, 285, 288, 290, 292
    protections   17, 141, 152, 268
    violations of   10, 141, 145–151, 156–159, 161, 168–169, 173, 178
Humanitarianism   35, 98, 103, 106, 264
Humanity   54, 56, 103–104, 208, 211, 249, 256, 273, 318

Individual criminal responsibiity   50, 65, 233, 241, 253, 272, 279, 283–285, 293
International Commission on Intervention, State Sovereignty, and International Development Research Centre   17, 154, 215, 216, 245, 246, 247–248, 278
International Committee of the Red Cross   4, 12–13, 16, 18, 94, 97, 103–105, 108, 241–242, 250, 271–272, 277, 294–295
International Convention on the Elimination of All Forms of Racial Discrimination   265, 286
International Criminal Court   16, 120, 158, 160, 224–225, 263, 272–273
    Rome Statute of the   160, 263, 273
International criminal law   5–6, 19–20, 113, 116, 126–128, 138, 145–146, 156–157, 158–159, 161, 168–169, 172–174, 272–273, 292–293, 316–318

International humanitarian law   97–98, 100–103, 105–108, 116, 119–120, 121, 203–204, 208, 255, 261–264, 266, 287–288, 290
International Law Commission   18, 154, 159, 249, 256, 275–276
International organizations   16, 18–19, 154, 170, 188–189, 230, 264, 281, 285, 305, 310–311, 313, 318
International relations   61, 79, 112, 140–141, 177, 186, 208, 230–231, 247, 258, 291, 304, 313
Intervention   17, 154, 215, 224, 244–248, 256, 269, 278, 314
    humanitarian   15, 105, 111, 155, 223, 248
Institutes of Justinian   9, 38–41, 73, 86, 320
Iraq   97, 153, 160, 189, 191, 220, 254–255, 269, 272, 274, 295
    occupation of   272, 288, 295
Iverson, Jens   19, 46, 82, 138, 145, 234, 236, 282

Japan   97, 111, 268–269, 278, 299–300
Jus ad bello   2–5, 6–14, 47–48, 55, 58–61, 80–81, 91–95, 97–99, 101–103, 107–121, 128, 141–142, 153–154, 166–167, 175–177, 204–205, 206–208, 210–213, 232–233, 313–314
Jus ad bellum   8–10, 12–16, 55, 58–59, 61, 80–82, 91, 94, 103, 107–108, 110–116, 120, 138, 141–142, 155, 164, 165–167, 209, 210–211, 252–253
Jus ante bello   115
Jus cogens   249–250, 256
Jus contra bellum   108, 209
Jus durante bello   115
Jus gentium   3, 79–80, 81–83, 86, 171
Jus in bello   3–4, 9–12, 13–14, 16, 19, 24, 55, 58–59, 91, 97–99, 100–103, 107–108, 110–111, 113–119, 153, 165–167, 204, 206–208, 210–211, 213
Jus post bellum   1–12, 19–23, 25–29, 45–50, 79–84, 88–94, 112–133, 135–139, 140–142, 145–149, 153–158, 164–168, 170–175, 177–203, 211–216, 231–239, 268–270, 274–284, 287–291, 302–319
    content and contours   3–5, 7–8, 10, 122, 129, 135, 137, 230, 231, 277, 281–284, 288, 316

INDEX

critics   91, 233, 237
framework of   61, 189, 233, 282
functional definitions of   131–132, 182, 308
functions   1, 7–8, 64, 307
goals   232, 245, 309
historical foundations   7, 175, 179, 253, 316
normative principles   4, 281
norms of   4, 130–132, 147, 164, 168, 232, 256, 266, 276, 279, 288, 306, 310, 318
procedural   171
scholars   27, 74, 112, 180, 237, 308
transitional justice and   11, 19, 113, 126, 138–139, 140, 168, 174, 178
Jus terminatio   122, 126, 137, 164, 213–215
Justice cascade   161, 169

Kant, Immanuel   7, 9, 19, 67, 88–90, 91, 142, 145, 153, 289, 294, 295, 296, 298, 300, 305, 316, 317
Kenya   224, 272
Korea   228
Koskenniemi, Martti   139, 140, 142
Kosovo   219, 224, 255, 258, 305
Kunz, Josef L.   80, 140, 175, 252, 253, 264, 285

Latin America   161, 169–170, 175
Lauterpacht, Hersch   1, 6, 76, 107, 109–110, 139, 140–143, 148, 172, 176, 177, 179, 250
League of Nations   90, 91, 109, 176
Legality   11, 19–23, 67, 97, 109–110, 112, 130–131, 143, 152, 155, 177, 179, 237–238, 248, 307
Legitimacy   120, 154, 155, 160, 168, 179, 183–186, 187, 211, 282
Lesaffer, Randall.   49, 50, 61, 71, 72
Lex pacificatoria   17, 89, 113, 122, 137–138, 153, 165–166, 168, 189, 191, 214–215, 311, 315
Liberia   220–223, 247
Liberty   17, 33, 68, 87–88, 89, 211, 262, 280, 296
Linz, Juan J.   175

May, Larry.   4, 45, 46, 281, 311, 314
Meron, Theodor   103, 208, 250
Mexico   170, 268
Middle East   274, 297

Milanovic, Marko   102, 119, 266
Minorities   112, 151–152, 252, 258, 261, 264–266, 284–287, 289
  discrimination   152, 218, 249, 256, 261–262, 265, 286, 292
  linguistic   265, 286
  national   252, 264–266, 285–287
  protection of   252, 264–265, 285–286

Natural law   24–25, 40, 50, 51, 59, 68, 74, 80–81, 84–85, 87, 111, 144
Neff, Stephen C.   63, 109, 119, 164
Netherlands   76, 268
Non Liquet, judicial   1, 140, 179
Noncombatant   24, 137
Non-governmental organizations   86, 206, 243, 245–246, 262, 266, 287, 306, 315
Non-state actors   13, 19, 129, 132, 137, 152, 164
Non-state groups   214, 240
North Atlantic Treaty Organization   15, 111, 212
North Korea   97
Norway   268, 280
Nuclear weapons   97, 114, 268

Occupation   16, 18, 146–147, 153, 162–163, 183–187, 191, 203–205, 229, 237, 266–271, 287–288, 289–292, 293–294, 299–300
  alien   18, 210, 250–252, 277
  belligerent   167
  conduct of   253, 270, 294
  contemporary   235, 254–256, 258, 269–270, 290, 293
  laws of   5, 89, 166, 186–187, 236, 237, 254, 263, 269–270, 278–280, 290–291, 293, 300
  military   108, 259
  occupying force   74, 162, 268, 271, 290, 294–295, 299
  post-occupation   163, 229, 269, 284, 292, 299
  transformative   11, 67, 129, 132, 139, 153, 248, 253, 270–272, 284, 289, 293–295, 297–298, 300
Optional Protocol to the Convention on the Rights of the Child on the Involvement of Children in Armed Conflict   94, 263

Orend, Brian 23, 27, 92, 112, 131, 142, 164, 235, 308
Organization for Security and Co-operation in Europe 245, 306
  High Commissioner on National Minorities 266, 287
Organized Armed Groups 15–17, 105, 212–213, 228, 236, 240, 266, 287

Pacifism 23, 46–48, 108, 282, 314
Pakistan 170, 212
Peace
  accountability matters for 148, 214, 242
  agreements 16–17, 49–50, 112–113, 122–123, 132, 137, 146–147, 151–153, 155–158, 165–166, 187–188, 214, 217, 219, 222, 229–230, 239–242
  early 11, 30, 123, 132–133, 135, 137, 211, 214, 298, 309, 319
  international 15, 26, 31, 36, 230, 254, 257, 298–300
  law of 17, 113, 117–119, 122, 153, 164–165, 176, 189, 235, 280, 305
  negative 5, 12, 63, 117, 145, 312, 314, 318
  negotiations 5, 63, 75, 91, 113, 129, 167, 187, 188, 215, 219, 239, 298
  operations 15, 318
  perpetual 83, 85, 88–90, 91, 295–296, 300
  positive 5, 12, 16, 28, 93, 116–117, 143, 145, 148, 212, 223, 258, 289, 314–315, 319
  processes 16, 152, 217–218
  security and 45, 48, 52–53, 58, 90, 216–218
  sustainable 7–11, 18–19, 45–47, 65–67, 87–90, 122–123, 129–131, 132–133, 136–138, 142–143, 145–146, 148–149, 165–168, 178–179, 190, 245–248, 287–289, 298–301, 309, 315–317
  treaties 16–17, 49–50, 58, 69–75, 76–78, 82–89, 90, 92, 132, 146–147, 155, 166–167, 214, 238–241, 249–250
Peacebuilding 123–126, 129, 132, 139, 146, 178, 217–218, 247, 266, 287, 305–306, 310–312, 314, 315, 318
Peacekeeping 2, 15, 132, 136, 146, 154, 170, 223, 229, 266, 287, 305
Peacemaking 29, 30, 37, 71, 76, 82, 86, 113, 137, 142, 280, 287, 299

Peoples 30, 33–34, 39–41, 43, 65, 67, 162, 209–210, 250–252, 254, 256–257, 274, 276–277
Peru 268
Post-Cold War World 35, 88, 90, 129, 139, 175, 296
Post-conflict 189, 191, 216, 218–219, 260, 269–270, 280, 282, 288–289, 307, 310, 311–312, 315, 316
  justice 5–6, 11, 53–54, 58, 64–65, 113, 123–126, 136, 138, 256, 319
  peace 11–12, 60, 91, 146–147, 189–190, 218, 246–247, 281, 292, 310
  phase 27, 168, 217
  reforms 142, 189–191, 234–236
  settlement 11, 143, 248
  societies 11–12, 146–147, 219, 282, 288, 299
  zones 185, 235, 254–256, 258, 269
Prisoners 4, 13, 69–70, 73, 86, 104, 149, 213, 242, 280
Property 53, 73–74, 78–81, 85, 139, 211, 258, 260, 270, 271, 290, 293, 295
Proportionality 4, 65, 120, 130–131, 254, 256, 258, 269, 277–279, 282, 307
Public order 223, 270, 290, 293

Raymond of Penafort (Decretals of Gregory IX) 41–42
Rebellion 29–30, 36–38, 68, 73–75, 83, 89–91, 204, 208
Reconciliation 4, 146, 174, 218, 222–223, 244, 247, 258, 279, 282
Reconstruction 185, 191, 247, 280
Refugees 94, 121, 162, 247
Regime 109, 149–150, 156, 159, 160, 163, 167, 169, 173–174, 191, 291, 297
  change in 10, 141, 145, 147–148, 150–151, 155–157, 158, 160–162, 171, 173–174, 178, 227, 282, 292, 298
  colonial and alien domination and racist 209, 251
  predecessor 10, 128, 135, 144–145, 146–147, 149–151, 157–159, 161, 169–170, 178, 292
  racist 18, 204, 209–210, 250–252, 277
Religion 24, 28, 45, 51, 67–70, 110, 246, 254, 261–262, 265, 286
Reparations 4, 66, 141, 147, 149, 153, 154, 168, 171, 229, 252, 279, 282

INDEX 359

Repatriation   156, 217, 247
Responsibility   5, 17–18, 20, 154–155, 159, 215, 233, 236, 244–249, 255–256, 278, 283, 311
Responsibility to Protect   17, 20, 25, 111, 154–155, 165, 215, 233, 244–248, 278, 283, 311
Restitution   4, 73–74, 75, 91, 282
Rodin, David   122, 137
Roht-Arriaza, Naomi   148, 149, 170

Secession   152, 155, 214, 230, 276
Schwarzenberger, Georg   58, 129, 152, 166
Scott, James Brown   26, 50, 58
Security   52–53, 57–58, 216–219, 234–235, 244, 254–255, 257, 271, 287, 289, 294–295, 298, 300
Self-defence   31, 46, 108, 114, 120, 167, 209, 213, 250, 299
Self-determination   18, 152, 209–210, 249, 250–252, 253, 256–257, 264, 266, 277, 279, 285, 287
    self-government   219, 254–255, 257
Sen, Amartya   5, 258
Slavery   39–41, 55, 67, 152, 229, 249, 256, 261, 273
South Africa   255
South America   175
South Sudan   212
South West Africa   255
Southern Europe   175
Sovereignty   17, 43–44, 49, 56–57, 59–60, 62, 66, 70, 73–75, 77–78, 83–85, 87, 173–174, 215, 230–231, 244–250, 253–255, 267–268, 278–279, 290–292
Soviet Union   175, 274, 276
Spain   76, 161
Stahn, Carsten.   80, 88, 92, 165, 175, 223, 232, 233, 235, 269, 278, 279, 280, 283
State
    recognition   214–216
    responsibility   146–147, 153, 154, 166, 229, 239, 252, 279, 305, 318
    succession   18, 50, 61–62, 74, 258–260, 273–276, 279, 281, 310
Suarez, Francisco   50, 58–59, 91
Sudan   170, 212, 224, 272
Syria   30, 97, 213

Teitel, Ruti G.   10, 135, 142, 144, 146, 150, 158, 160, 161, 175
Territorial administration   153, 255, 257
    international   19, 153, 233, 253–254, 257, 282, 318
Territory   44–45, 55–56, 116–117, 203–207, 212–213, 229–230, 242, 253–254, 257–260, 267–268, 271, 273–276, 279, 290, 292, 294–295
    administered   255, 256–257
    occupied   153, 268, 270–271, 290, 294–295
Terrorism   18, 243, 312
Torture   18, 33, 205, 243, 249, 256, 261, 273
Transitional justice   6, 10–11, 19–20, 113, 123–128, 135, 138–139, 140–141, 144–151, 156–163, 167–175, 177–179, 228–229, 290, 292–293, 315–316
    definition of   136, 159, 169, 172–173, 175, 178
    mechanisms   150, 161
    practice of   157, 161–162
    truth commissions   126, 149–150, 160
Trusteeships   5, 153, 209, 233, 251, 253–258, 269, 279, 283

Ubaldis, Baldus de   48–50, 71, 90
Uganda   126, 150, 224, 267, 272
Unconstitutional Change of Government   273
United Kingdom   104, 148, 262, 280
United Nations   4, 12, 15, 95–96, 109, 162, 207–210, 216, 219, 223, 226, 227, 238, 246, 249–258, 259–262, 265, 280–281, 286, 291
    Charter   4, 111, 120, 208–210, 216, 230, 246, 251, 256–257, 291
    General Assembly   17, 154–155, 209–210, 215, 244, 251
    High Commissioner for Human Rights   265, 286
    Security Council   13, 15, 110–111, 153, 156, 213, 216–219, 223, 224, 252, 255, 269, 272
    Uniting for peace resolution   15, 111
    Trusteeship Council   253–254
United States of America   126, 149, 165, 205, 208–211, 212, 251, 268, 272, 276, 291, 295

Use of force   12–13, 15, 17, 110, 114, 154, 155, 208–209, 210, 212–213, 237–241, 314, 317

Vattel, Emer de   81, 83, 84–87, 90–91, 204, 239
Victims   13, 18, 97, 104–105, 120, 206, 210, 250, 252, 264, 268, 277, 280
Vienna Convention on Succession of States in Respect of Treaties   258–259, 260
Vienna Convention on Succession of States in respect of State Property, Archives and Debts   258, 260, 275
Vienna Convention on the Law of Treaties   17, 120, 154, 155, 156, 214, 215, 238, 239, 240, 249, 263, 279
Vitoria, Francisco de   50–58, 59, 91, 204

Walzer, Michael   269, 313
War
    civil   11–12, 31, 83, 99–100, 170, 204, 212
    crimes   12, 112, 169, 273
    debts   275–277
    just   23–25, 46, 164, 235, 245
    justice after   128–129, 131, 308
    methods of waging   23, 29–30, 37, 42–43, 47, 57–58, 70, 81, 110, 112, 176
    termination   122, 137, 164, 186–188, 281
    theory   6, 23, 30, 43, 110, 131, 143, 164–167, 171, 186, 188, 308, 313–314
West Africa   221–222, 225, 306
Westphalia   79, 86, 173–174, 230–231, 264, 285, 288
Wolff, Christian   79–87, 91, 239
Women   35–36, 71, 94, 156, 162, 217–219, 266, 284, 287, 289, 297–301, 307
World Wars
    First World War   97, 99, 117, 139, 173, 209, 251–252, 264, 285, 318–319
    Second World War   1, 12, 99, 109, 119, 173–174, 177, 228, 271, 295, 299, 314, 318–319

Printed in the United States
by Baker & Taylor Publisher Services